Best wishes
Fred Simpson

CLAY CO. LIBRARY
CELINA TENN.

The Sins of Madison County

Fred B. Simpson

With
Mary N. Daniel
Gay C. Campbell

Triangle Publishing Co.
2000

TRIANGLE PUBLISHING COMPANY
105 NORTHSIDE SQUARE
HUNTSVILLE, ALABAMA

Copyright 1999 by Fred B. Simpson

All rights reserved. This book or parts thereof, may not be reproduced in any form or by any means, electronic or mechanical, including photocopy, recording, scanning, or any storage and retrieval system, without written permission from the author. Inquiries should be addressed to Triangle Publishing Company, 105 Northside Square Huntsville, Alabama 35801.

Library of Congress Catalog Card Number: 99-97386
Hardcover: ISBN: 0-09675765-0-4

Cover Painting, *"The Tree"* by Fred B. Simpson
Oil On Canvas, 20 X 24, Private Collection.
Cover Design by Gay Campbell

First Edition

Printed in the United States of America.

> There is no grievance that is a
> Fit object of redress by mob rule.
> Abraham Lincoln,
> Springfield, Illinois
> January 27, 1837

I'm just so lonesome that I don't know what to do.
Lonesome as a daisy that's a wishing for the dew.
I'm bluer in my feelings that the violet so blue,
    Jean's gone with Johnny to the hanging.
She dressed up in her cloke, red ribbons on her hat,
He bought her lots of candy, chewing gum and like of that,
And I'm just so frustrated that I don't know where I'm at,
    Jean's gone with Johnny to the hanging.
O this year love is painfuler than splitting rails in spring,
When the river's ripe for fishing and the birds let out and sing,
For Jean she's got my true love and what's more she's got my ring,
    And Jean's gone with Johnny to the hanging.

    Frank L. Stanton
    1900

About the Author

Fred Bryan Simpson was born in Birmingham, Alabama, but was educated by Montevallo Public Schools until joining the United States Air Force. During the Korean Conflict, he served in the Far East Office of Special Investigations. He financed his college education at Samford University by working as a Birmingham Police Officer. While at Vanderbilt Law School in Nashville, Tennessee, he paid his expenses working as a private investigator. He was District Attorney of Huntsville-Madison County during the decade of the seventies. He is now in private practice, specializing in murder cases.

Fred has been compiling information on murder cases in Madison County for over twenty-five years, and hopes to find time to publish more about these historical events. Interested in genealogy since a boy, he has compiled and plans to publish information about his family. Fred and his wife, the former Peggy Holloway, have been married for forty years and have three children: Bryan Simpson, Derek Simpson and Cindy Simpson Howard. They have also been blessed with four grandchildren. Besides writing, Fred enjoys his family, the law, painting portraits, and historical research.

About the Research Assistants

Mary Neyman Daniel was born in Chattanooga, Tennessee but has lived most of her life in Alabama. She graduated from the University of North Alabama with a degree in Elementary Education, and received her Masters Degree from Alabama A & M University. Mary was selected to work in Canada as a Fulbright Exchange Educator in 1993. She retired from the Huntsville City School System after teaching thirty-two years, but returned to teaching English as a Second Language, part-time. She has been married for thirty-five years to Frank (Kenny) Daniel, and they have two children, Trent and Kendra Daniel. Mary is an avid reader, and also spends much of her time in her garden when not traveling, performing public service or looking for information on local history.

Gay Cushing Campbell was born in Huntsville, Alabama. She received her degree from the North Alabama College of Commerce in Huntsville, Alabama. She retired from the Kroger Company in 1995. She was the Historian-Archivist for the John Hunt Morgan Chapter United Daughters of the Confederacy in 1997 and the President of the Tennessee Valley Genealogical Society 1996-2000. Gay is a public speaker, lecturing on topics of historical and genealogical interest of the Tennessee Valley. She has taught at the University of Alabama, Huntsville, and the Huntsville Madison County Public Library and for many historical societies. She is the mother of three children: Tony Coulson, Kristina Coulson and Kathie Campbell, and the grandmother of Alexis and Kenysha Coulson. Her hobbies are many, but her spare time is spent traveling to genealogically significant and historical places.

Many Thanks
Jay Campbell

To The Family

Acknowledgments

This book was written over several years, so any applause must be shared by the many great people who contributed to its completion. I lost track years ago of the number of people who willingly shared their time and information with me. I acknowledge with gratitude and pleasure, the assistance of these generous people and apologize beforehand to the many people whom I will unavoidably omit.

It is certain that errors have crept into such a large gathering of data, but I have not found any way to share the responsibility of any oversights, misstatements, or untrue facts found in this book. Years of research could be spent unraveling the lives of the people involved. All errors are unintentional and I will gladly accept any substantiated corrections for a revised edition.

Books that are well documented take considerable time to research and write, making a great library essential. I used the Heritage Room of the Huntsville-Madison County Public Library as the main source for historical reference materials. Having wonderful historical material is one of the greatest gifts from our past and one of the best gifts we can leave to future generations.

Not enough thanks can be given to the many family members whose ancestors are included in this work. They gave of their time, photos, and memories in order that all the facts be published. For some of these people it would have been less painful if certain memories had been left unmentioned.

During the time I have worked on this book, many great ladies on my staff have *"kept the wolves at bay."* Many thanks to Deborah Johnson, Angie Blocker, Lois Shering, Ann Lifer, Monica Waldon, Jan Lassiter and Jeanette Costantino.

Bob Willisson, my law partner, has been looking up law for me since my first year as a lawyer. He researched and found the rulings in the appellate cases cited, for which I am grateful.

My son and law partner, Derek, tried many cases and spent many extra hours in the office to allow me the time to work on my "hobby."

Brenda Webb, the Director of Maple Hill Cemetery, was kind enough to share countless hours of her time to help me find needed information.

Mickey King was not only interested in helping me find the history of Huntsville, but sometimes took over and got ahead of me. She always had the energy and intelligence that a good writer needs.

Tina Patrick was my paralegal (boss) for some years. After she finished our legal work she often went with me to interview people and look for some long-lost facts. She went to law school and now practices law in another state, but still seems like part of the family.

Tom Carney is a valuable friend who paved the way for me. He is the best person I know for researching and writing about Huntsville's history. He published several books and gave me space in his *Old Huntsville* magazine. I appreciate all the good advice he gave me.

Melissa Heron ran my office until she returned to law school. She became my law partner then moved on, and is now a great prosecutor in the District Attorney's office. We have tried murder cases together and against each other. She is my good friend who did not complain when she had to work late so that I could have time for research.

Sonya Brasher has been a paralegal and office manager in my law office over the life of this book. She has kept my office running smoothly during some very trying times. She has been my chief supporter, critic and friend. She has my lasting gratitude.

Mrs. Dorothy Scott Johnson allowed me to use her private collection of records for research about Huntsville's history. She was a tremendous help with her instant knowledge of the county history. She was kind enough to read and edit the work while it was in progress. Thanks to her careful scrutiny, many errors were found and corrected. Her continued encouragement has been a great source of strength.

Raneè Pruitt, Archivist, and the acknowledged expert in the Heritage Room of the Huntsville-Madison County Public Library, always has time to supply authors with details that would be unknown to anyone else. She has knowledge of the records and the history of Madison County that far surpasses that of any other source. It would be impossible to adequately thank her. She is a great lady.

Dr. Frances Roberts read the manuscript in its raw form, and contributed her insight to help me write a better book. James Record read the early version of the manuscript and offered suggestions and improvements.

The Honorable Joseph L. Battle reviewed the final chapter and the legal preceedings. I appreciate his input and his friendship in doing so.

Attorney Shannon Simpson and Don O'Halloran assisted in the proofreading. Thanks to their skills many mistakes were spotted and corrected.

Richard Smallwood assisted me in proofreading, as well as being an on-call advisor throughout the layout procedure. I am truly grateful to have had his expertise.

Gay Campbell joined me during the last two years of research and writing. She knew more history about the people of Huntsville from personal knowledge than I could find in books. She is a master on the computer and is responsible for the look of the finished work. I appreciate her patience; it has been a pleasure to work with her. There is no way to repay her for all that she has done for me.

Mary Daniel has been helping me for many years to gather facts and write a readable story. I am unsure if all this is my work or simply a rewrite of her corrections! Her red pen has been famous. I always gave her the hard problems, and I thank her for being such an encouraging taskmistress. She has been a close friend and supporter. I am grateful to have had this gracious lady assist me.

The support received from my sister, Dorcas Pilgreen, has been a blessing. I hope she knows the depth of gratitude I feel for all she has done.

A special thanks is given to my wife, Peggy, for her faith in me and her support over the years. We were always in the same room while I was writing and she was a great help. She was my spell checker before the days of the computer, and even now is still faster than the latest technology. She has been patient, understanding and forgiving when I spent too much time in the library or was away seeking an interview with someone's long lost relative.

Mary, Gay and I thank our families for putting up with our lack of attention to anything other than this *"Lynching Book."* Their support and understanding helped ease the long nights at the computer, the library, and trips to the archives or to interview knowledgeable people.

Thanks must also go to future generations for giving us the desire to leave something behind, so that they may know us better.

Fred B. Simpson

Table of Contents

About the Author IV
About the Research Assistants IV
Dedication VI
Acknowledgments VII
Table of Contents XI
Introduction XIII
Foreword XVII
Origin of the Term "Lynching" XVII
Definitions of Lynchings XVIII
Research Sources XVIII
Historical Perspective XX
The Lynching Era XXIV
Chapter One 5
    White-Evans-Hall 1878 5
        The Players 7
        The Killing 11
        The Testimony 21
        The Meeting 39
        The Lynching 44
        Epilogue 49
        Biographies—Chapter One 51
Chapter Two 89
    Wesley Brown-1883 89
        The Democrat 105
        November 1, 1883 105
        Epilogue 107
        Biographies—Chapter Two 109
Chapter Three 119
    Robert Mosley-1890 119
        Epilogue 129
        Biographies—Chapter Three 131
Chapter Four 139
    Mollie Smith and Amanda Franks-1897 139
        Epilogue 153
        Biographies—Chapter Four 155
Chapter Five 163
    Elijah Clark-1900 163
        Epilogue 191
        Biographies—Chapter Five 195

Glossary of Laws and Legal Terms 207
Trial Participants 209
Introduction to Chapter Six 211
Chapter Six 215
    Horace Maples-1904 215
    Wednesday September 7, 1904 241
    Friday, September 9, 1904 244
    Wednesday, September 14, 1904 247
    Thursday, September 15, 1904 248
    Friday, September 16, 1904 253
    Saturday, September 17, 1904 256
    Sunday, September 18, 1904 256
    Monday, September 19, 1904 257
    Tuesday, September 20, 1904 259
    Thursday, September 22, 1904 266
    Friday September 23, 1904 268
    Saturday, September 24, 1904 270
    Sunday, September 25, 1904 272
    Monday September 26, 1904 272
    Tuesday September 27, 1904 274
    Wednesday, September 28, 1904 276
    Thursday, September 29, 1904 278
    Friday, September 30, 1904 279
    Saturday, October 1, 1904 280
    Tuesday, October 4, 1904 281
    Later that Month 282
    Sunday, October 23, 1904 283
    Epilogue 285
    Biographies—Chapter Six 297
Bibliography 337
Index 343
Order Form 359

Introduction

The most exciting moments of my life have been when juries would return to the courtroom after deliberation and read their verdict, *"We, the jury find..."* There is nothing like it on television or anywhere else.

It became my duty as District Attorney in Huntsville, Alabama, during the decade of the seventies to ask for the death penalty in capital murder cases. I began to search the office for records of earlier capital punishment cases. These files were very interesting and I soon had a drawer filled with copies of them. After being returned to private practice by the public, there were death penalty cases to be defended. These cases were added to the files in the drawer. Collecting these files has led me to research murders of the last two centuries in Madison County.

On cold and rainy Saturday afternoons during the ensuing years it was my pleasure to explore past capital murder cases found in old newspaper articles at the public library. Articles were found in old dusty books of little interest to others. No one else was present—there were no waiting or long lines.

In my search for these murder cases, I found other cases of interest. These were the stories about the *"Sins of Madison County,"* during the lynching era, which occurred from 1878 to 1904. Initially, it was my feeling that surely a lynching could not have occurred in Huntsville's enlightened and law-abiding community. But there they were. This was a time of lawlessness and mob rule that prevailed for twenty-six years and produced six lynchings.

These stories described Huntsville's life in past years just as we see our life today. On each page I found an exciting, forgotten story of the past, written in great detail. Each article was filled with interesting facts and told a story about the community and its people. It was just like standing on the square today, asking—"what did you hear about this or that and did you see the story in the morning paper?" People accepted the realities of life and went on to tomorrow, just as we do today.

At the beginning, I felt the lynching stories could be quickly researched, compiled and published. I was mistaken. For years Mary Daniel and I attempted to locate and compile all of the information about the lynchings and the people involved. Gay

Campbell joined us in the last years of research. Even these two dedicated researchers could not locate all of the ever-growing facts. It became apparent that we had to stop the research, even though we knew there was much more information we could have found.

We are allowed to follow and report the actions of the people in the stories and also see into their future. These were real people who once led complicated lives. We follow several of the people's lives from birth to death, and the resulting events would require several books to report.

The stories read like a lawyer's brief because I am a lawyer and I don't know any other way to write. My intent has been to write about what happened or at least the way it was remembered and reported.

Each chapter contains carefully researched biographies to assist the reader in the background of the characters in the stories. Placing biographies at the back of the book was considered, but later I decided to place the biographies at the end of each story for the convenience of the reader.

The reader will note that there is more information in some stories than in others, but this was not intentional. I was limited in my search by the lack of information available in the accounts of some of the lynchings. While researching, I found rumors of other lynchings, but they could not be documented and therefore are not included.

I cannot explain why things were done or not done and there is no intent to imply anything—not after a century has passed. It is possible that what I found is not what happened at all. I just don't know. I attempted to record the facts as accurately as possible. There surely are facts that I have missed. I had no intent to invent scenes; you can do that yourself.

It is almost impossible to know what people of long ago thought or felt. Occasionally, we think we know, because there is no other way they could have felt, or their thoughts are revealed. A person about to be hanged will feel fear. A judge writes to the governor and tells him what he thinks and we can know his feelings from his writings. Anything else is only speculation and should not be found in this book. If I say, "*it was night,*" it is because it was reported that it was night. <u>This is not a novel</u>. Nearly everything in this book is taken from the newspapers or court records. If facts were taken from other sources I tell you so in the footnotes.

My dream is to take you back with me to visit the Huntsville of those days. I would like for us to know what really happened, to see behind the rumors and lies, and to somehow join the crowd and witness the same things they saw. We would be witnesses waiting for a participant to appear and perhaps hear them say something that adds to the story. The clothing would look odd, and the speech somewhat different, but the truths of human nature would be the same as today or any other time. The basic thinking of the people would be as we expect; with honor, truth, and integrity in the midst of lies and evil.

I would like to go back and stand in the middle of Meridianville Pike with Judge William Richardson as he faced over three hundred horsemen, trying to stop them from going into town with the intent to lynch three men. How interesting it would be to go back to the old Courthouse and be with Judge Paul Speake, Solicitor Erle Pettus, and the members of the Grand Jury as they set out to bring justice to the men who had been a part of an evil lynching. I would have loved to be the prosecutor in that fight! What did they say to their friends or to their wives when they went home at night? What led Speake and Pettus to take a courageous stand against the electorate and take an action that might lead to their ruin? For that matter, what led some people to take a leadership position in the violent killing of another human, and why did others allow themselves to be drawn into such a sinful event?

People have grown to maturity, died and others have taken their place. Buildings have been demolished and replaced by newer structures. However, the Courthouse Square is still here along with many structures that were standing at the time of the lynchings. Many homes are not only still standing but look much the same today as they did then.

These people were not exactly as we are today and the differences show in their actions. They did not know anything about a rocket to the moon or equal rights for women and minorities. People think and act within the framework of their own time and it is difficult to judge them with the standards of today or tomorrow.

We cannot change the facts or events related in this book. We can only learn about the sins of the past and hope that our actions of today are not found to be sins in the future.

Fred B. Simpson

Foreword
Origin of the Term "Lynching"

Lynching is associated with the brand of frontier justice practiced in Virginia and North Carolina during and after the Revolutionary War.[1] This conflict was not only a war between the American Colonies and Great Britain, but was itself a war between the states that consisted of continuous fighting between neighbors who were either American Patriots, or Torries loyal to Britain.

The prominent Lynch family of Bedford County, Virginia, produced at least two brothers. John Lynch founded Lynchburg, Virginia. The other brother, Colonel Charles Lynch, was an unexpected combination of a Quaker and Colonel of the militia during the Revolutionary War.

Colonel Lynch's home was a great distance from the colony's only court in Williamsburg, Virginia. The Colonel made his home into a courthouse, with himself as a self-appointed, presiding judge. This position allowed him to impose his own personal brand of justice to control the unrest that prevailed because of the distance from the courts and from the breakdown of the court systems.

Judge Lynch and his companions visited the British sympathizers and imposed their harsh brand of punishment on men, women, and children. Citizens were made to renounce their loyalty to England with the very real threat of receiving 40 lashes on their bare backs if they did not.

Lynch's punishment was so atrocious and cruel that his countrymen condemned him for his actions. Governor Thomas Jefferson was one of the many officials critical of Lynch and his self-fashioned rules of law.

After the war, there was an attempt to hold Judge Lynch and his companions accountable for their unlawful acts. The Virginia legislators took Judge Lynch to task, but nothing came of their investigations and no punishment was meted out to the Judge for his harsh actions. To the contrary, the legislators ratified the Colonel's actions, known as "*Lynch Law,*" and granted him immunity from prosecution or civil liability.

---

[1] Some think that a Captain William Lynch (1742-1820), of the Virginia militia gave us his infamous name. He formed a group to rid the country of criminals. His followers were called; "*Lynch's men*" and their actions became "*Lynch's law.*"

The action by the Virginia legislators and the criticism by high officials caused the practice of Judge Lynch to be discussed so much that this type of justice became known as *Lynch's Law*.

This phrase became part of our vocabulary and was broadened to describe a situation in which a person was punished by a mob, outside the judicial system.

When a person suffered at the hands of a mob, it was said that he was lynched. People attending to participate or watch were attending a lynching.

By the time of the War between the North and South, the term "lynching" was widespread.

Definitions of Lynchings

Definitions of a lynching are not always the same. Usually a lynching is murder with community approval. This could be by general participation of local citizens and the condoning of the acts of the mob. Approval could also involve action or inaction of public officials. There could be an acceptance of the conduct or acquittal of the killers with or without a trial.

Generally, lynchings were the act of a mob. These mobs were people acting outside the legal system to obtain what they felt was justice.

A lynching, sometimes but not always, consisted of a chase, a capture, a killing, and the display of the body to the public.

Sometimes called "popular justice," all lynchings shared one similarity: ordinary people choosing to circumvent their criminal justice system in order to punish those thought by them to be guilty of a crime.

Research Sources

Official sources are scarce because there are no official records on the lynchings themselves. There were court records when officials attempted to bring to trial those citizens participating in the lynchings. Some official letters from the office holders of those times give details that are helpful. Because of the personal accounts and detailed statements, newspapers are usually the best source of materials that are available. There are few written personal accounts of the situation around "*the tree*."

Passage of time prevents first-hand accounts from the participants and those attending the lynchings. All who were involved are long dead. The participants protected each other. Even those who disapproved of the lynchings would withhold information for fear of their own personal safety or for fear of being ostracized by their fellow citizens.

Many studies have been undertaken and books have been written about mob violence in the South and across the nation. It would take a library to hold all the material available about violence, lynching, hangings, etc. Generally, there are two methods of investigating the history of lynching: collective studies and individual studies.

Collective studies are the compiling of information about as many lynchings as possible throughout any given span of time. These studies are used to look for statistics, similarities, or facts in common in order to seek answers and explain the violence.[2]

Individual studies are detailed investigations of a single event. A detailed study is made about the motivation, circumstances, and people closely related to the lynching of a single victim.[3]

Throughout history and in all parts of the globe, there have been attacks against minorities, children, the underprivileged, the different, and the weak. Anywhere there is a large minority, there is dislike and many reasons given for mistreatment.

The good people of the Southwestern states not only lynched blacks but committed acts of violence against Hispanics and horse thieves. Native Americans in the Western states were killed without a second thought. The Chinese were not always treated with respect in California and in other parts of the United States. The Irish and Jews were not treated well in the Northeast.

---

[2] Examples of collective studies include: National Association for the Advancement of Colored People. 1919 (1969). *Thirty Years of Lynching in the United States,* 1899-1918, New York: Arno Press. Ginsburg, Ralp*h; 1962. 100 Years of Lynching.* Baltimore, Maryland: (1962) Black Classic Press,. *White, Walter. 1969. Rope and Faggot. A Biography of Judge Lynch*, Salem, New Hampshire: Ayer Company Publishers, Inc., Ames, Jesse Daniel, 1942. *The Changing Character of Lynching*; Atlanta, Georgia: Commission of Interracial Cooperation, Inc., Tolnay, Stewart E., 1992. *A Festival of Violence; An Analysis of Southern Lynchings*, 1882-1930, *Urbana and Chicago: University of Illinois Press.* Brundage, W. Firzhugh, 1993. *Lynching in the New South, Urbana and Chicago: University of Illinois Press.*

[3] Examples of individual studies include: McGovern, James R., 1982, Anatomy of a Lynching, The killing of Claude Neal, Baton Rouge: Louisiana State University Press; Smeal, Howard, 1986. *Blood Justice*, The lynching of Mack Charles Parker, Oxford University Press; Downey, Dennis B., 1991. *No Crooked Death*: Pennsylvania, and the Lynching of Zachariah Walker; Urbana and Chicago University of Illinois Press.

Historical Perspective

Madison County lies in North Alabama between the Tennessee state border on the north and the Tennessee River on the south. The southern part of the Appalachian Mountains rolls through the eastern half of the county.

Huntsville is located in the center of Madison County, at the foothills of the mountains, in a beautiful valley.

Southwest of Huntsville and into the Mississippi Valley is the flat Piedmont region where evidence of the cotton civilization still can be felt and seen. This region and the sandy soil of the coastal plains make up the black belt of farming land that cuts across several deep southern states.

This cotton-growing region was dominated by a plantation system that survived only because of a concentration of a large enslaved black population. Slave labor was thought to be necessary for the survival of the cotton economy.

The first blacks did not come from Africa as slaves, but as indentured servants. This system was soon found to be unprofitable, and was replaced by slavery. There was a profit to be made for the northern shipping industry by encouraging the slave trade. Most of the slaves were sent south to work on plantations such as those found in Madison County.

Slaves were separated from white society and from the white court system established to protect citizens from each other. Masters of the plantations provided a type of court system in which they were the judges, juries and sometimes executioners.

Before 1860, Huntsville was one of the small towns in Madison County that supplied the needs of the surrounding plantation community. This beautiful little town had the same characteristics of other small communities; unpaved streets, churches, small businesses and banks. It was the center of the county's government, trade, legal and medical services, and entertainment. The town's most distinguished feature was the Courthouse, which was literally and figuratively, the center of town.

There were numerous fine old homes where prominent citizens lived. Some local merchants and professional people had widely traveled and were sophisticated, educated, and well read.

The middle class lived in a different section of town in smaller homes, but contributed to the town from their shops and businesses. Blacks served the upper and middle classes as laborers and house servants. The lower class whites took care of themselves the best they could. When the cotton mills arrived, a new class of people was created.

During the War Between the States most of the men were away fighting and it was difficult to maintain a normal judicial system. At this time, there was some vigilante activity in Madison County that resulted in executions, but the proceedings were held under some semblance of control. The rules of criminal practice were followed and punishment was carried out only after a proper hearing.

Huntsville was an important railroad community soon occupied by the hated Yankees. The Northern occupation forces took complete control, including the responsibility of the courts. No local authorities were allowed to participate in maintaining law and order.

The loss of the war brought radical change to Madison County and the entire South. Four million blacks were suddenly transformed from being personal property to having equality with whites. They were quickly perceived as a threat against the southern whites' safety and authority.

The southern myth of the contented and wise "Mammy," and the faithful, obedient servant faded, and was replaced by a new image of the threatening black as a sexually depraved criminal.

Carpetbaggers from the North assisted the occupying Federal troops in intimidating southern whites. Even more humiliating was the power given to the newly freed slaves.

The Fourteenth Amendment to the Constitution extended the full rights of citizenship to black men. The Fifteenth Amendment guaranteed black men the right to vote.

Election boards in each state registered all adult black males as voters. Thousands of blacks voted to form the new Reconstruction governments. Women, regardless of race, were not given the right to vote, in the South or the North, for years to come.

White southerners felt they were disenfranchised. They had lost control of their government and their destiny to the two groups they hated the most: Yankees and former slaves.

Whites thought that blacks were ignorant, lazy, inferior and given to lawlessness. Most blacks had been forbidden an education and were accustomed to being told exactly what to do. The new freedom to do as they pleased sometimes led them to violate the law. Whites were forced to live with blacks as part of their society, and have the court system to control the black criminal element.

The Southern judicial systems were forced to assume the responsibility not only for white offenders but also the black offenders. New methods were sought that would be as effective as slavery had been in controlling the black population.

The Reconstruction Era heightened the angry feelings of both races. Southern whites thought themselves under siege, and they began to fight the Northern occupation and oppression. They devised means to regain control of their government, their lives and their supremacy. They refused to share political power with people they felt were inferior.

The Ku Klux Klan evolved for the purpose of controlling blacks, carpetbaggers and scalawags who sought to force drastic changes on society. Members of the Ku Klux Klan did not feel inclined to honor constitutional guarantees and used violence successfully to control the black population. The lessons were not soon forgotten. However, Ku Klux Klan involvement was not mentioned, in any source, regarding the mob violence associated with the events in this book.

At the end of Reconstruction, northern oppression, through occupation, lessened. White southerners began to disenfranchise blacks, regain control of their government, and attempted to return blacks to "their place," if not as slaves certainly not on an equal level with white people. White southerners were obsessed with racial superiority and maintaining the "color line" in the South.

In 1873, the United States Supreme Court ruled that the Fourteenth Amendment did not apply to the rights of individual states, but only to those rights of the United States. In 1876, the United States Supreme Court ruled that local states and courts were responsible for prosecuting civil rights violations. This allowed local officials to make decisions without intervention by the Federal Government. The stage was set for what was to follow.

In the presidential election of 1876, a Republican, Rutherford B. Hayes and a Democrat, Samuel J. Tilden, sought the election which ended in a tie. The turning point against blacks occurred during this contest when southern men made a deal to support Hayes in exchange for an end to Southern Reconstruction. Hayes delivered on his promise and southern Democrats began implementing laws and policies designed to take back control of their governments.

As the influence of the hated North declined, a white controlled political climate allowed the enactment of "Jim Crow" laws. Political districts were devised and the separation of blacks was begun, by removing them from public institutions. They were segregated in transportation, residences, business opportunities, and education.

By the 1880's, white society had regained its power and blacks had lost their political positions, their influence in government, and even, in most cases, the right to vote. By the 1900's, southern blacks had lost almost all the rights they had gained.

The votes of working class whites and blacks were soon taken for granted as the special interest took over. The lower black and white classes were now simply a group of disadvantaged people whose voice would not be heard.

This was an extraordinary period in American history. It was a time of tremendous change and unrest, when ordinary people did unspeakable things.

We can look back now, over these long years, and condemn the evils of that period, but at that time, vigilante action was common and accepted across the nation.[4][5]

It is easier for us to judge the people's answer to the flood of barbarism of yesterday, than the flood of barbarism that threatens our society today. We have little reason to be critical of the citizens of the past when the present loss of moral and cultural fiber of our nation cannot be corrected.

Southern lynching did not mean that all the white people of the South planned to use this type of violence just to keep others under control. Apparently their contact was from information they received concerning lynchings across the South as reported by the news media. Whites across the South did not know each other and there were no seminars or master plans devised to educate the white population on the *"ways to properly lynch."* Lynchings were nonexistent or extremely rare in most counties in the South.

Not everyone participated in or condoned mob violence, but in general, the public condoned lynchings. There was a feeling that criminal acts should be controlled, and that the court system did not move fast enough to prevent crimes. It appeared that the South had lost its respect for the judicial system and believed that government would not, or could not, prevent crime.

---

[4] President Andrew Jackson advised Iowa settlers that lynching murderers was acceptable conduct. (*Lynch Law*, James Cutler, page 87)

[5] "In many of the cases of Lynching which have come to my knowledge, the affect [sic] had been healthy for the community." (Theodore Roosevelt; *The Winning of the West*, Vol. 1, Page 132.)

The Lynching Era

The decades after the War Between the States and prior to the Great Depression have been called the Lynching Era. Lynch mobs throughout the nation, but mostly in the South, claimed more than three thousand victims.

The Lynching Era arrived in Huntsville, Madison County, Alabama, in 1878, and continued until 1904. There were six documented lynchings. Some lynchings involved more than one victim. A total of nine people were lynched during this twenty-six year period.

Many groups and individuals protesting lynching used an emotional appeal that lynchings were caused only when a black man was accused of raping a white woman. However, in this *Lynching Era*, murder, not rape, was the most common reason for lynching.

In Madison County, of the nine people lynched, only one was accused of rape, one was accused of kidnapping, and the other seven met their untimely deaths because of the accusations of murder.

The mob's behavior was not always the same. Some lynchings were straightforward, disciplined affairs, executed with little ceremony or celebration. Other lynchings were prolonged situations that took on the atmosphere of a county fair.

Some mobs were composed of poor white mill workers, field hands and the like. Other mobs were composed of prominent citizens and leaders of the community. They must have been caught up in very strong feelings to justify the atrocities committed against their neighbors.

The Lynching Era in the United States lasted until the 1960's, but the actual number of lynchings declined yearly. Across the nation, thousands of blacks and whites lost their lives because of the lawlessness of the times.[6]

There would be other killings in Madison County after 1904, but none that can be classified as a lynching.[7]

It is impossible to determine, definitely, what motivated lynch mobs a century ago. All mobs claimed to have a good reason for their

---

[6] Statistics about lynchings should be used cautiously since there is no guarantee that an accurate count was made.

[7] In 1915, Herman Neely, a Negro field hand, shot at a white boy on a mule. He missed the boy and the mule and wounded a white man, Arthur Craft, in the knee. Deputy Sheriff Silas Hunt arrested Neely and was at the Whitesburg railroad depot when six men took the prisoner and shot him to death. This was not a lynching, but a murder committed by a small group of men.

violence, whether it was to kill a black or to burn a city. The day after such violence occurred, blacks and whites went back to working side by side.

Why would otherwise law-abiding citizens take the law into their own hands and carry out their version of the law outside the framework of the judicial system? What were the reasons that mob violence came to an end and people again became law-abiding citizens?

Look at old photos of that time period and note that all men were wearing hats, while today men rarely wear hats. What happened? Did mob killings, like hats, go out of style?

Capital punishment, throughout the ages, has been carried out for a reason and has been condoned by communities everywhere. The killing of a criminal, by a lynch mob or by the state, was, and is used to send a message that criminal acts will not be tolerated. Whether either method was, and is, a valid deterrent to murder has not been decided and the debate still goes on.

Did lynching stop the murders? It did not. Has the execution of criminals today stopped people from killing each other? It has not.

Did the experiences of the past prove to an enlightened world that mob violence was a sin? It did not. Let us look at modern news accounts about mob violence.

Citizens of Quito, Ecuador burned a man alive after he was accused of stealing five head of cattle. They tied him to a tree poured gasoline on him and set him on fire. Another village burned five men who were accused of killing a taxi driver.[8]

After white rule ended in Cape Town, South Africa, new black leaders faced spiraling crime. People were frustrated because the criminal justice systems took too long to react. The frustration boiled over into violence and was not unexpected. Gangsters were executed by mobs of working class people who shot them or set them on fire.[9]

Two police officers in St. Petersburg, Florida, were shot, twenty-nine fires were set, and more than one million dollars in damage to property was reported, hours after a Grand Jury cleared an officer in the shooting of a black youth. A black man called for the execution of a white officer and threatened to burn down the city

---

[8] *Birmingham News* (November 15, 1996).
[9] *The Huntsville Times* (1996).

unless the officers who killed the youth were charged with the crime and fired.[10]

In Gary, Indiana, vigilantes beat to death a recently released ex-convict known as the "Pillowcase Rapist", after he broke into a neighborhood home. The vigilantes were not identified and never arrested.[11]

Could the lynchings of long ago have been caused by the ignorance of the rednecks of the South? They were not. Let us look at the present conduct of what should be our most intelligent segment of the population.

Three thousand students at Michigan State University, resorted to mob violence, not over human rights, poverty or civil rights, but because they were not allowed to get drunk at their favorite gathering spot before football games. There were the usual bonfires, accusations of police brutality, tear gas, injuries and arrests.

Experts were puzzled over the meaning of this mob violence. Some experts found the incident troubling but did not attach much significance to the events. They felt that students had a right to feel that something was being taken away from them; there was nothing wrong with the students fighting for their " right to drink".

Because of crackdowns on alcohol at fraternities, two thousand students at Washington State University in New Hampshire, were involved in a confrontation with police. Twenty-three police officers were injured.

A festival at the University of Connecticut turned into mob violence when students set fire to cars and confronted police because of a crackdown on underage drinking.

Students at Ohio University turned into a mob when bars closed an hour early. Because of the switch to daylight-saving time, one hundred seventy-five students went to jail.[12]

A mob caused a riot during the annual Classic Car and Music Festival in Reno, Nevada. Two thousand members of the mob beat unprotected citizens. At least fifteen thousand people were on downtown streets. One thousand people took over an intersection, jumping on cars and beating people.[13]

In Denver, Colorado, John Elway led the beloved Broncos to a win over the Green Bay Packers in the Super Bowl. Ten thousand people took over downtown, overturned cars and injured people.

---

[10] *USA Today* (November 15, 1996).
[11] *The Huntsville Times* (August 17, 1996).
[12] *USA Today* (May 6, 1998); *The Huntsville Times* (May 31, 1998).
[13] *The Huntsville Times* (August 10, 1998).

Bottles were thrown and bonfires lit. Police fired tear gas to move the mob. Said one member of the mob, *"The police moved in without any warning at all, they started throwing tear gas. I can't believe it!"*[14]

Should we conclude that because juries in the South found lynchers, *"not guilty"*, that they didn't do anything wrong? Can we assume that regardless of evidence presented, the judgment of twelve men must be accepted?

A jury found O. J. Simpson, a nationally known black football player, *not guilty* in the death of his white ex-wife; and the public is asked to accept the verdict without question?

A jury found the white police officers in Los Angeles who beat a black suspect, Rodney King, *not guilty*. The reaction of blacks was an attempt to burn *their* city to the ground.

Throughout history there have been excuses for mob violence and the abandonment of our judicial systems. Where would our civilization be today without the law and our system of investigation and trial for the accused that is presumed not guilty, until a judge or jury says otherwise?

Mob violence will remain with us as long as the civilized world believes, not in self-government, but in *self-gratification*.

---

[14] *The Huntsville Times* (February 1, 1999).

XXVIII

Chapter One
White, Evans & Hall
1878

The Independent.

THE LARGEST CIRCULATION IN NORTH ALABAMA.

THURSDAY, APRIL 18th, 1878

Brutal Butchery!

Geo. Schoenberger Assassinated by a Gang of Cattle Thieves.

Great Indignation in the Community.

Eph. Hall and Ben Evans, accused, Commit the Deed.

Mike White The Moving Spirit of the Outrage.

The Citizens Take the Law into their Hands.

Hang all three on one Limb.

EVERYTHING DONE WITH COOL DELIBERATION.

Sunday's Quiet now Prevailing.

Full Details, from Beginning to End.

IMPETUOUS JUSTICE HASTENS WHAT THE LAW WOULD HAVE DONE.

White, at the Gallows, Partially Fails to Deny Knowledge of the Deed.

First Meeting at Court-House.

Pursuant to a call published in the Huntsville papers, a meeting of citizens was held at the court house, last Saturday at 12 m. As the object of the meeting was to secure general co-operation to break up the cattle stealing which has been going on, there was a large crowd present. Mike White had just been arrested and the gravest rumors were prevalent. When the meeting was called the court-room was filled rapidly. Col. Geo. P. Beirne was called to the chair, and W. L. Clay, Esq., was chosen secretary.

The excitement, however, continued and about four o'clock same evening a large crowd made their way to the jail. Officer Hardy got up on the jail fence and told them that there were fifty men inside who would not allow them in. The crowd then retired. A large guard was put at the jail, Saturday night. Sunday the excitement was stronger than ever, and when it became rumored that White would be rescued from the jail Sunday night, additional good citizens volunteered to watch as guards, to see that nothing happened. The officers of the law did their duty in all respects throughout but it was impossible not to see that nearly every one thought the criminals could not be hanged too soon. Monday and Monday night all was comparatively quiet. Tuesday was likewise quiet. The sheriff notified the U. S. Marshal that he could no longer be responsible for the safe keeping of U. S. prisoners, and that they were in direct danger, but as they were in jail, something might accidentally happen, should a crowd come to the jail to lynch the murderers of Schoenberger. Accordingly a U. S. posse was placed at the jail. The prime object was to prevent anything wrong in connection with Government prisoners, but it was likewise hoped that the mere presence of men by the authority of the Government would serve to prevent any movement against any in the jail. It was never thought for a moment that there was any real danger to U. S. prisoners.

But the tide of indignation swelled in the country. The very best citizens entered into the plan to execute the three men.

Near three o'clock, last Friday morning. George Schoenberger was murdered. We give full particulars. The gun which killed him was loaded with two pewter balls and a cartridge, thimble and all. We give a correct diagram of the scene of the awful assassination.

1. Schoenberger's house.
2. S's slaughter house.
3. Gate on pike and road from S's slaughter

The Huntsville Independent

2

1878

During the years surrounding 1878, many interesting historical events happened in the World, the United States, the State of Alabama and locally in Madison County, Alabama.[15]

World

Queen Victoria ruled England.... Japan recognized Korea as an independent country... Canada introduced ballot voting... The British Parliament passed a public health act... Peter Tchaikovsky composed *Swan Lake*... Charles Darwin's *The Descent of Man*, applied evolution to humans... London's first telephone exchange was established... The first intelligible message was heard over a telephone... Jules Verne authored, *Twenty Thousand Leagues Under the Sea* and *Around the World in Eighty Days*...Arthur Sullivan composed the hymn, "Onward Christian Soldiers"... Strauss wrote the "*Blue Danube*"... The Suez Canal was opened... Debtor's prisons were abolished in Britain... Victor Hugo's *Les Miserable* had been published.

United States

Rutherford Hayes was President of the United States... The United States Senate passed a bill to repeal the bankruptcy law... The Reconstruction Era ended when the last Federal troops left the South... Two-hundred-sixty-four cavalrymen, under the command of Gen. George A. Custer, were killed by the Sioux at Little Big Horn... Mark Twain authored *The Adventures of Tom Sawyer*... Alexander Graham Bell patented the telephone, the phonograph, and invented the first electric lamp... George Eastman patented a process for photographic plates.... Saccharine, an artificial sweetener, was discovered... Billy the Kid killed a sheriff in Lincoln County, New Mexico... Lawyers met in New York to form the American Bar Association...

---

[15] Information was gathered from local and state history books and local newspapers. Information was also obtained from, *A Dream Come True, Vol. II*, James Record, 1978, John Hicklin Printing Co. Huntsville, Alabama, Library of Congress Card Number:76-11880.

State

George S. Houston, a former Florence attorney, was the Governor but was soon to be replaced in late 1878, by Rufus W. Cobb... Alabama's population was over one million...Cullman County was created... Tuition fees at Auburn, with free room and board, were $12 per month, the number of students attending was two hundred and fifty... There were 688 prisoners in the state prisons... The Yellow Fever epidemic disabled Alabama... The Alabama Bar Association was organized... Daily mail began to be delivered between Huntsville and Guntersville... The unjust reconstruction debt was $30,037,563, but the Bondholders settled for $9,000,000... Federal Troops were withdrawn from the State ... Convicts were rented out to farms and factories to bring in revenue to the State.

Local

A fifteen-inch snow fell and was accompanied by a minus twelve temperature. Ice covered much of the Tennessee River... William H. Council, the First President of the Normal School, started the first black newspaper, *The Herald*... The Catholic Church on Jefferson Street was dedicated... The Anheiser-Lager Saloon opened in the Hickman Building on the northeast corner of the Square... John Ford killed J. McCalley with a knife during a fight in the Courthouse corridor... A newspaper added hope that someone would find a large cameo pin lost between Adams Avenue and the Episcopal Church... Huntsville's city limits were only one mile square... East Side Square was known as "Cheap Side Row,"... 35,000 people lived in the county.... A violent storm hit, causing the tall steeple of the Presbyterian Church to fall, crushing the roof and part of the wall at the front of the building, and otherwise damaging it. An appeal was made to the citizens for contributions to aid in repairing the building.... Five black Baptist churches were blown down. *"The only casualties were a cat killed stone dead, and the teeth of a child knocked out."*... George Kennedy established a blacksmith shop near the corner of Clinton and Greene Streets opposite the County Jail in Huntsville... The Memphis & Charleston Railroad train, due at 9 a.m. did not arrive till 2 p.m. because of a rock falling on the track at or near Lookout Mountain.

Chapter One
White-Evans-Hall 1878

Madison County was a farming community that depended upon livestock for survival. Theft of stock had become a widespread problem and was of great concern to citizens across the area. Cattle farmers were not the only ones concerned about the situation. All families depended upon their small number of stock in order to survive. The citizens of Huntsville, the progressive town and center of the farming community, were also interested.

There was much talk about the theft problem and several leaders decided to take action. On Wednesday, the tenth of April 1878, Huntsville's *Weekly Democrat*[16] published a notice, submitted by twenty-one prominent men, informing the community of an upcoming meeting the next weekend.[17]

The meeting, to be held in the Madison County Courthouse at high noon on Saturday, the thirteenth of April, was called to take some concerted action to find and prosecute stock thieves. The citizens of Madison County were encouraged to attend this meeting and ask their leaders in law enforcement and in the judicial system, to investigate the theft and stop the wholesale plunder of cattle, hogs, and other stock. When people opened copies of *The Weekly Democrat* and read about the meeting, they started making plans to attend. They wanted something done about the thefts and wanted to get involved in any movement to stop them.

Theft of stock was not a new problem. There have always been people who felt the need to take what was not rightfully theirs. The problem was in small towns and communities everywhere. However, during April of 1878, unusual circumstances surrounding the thefts in Huntsville, would set this community apart from others.

---

[16] Most of the information for this chapter was found only in articles in two weekly newspapers *The Weekly Democrat* (April 18, 1878); *The Independent* (April 18, 1878). Each fact or quote will not be repetitiously footnoted individually.

[17] The citizens concerned enough to call a meeting were; John B. Anderson, Jacob W. Battle, Col. George P. Bierne, Judge Edward C. Betts, Thomas B. Crawford, Peter M. Dox, C. K. Ellis, J. J. Hammond, B. H. Hardin, Dr. George M. Harris, J. P. Haw, Thomas S. McCalley, F. A. McClung, James M. Moss, V. Augustus Nuckols, Daniel H. Turner and Isham Watkins. (*The Weekly Democrat*, March 27, 1878 and Wednesday, April 10, 1878)

Market on Washington Street-Late 1870's
Photograph Courtesy Huntsville-Madison County Public Library
Market House on Clinton Avenue (lower photograph)

The Players

There were two slaughterhouses in Huntsville. One of the slaughterhouses belonged to George Shoenberger,[18] the other to Mike White. Controversy concerning stock theft centered upon these two businesses. Suspicion pointed to White's establishment when rumors circulated that he was using stolen stock to slaughter and sell at the Huntsville market.[19]

Mike White was thirty-eight years old. He had blue eyes, light hair, a fair complexion, and was five foot eight inches tall. He was originally from Rochester, New York, but came to Huntsville about 1860, and served in the Confederate Army during the War Between the States. He served along with other men from Huntsville in the Fourth Alabama Cavalry.[20] He was a well-thought-of-citizen and was respected as a businessman. White did not have children by Elizabeth, his young and very beautiful wife.

At this time there were several Negroes[21] who worked for Mike White and lived near his slaughterhouse. Ephraim Hall also worked for White, but lived across Pinhook Creek in the Old Burchfield house. Hall was described as being a very stout, dark mulatto about fifty-five years old. His hair was tinged with gray around a most brutal face. He was born in North Carolina, and had many masters prior to the War Between the States. He had lived at Selma, Alabama, where he worked at the Ironworks, before coming to Huntsville after the war.

Ben Evans and his wife, Josie, lived in a small house near Pinhook Creek, adjacent to the slaughterhouse. Both were about forty-five years old. Ben was a medium sized man weighing about 150 pounds. He was raised in Lexington, Kentucky, and did not come to Huntsville until after 1865. He had worked at White's slaughterhouse for about one and one half years. Josie served as Mrs. White's maid.

---

[18] George Shoenberger's name has been found with two spellings (also Schoenberger) throughout the research material. The spelling of Shoenberger was chosen because that is the way "he" signed his name on his will.

[19] The Huntsville Market was located on the southwest corner of Clinton Avenue and Washington Street. The city-parking garage presently occupies this site. <see photograph on previous page>

[20] C.S.A. regimental records for Company F of the Fourth Alabama Cavalry; Microfilm, Huntsville Public Library.

[21] The word "Negro" has been used because it is true to the times, historically. While it may not be politically correct today, it was used during the time of the events in this book.

Frank Kelly and Lilly Mitchell lived with Ben and Josie. Kelly was a young man of nineteen described as being 'almost white.' Kelly had worked for Shoenberger for about a month, two and a half years earlier. Now he worked for White, loading the meat wagon and helping him at the Huntsville market. Lilly was Josie's niece.

Mike White's home and business was located about a quarter of a mile from the Shoenberger property.[22]

George Shoenberger was sixty-seven years old, and was a large man. He was born, May 8, 1820, in Glaurus, Switzerland, where he spent his youth. At seventeen, he became a member of the reformed Presbyterian Church in that country. He came to the United States in 1848, and served in the Indian Wars as a soldier on the Texas frontier.

Shoenberger arrived in Huntsville in 1853, and opened a slaughterhouse. Shoenberger married Cassender LaMar, and they had a daughter, Sallie. In 1856, Cassender died and she was laid to rest in Maple Hill Cemetery.

Later, he married Fannie Strong Davis. Their child, Annie, was born in 1864. Shoenberger became a member of the Cumberland Presbyterian Church during the ministry of Rev. Dr. Stainback. At the time of his death Shoenberger's mother and father had already died in Switzerland, but he had a brother and sister still there.

Frances "Fannie" Petrey Strong Shoenberger
Courtesy of the Burwell-Penny Family

---

[22] The slaughterhouse was located on what is now Oakwood Avenue. It was on the east bank of Pinhook Creek, west of Meridianville Pike. Sale of livestock was conducted there until the late 1970's, over 100 years beyond the time period of this story. Going north on Washington Street, after crossing Oakwood Avenue, one can still see the open space that was the stockyard and the concrete platform used to load cattle.

He, Fannie, and the two daughters, Sallie, twenty-two years old and Annie, fourteen years old, lived on Meridianville Pike, just outside the Huntsville Town Limits. His slaughterhouse was on his home premises. Shoenberger was a citizen who was politically active, a substantial businessman, and was respected by those who knew him.[23]

George Shoenberger openly discussed the problem of missing stock with others in the community and decided to do something about the situation. He became a leader in the fight and the community was behind him.

As time went on, rumors that Mike White had something to do with the missing livestock began to circulate more freely. Apparently, George Shoenberger made open accusations about missing stock being found at White's slaughterhouse. Competition between the two, mixed with the widespread theft of stock in the surrounding countryside, would soon lead to trouble.

On Thursday, April the 11th, 1878, the sun set on a southern community of 19,000 people beset with suspicion of thievery among its citizens. The sun would rise the next morning to startling circumstances.

Annie Shoenberger Hamplett photograph Courtesy of Burwell-Penny Family

Sallie Ophelia Shoenberger Penny photograph Courtesy of the Burwell-Penny Family

---

[23] Shoenberger's obituary notice, *The Weekly Democrat* (April 24, 1878).

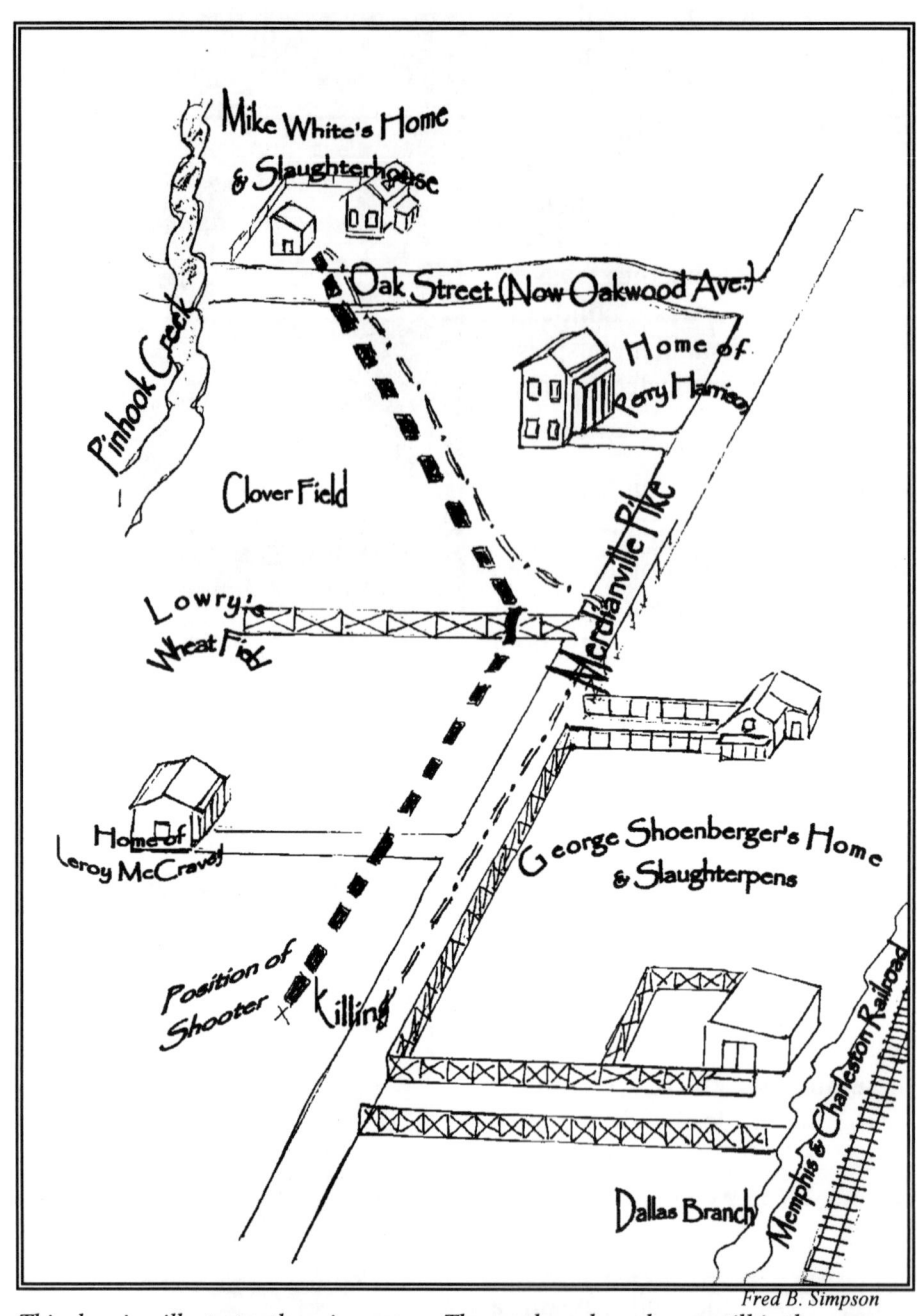

Fred B. Simpson
This drawing illustrates the crime scene. The roads and creeks are still in the same place, and the train still travels the same tracks today as it did the morning of the killing.

The Killing

Forty-two year old Henry Huddleston left his eight children, and his thirty-six year old wife, Amelia, and stepped out into the darkness. It was just after two o'clock on a fine spring morning, Friday, the twelfth of April. Carrying a lantern to show the way, he walked north up Meridianville Pike. A spring rain had caused a fog and the road was muddy.

He crossed the Memphis & Charleston railroad tracks and passed out of the Huntsville town limits. His destination was George Shoenberger's slaughterhouse located about one mile north of the Madison County Courthouse. Huddleston had, for some time, worked for Shoenberger as a butcher in his slaughterhouse, and he helped sell meat at the Huntsville market.[24]

As he neared the gate to the Shoenberger property, he saw movement in the darkness. He could not make out what it was, but felt that it was a person. Beyond the light of his lantern, the darkness loomed before him, but in his mind's eyes, he could see the surrounding countryside. This was a place he had seen many times before.

Meridianville Pike stretched northward over the flat land for more than a quarter of a mile then went over a small hill and out of sight. The railroad tracks and Pin Hook Creek ran parallel to the Pike to its east.[25]

Shoenberger's slaughterhouse was beyond a gate on the east side of the Pike crossing a lane leading down to the buildings and cattle pens. The property backed up to the creek and the railroad was across the creek.[26]

Continuing north on the Pike, Huddleston knew the next wagon road to the left would lead through a field to the home of a neighbor, Leroy W. McCravey. Next on the road would be J. T. Lowry's wheat field.

Further up the Pike, about one fourth of a mile, a wagon road led off to the left[27] just over a slight hill by the home of Perry Harrison. The road went south of Mike White's home and

---

[24] The market was located at the southwest corner of Clinton Avenue and Washington. This site is presently occupied by the city's parking garage.
[25] The land looks the same today. The Pike still runs along the same route. The Dallas Branch of Pinhook Creek and the railroad have not changed locations.
[26] The location today would be at the intersection of Meridianville Pike and Abingdon Avenue at the present site of Lincoln Public School.
[27] This road was first called Oak Road. About 1902, it became Oakwood Avenue, Huntsville Land Plat Book, No. 1.

11

slaughterhouse, and continued across Pinhook Creek. Mike White's house was located about three hundred yards from the Lowry home.

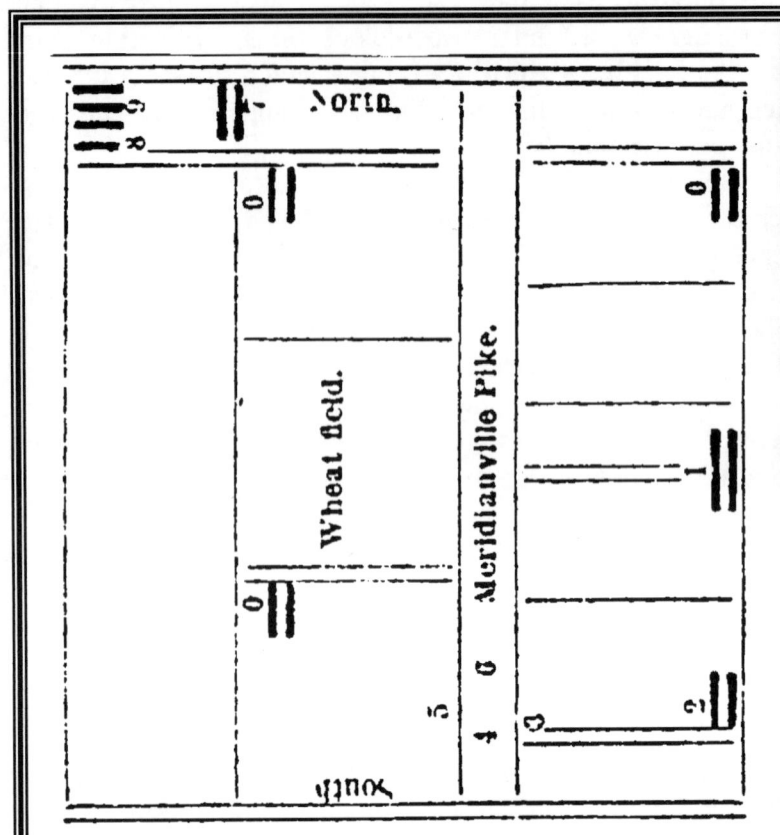

1. Schoenberger's house.
2. S's slaughter house.
3. Gate on pike and road from S's slaughter house.
4. Where wagon was in which S. was shot.
5. Where party was who shot musket.
. Eph's position at the time.
7. White's home.
8. Negro cabin in White's slaughter yard where Ben lived.
9. White's slaughter-house.
0. 0. 0. Residences of neighbors. The double lines show wagon roads: single lines show division fences.

This drawing appeared in the April 18, 1878 newspaper, The Independent, to show the readers the site of the murder of George Shoenberger.

Huddleston was again startled by a sound. Looking toward Shoenberger's gate he saw two men in the distance. A low mist still hovered over the ground from the rain and it was too dark to recognize either of them. He wondered who would be on the Pike at this early hour, but he did not speak to the men.

Huddleston opened the gate and walked down the lane to Shoenberger's slaughterhouse. While loading the wagon he told Shoenberger that he had seen two men at the gate. Shoenberger called to Charlie, one of the Negro helpers, to *"Remain in the pen until daylight. Ben Evans is watching for a chance to steal some more cattle."*

Before three o'clock in the morning, Huddleston and Shoenberger began their usual trip toward the market in Huntsville. Shoenberger climbed up on the step of the wagon and swung himself onto the driver's seat. Taking the reins in hand, he directed the two mules down the lane and onto Meridianville Pike.

Huddleston walked in front of the wagon to open and shut the gate. When Shoenberger reached the Pike, he drove through the gate, turned on the Pike toward Huntsville and stopped the wagon to allow Huddleston time to close the gate and climb on board.

Suddenly a shot rang out from the darkness. Huddleston looked in time to see the flash of gunfire from a man who stood across Meridianville Pike, in McCravey's field. He fired what appeared to be a musket.[28] Huddleston turned just as another man standing behind the wagon shot a pistol twice. Even though Huddleston saw everything that happened, he was unable to prevent the fatal action.

As the sound of the shots died away, the man in the field ran in a northerly direction, parallel to the Pike. Crossing the field he set the musket down next to the fence, crossed over, picked up his weapon and continued to flee through Lowry's wheat field. He ran toward the Pike, jumped a smaller fence and joined the other man who was running through the clover field[29] behind Perry Harrison's house.

Suddenly, breathing was difficult for Shoenberger. Attempts to grasp what had happened eluded him as his body began to yield to the inevitable. He fell back onto the wagon seat. Huddleston

---

[28] A musket is a smooth bore, rifle, loaded with powder usually from a container made from the horn of a cow, called a powder horn. It was fired with the aid of a percussion cap.

[29] The *Huntsville Independent* ran an article in the March 28th, 1878, issue advising farmers that clover fields were needed to provide nutrients to the soil.

attempted to help but the big man's life flowed from the three wounds in his back and side. Shoenberger's only words were *"Who hit me in the back?"*

Across the Pike, forty-two year old merchant and auctioneer, Leroy W. McCravey was asleep beside his thirty-two year old wife, Sarah. He did not hear the shots but Sarah did, and she woke her husband. Around 2:45 o'clock in the morning, McCravey hurriedly dressed and immediately ran to the Pike.

The sound of the shots carried across the countryside for a mile and could be heard throughout the town. On-duty Huntsville City Policeman, thirty-six year old G. W. Kennard was at the Courthouse at 2:40 o'clock in the morning when he heard the three shots. Because the report was so loud, he thought that the first shot sounded like a shotgun, but the other 'shots' sounded like pistol shots.

Mrs. Shoenberger heard the shots and ran out of her home. She ran down the lane, toward the wagon. She began to scream before she could see the bloody body in the wagon. The screaming went on for an inordinate length of time through the still morning air and could be heard at a great distance.

Further up the Pike, forty-nine-year-old tax collector, Perry L. Harrison, rose out of bed when he heard the three gunshots. His wife, Elizabeth, and their seven children became upset because of the screaming. He hurriedly calmed them and, giving a pistol to one of his workmen, he ran in the direction of the Pike toward the noise.

Perry Harrison's daughters, Sue, eighteen years old, and Hattie, fifteen years old, were awakened by the shots and, looking out one of the upstairs windows, saw two men running through the field of clover next to their house. They watched two Negro men run in the direction of Whites' place and, in loud voices, let everyone know what they had seen.

Todd Harrison set off for town to alert the authorities. The screaming continued.

As McCravey reached the Pike, a young boy[30] told him that Shoenberger had been shot, and that he was dead. McCravey looked in the wagon and found Shoenberger in a natural position, as if he was driving, but he was no longer alive. Perry Harrison arrived at the wagon soon after McCravey.

---

[30] There is no further information on who this boy was or how he came to be on the Pike at this hour with so much information.

Elizabeth Harrison [everyone called her Lizzie], and some of the children, along with Lurind, their old Negro cook, William, a nine-year-old house servant; and laborers, George and Sara Baubaugh stood at the front of the house awaiting news of the unusual events on the road. Lizzie was not afraid, because George was there with a pistol.

Other men who lived nearby heard the noise and came outside to search for the problem. Milton Humes, a thirty-three-year-old lawyer; George B. Gill, a thirty-one year old real estate agent; and sixty-one-year-old farmer, John Patton, hurried to the scene. Another neighbor, John Tate Lowry, a fifty-six-year-old farmer, and his twenty-six-year-old son, Dr. Samuel Lowry, arrived. Dr. Lowry attempted to put his skills to use, but could see at a glance that Shoenberger was not alive. Herman Humphrey, another neighbor, arrived soon after.

As the group of men stood around Shoenberger's wagon, they heard the noise of an approaching wagon. They soon made out Mike White's mule-drawn wagon coming down the Pike on the way to the Huntsville market. In the glow of the lantern they could also see Frank Kelly in the wagon.

Harrison called out, *"Who's there?"*

Mike White did not answer, but posed a question himself, *"What's the matter?"*

White did not get down from the wagon, nor did he ask any of the particulars of the killing.

He asked, *"Do you want to send anything to town?"*

When Harrison said, *"No,"* White drove on toward town.

Officer Kennard was still at the Courthouse when Todd Harrison came in to spread the word about the shooting. The officer hurried down Meridianville Pike to join the other men at the scene at the gate. The neighbors did not know what to do. They stood in the road talking to each other and to the officers who rushed to the scene.

Some of the men assisted in placing Shoenberger's body in the back of his wagon. They turned the wagon around, and he was carried back up the lane to his home. Mrs. Shoenberger accompanied the wagon. Her distress was evident to all.

Thus, George Shoenberger died on an early spring morning far from his native land. His death was not so different than any other of a thousand murders throughout the world, but the next week found events originating from his death that were very different.

Two Huntsville Police Officers, Alfred Sweeney and Joseph P. Parton, joined Officer Kennard. They waited until Brittain Franks, the County Coroner[31] and Town Marshall, joined them at the scene.

At daybreak, the police officers were in charge and listened to Huddleston's story of what happened. Huddleston pointed out where the musket was fired in McCravey's field.

Fred B. Simpson
Present Day Photograph of the Scene of the Shooting
Taken at Daybreak April 1999—
121 years after the murder.

---

[31] A public officer who must determine the cause of any death not due to natural causes.

The Tracking

When all of the law enforcement officers were assembled, the men went into the field and struck a trail where the shooter had been standing. The tracks could be seen distinctly. McCravey pointed out that the tracks showed that the person making them had long strides, four to five feet in length. The impression of a run-down shoe print was clearly visible. The tracks ran north along the Pike. Where the footprints stopped at a fence, the fresh impression of the butt of a gun appeared next to the fence where the shooter had set his gun down to cross. The tracks then continued into Lowry's wheat field where they were joined by another set of tracks.

As the trackers neared the Harrison home, Sue and Hattie Harrison told of seeing two men cross from the Pike near the back of their house, then across Cox's oat field in the direction of White's slaughterhouse. The trackers followed the tracks further north where the tracks of the run-down shoe led into a ditch while the other clearly went to Ben Evan's house.

Coroner Franks discussed this turn of events with the officers and directed them to look for the suspects and the murder weapons at Mike White's place. The group of officers mounted their horses and headed over to White's slaughterhouse.

Being detectives, they knew what to look for. Since tracks led to Ben Evans' house they knew someone in the house had to be involved. His pants would be wet from the wheat field and there would be fresh mud on his shoes. There should also be a musket somewhere in the house with items needed to fire the musket, such as powder horns, ramrod and caps.

The group split up for the search. Some went into a room by the slaughterhouse where salt was stored. Behind a barrel, they found powder horns. Others searched Ben Evans' house, where Officer Parton found a ramrod in the corner of the kitchen. Officer Kennard found some dry pants in the kitchen, but they knew the pants the person had on earlier that morning should be wet, so they continued to search.

Hoping for some additional information, the Coroner and Officer Kennard walked over to Mike White's house to talk to Ben Evans' wife, Josie. Officer Kennard asked Josie what she had done with the pants but she gave the men no answer.

The men returned to Evans' house and continued their search. After looking around and behind everything, Officer Kennard found the pants rolled up into a knot in Kelly's bedding. They were wet nearly to the waistband and spotted with grass stains and fresh mud.

Kennard saw kick marks on the front door. This caused him to look closely at the floor beneath the door, where he found other kick marks. Pulling the boards aside and looking under the floor, he reached into the darkness and pulled from its hiding place the suspected murder weapon, an old musket. A fresh, just burst cap was still on the gun and there was moist dirt wedged into the muzzle. On the stock of the gun was a leaf of fresh green wheat. The gun was loaded with two pewter balls and a cartridge, thimble and all.

As the men continued the search of the house, they found a box of caps in the bottom drawer of Josie's wardrobe.[32] Next, Kennard saw a hogshead.[33] He opened it and, with a stick, dug around in the straw until he found a pair of shoes that were damp and muddy.

After gathering the items found in Ben Evans' house, the officers took care to preserve them to be used as evidence in court. They took the muddy shoes and musket back to the fields where they had found the shoe prints. Officer Patton took the shoes and fit them into the shoe prints with ease. The butt of the gun from Ben's house was an exact fit into the impression by the fence.

They had enough evidence. The next step would be to arrest and question the people involved. Policeman Sweeney went with the Coroner back to White's slaughterhouse to arrest Ben Evans.

Coroner Franks said, *"Ben, I will have to search and arrest you."*

Ben replied, *"What am I being arrested for? I can prove where I was all night. I have not had a gun for five or six years!"*

Policeman Sweeney put Ben Evans up on the horse behind him and started toward town.

Ephraim Hall hid in some weeds and watched the officers coming toward Mike White's slaughterhouse. At first opportunity he ran inside and hid in the slaughterhouse loft while the officers searched Ben Evans' house. After the officers departed, he came back and found Lilly at Mike White's house along with Mrs. White, who was sewing. Aunt Mariah Cabaniss[34] was also there. Ephraim called Lilly outside and asked her where Ben was. Lilly said he had been

---

[32] Since closets were considered a room to the home during this period of time, and taxed as such, large wooden cabinets called wardrobes were built and used to store a person's clothes.

[33] A large cask, an old measure of capacity, containing 64.85 gallons of liquid, or other material. 1986 Webster's Third Unabridged International Edition Dictionary

[34] No information could be found regarding Mariah Cabaniss.

arrested. Ephraim ran across the creek toward his house but he would not escape the officers of the law for very long.

The officers returned to White's slaughterhouse and arrested Lilly and Josie and they too were taken to jail.[35]

A murder had occurred. It was still early, the sun not long up, before the evidence was found, and those involved questioned and arrested.

George Shoenberger's body was stretched upon the bed in his home. Modesty held no place under the physician's stare. Local doctors examining him were: Dr. John J. Dement, Dr. Samuel H. Lowry, Dr. Christopher A. Robinson, and Dr. James P. Burke.

Those involved in the investigation had finished examining the crime scene, determined the facts, and gathered evidence from the suspects' residences. The recently fired musket, muddy shoes, wet pants and known suspects were in custody. All this would be presented to a jury at a Coroner's Inquest to make an official record of the proceedings. The hearing had to be conducted by the Coroner in the prescribed lawful manner.

The Coroner's Jury[36] was called to meet at the Courthouse at 12 noon, on the day of the murder. This was little more than eight hours after the killing had occurred. Coroner Franks selected six men to serve on the Coroner's Jury for the inquest. All six were close friends and neighbors of the victim. Some had been a part of the investigation and one was an officer of the law. Some of the men were to testify and also sit in judgment.[37] These jurors were: Milton Humes, L. W. McCravey, J. T. Lowry, G.W. Kennard, S. H. Lowry, and P. L. Harrison.

---

[35] The jail was located downtown at the intersection of Clinton and Greene Streets.
[36] A judicial inquiry is usually before a jury as a Coroner's investigation of a death. (Black's Law Dictionary) Code of Alabama, 1852, page 658-660, #3765, "Coroner may subpoena witnesses and call in a physician to advise professionally." #3765, "Coroner may examine as a witness any person who, in his opinion, may have knowledge of the facts." #3767, "Any person who refuses to answer any question, except by the grounds that it may incriminate himself, is guilty of a misdemeanor, and must be committed to jail unless he give bail if $550 and appear at the Circuit Court." #3770, "If the jury finds that the deceased came to his death by the act of another by unlawful means, the Coroner may issue a warrant for his arrest."
[37] This would not be allowed today. As an agent of the government, a detective would not be allowed to be the judge or sit on the jury of a case he investigated. Close friends of the victim would be declared biased and not allowed to sit in judgment. Today, the first hearing to determine probable cause would be in the district court in a preliminary hearing before an impartial judge.

Neighbors of the deceased, who had been selected for the jury, saddled up their horses or hitched up their wagons and traveled down Meridianville Pike toward Huntsville. They turned onto Washington Street, went up to the Courthouse, tied their horses to the fence that surrounded the Courthouse yard, and went into the imposing building that sat in the middle of the town.

They talked among themselves about the morning's events, and about the loss of their friend and neighbor while those in charge set up the room to display the evidence and question the suspects.

As these men gathered for the proceedings, the accused were taken from jail and marched, under guard, down Clinton Street, up Washington Street, across Commercial Row and into the Courthouse. The Negroes were kept separate and were not allowed to talk to each other before or after their testimony.

It was Friday, near lunch hour. The crowds along the sidewalks stopped to watch the group of prisoners being taken to the Courthouse. Rumors surely circulated about what the community's reaction would be to the death of George Shoenberger. Most citizens would be outraged that a noted member of their community had been viciously murdered. To be murdered, as it was rumored, by Negroes, was unthinkable.

Mike White was informed upon his return from market, that officers of the law had searched his property and arrested his employees. His wife sensed his apprehension and became upset. He was, therefore, not surprised when the Sheriff knocked at his door and said that he had to appear at the inquest.

Kelly was arrested and placed in the jail with the others.

It probably seemed a long ride into town for Mike White. He must have wondered if he was suspected but he knew Negroes would not be believed in court against a white man.

Huntsville-Madison County Public Library
The Madison County Courthouse

The Testimony

The Inquest lasted all afternoon and into the night.[38]

J. Withers Clay, editor of the *Huntsville Weekly Democrat*, was allowed to be in the courtroom. His job was to record facts from the testimony of each person as fast as he could, for the benefit of his readers. This was the stuff that put bread on his table and paid the rent, but for a few reporters like J. Withers Clay, it was more. One minute he was scratching out the weather and crop predictions and the next he was writing copy that would be read by all of America. Today J. Withers would savor the opportunity to be the eyes and ears of his readers.

The first witnesses were the doctors. The men of the jury listened intensely as they heard the technical evidence from the physicians about the cause of death.

---

[38] All of the reported testimony was in the form of answers only. All of the questions asked by Coroner Franks in the story are the opinion of the author based upon a logical question for the answer.

"We find three wounds in the right side of the back. One large wound was one inch from the spinal column ranging upward and slightly forward, to the left, passing through the ninth and tenth ribs, through the heart, the right lung, and lodged in the wall of the left chest. One smaller wound, about five inches from the spinal column, entered the right side of the back, passed through the diaphragm and liver, and lodged in the front wall of the chest. Another ball seemed to have entered the large wound, took the same direction and was also found in the walls of the chest." It was from the effects of these wounds that the doctors concluded that George Shoenberger came to his death.

Henry Huddleston took the stand to describe what he had seen that morning.

L. W. McCravey had been part of the team tracking the suspects and related his actions. He had followed the tracks and he believed that Ben Evans' shoes fit the imprints found in Lowery's wheat field.

Perry Harrison stated for the record that he heard three shots and hurried to the Pike.

Police Officer Joseph Parton and Officer G. W. Kennard related their search of the slaughterhouse and of the items they found.

Officer Sweeney testified that he went with Marshall Franks to Mike White's slaughterhouse to arrest Ben Evans. Ben would not tell them anything about the gun that was found, so he was arrested and placed in jail.

Members of the jury knew all the facts of the investigation before they began to question those involved. They had been part of the investigation. They knew that the killer's tracks led to Ben's house, where other evidence was found and that the people in the house were involved. They knew one of the men had shot the victim. The jury would know the subjects were lying if they denied any involvement in the killing.

Mike White arrived at the Courthouse and walked through the lunch hour crowd into the building. He was shown into the courtroom and faced the jury.

He was first asked if he knew anything about the killing of George Shoenberger. He asserted that he knew of no circumstance that would show who had killed Shoenberger.

When asked about his actions of the previous night, he stated that he went inside his house about seven o'clock and went to bed early. He woke up around two-thirty, but fell back asleep again and did not intend to get up again until three o'clock. His clock had been 'out of fix' and he really wasn't sure of the actual time. When he awoke the second time he looked at the clock and it was ten minutes until three.

He got out of bed, pulled on his pants and boots, and was washing his face when he heard what he believed to be, one gun shot. He finished getting dressed and lit his lantern, intending to go to the market. When he opened the door to go out he heard screaming coming from the direction of Merdianville Pike. He thought to himself that it seemed to be coming from McCravey's house and realized something must be wrong.

His wife, Elizabeth, became distressed and asked him not to go to the market, detaining him about ten minutes. He went to Ben's house to tell Josie Evans to go to his house and stay with his wife. When he got there, Ben, Josie, Lilly and Kelly were asleep in bed. He told Kelly to get up and help him load the wagon. He told Ben to get up and hitch up the team of mules.

The Coroner knew one of the Negroes had not been in bed sleeping and questioned White closely to determine which one of them had been outside. White began contradicting himself by stating that he didn't know if Ben or Kelly was actually in bed when he got there. It now became his recollection that Ben came out of the house immediately when he called.

White stated that he left his house at 3:10 in the morning, stopping by his slaughterhouse at 3:15 and picked up Kelly before heading into town. They left the slaughterhouse and turned right onto Meridianville Pike. Shortly, they came upon the group at Shoenberger's gate. White stopped and asked one of the gentlemen if they wanted to send anything to town. He stayed and talked to them two or three minutes before leaving for market.

Coroner Franks showed the musket to Mike White, asking him if he had seen the gun before.

White responded, "*I do not know whether I saw the gun or not. I bought a gun like that about three years ago from Tom Green.*"

Franks: What kind of gun was it?

White: "*It was a musket like this one that I have in my hand.*"

Franks: What did you do with your musket?

White: "*I first gave the musket to Jimmy Ridge. He kept it while he worked for me. He quit about nine months ago. He lived in the same room Ben Evans now lives in, in the slaughter yard. It then fell into the possession of a man who worked for Rudolf Beidermann. He kept possession of the gun for four months.*"

Franks asked if he gave the gun to anyone else. White replied, "*I did not turn the gun over to anyone! I don't know for certain that the gun was at Ben Evans' house. Ben Evans had charge of it, if it was there.*" He stated he didn't know of it being at his place in the last year.

White was asked about the employment of Ben Evans. White stated that Ben Evans had worked for him for about two and a half years and that if the gun were on the property Ben would be the one in charge of it. White was asked about Ben's muddy shoes and he explained that yesterday Ben had plowed the west part of the field, the lower bottoms, next to the creek.

Franks asked White if Ben had any bullets, to which White replied that Ben did not, but that he allowed his employees to use guns to shoot the stray dogs that would hang about the slaughterhouse yard. White acknowledged that he owned a small pistol, and that he had planned to take it with him that morning but it was not to do any killing.

After answering the questions put to him, Mike White left the courtroom in downtown Huntsville. He was probably worried about the turn of events and he certainly was given cause for deep thoughts as he traveled back home.

Frank Kelly was brought into the courtroom. He was belligerent, arrogant and would attempt to cover himself, and his friends, by lying.

Under opening questioning, Kelly stated that he had worked for Mr. White for about two and a half years. During that time he lived on Mr. White's place except for about one month when he had worked for Mr. Shoenberger. For two or three months he had lived with Ben Evans and his wife, Josie, and Lilly Mitchell. They all stayed in the small house in the same room.

Everyone knew someone in that room had gotten up and gone out to kill Shoenberger. Coroner Franks asked about the specific sleeping arrangements. Kelly could not remember if there were one or two beds in the room but he stated that he slept on the floor. Lilly was in the same bed as Ben and Josie.

He was asked if he heard the noise of someone moving about around two o'clock that morning. He said he woke up about two o'clock but not because of any noise. He was asleep when Mr. White called him about three o'clock. "*Ben said he was going into town, but was in the room when Mr. White called. I called to him and he answered. He could have gone out when I was asleep but Ben didn't get up until Mr. White called him. I came out before Ben. He had his shoes on.*"

Kelly continued, explaining to the jury that he was walking across the horse lot to the slaughterhouse with Mr. White about three o'clock in the morning, when they heard screaming. It was loud and sounded like a woman hollering. According to Kelly, it sounded like it came from the creek. Mr. White did not know where the screaming was coming from but thought it was over toward McCravey's.

Kelly stated that they always left the slaughterhouse for the market about three, but that morning they started about twenty-five minutes late. Kelly denied over and over that he knew who shot Mr. Shoenberger. He denied that Ben had a gun or a pistol or that he ever saw a gun at Mr. White's. He didn't know anything about shooting at dogs. And no, he hadn't heard any shooting that morning.

He was asked if Jimmy Ridge had the musket. Kelly answered that he knew Mr. Ridge because he once stayed at White's for a year but he had not lived there for several months. He had not stayed in the same room with Mr. Ridge, and he saw no gun present while he was there. Kelly did not know if Mr. White had ever given Mr. Ridge the gun. In fact, he had never seen a gun kept there by anyone except a pistol that he had seen lying on a bureau in Mr. White's house.

He was shown the musket. Kelly denied having seen the gun before; not the previous night or ever at Mr. White's house. He had no knowledge about where the gun stayed. He also denied owning or seeing any powder horns or that he had given Ben a cartridge the night before. He never heard Ben say a word about Mr. Shoenberger accusing him of stealing his stock.

He was shown the muddy shoes and wet pants. He agreed that the shoes and pants looked like Ben's. He stated that Ben had been ploughing the day before but he didn't wear the pants in question. Kelly didn't know who could have put the pants in his bedding or who the pants belonged to. He was wearing the same pants he had worn all morning.

Kelly had been under questioning for a long time and didn't know the right answers. He was again shown the musket and this time he seemed to remember having seen the weapon, but didn't know where it stayed. He said he had never seen the musket in the room where the salt was kept, but then admitted that he had seen guns sitting around the slaughterhouse, once or twice. He denied that the gun was kept in the room where he stayed, but admitted the musket he had seen looked like the one on the table now.

Kelly was led from the courtroom and the next witness was brought in.

Lilly Mitchell was frightened as she began her testimony. She said she had been staying at Ben and Josie's house for about two weeks and was there the previous night. She had been to Lowry's place after supper and returned home about seven-thirty. She slept by herself on a tick[39] on the floor, and when she went to bed about nine o'clock, Ben and Kelly were already in bed.

Lilly stated that Ben was in bed when she went to sleep and in bed when she woke up. She woke up when Mr. White called Kelly to go to the market. The Coroner asked about the screaming. She said she heard someone holler when Mr. White came in. They did not know what was the matter. After Kelly went out they heard screaming, but the market wagon was gone when she went to the door.

Mr. White told Josie to go and stay with his wife until he came back. About seven-thirty, Josie and Lilly went back up to Mrs. White's house so that Josie could do the ironing.

When asked about the search of the house by Coroner Franks; Lilly said; *"I seen a crowd this morning but didn't ask no questions. I didn't know what them men wanted when they come to the house. Mr. Franks was there and asked about a gun."* Josie told him that Mr. White had an old gun there.

She was shown the murder weapon. She said she had never seen the gun, and denied telling anyone where the gun was, or that it was in the house. She did not know how the gun came to be under the floor or how the shoes came to be in the hogshead. She knew the powder horns belonged to Kelly and she had seen him put them behind the barrel.

She identified the shoes and pants as belonging to Uncle Ben, but could not explain why they were wet or in Kelly's bedding. She did not know who could have put them there. She did not know who put Kelly's bed down that night but she took the bed up that morning while cleaning up. She knew those were the pants Ben had worn but he did not wear them the day before. She did not know who wore the pants last night. She did not know when the pants were put in the bedding under the bed, or who took the pants from under the bed and put them in the trunk. She admitted that the pants were wet from someone wearing them.

---

[39] A cloth covering stuffed with materials, sometimes straw or feathers to make a mattress or bed.

She confessed that she knew something was wrong. When she saw the pants she knew they were Ben's and said, "*I didn't want nothing to do with them.*"

Lilly had been found with three dollars and Franks wondered if someone had paid her for her part in the cover up. She was questioned about where she had acquired the money and she stated that Miss Lizzie White[40] had given her three dollars that morning in order to pay Aunt Minerva Malone,[41] Mrs. White's washerwoman. Miss Annie and Miss Mary[42] were there, but Lilly wasn't sure if they had seen Miss Lizzie give the money to her.

The Coroner was finished with Lilly and Josie Evans replaced her on the witness stand.

When Josie Evans appeared, she told the jury that she had worked at Mr. White's since Christmas, doing the washing and ironing for Mrs. White. She had lived there two years before, and came back because Mrs. White's maid, Anna White, had moved to town, and stopped taking in Mrs. White's washing. Coroner Franks asked if Minerva Malone was the washerwoman for Mrs. White. He trapped Lilly in a lie when Josie replied, "*Aunt Minerva never did any washing for Mrs. White.*"

She was asked about the sleeping arrangements at their house that night. She stated that she, Ben, Kelly and Lilly stayed in the same room and that Ben and Kelly had gone to bed after supper, but she stayed up until about ten or eleven o'clock that evening. She made a pallet for Lilly, but Lilly had gotten in the same bed, behind her, when she got home from Lowry's.

Mr. White woke her up that morning by calling for Kelly and said there was a noise down on the Pike. She went to Mr. White's house with him that morning to stay with his wife because Mrs. White was upset about the fuss at the Pike. Josie was asked about hearing a gunshot. She replied that she did not hear the report of a gun or any screaming, but Mrs. White told her that she had heard the report of the gun. Josie told the jury that she had stayed at Mrs. White's until about six o'clock that morning. She lied when she told them that she did not learn about the shooting until Mr. White came back from the market. She had talked to Mr. Franks and Mr. Kennard at Mrs. White's house. They had asked her about the pistol and she

---

[40] Mike White's wife, Elizabeth White.
[41] No additional information could be found regarding Aunt Minerva Malone.
[42] These names are listed in *The Independent* (April 18, 1878); but their identification is unknown.

told them Mr. White did not take his pistol off the bureau that morning.

Josie told the jury that she believed the powder horns belonged to Kelly and she knew the shoes belonged to Ben, but could not remember if he had worn them the day before. When asked how the pants got wet, or why they were under Kelly's bedding, Josie replied that she did not know, but that Lilly had "taken up" Kelly's bed, so she had no way of knowing if she also picked up the pants.

Josie was asked who used the salt room and she replied that Ben and Kelly went into the salt room to salt hides; they would be the ones who would know if a gun was kept there. Ben, Kelly and "Wils"[43] were the only ones who ever went into the salt room.

She was told to look at the weapon lying on the table in front of her. She stated that she did not know who placed the weapon under the floor or who took it from the salt room.

The Jury knew that the musket had been at the slaughterhouse and that it was used in the killing. They knew it had been stored in the salt room and that it was found under the floor in her house. They all knew she was lying when she stated that she did not know who placed the weapon under the floor or who took it from the salt room.

She suddenly pointed to the murder weapon and said, *"That's Mr. White's gun, it sets in the next room to me and it was there two years ago when I stayed there."* The jury heard now that the weapon belonged to White and, unless the Negroes had stolen it from him, he would be implicated in the killing. The remainder of the hearing would be focused on White's involvement in the murder.

The jury had heard enough from Josie and went on to the next witness.

Ben Evans was called before the jury. When asked by Coroner Franks about his whereabouts on Thursday night, he said he had wanted to go to a dance that night but did not know of one. At about seven, he left Mike White's property where he had lived for three years, and rode into town to see Ella Lowe at the brickyard in Georgia.[44] He went there to sleep with her, but her children were there and he could not. Instead, he decided to go over to Patsey Henry's bawdy house, where he arrived about eight o'clock that night. He did not get down from his horse but went over to Aaron Kelly's house across the creek from Mr. White's. About ten o'clock,

---

[43] The name is spelled as it appears in *The Independent* (April 18, 1878). The identification of this person is unknown.
[44] A section of town that was predominantly of a black population. It was located where the Huntsville Hospital is today.

he went home, unsaddled the horse, put it in the horse lot, and went to bed.

Ben told the jury that he and his wife stayed in the house along with Josie's niece, Lilly, and Kelly. Narrowing the questioning to the night's events and knowing that they all would know if someone got up and went out that morning, Coroner Franks asked about the sleeping arrangements. Ben stated that he went to bed before Kelly and Josie but remembered that Lilly got in bed behind Josie. When Mr. White came in to wake up Kelly, nobody was in bed.

Until now, his testimony was short of a confession but revealed his lying and deceit. Coroner Franks asked Ben, Did you hear anything unusual last night? To which Ben replied, *"No, but Lilly said, "I hear someone crying." Mr. White and Kelly left on the wagon, going to the market, but I didn't hear any crying after the wagon started."*
Coroner Franks, showed the musket to Ben and asked him,
When did you see this last?
Ben replied that he had seen the gun Wednesday.
Coroner Franks, Have you ever shot the gun?
Ben replied no, that he had not, but realizing the Deputy would know it had been recently fired, stated that Kelly had busted a cap on it.

He was asked about the bullet moulds and the ramrod that were in the house. Evans was beginning to see that the jury was focusing in on him, hard. In desperation, he stated that he was unaware of any bullet moulds in the house, that the gun was never loaded and he didn't know if it had a ramrod. Franks asked again, Ben where do you keep the gun? Ben answered, *"Under the floor."*

He was asked about wearing wet pants on that day.

Ben replied, *"Those are the clothes I wore in the fields, I don't wear them except in the fields."*

Coroner Franks showed Ben the powder horn and asked, do you recognize these powder horns? Are they your powder horns? Ben said that he did recognize the powder horns. In fact, he knew that he had held them in his hands within the last twenty-four hours. Ben stated, *"They belong to Kelly."*

Ben was shown the mud-caked shoes. He replied that those were the ones he wore yesterday, he pulled them off yesterday. Coroner Franks posed the fateful question—Do you know of anyone who would want to shoot Mr. Shoenberger?

Ben knew he was in a lot of trouble. At that time the members of the jury did not know Ephraim Hall was involved. Ben hoped he could gain some advantage implicating his co-partner in crime. He said, *"I heard Ephraim Hall often say, "I intend to kill Mr. Shoenberger;" the last time I heard it was on Monday."*

This was the first time the jury had heard about Ephraim Hall's involvement. They knew of him, but his name had not been given so far and they had not asked any questions of the other witnesses about him. The jury had now heard a statement that indicated the murder was premeditated.

When Franks asked Ben when was the last time he had seen Ephraim, Ben told him that he had not seen Ephraim this morning, but had seen him yesterday in the slaughterhouse right before he went to dinner. Then Ben connected Ephraim to the morning killing by saying. *"Ephraim had come to the house last night, but I did not go out with him."*

Then Ben dropped the bombshell. He implicated Mike White when he stated that Ephraim told him there was a man who had offered him money to murder Mr. Shoenberger but he had not been told exactly how much money.

Coroner Franks then pressed for more details from this witness who was more than willing to lay the blame elsewhere. The Coroner asked Ben if he could tell them who the person was that offered the money to Ephraim to kill Mr. Shoenberger.

Ben said, *"I think it was Mr. White that offered him the money."* Coroner Franks asked, Well Ben, what did Ephraim say he was going to do about that? Ben said, *"Ephraim did not say, but I got the idea that he was going to do what he did do."*

Ephraim Hall was summoned and arrested. It was not long before the Sheriff returned with him in custody, and brought him into the courtroom.

As Ephraim Hall approached the witness stand, he had no way of anticipating that his worst nightmare was just beginning. The jury had just heard that Ephraim was probably paid to kill Shoenberger.

He was asked where he lived. Ephraim told them he lived next to the creek, at the old Burchfield house. When asked what he did the night before, he told the jurymen, quite boastfully, that he had slept with his sweetheart, Ada Sledge.

Coroner Franks went straight to the point and asked Ephraim what was his involvement in the murder of Shoenberger. Ephraim told the Coroner's Jury that he had seen Ben late that evening at the slaughterhouse gate. The conversation had turned bitter as Ben made the statement, "*I am going to town to get the powder to kill old Shoenberger. He accused me of stealing his steer.*"

Ephraim had returned Ben's favor and had now placed the killing on him. Ephraim and Ben took the route used by most people throughout history who have been caught in a crime with a co-defendant. They admit that they were present, but place the actual killing on their partner. Ephraim admitted being near the scene of the crime about the time of the killing, with no apparent excuse. That was enough for the jury. They knew the victim had been shot three times, by two men, and could assume that both men had shot him.

Ephraim next said that he was passing by Mr. White's slaughterhouse before daylight, about three o'clock in the morning, when Ben came riding up on a horse. It was after he returned home that he heard the report of the gunfire. He continued to lie, by saying that he did not know anything about the killing until he returned to the slaughterhouse, about seven that morning, where he saw Mrs. White and Aunt Mariah Cabannis. At that time, Lilly told Ephraim that Ben had been arrested.

The Coroner began to ask questions about the events that led up to the killing of Shoenberger. Ephraim said that he had not been offered any money to do the killing. He became confused and began to stumble around, first remembering that he had a gun that night, and then not remembering what he had done with it. Loss of memory was not a good answer under the circumstances.

In his fright he began to give all the details. He admitted that he had given Josie Evans his pistol that morning. With that admission Ephraim had no choice but to lay out the events, piece by piece, finally telling the story the jury wanted to hear. Ephraim said, "*We went down there. Ben shot the gun and killed Mr. Shoenberger. I shot my pistol twice to keep anyone from following us. After Ben shot Mr. Shoenberger, we ran through the field.*"
Coroner Franks showed the musket to Ephraim.
Franks asked Ephraim if this was the musket that was used.
To which Ephraim replied, "*Yes, that is the gun that Ben shot Mr. Shoenberger with.*"

The jurymen were startled by the testimony they had just heard. If the testimony were to be believed, even if it were surrounded by lies, it would still appear that the two Negroes had indeed killed George Shoenberger. It would also appear that Mike White was involved.

Ephraim was taken from the Courtroom. The hour was late, everyone was tired, so the hearing was continued until the next morning.

It would be interesting to know all that happened in this progressive little community the Friday night of George Shoenberger's murder. The obvious thing that happened was that friends and family surrounded Fannie Shoenberger as she prepared for her husband's burial. Her house was surely filled with friends. Perhaps, many people slept from exhaustion that night.

Mike White probably did not sleep with much satisfaction and was contemplating what tomorrow would bring.

Downtown, at the jail, the scene could not have been pleasant. Lilly Mitchell's mother came to the jail. She brought her daughter a quilt and pillow and insisted she tell the truth.

Sometime during that night, John Spence visited Lilly in jail. He advised her to tell what she knew. Evidently the visits from Spence and her mother were enough to convince Lilly that she was not doing herself any good by lying.

The records do not show who, if anyone, went to the jail to visit Josie Evans.

Ben felt that he could further convince the jury that all this was Ephraim's doing. He thought he had discovered something new to use, but this same plan had been used throughout history and will probably be used into the future. People who commit crimes together will turn on each other at the first threat of the loss of their freedom.

Kelly decided he would tell the jury all that he knew when he went back the next morning. [45]

The people of the town awoke early Saturday morning, April 13th, eager to learn about the next phase of events. Men made their way downtown to the Square, where people always congregated when special events occurred, just to gather any new bits of information.

A large crowd of people gathered around the square to attend the stock-stealing meeting. The public square was crowded with wagons and the horses were tied to the fence around the courtyard. Upon arriving from the country, some would learn the fast breaking news of Shoenberger's death. Most were undoubtedly shocked to

---

[45] There is no record of what the prisoners said or thought, but they must have spent a sleepless night.

hear, for the first time, how their fellow cattle farmer and friend had met his death the previous morning.

Newspapers were published weekly and the editor, J. Withers Clay, of the *Huntsville Weekly Democrat,* set out to cover this fast evolving story. Today this was not a community interested in world affairs: today the world was interested in the affairs of this community.

The early morning crowd watched Sheriff Hardy march the prisoners—Ben Evans, Josie Evans, Lilly Mitchell, Ephraim Hall and Kelly, out of the jail and across Clinton Avenue. They marched up Green Street, turned right by the Methodist Church, and headed down Randolph Street. Crossing the Square, they made their way through the gathering crowd and into the Courthouse.

One by one, the prisoners were led into the courtroom and again would face the jury of white men and the intense questioning by Coroner Franks. They began to tell their story, only this time, each story would be told a little differently.

Kelly was more subdued this morning. Gone was the arrogance and belligerent attitude that was so prevalent in his first appearance.

Kelly told the jury that he had overheard a conversation between Ben and Ephraim Hall at the gate near the slaughterhouse. Ben had said, *"I sure wish I had some buck shot."*

He also stated that Ephraim and Ben had been talking together at dinner that night, and Ephraim had been fooling around with a pistol after supper. Ben was seen greasing the lock of a gun he had gotten from the slaughterhouse. Kelly could not say if Ben had loaded the gun. Kelly saw Ben set the musket in the corner of the room when he went to bed the evening before.

Kelly said Ben had stayed in bed until about one o'clock when someone called to him. The voice sounded like Ephraim Hall. Ben got up and went out of the house taking the gun with him. Ephraim came into their house about two hours later, at about three o'clock, just before Ben arrived. When Ben arrived he did not bring the gun back into the house with him. Ben was blowing [out of breath], when he came back in, as if he were tired. He took off his clothes and got into bed.

Shortly after this, Kelly remembered Lilly as saying, *"I hear someone hollering."* Kelly said it was very plain, distinct and coming from the creek. Kelly remembered Ben saying, *"Someone has shot a hog, I reckon."*

Coroner Franks inquired more about the part Kelly had played in the plotting and the murder. Kelly was very emphatic that he had not taken part in it. He had heard things, but Ephraim must have done the shooting. Kelly covered for Ben blaming Ephraim for the entire deed.

According to Kelly, Ephraim had said, *"I got him! Didn't I?"*
To which Ben replied, *"Yes, you did get him!"*

The jurymen were finished with Kelly, so he stood down and was replaced by Lilly.

Incarceration must have been an enlightening experience for young Lilly Mitchell. In her testimony she eagerly acknowledged to the Coroner's Jury that she had told a lie the day before.

Now she told them that she had gone to Lowry's about eight o'clock the night before but only stayed about an hour. Then she went home and got into bed with her Aunt Josie.

She saw Kelly get the caps out and get the gun from the next room. Kelly and Ephraim loaded the gun and she knew something was up.

She heard Ephraim call Ben sometime during the night. Ben got up, dressed and they went away. Kelly did not go with Ben and Ephraim. Later, when Ben came back home, he came in barefooted and wanted a dry pair of breeches. Ephraim came back and whispered something low to Kelly, then left. When Mr. White came in, Ben had just arrived and was putting on a pair of dry shoes.

She was questioned about the money that had been found in her possession. When they asked if she had been paid to keep quiet, she quickly admitted telling a lie about the money. She said she had stolen it from her Aunt Josie to buy a pair of shoes.

After being questioned about why she had changed her story she explained that her mother had visited her in the callaboose [sic]. Her mother had admonished her for participating in the activities and had given her daughter the advice that "honesty is the best policy." Also, John Spence had told her that it would go better for her if she told all that she knew.

Lilly was happy to get away from the questioning but worried about Josie who was entering the courtroom as she left.

Josie's statement was short. They wanted to know the details about who left the house to go to the Pike that morning. Josie attempted to convince the jury that she did not know anything about the killing before hand and that she only covered for the killers after the deed was done.

Josie now admitted that Ben had gone out that night but she could not, or would not, remember the time. She did remember that Ephraim came back to the house first and asked Kelly if he had heard the alarm. She was curious and asked Ephraim, *"What alarm?"* to which he replied, *"Hush, you have nothing to do with it."*

Ephraim had left before Ben returned home. When Ben came in he was barefooted. He said, *"I want a dry pair of breeches, I'm wet."* Josie said Ben was blowing as if he had been running and so was Ephraim. Obviously aware something bad had happened, she did not return to sleep before Mr. White arrived to tell her to get up and go up to the house to stay with his wife.

Coroner Franks handed the pistol to Josie and asked her who it belonged to. Josie looked at the gun and told him that it looked like Ephraim's pistol. When asked if she knew about Mike White owning a gun she replied that she had seen Mr. White shooting a pistol some time before, but she remembered that his gun shot small cartridges.

After this, the jury was finished with Josie Evans and she was escorted out of the courtroom.

Ben Evans was brought into the room before the group of men. He was very frightened. His second examination revealed a great awareness of his circumstance and the need to lay the blame on someone else. In a heated tone he exclaimed, *"Mr. White was the first to start it! He knew very well what was done and was the cause of it."*

He continued by saying that Mr. White had been talking about it for two or three weeks. Sometimes Mr. White would come into the fields and talk to him about it. Ben said, *"Mr. White would say, why don't you go with Ephraim and attend to that business."* Ben said that Ephraim had told him that Mr. White had talked to him last Saturday about it. Then on Sunday, Ephraim came to Ben's house and talked to him and Kelly.

Ben said that Ephraim had asked the whereabouts of the old gun. Kelly told him that Ed Rainey now had it. So it was left up to Kelly to go to Rainey's and get the gun then to go to Adaline Posey's and get powder horns. The gun was stored at the stable until Thursday evening.[46]

Mr. White told Kelly that Mr. Shoenberger had implicated all of them in the cattle thefts, and it was best that they kill Mr. Shoenberger to avoid being prosecuted.

---

[46] We were not successful in finding information regarding Ed Rainey or Adaline Posey.

Ben set the scene for the jury. Monday night at about seven o'clock, Mr. White came down to the platform of the slaughterhouse. He began talking to them saying, *"Me and Shoenberger are no friends. Why don't you and Ephraim go and kill him?"*

Then on Thursday night, Mr. White told Ben, *"Ephraim will be there and if you are going to do it, you better do it now."* Ben told the jury that Mr. White said, *"Ephraim has his place all picked out; you do just like he tells you and he'll shoot him."*

Ben continued; *"Ephraim took the gun out and greased it at the slaughterhouse. I loaded it. I had the pistol in my coat pocket. When I got back home Kelly asked me if we got him and I told him yes, Ephraim got him."*

The jurymen listened as Ben continued to lie about the evidence that was before them. They knew that the person who stood in the field was the person who fired the musket. The tracks led to Ben's house and the shoes and wet pants were his. Even his wife had identified his shoes and clothes. Ben seemed oblivious to the fact that the men knew the tracks through the field were caused by his shoes. He had admitted that he had the pistol in his coat pocket, but did not say he had the musket. All of the other prisoner's statements placed Ben with the musket and Ephraim with a pistol.

The jury recognized the implications of White's involvement in the situation and had listened with intense interest to the testimony presented. Should they believe the word of the Negroes to implicate Mike White? There was little evidence against White, only the statement of Negroes who had lied with every breath.

As Ben's testimony came to an end, the jurymen wondered how deeply White was involved. They could only believe that White had used the Negroes to do his dirty business— or had he?

As Ephraim Hall began his second examination, it was obvious that fear had gotten the best of him. In chilling testimony, Ephraim explained the reason for the killing.

Ephraim testified that on that Saturday he spoke with Mr. White while at the market house in Huntsville. Mr. White had told him that Mr. Shoenberger had been accusing him, Ephriam, of stealing cattle and that if he would kill him not only would it rid them of the problem but he would pay him money to kill him. Mr. White then threatened that he would, himself, prosecute Ephraim if Shoenberger were not killed.

After giving the statement implicating White, Ephraim had to admit that this was the only time he had spoken to Mr. White about the killing. His position was that Mr. White had forced him to kill

Mr. Shoenberger when he made this one statement at the Huntsville Market. However, he believed White had spoken to Ben Evans many times.[47] Ben had told him that they would all be prosecuted if Mr. Shoenberger were not killed. Since prosecution for cattle thieving held high fear with the Negroes, they felt it necessary to kill Shoenberger to take care of the problem.

Ephraim testified next about how the men planned the murder. Ben went into town to get powder and gave Kelly two balls and a brass cartridge. Kelly loaded the gun and told them he thought those balls would kill Shoenberger. Kelly supplied the caps and knew they were going to kill Shoenberger. Ephraim was shown the bullet moulds that he said he got from a man named King and used them to mould the bullets.

On Thursday night they began to lay plans for the murder. Ephraim came through the darkness, to Ben's house Friday morning in order to carry out their plan. He called to Ben and they went down the Pike to Shoenberger's gate carrying a pistol and musket. They decided that the best way and the best place to do the shooting was at Shoenberger's gate as he entered the Pike on his way to market.

Ephraim said, *"We saw Mr. Huddleston as he came up the Pike going toward the gate. After Mr. Huddleston went down to the slaughter pen, we hid and watched. Before Mr. Shoenberger got to the gate he hollowed to Charlie to stay around because someone was lurking about."*

Ephraim continued, *"Ben was behind a post over in Mr. McCravey's field to keep Mr. Shoenberger from seeing him. Mr. Shoenberger had turned the horse toward town and stopped on the Pike when he came out of the gate. He had his right side to Ben when Ben shot. Mr. Huddleston was at the gate and Shoenberger was on the wagon seat when Ben shot."*

Ephraim said, *"I was standing in the road when Ben fired the musket and I shot right after Ben shot. He shot once and the cap busted once. Ben ran through the wheat field, I ran up the Pike."* Ephraim said he ran to Ben's house. Ben had already gotten there and was pulling off his clothes when Ephraim went in. He heard the screaming after he reached Ben's house. He gave his pistol to Josie and she said she would put it where nobody would find it.

Next Ephraim restated that Kelly asked Ben if he had hit Shoenberger and Ben replied, *"Yes, I did!"* Then he added that he

---

[47] In most cases, this would be viewed as third hand knowledge or hearsay.

said, "*I think I got him.*" Ephraim said, "*The women should have heard that.*"

Ephraim, in a sorrowful, remorseful tone told the jury that he wished he had never done it. He said that he, "*would never have gone to kill Mr. Shoenberger if Mr. White hadn't said what he did and I would give a million dollars if I was not in it.*"

There was no need for any more questions. Sheriff Hardy took the prisoners back to the jail and appointed guards to stay with them.

Coroner Franks and the members of the jury had spent the better part of two days listening to testimony in the investigation. They discussed the startling developments and the statements made by the witnesses. It was time to write their report. With the help of Coroner Franks, the men composed the verdict of the Coroner's Jury. They signed their names denoting that the report reflected their opinions and judgment.

The members of the jury stopped the questioning and left the Courthouse to attend Shoenberger's funeral.

The Sheriff went to arrest Mike White and place him in jail along with the others involved in the killing.

There was an overflowing crowd attending services at the Cumberland Presbyterian Church, located on Randolph Avenue. Shoenberger's suffering family and hundreds of friends gathered in Maple Hill Cemetery at eleven o'clock in the morning, after one of the largest processions ever witnessed in Huntsville. Many tributes to the memory of this kind man were given, expressing the heart of Huntsville toward him for his quiet and amiable life. It was a manifestation of the respect in which he was held, the esteem for his family, and the deep sense of the wrongfulness of his death.

The people moved from Maple Hill Cemetery over the hill and back to downtown for the livestock-stealing meeting. The crowd, some still dressed in their funeral finest, had continued to grow around the town square. The testimony of that morning's Coroner's Jury was released and spread throughout the crowd. Everyone was surprised to learn that Mike White had just been arrested, and the gravest rumors were prevalent.

The Meeting

When the livestock-stealing meeting started, the courtroom filled rapidly. Col. George P. Beirne was called to lead the meeting and W. L. Clay, Esquire, was chosen secretary.

J. Withers Clay offered the following resolution:

"Resolved that a committee of ten members be appointed by the chairman to prepare a plan of organized movement to aid the courts of the state in the suppression of stock stealing, to report to a meeting, to be held in the courthouse in Huntsville on Saturday, April Twentieth."

A discussion about the Resolution was not well received. The only discussion in which anyone seemed interested was the killing of George Shoenberger. Several people had their full say about the subject. George Bierne must have felt that he was fast losing control of the meeting because the crowd was extremely upset at the loss of a good friend.

Judge Edward C. Betts rose to speak. He spoke against the present justice system. In his opinion, elected officials were indifferent to the way the courts dragged their feet in bringing criminals to justice and, as long as this continued, justice would be poorly served.

John J. McDavid, Esq. opposed this vigilante notion. He insisted that the law should handle this matter and that the people should respect the law and honor its authority in meting out justice to criminals.

Mr. Sanders, a gentleman from Indiana, was a most excellent citizen. He spoke of the general thieving that was ongoing and urged the appointment of a vigilance committee that would procure change.

Solicitor Daniel Coleman got the floor and zealously approved of the resolutions. He reminded the men that if the town's citizens had made a move such as the present one twelve months ago, the terrible tragedy that had just occurred would have never happened. The active aid of good people was the thing the community needed. He talked to the crowd about how George Shoenberger had stepped to the front and was laboring to get to the bottom of the thieving. He insisted that a popular effort, properly directed, was always the best guarantee of vindication of the law. He urged that the law be allowed to have its course.

Some unimportant amendments to Clay's resolutions were offered but later withdrawn. The resolution was adopted with only one dissenting voice. A committee composed of the very best material was appointed; J. J. Hammond, Harris Toney, Hugh L. Toney, Dr. O. R. Hatcher, B. Terry, Dr. J. P. Hampton, G. P. Bone, and W. F. Whitman.

It was urged that all citizens who had any information or interest in the thefts should attend the upcoming meeting set for the next Saturday. However, after the meeting, the crowds did not leave, but milled about the town square in the numerous taverns and restaurants to discuss the committee meeting and the community's situation.

Excitement in the crowd grew with each passing hour. There was much talk about the immediate punishment of those connected with the killing. There was talk of a lynching and this talk spread with obvious approval through the majority of the crowd. Most felt that it was up to them to see that it was carried out. Even those who spoke in favor of law and order could understand the sentiment that was being widely expressed.

There was a movement to learn more about the guilt of those being held in the jail. Information was given to some about the verdict of the Coroner's Jury and there was a demand that more information be given about the verdict.

Leaders were eagerly surfacing who were interested in swift punishment and everyone was informed to regather in the courtroom right away to demand the results of the inquest.

The crowd openly ex-pressed its feeling that the *Lynch Law* could not be used soon enough.

There was a loud outcry for the Coroner's Jury report to be read for the crowd.

Judge William Richardson

40

It now became evident to those in charge that the citizens were favoring immediate punishment of those connected to the crime. Unless something was done to soothe the tempers, and done fast, they could have a mob on their hands.

Judge William Richardson arose as the chief officer of the county, and addressed them on behalf of law and order. He advised them to counsel well among themselves and let the law have its course. He told them that the resolution, which had been adopted that morning, met his most hearty approval. He believed that justice would be meted out in the courts. It would not be advisable, in their inflamed state, to hear the verdict of the Jury of Inquest. They would all know the judgment in due time. He called upon them to see that law and order prevailed, and to make sure that no mob violence be visited upon the prisoners. He stressed that he intended that the law be upheld.

The crowd would not be put off. They demanded the results of the jury. The leaders could see that the citizens would wait no longer and the decision was made to give the crowd what they wanted.

The verdict was read aloud to the crowd.

Verdict of the Coroner's Jury

State of Alabama

Madison County

"We the undersigned Jury of Inquest summoned and duly sworn by Brittain Franks, as Coroner of Madison County, Alabama, to inquire into the cause of the killing of George Shoenberger, do hereby render the following verdict, after an inspection of the body and hearing the evidence, namely: that George Shoenberger was murdered on the Twelfth Day of April 1878, at the hour of about 3 a. m., on the Meridianville Pike, about one mile from the Court House in the City of Huntsville, Alabama, by Ben Evans and Ephraim Hall, colored, by shooting the said Shoenberger in the back with a musket, the property of one Mike White, and that said murder was committed by lying in wait. The Jury further finds that said Evans and Hall were instigated to the commission of said murder by said White; and that said White and one Kelly, colored, were accomplices and accessories of the said Evans and Hall, in the perpetration and commission of this crime. This done in Madison County, Alabama, on April 13, 1878; Milton Humes, L.W. McCravey, S. H. Lowry, G. W. Kennard, J. T. Lowry, P. I. Harrison."[48]

---

[48] The Independent (April 18, 1878).

The crowd left the Courthouse but remained in the courtyard and around the square. There was much anger and the excitement flamed stronger every minute. For an hour, there was loud and violent talk, shouting, and angry words. Speeches were made for and against law and order. The crowd started making its way from the Courthouse, down Washington Street, onto Clinton and toward the jail.

In the distance of one block, the crowd became a mob.

Large numbers of citizens stood along the walkways and lined the streets in front of the stores to watch the passing mob. Many joined those in the street. The mob began to crowd around the jail and started to demand the prisoners be released to them. Officer Hardy climbed on the jail fence to get a better command of the situation and make his voice heard to the hundreds that had gathered. He told the mob to leave because he intended to see that the law was sustained—there were fifty men guarding the jail and they would protect the prisoners. The unarmed mob saw the men awaiting them inside and began to leave in small numbers until only a few remained outside the jail. Even those soon left to return home.

Sheriff John C. Thomas began to increase the number of guards at the jail. He deputized a large group of men to secure the safety of the prisoners.

As soon as it was reasonable to do so, Sheriff Thomas released the imprisoned women. The prisoner's families were allowed to visit. Elizabeth White was allowed to see her husband.

Saturday night remained quite calm.

The excitement was still strong on Sunday, April 14th, but there were no crowds in the streets and the city went about the normal Sunday activity. The general atmosphere of the people appeared calm and normal.

However, late in the day, a rumor began to circulate that Mike White would be rescued from the jail that night. Citizens volunteered to serve as guards to see that all remained calm. Those in law enforcement were at their posts and all believed the law would carry out its duty to the community. But it was impossible not to know that the majority of the citizens believed the criminals should be hanged as soon as possible.

Large crowds of curiosity seekers rode out Meridianville Pike to see the place where the shooting occurred.

Monday, April 15th was quiet. The town went to work, but talked of nothing but the events of the past days.

Mike White, realizing the seriousness of his situation, asked his wife to bring the necessary papers to transfer his land back to the original owner, since he still owed money on it. In 1869, Mike White had purchased the twenty acres where his slaughterhouse was located from Worley White. Title was to be passed when the deferred payments were paid in full. Worley White visited the jail and they completed the paperwork to return the property.

On Tuesday, April 16th, a great storm arose and may have been perceived as an omen of hope to sweep the city clean of its moral shortcomings. The steeple of the Presbyterian Church was blown off and would cost much to repair. On the surface, the people were busy recovering from the storm and appeared inattentive to the business of accusations. The calm after the storm was a facade on the undercurrent of unrest.

With several United States Federal prisoners in the jail, the Sheriff notified the U. S. Marshall that the sentiment of the crowd had reached epic proportion and he could no longer be responsible for the safe keeping of the United States prisoners. *"Not that they are in any danger, but they are in jail with the prisoners charged with the murder of Shoenberger."* A Federal posse was sent to the jail to protect the Federal prisoners that were housed there, and to help prevent any danger to the other prisoners.

The Lynching

The voices in favor of lynching the three would not be stilled. Since the meeting, there had been time to allow an opportunity for some of the very best citizens, throughout the county, and south Tennessee, to enter into a plan to take charge of the men and lynch them. Hundreds would join them to carry out their plan. The men felt that if they were technically wrong, they were morally right in what they were doing.

Farmers from Madison County and citizens from Tennessee were up early on Wednesday, April 17th. They saddled their horses and met with friends and neighbors on the Pike. More and more horsemen soon joined them until the roadway was filled with them. They were all headed toward Huntsville to witness the punishment of those men whom they felt had made them suffer loss.

Some said that the citizens were interested in the hanging, not because of the killing of George Shoenberger, but because of the thefts. The people felt this action must be taken because the courts would not punish criminals properly.

By ten o'clock in the morning, citizens of Huntsville became aware that there was a tremendous troop of horsemen approaching Meridianville Pike. There were as many as three hundred fifty men, all armed with shotguns and other weapons.

The citizens of the County knew what was about to happen. Four brave men went out to meet the riders. They were: Judge William Richardson, the county's probate judge; Septimus Cabaniss, who had been Huntsville's mayor many times; business leader William Cox, and the town's present mayor, Zabulon Davis. The four stopped at the town limits, on Meridianville Pike, and watched the men approach.

The four men stood alone in the road before the mass of horsemen. Judge Richardson motioned the men to stop and listen to him. The riders surrounded the four men and listened to what the Judge had to say.

Judge Richardson urged the men to cease in the name of law and order, and disperse.

But the men would not listen to reason from these wise leaders, and insisted their plan would not be changed and there was no turning back

None of the men were disguised; but their names were not recorded. It was a popular revolution against thieves such as Mike White and his cohorts.

Seeing that they could not stop the men, the Judge urged the leaders not to harm to the young boy, Frank Kelly. It might be possible that he was not guilty, and the men were urged not to kill him. The men agreed to spare him from harm.

The four men stood helpless in the middle of Meridianville Pike and watched as the hundreds of horsemen flowed silently around them, heading down the Pike toward town. As the men passed the home of George Shoenberger, ladies were on the fence pleading with them not to stop and not to turn around, but to carry out their plan.

The scene at the jail for White and his wife, Elizabeth, was a sorrowful occasion. Knowing the men were coming to complete their designated task made the last few moments surely unbearable for Elizabeth. She was young, beautiful and in love with her husband. Conscious of the horrible end her husband was about to face was unthinkable. She had to be physically removed from the jail just before the lynchers arrived.

The horsemen made their way down the Pike then followed Green Street to the jail. They completely surrounded the building and blocked the adjoining streets. The guards in the jail could not defend the prisoners against the great throng of men with weapons. Crowbars and sledgehammers were used to beat down the jail door. After that, they entered the jail with no resistance and there was little need for force against the guards. They forced open the cell doors of White, Evans, and Hall and each man was taken out into the street. Every precaution was used to prevent the other prisoners from being allowed to escape or be harmed.

With their hands tied behind their back, the prisoners were marched down Clinton Avenue to Church Street and then to the Big Spring Branch. Men on foot and on horseback guarded the men, while tremendous crowds began to follow.

A large willow oak, located about five hundred yards down the Big Spring Branch, was selected as the hanging tree.[49] Careful plans had not included a wagon on which to place the men, and there was a delay until one could be brought to the tree.

---

[49] In 1878, the Big Spring Branch ran straight until it reached Pin Hook Creek. Canal Street ran along the west bank. In the Urban Renewal of the 1960's the branch was turned and two lakes were formed. The location of the hanging tree would be approximately where the marquee for the Von Braun Center is now located, near the intersection of Williams and Monroe Streets.

Huntsville-Madison County Public Library
1878 Scene of the Big Spring flood

Newspapermen had gathered to chronicle the event. They dared not approach the men in charge of the lynching, but ventured on in the name of history, to seek an interview with the men about to be hanged. While waiting for the wagon to be brought around, the newsmen began to question the condemned prisoners.

The first to be questioned was Mike White. He appeared for the most part rather firm. He would only speak when spoken to. He told them he was thirty-seven years old. He had no children, and he saw his wife in jail that morning. He came to Huntsville in 1860, and as he glanced at his compatriots in the crowd, he stated that he was a good Confederate soldier. He refused to acknowledge that he played a part in the killing. He never admitted his guilt, but also did not deny any wrong doing, saying only that he did not have any messages that needed to be sent to anyone because Mr. Edwards[50] would look after things.

The reporter asked, Do you know who killed Mr. Shoenberger?

To which White replied; *"I did not kill Mr. Shoenberger."*

He was asked again by the reporter,

Do you know who killed Mr. Shoenberger?

To which there was no answer, but only an averting of White's head.

Ephraim Hall was stoical, unrepentant and not disposed to talk much. He said he had already told as much as *"needed to be told, but that all four of them were in it, including Kelly."*

---

[50] Information could not be found regarding "Mr. Edwards."

Ben Evans, as usual, talked away, He said, *"There isn't any use to talk anything but the truth. I know I am going to be killed. Mr. White and all of us was into this thing. It's just like I told before Kelly loaded the gun. Mr. White worked this thing up. There isn't any use to lie. Ephraim shot the gun."*

Ephraim Hall replied, *"No Ben, I was there, but you shot the gun."*

Ben Said, *"Well, we were all in it. Mr. White was always saying to us, dead men don't tell no tales."*

Ben turned to White and said, *"Now see, Mr. White, what you have brought us to!"*

To which White replied, *"Don't talk to me about bringing anything!"*

Evans and Hall asked to have a minister pray for them. White made no such request. Reverend E. C. Gordon came forward at the two men's request and prayed for them.

The reverend said:

"Oh Great God, In the rich provision of your mercy pour out on the guilty three, the sprit of repentance, that he would make them to feel their great guilt and horrible crime. Enable them to see that they have sinned against God and man. Enable them to realize that there is a balm in Gilead, and even the murderer may hope to be pardoned of his guilt."

A wagon arrived through a parting of the crowd. It was placed under the tree and the three men were assisted onto the wagon. Three ropes were thrown over a limb and a noose was made in each. Black cloths were tied very properly over the men's faces. Mike White asked to keep his hat on, and was allowed that. The three ropes were brought to the men. The noose was placed around each of their necks. The horses were whipped and at about three o'clock in the afternoon, the men swung clear and dropped into eternity.

White and Evans died quickly, but Hall fought the inevitable to the end. The newspaper reported that he contorted in a most revolting manner. They all died from strangulation.

The large crowd was quiet and orderly during the hanging watching the men fight the empty air until they became still. All things had been done without any evidence of brutality, other than to the necks of the three dead men. After seventeen minutes, a physician approached and pronounced that all three were dead.

A gentleman who seemed to be in charge told the crowd, *"Now, men, go to your homes in perfect order and peace. There is nothing more to be done.*" The large crowd quietly dispersed but there were many who stood and watched as the bodies twisted in the wind as if they might turn, face them, and make one last statement.

After hanging for two hours, the men were cut down. They were delivered to their families and friends who carried them away.[51]

A Coroner's Jury held an inquest concerning the lynching and returned a verdict in accordance with the facts as known by everyone.

Mike White's funeral took place Thursday evening with the Rev. Hearn officiating. Many citizens were present. There was a divided opinion about the guilt of White in the matter.[52]

Frank Kelly's life was spared, but he remained in jail pending a trial for the charge of murder. The Madison County Grand Jury indicted him for murder in July of that year. His lawyer moved for a change of venue on grounds that the prisoner could not receive a fair trial in Madison County. The motion was granted, and the trial was moved to the Circuit Court in Limestone County. The case was tried in the Spring Term of 1879, in Athens, before a jury of twelve white men; found "*Not Guilty*" and released.[53]

Elizabeth White suffered greatly from the unhappy end of her marriage, and it was only later that a report circulated that she was beginning to recover from her extreme illness. Mike White's lynching had an impact on Huntsville long after his death. Mike White had purchased a life insurance policy for $10,000, making Elizabeth the beneficiary. The company sued the City of Huntsville for the amount. The case went into a lengthy litigation, but eventually Elizabeth was awarded $7,500.

The very best and leading citizens had taken unlawful, violent action. As would be expected, this action did not stop murder or theft in the community then, or ever.

Less than five years later, George Steele was shot and instantly killed by H. F. Fuston, on Meridianville Pike, near the spot where George Shoenberger was assassinated. Mr. Fuston had a hearing before Justice Barclay and was discharged; his defense being that Steele had made improper advances to his wife the same evening.[54]

---

[51] There is no record of a funeral or burial of either Ephraim Hall or Ben Evans.

[52] "There is no room to doubt his guilt, at least that is the universal belief." *The Independent* (April 18, 1878).

[53] Limestone County Alabama Circuit Court Minutes, General State Docket Book, Fall 1865-Fall 1882, no page numbers and the book is not indexed.

[54] The *Huntsville Gazette* (October 7, 1883).

Epilogue

Septimus D. Cabaniss remained active as a practicing attorney after the 1878 incident. Historians, who study Huntsville's role during the time of the War Between the States, have used his detailed description of events occurring in Huntsville. Cabaniss died on March 19, 1889, and was buried in Maple Hill Cemetery.

John Withers Clay remained the editor of *The Huntsville Weekly Democrat* until his death on March 29, 1896. After his death, his two daughters continued to operate the paper in the roles of editor and business manager. The letters John W. Clay sent home to his family during his service for the Confederacy provide us with many interesting facts regarding the events and hardships of the war.

Zebulon Pike Davis served as Mayor of Huntsville eight times. Before the War Between the States, he served five terms as a Whig candidate. After the war, he served three terms as a Republican candidate during the years of Reconstruction. In 1881, Thomas White defeated him. Davis died January 3, 1882, and was buried in Maple Hill Cemetery.

Josephine Evans was found listed in the 1911 Huntsville Directory, working as a laundress at a private home on Blue Springs Road.

Brittian Franks continued to serve his community until his death in 1891.

Frank Kelly remained in jail for almost one year until his trial in Athens. He was never heard from after his *"not guilty"* verdict in Limestone County.

Nothing more was found regarding Lilly Mitchell.

Judge William Richardson was the Madison County Probate Judge during the 1878 lynchings and remained in that office until 1886. In 1890, he ran for Governor on the Democratic ticket. He carried each county north of Birmingham but withdrew his name in order to stop dissension in the Democratic Party. In 1900, Judge Richardson was appointed to represent the people of the Eighth

Congressional District after General Joe Wheeler resigned. Judge Richardson remained in that position until his death. He served on many important committees and was a leader in the founding of the Tennessee River Improvement Association, which was the forerunner of TVA. At Richardson's death, Governor O'Neal ordered all the flags of Alabama flown at half-mast and the State Capital building was to be draped in mourning cloths. Judge Richardson died on May 31, 1914, and was buried in Maple Hill Cemetery.

George Shoenberger's remains were supposedly placed beside his first wife, Cassander [sic], however there was never a gravestone placed there. His second wife, Fannie, later married James H. Jackson and is buried beside him. Sallie Shoenberger married W. E. Penny. She later sued her stepmother and half-sister for her share in Mr. Shoenberger's estate.

Mike White is supposedly buried in the White family plot near Worley White in Maple Hill Cemetery. There is no marker on his grave.

Elizabeth White lived with her mother and sister in Huntsville, in 1880. After that time, there was no further information regarding Elizabeth White.

The Life Insurance Association of America refused to honor a policy in the amount of $10,000 for the death of Mike White. The widow, Elizabeth White and Worley White's estate (the person that held the note on Mike White's property) sued the insurance company for the value of the policy. After lengthy litigation, the insurance company settled with Elizabeth for $7,500.[55] The insurance company then sued the Town of Huntsville for the wrongful death of Mike White.[56]

---

[55] Madison County, Alabama, Probate Records, Trust Deed, Book YY, Page 215.
[56] *Life Insurance of America v. Nevelle, 72 Ala. 517.*

Biographies—Chapter One

The following short biographies are of the people involved in the preceding story. Every effort was made to find information on individuals no matter how small or large a part they played in the story. [57]

Anderson, John B.; Citizens Meeting.
John B. Anderson was born in Pennsylvania, March 4, 1826. In 1870, John was employed as a farmer and was forty-four years old. His wife, Amanda, was born in Ohio and was forty-three years old. They had seven children: Jenny C., fifteen years old; James, thirteen years old; Harvey, eleven years old; Charles, nine years old; Alice, six years old; William, five years old; and John, two years old. Also in the house was Abraham Kage[Cage], from Ohio, thirty years old, who was working as a farmer. By 1880, the couple had added another child, DeWitt C. who was now seven years old. John's farm was located in Section 4 Township 1 West.[58] Anderson died March 9, 1903. The Maple Hill Sexton's Records show that he died at seventy-seven years of age.

Battle, Jacob W.; Citizens Meeting.
Jacob William Battle was born May 2, 1842, near Huntsville in Madison County. He was the son of Josiah D. Battle from North Carolina. His mother's name was Mary, and he had five sisters.[59] During the War Between the States, Jacob entered the service as First Sergeant, January 2, 1862, at LaGrange Alabama, Co. H Thirtieth-fifth Alabama Infantry. Continuing in service until October 8, 1862, he was promoted to Second Lieutenant and was transferred to Co. C, Fiftieth Alabama. He was promoted to First Lieutenant July 5, 1863, and transferred to the Cavalry, September 9, 1864. He commanded a Scout Company under General Forrest until the surrender. He was paroled at Pond Spring, near Courtland, Alabama, May 16, 1865.[60] By the 1870's, Jacob had married. His wife, Kate E., was twenty-five

---

[57] A search was conducted using the Huntsville City Directories; 1900-1910 United States Federal Census; *Madison County Cemeteries*, Vol. 1 & 2; *Maple Hill Cemetery, Phase One;* and private manuscripts regarding the cemetery; Dorothy Scott Johnson; Merrimack *Cemetery*, Ann Maulsby; Confederate *Veterans Census*, Dorothy Scott Johnson; various military records; Madison County Probate and Civil Court Records.
[58] 1880 United States Federal Census, Madison County, Alabama.
[59] 1850 United States Federal Census Madison County, Alabama.
[60] 1907 Confederate Veteran Census for Madison County, Alabama, Page #1.

years old, and had been born in Alabama. They lived in the Meridianville area.[61] Jacob Battle lived at 315 Walker Street,[62] but by 1911, he was a planter who lived at 500 Randolph Avenue.[63] Jacob Battle died on November 14, 1912 at the age of seventy. He was still farming and lived at 500 Randolph Avenue. He was buried in Maple Hill Cemetery.

Beirne, George Plunkett; Citizens Meeting.
George Plunket Beirne was born in Virginia, July 8, 1809. He was a Huntsville attorney. His wife, Eliza Carter Gray, had been born in Virginia, September 12, 1811.[64] It is assumed that they were married in Virginia, as their first child, Elizabeth Gray, was born there on September 25, 1839. Before the second child, Lucey, [sic] was born in 1842, the couple moved to Huntsville, leaving a narrow margin of time for us to estimate the date of their arrival. By 1850, the couple had other children. Mary was born around 1843, and Jane Patton around 1847. Nona Plunkett was only four months old at the time. In the house with them was Eliza's sister, Maria Hunton, thirty-three years old, from Virginia. George P. Beirne continued working as an attorney.[65] His land was located at Township 4 South Range 1 West of Madison County.[66]

Prior to the War Between the States, George had acquired a very admirable estate. In the home with the family was daughter, Nona, and Ellen Beirne, a niece. Thomas Fearn,[67] a Madison County doctor, lived next door.[68] In May of 1862, during the occupation of Huntsville by the Federal forces, Beirne was arrested, along with several others, in retaliation for a bridge burning and the cutting of telegraph wires in the county. Afterward, as an honorary title, the locals called Beirne "Colonel." With the end of the War Between the States, things changed for the Beirnes. Eight other persons lived in the home with the Beirne family during 1870.[69] Little changed in the Beirne home through the next few years, except age. George Plunket

---

[61] 1870 United States Federal Census, Madison County, Alabama.
[62] 1896 Huntsville City Directory, Page 21.
[63] 1911 City Directory, Page 108.
[64] *Maple Hill Cemetery, Phase One*, Robey, Johnson, Jones, & Roberts, 1995, page 53.
[65] 1850 United States Federal Census Madison County, Alabama.
[66] *Old Land Records of Madison County*, Margaret Cowart, page #31.
[67] Fearn was responsible for establishing the waterworks in Huntsville Alabama.
[68] 1860 United States Federal Census, Madison County, Alabama, Page 213.
[69] 1870 United States Federal Census, Madison County, Alabama, Page 9, Ward 3.

Beirne died on July 14, 1881, and was buried in Maple Hill Cemetery.[70] The tombstone reads: "Blessed are the Pure in Heart." His wife, Eliza, died December 22, 1900, and was buried beside her husband. Daughter Eliza Gray Beirne died May 10, 1885 and was buried beside her parents. Nona Plunkett Beirne died at fifteen years of age, December 30, 1865. She was buried in Maple Hill Cemetery, Section 7 Row #12. Daughters Eliza Gray and Jane never married and lived with their parents on Williams Street.[71]

Betts, Edward Chambers; Citizens Meeting.
Edward Betts was a lawyer, planter and Commissioner of Agriculture. He was born August 13, 1820, ten miles from Huntsville in Madison County. He was born on the plantation of his father, Charles Edward Betts. His mother was Martha Cousins [Chambers] Betts, a former native of Luenburg, Mecklenburg County, Virginia. She later lived at Boydton, Virginia, but finally located in Madison County. She was a sister of United States Senator Henry C. Chambers, for whom Chambers County Alabama was named. Grandson of Elisha and Mary [Parrot] Betts, Edward Chambers Betts received his elementary education in the private schools in Madison County with private tutors. He then attended the University of Virginia to study and travel abroad and in the eastern United States. In 1850, Edward lived with two other businessmen: Hugh Easley, a forty-year-old cabinetmaker; and attorney, Vance M. Robertson from Maryland, thirty-five years old.[72]

Edward served several of the county courts of Madison County. He was also the first Commissioner of Agriculture of Alabama and Trustee of the University of Alabama for a number of years. He was a Democrat and an Episcopalian. Edward was married in Courtland, Alabama, to Virginia Augusta, in 1854. Virginia was born February 10, 1836. She was the daughter of John M. and Cyntha [Early] Swope of Huntsville, and the granddaughter of Peter Early and Ann Adams [Smith], great-granddaughter of Jeremiah Early, who emigrated from Donegal County, Ireland to Virginia about 1702. General Jubal A. Early and Bishop John Early were among his descendants and he was a lineal descendant of Carbri Lifcar, an

---

[70] *Maple Hill Cemetery, Phase One*, Robey, Johnson, Jones, & Roberts, 1995, page 53.
[71] 1880 United States Federal Census, Madison County, Alabama.
[72] 1850 United States Federal Census, Madison County, Alabama, Page 278.

ancient king of Ireland, who was born A.D. 225. The name was anglicized, as Early, during, the reigns of the Henrys and Edwards.

Edward's children were: Tancred, Victor [married Lucy Lee Winston], and Augusta Ada Kortrecht. During the 1850's, life was good for Edward. He and Virginia added a baby boy to their family and attained considerable wealth. [73] This would decrease, as did most southern property after the War Between the States. The family lived near Thomas Bibb in Huntsville during 1870.[74] After practicing law for some years, Betts retired to his plantation as his last residence.[75] Edward C. Betts died September 18, 1891. He was buried in Maple Hill Cemetery. Buried with him are his wife Virginia, who died August 13, 1892; Augusta, his daughter, who died August 25, 1894; son Tancred, who died May 24, 1921; and Tancred's wife, Maud M. Brown, who died January 2, 1940.[76]

Biederman, Rudolf (Henry); Neighbor

The 1880 United States Federal Census listed Rudolf Biederman, seventy-seven years old, employed as a gardener (family notes indicated that he and his son were in the floral business.) He was born in 1803, in Switzerland. His wife, Eliza, was born in 1820. Home with the parents were: son, Leo, thirty-eight years old, who also worked as a gardener; and daughter Adale, was thirty-five years old. Henry and Eliza had two other children, but their names are unknown. Before coming to Alabama, Henry had traveled to California and purchased a business called the Sierra Nevada Café. It was a restaurant and boarding house for which he had drawn the plans. Meticulous in his record keeping, Biederman kept records to the penny and even recorded the daily temperatures. He sold this property in 1855, and went back to Zurich. He came back to the United States with his wife and settled in Alabama so that they could be close to his daughter who was attending the Huntsville Female Academy.[77] The 1911 and 1916 Huntsville City Directories listed Henry and Leo Biederman as farmers with a home on Franklin Street.

---

[73] 1860 United States Federal Census, Madison County, Alabama, Page 60.
[74] 1870 United States Federal Census, Madison County, Alabama, Page 132.
[75] History of Alabama and Dictionary of Alabama Biography, Thomas McAdory Owen, LL.D. 1921 page141.
[76] *Maple Hill Cemetery, Phase One*, Robey, Johnson, Jones, & Roberts, 1995.
[77] *Old Huntsville,* Magazine, Issue #86.

The book, Maple Hill Phase One,[78] lists R.A.H. Biederman buried in Section seven Row 1, with his daughter Jennie [who married Carl Ernest Cramer July 8, 1873]. There are no tombstones from which to extract data.

Bone, Hugh Phillips; Citizens Meeting.
Dr. Hugh Phillips Bone was born June 8, 1838, in Todd County, Kentucky.[79] In 1860, he lived and practiced dentistry in the NE Section of Madison County (Gurley). Dr. Bone lived with his father, Reverend M. H. Bone, his mother C. P., and his sister Martha. Miss Louisa Bone, seventeen years old, and the Reverend's sister, Lane Bone, sixty years old, also lived there. Rev. Bone was born in Tennessee and Mrs. Bone in Georgia.[80]

During the 1870's, Dr. Bone married. He and his wife had three children. However, his wife was not in the home by 1870. His sister, Louisa, forty-one years old, who was born [1829] in Mississippi, lived with Hugh. She appears to be taking care of the children: Annie L. eight years old; Houston, six years old; Lily, three years old; and one-year-old, Mary. In 1870, Dr. Bone, thirty-one years old, was a dental surgeon.[81] In 1880, Dr. Bone lived with his sister, Louisa, and his mother, Martha H., seventy-seven years old. In addition, there were the children, Annie L. eighteen years old; Matthew H., sixteen years old; Lillian, thirteen years old; Mary, eleven years old; and James [whose age is unreadable].[82] Dr. Bone is probably buried in the McCartney-Bone Cemetery with his parents; however there is no tombstone to mark his grave. Absent also is a marker to indicate that he served in the Confederate Army, fighting with Company A, Todd Company of Kentucky. The cemetery is located two miles northeast of Maysville on the old Wilson Indian Reservation. The tiny cemetery is located near the old antebellum style Bone home.[83] Laura G. Bone is buried in Maple Hill in Section 10, Row 4, but there is no tombstone data to use to prove that this was his wife.

---

[78] *Maple Hill Cemetery, Phase One*, Robey, Johnson, Jones, & Roberts, 1995, page 45.
[79] Kentucky Confederate Soldiers Pension Records.
[80] 1860 United States Federal Census, Madison County, Alabama.
[81] 1870 United States Federal Census, Madison County, Alabama, Page 197.
[82] 1880 United States Federal Census, Madison County, Alabama, Page 203.
[83] Cemeteries of Madison County, Dorothy Scott Johnson, Vol. III Page 300.

Burke, Dr. James P.; Doctor/Inquest.
James Burke was born in Alabama on October 31, 1832. In 1870, James was thirty-six years old, and a practicing physician in Madison County, Alabama. His wife, Ella K., was thirty years old. They had one child, Mat O., who was three years old. The couple had a servant, Julia, who was white, eleven years old.[84] Ella K. Burke died, November 21, 1871. Her tombstone reads, *'He giveth his beloved sleep.'* On the back of her tombstone, is another tombstone of five-month-old, Willie Kirkland Burke, which leads one to believe Ella died in childbirth.[85] Dr. James P. Burke then married Henrietta E. Strong, September 30, 1873.[86] By 1880, James and Henrietta had two children: John, born 1875, and Thomas G., born 1877. Mollie Tarks, twenty years old, black, and lived with them. They lived at the end of the Meridianville, Alabama precinct.[87] Dr. Burke died February 12, 1911, and was buried in Maple Hill Cemetery. His wife died on October 18, 1918, and was buried next to her husband. Carolyn Burke, (possible daughter) was born February 9, 1885. She died April 4, 1963, and is buried in the family plot.[88]

Cabaniss, Septimus; Stand in the Road.
Septimus Cabaniss was born October 1, 1824, in Virginia. His family was one of the original settlers of Madison County, Alabama. He married Virginia Shepherd on June 19, 1843, in Madison County, Alabama.[89] By 1850, Cabaniss was a prominent practicing attorney in Huntsville. He and Virginia had three children: Charles E., Virginia C., and Ellen.[90] He and his wife endured the loss of several children. The 1860 census[91] listed children: Charles; Lucy; Septimus D.; Fanny; and William. During the 1870's, neighbors of Cabaniss were: Matthew Steele, the architect; William and Reubin Street; William Mastin, Mayor of Huntsville at the time; and George Shoenberger.[92]

---

[84] 1870 United States Federal Census, Madison County, Alabama, page 17,

[85] *Maple Hill Cemetery, Phase One*, Robey, Johnson, Jones, & Roberts, 1995, page 64.

[86] Madison County, Alabama Marriage Records, Book 7 Page 11.

[87] 1880 United States Federal Census, Madison County, Alabama, page 212 Section 2, Range 1East.

[88] *Maple Hill Cemetery, Phase One*, Robey, Johnson, Jones, & Roberts, 1995, page 65.

[89] Madison County, Alabama Marriage Records, Book No. 4 Page 695.

[90] 1850 United States Federal Census, Madison County, Alabama.

[91] 1860 United States Federal Census, Madison County, Alabama.

[92] 1870 United States Federal Census, Madison County, Alabama, page 17, Ward 2.

By 1870, Charles was twenty-four years old; Lucy was nineteen years old; (Septimus) Douglas was seventeen years old; Frances (Fanny) was fourteen years old; William was ten years old; and Bud was nine years old.

During his lifetime, Cabaniss accomplished many things. He was a lawyer, State legislator and Colonel in the Intelligence Division of the Confederacy. Cabaniss' Presidential Pardon Application, dated August 18, 1875, is of particular historical significance because of its detailed description of events surrounding Huntsville at that time. S. D. Cabaniss died on March 19, 1889 and was buried in Maple Hill Cemetery.[93] His wife, Virginia, died on March 21, 1907, and was buried beside her husband. The City Directories of 1911 and 1916 listed daughter, Miss Frances Cabaniss, as the Register in Chancery and lived in the family home at 505 Randolph Avenue.

Clay, John Withers; Editor of *Weekly Democrat*.
John Withers Clay was the son of one of the first and most distinguished citizens of Madison County, Clement C. Clay. John Withers became the editor-publisher of the town's leading newspaper, *The Huntsville Democrat*, which was continued after his death by his daughters. J. Withers Clay married Mary Fenwick Lewis on November 11, 1846.[94] She was the daughter of John Lewis, who had graduated from the University of Tennessee with two degrees and settled in Huntsville at the time of statehood, 1819. Mary Lewis was fortunate in 1842-44 to finish her education at a boarding school in Paris, France. Withers expressed his love for Mary in many of his personal writings.[95] They began their family with a son, Clement, who was born around 1848. They named him after J. Withers' father. Next to be born was William L. in 1853; Mary Louisa in 1854; and Susanna W. in 1858. In 1860, Maxwell Greene lived in the house with the Clay family.[96] There are many Greenes buried close to the family in Maple Hill, so it is assumed they are related. During the War Between the States, Clay was a member of the Forty-ninth Infantry Co., D of the Confederate Army. He served as a Second Lieutenant. The letters he wrote to family members during this time provide us with many interesting facts and much information

---

[93] 1870 United States Federal Census, Madison County, Alabama, page 17, Ward 2.
[94] Madison County, Alabama Marriage Records, Book 4 A, Page 147.
[95] The Huntsville Historic Review, Winter-Spring 1995 Vol. 22, No.1, page 18.
[96] 1860 United States Federal Census, Madison County, Alabama, Page 220.

regarding Huntsville and her citizens.[97] The 1870 census shows that Clay returned to Huntsville after the war and continued as editor of the paper. The family lived in Ward 2, on Eustis Avenue. The children at home were: Willie (William Lewis Clay); Mary; Susan; John; Jennie; Elodie; and Lucy Lewis.[98] J. Withers Clay died March 29, 1896. He was buried in Maple Hill with the following inscription on his tombstone: *"Our precious father, John Withers Clay, son of Clement C. and Susanna W. Clay, born January 11, 1820. Entered into Rest, Palm Sunday, Thy faith hath made thee whole."* Clay's daughters continued to operate the *Huntsville Weekly Democrat* into the next century.[99] In 1911, Susanna was the business manager; and lived on Eustis Street. Virginia was the editor and lived with her sister.[100] Virginia died shortly after, in 1911; and Susanna was left to carry on the family business until her death in 1928.

Coleman, Daniel; Solicitor.
Daniel Coleman was born September 7, 1838, in Limestone County, Alabama. He came to Huntsville in the early 1870's when he began practicing law. During the War Between the States, he served with the Forty-second Inf. Co. D as Captain in the Confederate Army.[101] Daniel married Claude LeVert on June 17, 1873.[102] Signing on the marriage bond for the marriage with him was William Richardson [Madison County Judge]. The couple had a stillborn child, Daniel Coleman Jr., born October 10, 1876.[103] The Colemans had two other children: LeVert and Vera. Coleman's law practice was at 117 Eustis, and his residence was at 517 Adams.[104] He continued practicing law, but became very politically active. He became a Representative in the State Legislature, Madison County Solicitor, and during President Grover Cleveland's first term, was appointed Consul to St. Etienne, France. He was also very active in the Episcopal Church of the Nativity, serving as vestryman and succeeding the late Judge I. M. Dox as Senior Warden. In his obituary, he was described as *"A brave,*

---

[97] 1907 Confederate Census, Limestone, Morgan & Madison County; Johnson Historical Publications, (1981).
[98] 1870 United States Federal Census, Madison County, Alabama, page 4, line 14.
[99] *Maple Hill Cemetery, Phase One*, Robey, Johnson, Jones, & Roberts, 1995, page 26.
[100] 1911 Huntsville Alabama City Directory Page 128.
[101] *1907 Confederate Census, Limestone, Morgan & Madison Counties Alabama*, Johnson Historical Publications, Page 12.
[102] Madison County, Alabama Marriage Records, Book No. 6, Page 566.
[103] Maple Hill Sexton's Records.
[104] 1896 Huntsville Alabama City Directory, page 27.

Confederate soldier and loved with a loyalty born of true patriotism to his native Southland and the cause for which he fought." Coleman died at his home June 29, 1906, with Mrs. Coleman and their son, Captain LeVert Coleman at his bedside. His daughter, "Miss Vera" was in Europe [having sailed with a party of friends, in June, for a tour of several months]. Daniel Coleman served the Egbert G. Jones Confederate Veteran's Camp as commander for a number of years. At his death, members honored his memory by carrying his body from the Episcopal Church to his final resting place in Maple Hill Cemetery. As a lasting memorial, they dropped a sprig of evergreen into his grave. The inscription on his tombstone reads: *"Fearless in the Fight."* Claudia L. Coleman lived in the family home at 425 Adams Street until her death on November 27, 1931.[105]

Crawford, Thomas B.; Citizens Meeting.
Thomas B. Crawford was born in Pennsylvania in 1818.[106] According to the United States Federal Census in 1870, he was a farmer on the western boundary of the City of Huntsville. He was married to Sarah, age forty years old. Their children's names were: Emma, twenty years old, who was born in Ohio; Austin, nineteen years old, also born in Ohio; Frank, sixteen years old, born in Alabama [which tells us that Crawford came to Alabama sometime between 1851 and 1854], and Fletcher, twelve years old, born in Alabama.[107] During the War Between the States, Thomas served in Hardee's Cavalry Battalion, Companies A and K of the Confederate Army. Thomas Crawford is buried in Maple Hill Cemetery.[108]

Davis, Zabulon P.; Mayor/Stand in the Road.
Zabulon Pike Davis was born in Kentucky around 1816. Zabulon married Willimetta Davis Eason on December 22, 1840.[109] "Zab" was a timber agent for the United States Government. He and Willimetta were blessed with a daughter, Martha H. in 1843, a son George Lane in 1845, and another daughter Effie in 1848, and Anna E. in 1849.[110]

---

[105] *Maple Hill Cemetery, Phase One*, Robey, Johnson, Jones, & Roberts, 1995, page 15.
[106] Madison County, Alabama Birth and Death Records, Hunstville-Madison County Public Library Archives, page 38.
[107] 1870 United States Federal Census, Madison County, Alabama, page 9.
[108] Madison County, Alabama Birth & Death Records, Huntsville-Madison County Public Library Archives, page 38.
[109] Madison County, Alabama Marriage Records, Book 4-4B (1826-1865).
[110] 1850 United States Federal Census, Madison County, Alabama Page 279.

He was the Mayor of Huntsville from 1856-1859. By 1860, four more children had been added to the family: Henrietta, born in 1852; Nicholas, born in 1854; Zabulon Jr.; born in 1857; and Williametta, born 1859.[111] He was elected Mayor again in 1861 [resigned in September], elected again in 1866, serving until 1867. Davis did not serve in the War Between the States, but remained active at home.[112] By 1870, two more children had been born: Nora, 1861, and Effie, 1867 [The Effie above, born in 1848 was not in the household. It is assumed that the older child died and they named this younger child born in 1861, Effie]. There is no further mention of son Nicholas, now sixteen years old. However, a newspaper account tells of his being involved in stabbing a man. Further information could not be found regarding this story. Zabulon Davis was elected Mayor again in 1878 and served until 1881, when Thomas White defeated him. The family plot in Maple Hill Cemetery provides us with insight into the family trials and troubles. Zabulon Davis died on January 3, 1882, at his residence.[113] Zabulon was called "Colonel," however it is believed this was an honorary title since no military record has been found. Daughter, Effie died of consumption [tuberculosis] in May of 1893 at the age of twenty-six years old. His wife, Williametta died May 4, 1889. George Lane, Henrietta E., Williametta, Martha H., Nora, & Effie are all buried with their parents, with no indication of a spouse, leading one to believe they never married.[114]

Dement, Dr. John Jefferson; Doctor/Inquest.
John Jefferson Dement was born May 13, 1830.[115] He received his early education in Madison County, Alabama, then began his formal medical training in Kentucky. He received his medical degree from the University of Pennsylvania in Philadelphia in 1853. He had become a promising physician by age thirty. John joined the Confederacy as a surgeon in the Confederate Army with the Twenty-seventh Alabama. The Union Army at Camp Chase imprisoned him. However, upon his release he returned to the Confederate Army.[116]

---

[111] 1860 United States Federal Census, Madison County, Alabama Page 197.
[112] 1870 United States Federal Census, Madison County, Alabama Page 1 Ward 4
[113] *The Weekly Democrat* (January 4, 1882)
[114] *Maple Hill Cemetery, Phase One*, Robey, Johnson, Jones, & Roberts, 1995, page 46.
[115] *Maple Hill Cemetery, Phase One*, Robey, Johnson, Jones, & Roberts, 1995, page 101.
[116] Medicine Bags and Bumpy Roads, Goldsmith and Fulton, 1985 page 139

He returned to his medical practice in Huntsville at the end of the war.

On January 26, 1869, John Jefferson Dement and Cornelia Clopton Binford were married.[117] Mrs. Dement was the daughter of Dr. Henry Binford. At the time, John was forty-four years old, and Cornelia, was thirty-four years old. The couple had a son, Henry, in 1870. Cornelia's father lived with them, as was her brother, Henry Binford, twenty-two years old, and her sister, Sarah Binford, twelve years old.[118] John J. Dement served on the first Madison County Health Board and was the first county health physician. He was the first physician from Madison County to serve as President of the Medical Association of the State of Alabama, 1876-1877. He was a Trustee of the Board of Trustees of Vanderbilt University, and a Trustee of the Huntsville Female College. He was also a Sensor of the Madison County Medical Society.

Dr. Dement died in Sithia Springs, Georgia, on August 10, 1891.[119] He was buried in Maple Hill Cemetery.[120] In later years his widow, Cornelia, lived at 416 Holmes Avenue, with son, Robert S. Dement (who worked as a cotton buyer[121]), until her death October 13, 1918. Seven of the Dement children are buried in the family plot with their parents.[122] Dr. John J. Dement was the father-in law of Dr. Riley Marion Mormon, the Grandfather of Dr. John Dement Mormon, and great-grandfather of Dr. Robert Circy Mormon.[123]

Dox, Peter Myndert; Citizens Meeting.
Peter Dox was born in Geneva, New York, on September 11, 1813. He was a New York State Legislator and Judge before he moved to Alabama in 1856.[124] On the 1860 United States Federal Census, he was listed as a farmer. He was married to Matilda M [argaret], aged thirty years old at the time of the census. She was born in Alabama.

---

[117] Madison County, Alabama Marriage Book No. 5, Page 633.
[118] 1870 United States Federal Census Madison County, Alabama, Ward 1.
[119] Madison County, Alabama Birth and Death Records, Huntsville-Madison County Public Library Archives.
[120] *Maple Hill Cemetery, Phase One*, Robey, Johnson, Jones, & Roberts, 1995, page 10.
[121] 1911 Huntsville Alabama City Directory page 139.
[122] *Maple Hill Cemetery, Phase One*, Robey, Johnson, Jones, & Roberts, 1995, page 101.
[123] *Medicine Bags and Bumpy Roads*, Goldsmith and Fulton, 1985 page 101.
[124] *The Huntsville Historic Review*, Winter-Spring 1995 Vol.22 No.1, page6.

Also in the home was her mother, Eliza E. Pope, sixty-one years old, who was born in Virginia.[125] Dox was a member of the State Constitutional Convention of 1865 and a member of Congress from 1869-1873, as well as a noted Jurist.[126] On May 9, 1876, he married Miss Margaret Simpson. He was sixty-three years old and she was forty-one years old.[127] Dox was employed in Huntsville, as an attorney. He died April 2, 1891, in Huntsville at age seventy-seven. Margaret Dox continued to live at their home at 416 McClung Avenue.[128] until her death in January 17, 1925. She was buried next to her husband in Maple Hill Cemetery.

Ellis, Clarence K.; Citizens Meeting.
During the 1870's, Clarence Ellis was a twenty-two-year-old farmer from Massachusetts. He lived with his twenty-two-year-old brother in the western section of the county near Monrovia.[129] Ten years later, in 1880, he was working as a farmer. His wife, Lavisa, was thirty-one years old. They had five children: Kellogg, eight years old; Clarence B., six years old; Clara L., four years old; Nelson, two years old, and nine-month-old, Nettie.[130]

Evans, Ben; Lynched.
Ben Evans came to Alabama shortly after the War Between the States. He was born in Lexington, Kentucky. He was around forty years old, and weighed about one hundred fifty pounds. His wife's name was Josie. They lived in a house at Mike White's slaughterhouse until his lynching.[131]

Evans, Josie; Wife of Ben Evans.
In 1911, "Josephine" was working as a laundress at a private home on Blue Springs Road.[132]

Franks, Brittain; Madison County Coroner.
Brittain Franks was born August 15, 1807, in Tennessee. His wife,

---

[125] 1860 United States Federal Census, Madison County, Alabama.
[126] *Maple Hill Cemetery, Phase One*, Robey, Johnson, Jones, & Roberts, 1995, page 121.
[127] Madison County, Alabama Marriage Records.
[128] 1916 Huntsville City Directory, page 137.
[129] .1870 United States Federal Census, Madison County, Alabama, Page 7.
[130] 1880 United States Federal Census, Madison County, Alabama, Page 74B.
[131] *Huntsville Democrat* (April 18, 1878).
[132] 1911 Huntsville City Directory, Page 146.

Mary, was born in Georgia around 1822. In 1850, he was a grocery keeper and they had five children: Rufus B., eight years old; James, six years old; Alameda E., four years old; William W. three years old; and Eleanor P., was three months old. Mary's sisters, Nancy Hawkins, twenty-eight years old; and Elizabeth Hawkins, twenty-six years old; John Slaughter, a grocery keeper; and Henry Lemburg, a sixty-year-old, carriage maker from Prussia also lived in the home.[133] During 1854, Franks purchased 80 acres of land.[134] He served as Town Marshall from 1850-1866. Brittain Franks served in the War Between the States as a Private in the Fourth Alabama Infantry Company. Son, Rufus, now seventeen years of age, was a student, as was his younger brother James. The house was listed as a boarding house that housed eighteen people, reflecting the town's growing diversity with a wide variety of crafts and talents including shoemaker, blacksmith, painter, carpenter, harness-maker, butcher, seamstress and cabinet-maker.[135] In 1872, Franks was (appointed) Madison County's only cotton weigher, then served as Coroner from 1873 until his death in 1891. Franks also held the position of Maple Hill Cemetery Sexton (Superintendent) from 1862-1882 and from 1883-1901, and the Sexton for Glenwood Cemetery from 1880-1881.[136] [137]By 1870, the boarding house occupancy had diminished. His son, William lived with them and five other tenants.[138] Briton [sic] Franks and his son Rufus were buried in Maple Hill Cemetery. Each has a Confederate grave marker. There is a note that Brittain Franks was a widower, but a record of Mrs. Frank's burial could not be found.[139]

Gill, George B.; Neighbor/Farmer.
George B. Gill was born February 20, 1846 in Lincoln County, Tennessee. George joined the Confederacy as a Private in 1864 with the Fourth Alabama Cavalry Company E.[140] After the war, he returned to live in Huntsville. In 1870, he lived with his parents,

---

[133] 1850 United States Federal Census, Madison County, Alabama, Page 264.

[134] *Old Land Records of Madison County Alabama*, Margaret Cowart.

[135] 1860 United States Federal Census, Madison County, Alabama.

[136] *A Dream Come True Vol. II*, James Record, 1978, John Hicklin Printing Co. Huntsville, Alabama, Library of Congress Card Number:76-11880.

[137] *The Valiant Survivors: the United Confederate Veterans of Madison County—A Record of Their Services 1861—1865*; 2nd Edition, page 36, Charles Wells.

[138] 1870 United States Federal Census, Madison County, Alabama.

[139] *Maple Hill Cemetery, Phase One*, Robey, Johnson, Jones, & Roberts, 1995, page 39.

[140] The Confederate Soldiers Census of 1907, Page 9.

Thomas and Mariah.[141] George was selling real estate and working as a Pension and Notary Agent in 1896.[142] Not much is mentioned about George Gill's wife, Octie, except that she lived in Rome, Georgia until her death on June 20, 1889. She was buried in Maple Hill Cemetery. George Gill died on October 4, 1926. According to Maple Hill records, George Gill bought and erected many of his family's tombstones; however, one has not been found for him.

Gordon, E. C.; Minister.
Little information regarding Reverend Gordon was found. Records show that a child of E. C. Gordon's died on November 22, 1874 and was buried in Maple Hill Cemetery.[143] A marriage was also noted that Rev. Gordon performed for Joseph J. Parton, in 1874.[144]

Hall, Ephraim; Lynched.
Ephraim Hall was estimated to be about fifty-five years old when he was lynched in Huntsville. He was born in North Carolina. He lived next to the creek at the old Burchfield house.[145]

Hammond, John J.; Citizens Meeting.
John J. Hammond was born in Virginia on July 20, 1845.[146] He was a farmer who lived in Huntsville District #2. During the 1880's, he worked as a farmer. Children at home were: Etta, twenty-six years of age, who was born in Virginia; Hubert, twenty-two years of age, was born in Virginia; Otho, twenty-one years old, was born in Alabama; and Bertha, seventeen years old was born in Alabama.[147] J. J. Hammond was part of the Twenty-fifth Infantry of Co. K in the Confederate Army. He died on July 21, 1884, and was buried in Maple Hill. Also buried there are Nancy McCrary Hammond [1861-1947], and Otho Conrad Hammond [1861-1954].[148] It is not known if Nancy was a younger wife of John, a daughter-in law, or a child not listed on the 1880 census.

---

[141] 1870 United States Federal Census, Madison County, Alabama.
[142] 1896 Huntsville Alabama City Directory, page 36.
[143] Maple Hill Sexton's Records.
[144] Madison County, Alabama Marriage Records, Madison County Courthouse.
[145] *The Huntsville Weekly Democrat*, April 18, 1878.
[146] Huntsville Alabama Birth and Death Records, Page 16.
[147] 1880 United States Federal Census, Madison County, Alabama.
[148] *Maple Hill Cemetery, Phase One*, Robey, Johnson, Jones, & Roberts, 1995, page 84.

Hampton, Dr. John P.; Citizens Meeting.
John P. Hampton was born in Alabama on January 22, 1825. He married Mary T. Battle on November 3, 1868, in Madison County, Alabama.[149] In the 1880 Census, Dr. Hampton's occupation was listed as farmer. His wife, Mary, was thirty-six years old; son, William B., was twenty-one years old; and son, Placebo, was sixteen years old. They were farming.[150] John P. Hampton died on June 8, 1907, and was buried in Maple Hill Cemetery. His grave is marked with C. S. A. marker # 38. His grave is located in Section 23 Row 14. Mary T. [Battle] Hampton died May 5, 1884 and is buried in Maple Hill Cemetery.[151]

Hardy, [Hardie] John Bryon; Policeman.
John Byron Hardy (Hardie) was born in Huntsville, Alabama, on December 3, 1849. His father, John Hardie, married Harriet M. Saxon, on May 22, 1844, in Madison County, Alabama.[152] John, twenty years old, lived with his parents during the 1870's.[153] John lived in Huntsville and was the Deputy Marshall. John's father died December 16, 1877. However, he continued to live with his mother Harriett, until his death. John Hardy died December 8, 1880, at the age of thirty-one. No information is available regarding his death or the death of his mother.[154]

Harris, Dr. George M.; Citizens Meeting.
Dr. George Milton Harris was born in Madison County, on July 11, 1820. He was the son of Epps and Mahala Harris who were from Appomattox County, Virginia. They settled at Blue Springs [now Blue Springs Road]. His grandfather had been a Revolutionary War soldier who came into the county in the early part of the 1800's, acquiring a large tract of land from the Federal government. George M. married Mary A. E. Ford, on May 6, 1842. Also, in 1842, Dr. Harris received his medical degree from the Louisville School of Medicine in Kentucky. He began his medical practice at Bellefonte,

---

[149] Tombstone Data at Battle Cemetery, *Madison County Cemeteries*, Vol. 2 page 236, Dorothy Scott Johnson.
[150] 1880 United States Federal Census, Madison County, Alabama, Township 2 Range 1W.
[151] *Maple Hill Cemetery, Phase One*, Robey, Johnson, Jones, & Roberts, 1995, page 19.
[152] Madison County, Alabama Marriage Records, Book 4B, Page 29.
[153] 1870 United States Federal Census, Madison County, Alabama.
[154] *Maple Hill Cemetery, Phase One*, Robey, Johnson, Jones, & Roberts, 1995, page 19.

in Jackson County, Alabama. He remained there until 1852, when he moved to Meridianville. Dr. Harris practiced medicine and was involved in the mercantile business until 1863. He also owned a large farm in Arkansas. In 1870, he moved his family into Huntsville. George and Mary had a son, Arthur L., who married Lula Allen Weaver. Dr. Harris was one of the organizers of the Huntsville Light Company. It was said that *"he could be generous with his personal influence for all those who needed it and that he portrayed a broad minded, wide awake, enterprising public spirited physician, who enjoyed a large personal acquaintance and friendship throughout Northern Alabama."* He spent his retirement years in his home that he built in 1888, at 526 Adams Street. Five months after Mrs. Harris passed away, Dr. Harris died on April 26, 1900. Their son, Arthur, had died eight years earlier. They all were buried in Maple Hill Cemetery.[155]

Harrison, Perry L.; Tax Collector/Neighbor.
Harrison, Elizabeth, Hattie and Sue.
Perry Harrison was born on May 28, 1829. He married Elizabeth L. Daniel on September 20, 1855.[156] By 1870, the couple had five children: Kibble J., twelve years old; Susan, ten years old; Harriet, seven years old; Carrie, five years old; and Perry Jr., four years old. Elizabeth had personal real estate apart from her husband.[157] Ten years later little had changed in the family, except age and status. The family had acquired a cook, sixty-six year old Lurinda Irwin; William Cole, an eleven-year-old house-boy; and two laborers, George Bauhough, forty-five years old, and Sarah Bauhough, thirty-six years old. They both worked on the farm. Records show that Perry Harrison died on May 13, 1885.[158]

Harrison, Todd; Neighbor.
William Todd Harrison married, Florence Cochran, November 28, 1883.[159] Todd died September 23, 1915, and is buried with his parents

---

[155] *Medicine Bags and Bumpy Roads*, Goldsmith & Fulton, Page 131.
[156] Madison County, Alabama Marriage Records, Book No. 4 Page 124.
[157] 1870 United States Federal Census, Madison County, Alabama, Page 19 T2 R2W.
[158] Madison County, Alabama Birth and Death Records, Huntsville-Madison County Public Library Archives.
[159] Madison County, Alabama Marriage Book, Book 13, Page 200.

in Maple Hill Cemetery. His tombstone reads, "Captain Fifth United States Volunteers, Spanish American War. A Loyal Friend."[160]

Huddleston, Henry and Amelia; Employee/Neighbor.
In 1870, Henry Huddleston was thirty-four years old, married, and employed as a butcher. His wife, Amelia, was twenty-eight years old. The couple's children were: Willie, four years old; James, two years old; and Ora, born in October of 1869.[161] During the next ten years, Henry and Amelia had four more sons: Oscar, Bovell, Walter D., and Edgar, and a daughter, Mildred.[162]

Humes, Milton; Attorney.
Young lawyer, Milton Humes was born on April 4, 1844, in Abington, Virginia. He married Ellelee Chapman [daughter of Reubin Chapman, the ex-Alabama Governor], June 1, 1870. Ellelee had a turbulent time as a young lady. Her home-place, the Reuben Chapman home, had been confiscated during the War Between the States, and burned on the last day of the War by Union soldiers. It was then turned into a Freedman's Camp. Reuben Chapman was special envoy to France for the Confederacy, during the War, and upon returning to the States was arrested in Boston Harbor, where he was put into prison until the end of the war.[163] Milton Humes served the Confederacy during the War Between the States in Company A of the Sixty-third Virginia Volunteer Infantry, where he held the rank of Captain. He enlisted at Abingdon, Washington Co., Va., in 1861. Humes was listed for a promotion to Major of Battalions but did not get the commission due to the end of the War.[164] After their marriage, Milton and Ellelee resided at the Venable Hotel in Huntsville.[165] Later they made their home at Abington Place on Meridianville Pike, near the city limits.[166] The couple had plenty of servants to keep their lives comfortable. Thomas Power, sixty years old, from Ireland, was their gardener; Banister Reed, black, fifty-two years old, was their farm

---

[160] *Maple Hill Cemetery, Phase One*, Robey, Johnson, Jones, & Roberts, 1995, page 109.
[161] 1870 United States Federal Census, Madison County, Alabama, Page 3, Ward 4
[162] 1880 United States Federal Census, Madison County, Alabama, Page 55.
[163] *Maple Hill Cemetery, Phase One*, Robey, Johnson, Jones, & Roberts, 1995, page 32.
[164] *1907 Confederate Census, Limestone, Morgan & Madison Counties Alabama*, Johnson Historical Publications, Page 12.
[165] 1870 United States Federal Census, Madison County, Alabama, Page 16, Ward 1.
[166] 1916 Huntsville City Directory, Page 169.

hand; Creecy Reed, forty-three years old, was the cook; Mary Jones, twenty-three years old, was the wash-woman; Leonidas Cogswell, from Virginia was their carriage driver; and Kate Fleming, seventy-four years old, was the maid. Milton Humes worked as an attorney, with the law firm of Humes, Sheffey & Speake.[167] Milton Humes died in 1844. He and Ellelee are buried in Maple Hill Cemetery. His tombstone states, "1844-1908." Ellelee Chapman Humes' tombstone states "July 24, 1920, Perfect Peace."[168]

Humphrey, Herman; Neighbor/farmer.
Herman Humphrey was twenty-eight years old, and served the town of Huntsville as a Deputy Sheriff in 1880. He married Virginia Sneed on February 25, 1879.[169] His mother-in-law, Susanna Snow, lived with them in 1880.[170]

Humphrey, Thomas W.; Citizens Meeting.
In 1878, Thomas W. Humphrey was forty-two years old and was born in Kentucky. By 1870, he was a cotton merchant. His wife's name was Mary, who was born in Alabama. They had four children: Bessie, ten years old; Thomas, seven years old; Matthew, four years old; and two-year-old, Edie. Also in the home was sixteen-year-old Nannie Weaver.[171]

Kelly, Frank; Accused.
Frank was only nineteen when accused of being involved in the murder of George Shoenberger. He was kept in jail and not lynched because there was a doubt that he was guilty. It was stated that he was *"nearly white, and apparently unhardened by the crime."*[172] Kelly's lawyer moved for a change of venue and the trial was moved to Limestone County and tried in Athens. The verdict was not guilty. Thus, a trial transcript will not be found. After the trial, nothing more was heard of Frank Kelly.

---

[167] 1896 Huntsville City Directory, page 43.
[168] *Maple Hill Cemetery, Phase One*, Robey, Johnson, Jones, & Roberts, 1995, page 32.
[169] Madison County, Alabama Marriage Records, Book 10 Page 200.
[170] 1880 United States Federal Census, Madison County, Alabama, Ward 2.
[171] 1870 United States Federal Census, Madison County, Alabama, Page 15.
[172] *The Weekly Democrat* (April 1878).

Kelly, William Solon; Citizens Meeting.
William Solon Kelly was born in Madison County, Alabama, on May 22, 1835. He was home with his parents, David and Nancy Kelly, in Madison County.[173] This family appears in Chapter Four. William served in the Confederate Army in Co. K, Second Alabama Infantry, serving until March 1862. He entered service as a Private in March of 1861, at Huntsville, Alabama. He re-enlisted as a Private in May of 1862, at Corinth, Mississippi in Co. B of the Fourth Alabama Cavalry and continued until he was captured at Shelbyville, Tennessee, on June 27, 1863. He was sent to prison and remained there until the close of the war.[174] All of the children of David and Nancy are buried in the Kelly Cemetery except William Solon. He had one son, Clark Kelly, who was buried with him in Cameron Texas.[175]

Kelly, Aaron; Friend of Ben Evans.
In 1911, Aaron Kelly lived at 430 Half Street, in Huntsville with his wife Delia. He was a farmer.[176]

Kennard, George W.; Policeman.
George W. Kennard was born about 1842 His father, Lewis M. Kennard, a tailor, who was born in Tennessee. George was a part of the Madison Rifles unit when it left for Pensacola, Florida in March of 1861. He returned to Huntsville and married Maggie F. Pryor on November 21, 1862.[177] Twenty-seven-year-old George was employed as a printer by 1870.[178] However, by 1878, he was the town's constable and during the 1880's, George also worked as a policeman for the town of Huntsville. He and Maggie had two children: Thomas, thirteen years old, and Mattie, ten years old. His mother-in-law, Martha Pryor, lived in the home.[179] At the time of his death, George W. Kennard was a widower, and worked as a printer. His death was on March 27, 1888.[180]

---

[173] 1850 United States Federal Census, Madison County, Alabama.

[174] *1907 Confederate Census, Limestone, Morgan & Madison Counties Alabama*, Johnson Historical Publications, Page 15.

[175] Madison County Cemeteries, Vol. 1, Page 60, Dorothy Scott Johnson, Johnson Historical Publications.

[176] 1911 Huntsville Alabama City Directory.

[177] Madison County Alabama Marriage Records.

[178] 1870 United States Federal Census, Madison County, Alabama, Page 136.

[179] 1880 United States Federal Census, Madison County, Alabama, Page 34, Ward 1, Enumeration District 231.

[180] Madison County, Alabama Birth and Death Records, Page 20 Huntsville-Madison County Public Library.

Lowry, Dr. Samuel Hickman; Neighbor/Doctor/Inquest.
Dr. Samuel Hickman Lowry was the son of John Tate Lowry [see chapter one] and Virginia H. [Miller] Lowry. and was born October 16, 1850. After Samuel's early education in Huntsville, he attended the University of Virginia, and Bellevue Medical College in New York. He received his medical degree in 1873, then came back to Huntsville and began his medical practice with John J. Dement, becoming one of the leading physicians in Madison County. He served as a member of the board of censors of the Madison County Medical Society, grand senior censor and vice president of the State Medical Association, and served as Madison County jail physician in 1884 and 1885. He was a Mason, a member of the B.P.O.E. Lodge and Madison County Health Officer in 1888 and 1889. He married Lucy James Pulley of Huntsville on November 26, 1890. She was always fondly called "Miss Jimmie". Dr. Lowry's home was at One Bank Row. The Lowry children were: Elizabeth [Mrs. William Halsey, Jr.]; Georgia, [Mrs. Birnie Spraggins], and John Tate. Later the family lived at 220 Williams Street, but had a summer home on Monte Sano, enjoying the cooler days the mountain would provide. Dr. Lowry suffered a stroke several months before his death, which was June 7, 1906.[181] Jimmie P. continued to live in the family home until her death in 1940. Dr. Lowry was known as a kind man with a loving manner who felt an attachment to his patients. Famous artist Howard Weeden left him one of her most famous paintings. Dr. Lowry is buried in Maple Hill Cemetery, beside his beloved Jimmie in Section 12 Row 13.[182]

Lowry, John Tate; Neighbor/Farmer.
John Tate Lowry was born April 19, 1821. He married Virginia H. Miller, daughter of John and Mary Miller. Their marriage took place in Madison County on November 8, 1849. Reverend M. H. Bone performed the ceremony.[183] Sadly, Virginia died almost one year later on October 30, 1850, shortly after the birth of Samuel Hickman.[184] In the 1860's, John Tate lived in the section of the county called Madison. He was a substantial merchant. With him were his mother,

---

[181] *Medicine Bags and Bumpy Roads*, page 193, Goldsmith & Fulton, 1985.

[182] *Maple Hill Cemetery Phase One*, page 105, Robey, Johnson, Jones, Roberts; Huntsville-Madison County Historical Society.

[183] Madison County, Alabama Marriage Records, Book 4A, Page 327.

[184] *Cemeteries of Madison County, Alabama*, Vol. II, Page 127, Dorothy Scott Johnson, Johnson Historical Publications.

Elizabeth, age sixty-five, and his son, Samuel, age nine. John remained a widower until his death. His son, Samuel, lived with him for a while after becoming a doctor, as did his mother until her death. Eighty-five-year-old Elizabeth Lowry died on March 27, 1881, and was buried in Maple Hill Cemetery.[185] John Tate Lowry was seventy-five years old when he died, January 2, 1886.

Martin, John William; Citizens Meeting.
John W. Martin married Mollie [Mary] Wilmore October 8, 1868, in Madison County, Alabama. John was born in Madison County, Alabama in 1847. Mollie was born in Tennessee, in May of 1850. The couple had ten children: John William Jr., born 1869; Malisa E. born October 25, 1872; Peny born, October 1878; Seny, born, October 1878; Mattie L. born, April 16, 1882 [Grandmother of Gay Cushing Campbell]; Robert Eldridge born, May 10, 1883; Mary L., born March 1884; Ella F., born October 1887; Ausborne, born 1877; Emmett W., [unknown]. John W. Martin died July 1, 1914 and was buried in Hayden Cemetery in Madison County with his wife, Mollie. Mollie died January 7, 1911.[186]

McCalley, Thomas Sanford; Citizens Meeting.
Thomas McCalley was born February 13, 1807, in Spotsylvania County, Virginia. Three McCalley brothers left Spotsylvania County, Virginia, and relocated to Huntsville. Two brothers, Thomas and Robert married two sisters, Caroline Matilda Lanford, and Ann Lanford whose parents were Robert and Ann Lanford from Louisa Co., Virginia. Charles McCalley did not marry. Thomas lived in the area known as Triana. In 1850, his wife, Caroline Matilda, was born October 17, 1820. By 1850, the McCalley's had five children: Martha Ann, born 1840; Robert L., born 1842; Charles S., born 1844; Thomas, born 1846; and John, born 1848.[187] By the time of the War Between the States, his son, Robert was eighteen years old; Charles S. Jr., was sixteen years old; Thomas, was fourteen years old; and John, was twelve years old. The younger son, John, was too young to fight in the upcoming war, but the older sons fought for the Confederacy. The enemy occupied the family home during the war, and a photograph of Union Soldiers on the front porch may be found

---

[185] *Maple Hill Cemetery, Phase One*, Robey, Johnson, Jones, & Roberts, 1995, page 106.
[186] Gay Cushing Campbell's Family Genealogy Records.
[187] 1850 United States Federal Census, Madison County, Alabama, page 208.

in the archives photo collection at the Huntsville-Madison County Public Library.

Charles McCalley was buried next to his brother, Thomas S. McCalley, in Maple Hill Cemetery. Henry, a son of Thomas S. and Caroline, was also buried there after his death on November 21, 1904. Also buried in the same plot is Carrie L. McCalley [1861-1944], and Kate T. McCalley [1854-1936]. Thomas Sanford McCalley died in Huntsville on February 22, 1880. There was a small Confederate soldier statue about 18" tall that was tinted in authentic colors that stood in the middle of the graves between Thomas and Caroline. However, it has disappeared. Caroline Matilda died May 14, 1874. She was buried beside her husband.[188] The house that was the family home-place is no longer in existence. Many descendants of this family remain in Huntsville, including Charles Hooper, a prominent attorney.

McCravey, Leroy Wesley and Sarah; Neighbors\Farmer.
Wesley L. McCravey was born in Huntsville, Alabama, on February 14, 1835. He entered service as a Private in the Confederate Army at Memphis, Tennessee. He later re-enlisted as First Lieutenant at Huntsville, serving with General Forrest, in the Fourth Alabama Cavalry, Company F. He was a prisoner at Johnson Island, Illinois, for nineteen months and was not released until the close of the war. It is known that prisoners serving there endured excruciating cruelties. By the 1870's, McCravey had accumulated a good amount of money as a young clerk and ex-merchant.[189] His wife, Sarah, was twenty-three years old; ten years younger than her husband.

By 1880, Wesley had become an auctioneer. The couple had two children, Benjamin L., born 1875, and Cornelia, born 1878. They had a nurse, Willametta Trottman, thirteen years old, with them. Neighbors of the family were John Lowry and Henry Metz.[190] Sarah Elizabeth was born October 21, 1846, and died December 8, 1889. Benjamin Lowry McCravey was born November 27, 1874, and died July 19, 1896. A second wife, Rebecca L. [born August 26, 1850], died on December 17, 1910, is buried beside her husband. L. W.

---

[188] *Maple Hill Cemetery, Phase One*, Robey, Johnson, Jones, & Roberts, 1995, page 58.
[189] 1870 United States Federal Census, Madison County, Alabama, Page 12, Ward 2.
[190] Ibid.

McCravey died on April 28, 1919, at his residence in Farley. He was eighty-four years old.[191]

McDavid, John J.; Attorney.
Young lawyer, John J. McDavid was born in Tennessee, but in 1835, came to Huntsville. He shared a house with William Brickell, also twenty-five, and an attorney. A tenant of the house was Lee P. Hammonds, eighteen, and a college student.[192] During the course of the next ten years, he married Mary Thompson, who was born on October 21, 1882.[193] The 1870 census states the couple had two children; Robert, three years old, and seven-month-old, Neddie, born in October of 1869.[194] John's practice on Randolph Street grew and so did his family. Daughter Mary was born around 1872; Blanche and Edmund around 1874, and Mollie around 1877. Little Neddie is presumed to have died young, as she is not listed with the family in the 1880 Census.[195]

It is assumed that John and Mary are buried in the family cemetery, the McDavid Cemetery, which is located in Section 13 Township One South and Range One West. Dorothy Scott Johnson, who compiled information on the Madison County Cemeteries, wrote the following passage concerning the cemetery,

Note: "This cemetery was all but destroyed several months ago by neighborhood boys hunting rabbits, according to a near by resident. Cattle have now been let into the graveyard and have about finished the destruction the irresponsible boys began. I have spent several hours here attempting to find missing parts to the many pieces of tombstones but was unsuccessful for the most part. It was like trying to fit together a giant jigsaw puzzle."[196]

Moss, James M.; Citizens Meeting.
James M. Moss was born in New York in 1822. He came to Alabama between 1860-1867.[197] He was a successful farmer and lived in

---

[191] *Maple Hill Cemetery, Phase One*, Robey, Johnson, Jones, & Roberts, 1995, page 89-90.
[192] 1860 United States Federal Census, Madison County, Alabama, Page 219.
[193] Madison County, Alabama Marriages, Book 12, Page 310.
[194] 1870 United States Federal Census, Madison County, Alabama, Page 11.
[195] 1880 United States Federal Census, Madison County, Alabama.
[196] Cemeteries of Madison County, Alabama, Vol. II, Dorothy Scott Johnson, Johnson Historical Publications.
[197] This fact was arrived at by looking at the birth of children. Daughter Ella was born in Iowa and Jane is the first born in Alabama.

Township Three and Range One West. He was married to Ellen who was born in Indiana about 1831. The children in 1870 were: Hubert, twenty-one years old, born in Indiana; Gertrude, nineteen years old, born in Indiana; Rosalind, eleven years old, born in Iowa; Ella, eight years old, born in Iowa; and Jane T., three years old, born in Alabama.[198] James farmed in 1880. His wife, Ellen, was now forty-eight years old, and he was fifty-eight years old. Their daughter, Ella, was eighteen years old, and taught school. The younger children; Louisa, thirteen years old, and Grant, seven years old, attended school.[199]

Nuckols, Virgil Augustus; Citizens Meeting.
Virgil Augustus Nuckols was born in Alabama on December 9, 1841. His parents were Samuel O. and Eliza C. Nuckols. Nuckols served in the Confederate Army in Co. I of the Fourth Alabama Infantry. He married Martha Susan Allen. V. Augustus Nuckols died June 5, 1886, at his home near Maysville. His wife, Martha Susan, was buried beside him in Maple Hill Cemetery. She died April 9, 1924.[200] An Iron Cross, on his grave marks his Confederate military service.[201]

Parton, Joseph J.; Policeman.
Joseph J. Parton was a coach maker in Huntsville during 1860. He was born in Tennessee around 1835. He was a member of the Huntsville Guards during the War Between the States.[202] Joseph J. Parton returned from the war to make coaches and live in Huntsville. He lived in the home of Mary Burnett, who was born about 1838. Her son, Clark, ten years old, was born in 1870.[203] Joseph's brother, William Parton, who was born around 1828, also lived in the home. He was also a coach maker. On February 10, 1874, Joseph J. Parton married Miss Sarah A. Scroggins. E. C. A. Gordon, Minister of the Gospel, performed the marriage. Joseph J. Parton and Thomas W. Smith signed the bond.[204] Mrs. Parton was twenty-one years old, and Parton, was forty years old. By 1880, the Parton's lived on

---

[198] 1870 United States Federal Census, Madison County, Alabama, Page 147.
[199] 1880 United States Federal Census, Madison County, Alabama, Page 61A.
[200] Birth and Death Records of Madison County, Alabama, Huntsville-Madison County Public Library Archives.
[201] *Maple Hill Cemetery, Phase One*, Robey, Johnson, Jones, & Roberts, 1995, page 102.
[202] Madison County, Alabama, C.S.A. Pension Application Records, Microfilm.
[203] 1870 United States Federal Census, Madison County, Alabama, Page 10.
[204] Madison County, Alabama Marriage Records, Book 7, Page 212.

Meridianville Pike. They had two children: William, born 1875 and Joseph, born 1877.[205] Death or burial records have not been found for John J. or Sarah, however William J. Parton is buried in Maple Hill Cemetery. He died January 23, 1887.[206]

Patton, John; Neighbor/Farmer.
John Patton was a fifty-six year old farmer, born in Virginia but in Huntsville by 1870. His wife, Marion, was born in Virginia. Their children were: James, born in Alabama about 1853; Dicey, born in 1856; Robert, born about 1859; and Louise, born about 1862.[207] John Patton paid his Madison County, Alabama Poll Tax in 1875.[208] John Patton was sixty-eight years old and farmed in 1880. His wife, Mary, was fifty-six years old, their son, Robert H., was twenty-one years old. Jane H. Childs, eighty-four years old, a retired school ma'am from Washington, D. C., lived with the family. She died May 22, 1882 and was buried in Maple Hill Cemetery. John's home was ten dwellings away from Milton Humes and near the Shoenberger home.[209] John Patton died on July 11, 1888.[210] He was buried in Maple Hill Cemetery.[211]

Richardson, William; Judge.
William Richardson was born in Athens, Alabama May 8, 1839. His mother was the daughter of Capt. Nicholas Davis, who was one of the members of the convention that met in Huntsville to draft the constitution under which Alabama was admitted as a State in 1819. Richardson was educated at Wesleyan University in Florence, Alabama. When only a young man of sixteen, he enlisted in the Confederate Army as a Private but soon was promoted to Captain for *"conspicuous gallantry."* He was severely wounded at the battle of Shiloh and taken prisoner of war. Upon his recovery, he escaped and made his way to Nashville where he attempted to get through enemy lines to rejoin his command. However, he was recaptured and tried. On the night before he was scheduled for execution, Gen. Nathan B.

---

[205] 1880 United States Federal Census, Madison County, Alabama.
[206] *Maple Hill Cemetery, Phase One*, Robey, Johnson, Jones, & Roberts, 1995, page 71.
[207] 1870 United States Federal Census, Madison County, Alabama, Page 18.
[208] Alabama Poll Tax, Probate Records, Madison County, Alabama.
[209] 1880 United States Federal Census, Madison County, Alabama, Page 53.
[210] Madison County, Alabama Birth and Death Records, Huntsville-Madison County Public Library Archives.
[211] Maple Hill Cemetery Lot Ownership Records.

Forrest learned of his capture and rescued him. Again, he returned for duty but was seriously wounded in the battle of Chickamauga. He lay on the battlefield for six days and was kept alive by his faithful black servant.

By 1880, he had married Sallie [Elizabeth—tombstone data] who was twenty-five years old. They had a daughter, Sallie, born 1875.[212] He was the Madison County Probate Judge from 1875 until 1886. The 1896 City Directory listed Richardson as a lawyer who lived at 626 Franklin Street. His office was at #7 Bank Row.[213] In 1890, he became a candidate for the Democratic nomination for Governor. After carrying every county in the State north of Birmingham, he withdrew his name in order to harmonize the factional differences of his party. *"His natural eloquence and analytical mind made him an especially effective lawyer in jury cases and he was ranked by many of his brother lawyers as one of the leading criminal lawyers in Alabama."*[214] On July 2, 1900, Richardson was nominated to the United States Congress for a short term to succeed General Wheeler, who had resigned. From his election the following November 1900, until his death, he served the people of the Eighth Congressional District of Alabama. Richardson served on many important committees during his service.

Richardson's landmark work with the Tennessee River Improvement Association has greatly benefited the entire Tennessee Valley. One of his colleagues, John L. Burnett [also a representative of Alabama], said of the efforts of Richardson: *"If the scheme for water-power development and the opening of that great stream is ever consummated, the people of the Tennessee Valley ought to erect a monument to the name of William Richardson."*[215] While Richardson accomplished many great things in his lifetime, one of the greatest was when he introduced a bill to establish a home in Huntsville, Alabama, for disabled soldiers of the Confederate States. While the location of the home was changed on January 21, 1901 to Johnson

---

[212] 1880 United States Federal Census, Madison County, Alabama, Page 53.
[213] 1896 Huntsville Alabama City Directory, Page 65,
[214] *Memorial Address* delivered in the House of Representative of the United States of America, Sixty-Third Session, January 31, 1915.
[215] *Memorial Address* delivered in the House of Representative of the United States of America, Sixty-Third Session, January 31, 1915

City, Tennessee, Richardson heartily supported passage of $250,000 to open the home.[216]

The Honorable William Richardson's home was at 508 Franklin Street. However, he died in Atlantic City, New Jersey, on the 31st day of March 1914, at the age of seventy-four years, ten months, and twenty-three days. The Governor of Alabama, Emmet O'Neal, issued a proclamation and order that the State's flag was to be placed at half-mast on the Capital and the building was to be draped in mourning. All offices in the Capital building were closed on the day of the funeral in respect for Richardson. At his funeral services in Maple Hill Cemetery, Representative Mann of Illinois observed *"Richardson's compatriots as they marched around the burial plot. Among these was the distinguished Senator Thornton of Louisiana, and bringing up the rear of the procession was a humble old colored laborer; a procession of old men who had taken part in the war, and composed of those who loved him."*[217] He was buried beside his wife, Elizabeth B. Richardson (3/12/1853-10/24/1891), in Maple Hill Cemetery.[218] There was a C.S.A. iron cross, placed on his grave, but it is now gone.[219] The editor of the *Huntsville Mercury-Banner* prepared the following that is fitting for William Richardson's tribute;

"Huntsville has upon her roll of honor the names of many eminent sons, but it is doubtful if the death of any one was ever more generally regretted and the sorrow of our loss more deeply and keenly felt than in the death of William Richardson. The public is familiar with his long official career characterized by eminent ability, capable efficiency, and the most loyal fidelity to every trust. He was a man of unquestioned courage, mental, moral and physical. Perhaps the dominating element of the man was his strong, native common sense, which gave him almost unerring judgment. He was a positive character. In all of his, many political and legal battles he asked no quarter and gave none. As a citizen, he lived on a high plane, and in the thirty-one years we knew him, he never failed to respond to any call for the betterment and uplift of this home, city and county. He took great pride in beautifying and caring for the Court Square. And in no relation of life did his fine nature shine out more nobly than in his watchful, faithful attention to the interest of widows and orphans. He has won and richly deserves every respect and honor his people

---

[216] Ibid.
[217] Ibid.
[218] Maple Hill Cemetery, Manuscript records of Dorothy Scott Johnson.
[219] Madison County, Alabama Confederate Soldiers Records.

can pay his memory, and in this last tribute they do honor themselves. Peace to his ashes."[220]

Ridge, Jimmy; Neighbor/former employee of Mike White.
James Ridge lived one house above Mike White and was also a butcher who sometimes worked for Mike White. He was born in England in 1814. His wife, Elizabeth, was born in Tennessee in 1834.[221]

Robinson, Dr. Christopher A.; Doctor.
Dr. Christopher Robinson was listed in the 1859 Huntsville City Directory.[222] Records show he paid his Alabama Poll Tax in 1875.[223] Dr. Robinson married Joanna on October 21, 1875.[224] In 1880, Dr. Robinson was thirty-five years old, as was his wife Joanna. He was a physician and farmer.[225] The Robinsons lost a child on June 26, 1878.[226] In 1896, Dr. Robinson lived at 502 Randolph Street.[227]

Shoenberger, George; Victim.
George Shoenberger was born May 8, 1820, in Glaurus Switzerland. Before arriving in America, he relocated with his parents to the eastern part of Switzerland near the tiny county of Liechtenstein. George Shoenberger then came to America and became a naturalized citizen in 1838. Shortly afterwards, he joined the United States Army and served five years as a soldier on the Texas frontier.[228] He settled in Huntsville, Alabama, about twenty-five years before his death, which would have been about 1853. During the 1860's, his occupation was a butcher. His wife, Cassander Lamar, was born in Georgia around 1824.[229] His daughter, Sallie, was born in 1865. Her mother was not listed on the 1870 U. S. Federal Census, but it was found that she died August 6, 1870, and was buried in Maple Hill

---

[220] Huntsville *Mercury-Banner* April 2, 1914.
[221] 1870 United States Federal Census, Madison County, Alabama, Page 144.
[222] 1859 Huntsville Alabama City Directory, Page 79.
[223] Madison County, Alabama Poll Tax, Probate Records.
[224] Madison County, Alabama Marriage Records, Book #4.
[225] 1880 United States Federal Census, Madison County, Alabama.
[226] Maple Hill Sexton's Records.
[227] 1896 Huntsville City Directory, page 66.
[228] The *Weekly Democrat*, Obituary Notice (April 24, 1878).
[229] 1860 United States Federal Census, Madison County, Alabama, Page 295, Hayes Store.

Cemetery.[230] During that time, George, a carpenter, and his wife, Sallie Ruffin, (both were born in Ohio) lived there. Next-door neighbors were Mayor William Mastin, and his wife.[231]

George Shoenberger's second wife, Fannie, was born in 1839. Their daughter Annie was born in 1872. Annie Shoenberger married Ervin W. Hamplett. Sallie Shoenberger married Walter Eugene Penny on October 18, 1883.[232] Shoenberger's widow, Fannie P. Shoenberger later married James H. Jackson on October 27, 1886. There is no marker for George Shoenberger, for the occupied grave that is present beside Cassander Shoenberger. It is located in Section 9 Row 4. Second wife, Fannie, was buried beside her second husband, James H. Jackson, in another part of the cemetery.

Spence, John; Visited Lilly
John Spence served in the Confederacy as a private in Company A, Fourteenth Alabama Infantry.[233] During the 1870's, John served the town as the Foreman of the Volunteer Fire Department. The position is now called the Fire Chief. It was the only paid position of the Fire Department. John Spence was thirty-three years old and an agent for S. & M. in 1880. He was married to Sue, who had been born in 1853. They had four children: Lillian A., born in 1869; William H., born in 1872; Laura, born in 1876; and Emma born in 1878. Nancy Davis and Eliza, both black servants, lived with them.[234] John S. Spence was buried in Maple Hill.[235] He died October 1, 1890 of a gunshot wound. At the time of his death, he lived in Huntsville Ward One.[236] There was a C.S.A. Cross No. 158 on the grave recognizing his service to the South.

Sweeney, Alfred; Policeman.
Alfred Sweeney was born in Ireland around the year 1838. He lived with Frank Mastin in Huntsville in 1870. The home was located in

---

[230] *Maple Hill Cemetery, Phase One*, Robey, Johnson, Jones, & Roberts, 1995, page 63.
[231] 1870 United States Federal Census, Madison County, Alabama, Page 379.
[232] Madison County, Alabama Marriage Records, Book 13 Page 93.
[233] *The Valiant Survivors: the United Confederate Veterans of Madison County—A Record of Their Services 1861—1865*; 2nd Edition, page 116, Charles Wells.
[234] 1880 United States Federal Census, Madison County, Alabama, Page 376.
[235] *Maple Hill Cemetery, Phase One*, Robey, Johnson, Jones, & Roberts, 1995, page 104.
[236] Huntsville Alabama Birth and Death Records.

Township Three Range 1 West.[237] Sweeney married Catherine Neagle on February 21, 1871. P. M. Magennis (a Catholic Priest), performed the ceremony.[238] By 1880, Sweeney was forty-five years old and worked as a policeman for the town. His wife, Catherine, was thirty-five years old. They had one child, Mary, aged four, and the family lived on Holmes Avenue.[239] They lived next door to Harmon Humphrey. The couple lost a child in 1876, the same year Mary was born, leading one to think she may have been a twin.[240]

Terry, William B.; Citizens Meeting.
William B. Terry was born on June 6, 1823. The 1850 Census reveals that William lived with his parents George and Elizabeth Terry, and brother John, and sisters Eliza and Ellen.[241] He married Susan J. White on May 14, 1851. James C. Elliott, Minister of the Gospel,[242] performed the ceremony. William died February 14, 1892, at the age of eighty.[243] He and Susan [who died July 17, 1915] were buried in Hayden Cemetery.[244]

Toney, Harris; Citizens Meeting.
Harris Toney was born August 12, 1843. In 1850, Harris, seven years old at the time, helped his father stock the family store after school.[245] *A Dream Come True*, refers to the Toney family and their standing in the community as;

"There came to Madison County in 1818 three brothers, Harris, Caleb and Edmund and were the first to buy land in the Triana vicinity. These three brothers were men of considerable means (as judged by the standards of that time) and quickly identified themselves with the development of Triana. Harris was the eldest and the leader. He engaged in the merchandising and cotton business, later investing his ample means in farmlands and slaves. He was far in advance of this time in his methods of farm development and was

---

[237] 1870 United States Federal Census, Madison County, Alabama, Page 145.
[238] *Madison County Marriages*, Book #2, Dorothy Scott Johnson, Johnson Historical Publications.
[239] 1880 United States Federal Census, Madison County, Alabama Ward 2.
[240] Maple Hill Sexton's Records.
[241] 1850 United States Federal Census, Madison County, Alabama.
[242] Madison County, Alabama Marriage Book #4.
[243] Madison County, Alabama Birth and Death Records, Huntsville-Madison County Public Library Archives.
[244] Madison County Cemeteries, Vol. III, Dorothy Scott Johnson, Page 83, Johnson Historical Publications.
[245] 1850 United States Federal Census, Madison County, Alabama, Page 230-231.

laying plans so extensive they would have overshadowed all other agricultural enterprises of his time, but unfortunately, he did not live long enough to the fruition of this undertaking. He died in the prime of his manhood. He evidently never married and a Mrs. Coons and Mrs. Barclay inherited his lands and properties. Caleb died at a young age. The youngest of the three Col. Edmund Toney, was one of the best businessmen of his day, possessing excellent judgment and sound business sense. It has been said in his whole life, he never made a business blunder. The war stripped him of his slaves and land, which ran to waste at the close of the war. However, he was soon out of debt and able to embark in the General Merchandising business in Triana. He died in 1877 at the age of seventy-seven and is buried in Maple Hill Cemetery."[246]

Edmund's two daughters were educated in Philadelphia and both married Jewish men. His son, Harris Toney, was a graduate of the University of Virginia, along with brothers Edmund and Charlie. Harris also took special courses at Oxford and Heidelberg while studying abroad.[247] Harris served the Confederacy during the War Between the States. According to his service records, he entered service as a Private in May of 1861 at Courtland, Alabama, serving in Company D of the First Louisiana Cavalry. He continued with this unit until he was captured August 2, 1863. He remained in prison until February 25, 1865.[248] Harris married Mary N. Alexander from Georgia on December 9, 1868. By age twenty-seven, Harris ran the Triana retail dry goods and general merchandise store that his father had owned twenty years before. His father, Edmund, lived in the house with Harris and his family until his death in 1877. It is worth noting that someone other that Edmund must have answered the census questions, because they did not know Edmund was from Virginia.[249] By 1880, Harris and Mary had the following children: Matthew was eight years old; their daughter, Analon, was five years old; Mary Bell was four months old, and a nephew, Manly Boykin,

---

[246] *A Dream Come True Vol. II*, James Record, 1978, John Hicklin Printing Co. Huntsville, Alabama, Library of Congress Card Number:76-11880.
[247] *The Historic Huntsville Quarterly of Local Architecture and Preservation.* Summer 1997, *The History of Triana*, Page 119-121.
[248] *1907 Confederate Census, Limestone, Morgan & Madison Counties Alabama*, Johnson Historical Publications, Page 39.
[249] 1870 United States Federal Census, Madison County, Alabama, Township 5 Range 2W.

was nine years old and attended school.[250] In the center of the town of Triana is the Old Triana Cemetery. Harris Toney was buried there within a small plot surrounded by a rock wall. Two sons of Harris and Mary were also buried there as children: Harris Toney Jr., died at five months old, and Robert G., died at two weeks old.[251]

Toney, Hugh L.; Citizens Meeting.
Hugh L. Toney was born September 15, 1837. He married Sarah E. Biggers in Madison County, Alabama, February 12, 1865. The marriage ceremony was performed by J. J. Power, Minister of the Gospel.[252] Hugh lived in the Madison Cross Roads area by 1880.[253] Hugh and Sarah had a daughter, J. E., born in 1869. Hugh's brother, Elleck, lived in the home with them during the year 1880. Tombstone information reveals that Hugh died January 9, 1908.[254]

Turner, Daniel H.; Citizens Meeting.
Daniel Harris Turner was born on January 12, 1842 in Huntsville, Alabama. He was the son of Reverend Henry P. Turner and Lucy T. Powell. The family lived in the Madison Cross Roads area. In 1860, children at home were: Daniel, and brothers John, a fifteen-year-old student; John S. a thirteen year old student; and sister, Ann, who was nineteen years old..[255] Both Daniel and his younger brother Henry P., served in the Confederate Army. He entered service in the Confederate Army as a Private April 1861. He joined Co. Q of the Fourth Alabama Infantry and continued with this group until July 2, 1863. At this time, he was wounded at Gettysburg in the right arm. He was paroled at Greensboro, North Carolina, April 9, 1865, as Captain of that Company.[256] By 1870, Daniel had married Jennie who was twenty-three years old. They lived next to his parents.[257] Daniel and Jennie had three children during the next decade. Daniel's mother, Lucy, fifty-seven years old, lived with them.[258] Daniel Harris

---

[250] 1880 United States Federal Census, Madison County, Alabama.
[251] *Cemeteries of Madison County, Alabama*, Vol. 1, Dorothy Scott Johnson, page 300-302.
[252] Madison County, Alabama Marriage Records, Book No. 4 Page 193.
[253] 1880 United States Federal Census, Madison County Alabama, Page 42 Township 2 Range 2 West.
[254] *Cemeteries of Madison County*, Vol. I, Dorothy Scott Johnson, Page 28.
[255] 1860 United States Federal Census, Madison County, Alabama, Page 43.
[256] *1907 Confederate Census, Limestone, Morgan & Madison Counties Alabama*, Johnson Historical Publications, Page 39.
[257] 1870 United States Federal Census, Madison County, Alabama.
[258] 1880 United States Federal Census, Madison County, Alabama, Page 47B.

Turner died July 21, 1921. He was buried in Maple Hill Cemetery. His tombstone reads "Captain, Fourth Alabama Infantry C. S. A." Military Iron Cross, #221 was placed on his grave. His wife, Jennie H., died October 8, 1885. Her tombstone reads, "Asleep in Jesus, blessed sleep from which none ever wake to weep."[259]

Watkins, Isham; Citizens Meeting.
Isham Watkins was born in 1839, in Alabama. By 1870, he was married to America, who was born in 1845. They had four children: Cordelia, eight years old; James, five years old; three-year-old William; and ten-month-old, Sarah. The Confederate Veterans listed Isham as serving with Company K of the Fourth Alabama Infantry, as a Private. There is no record of America's death. He married Mrs. Jane Yeatman on April 20, 1875. The Maple Hill Cemetery Sexton's Records show that Isham died at sixty-nine years of age, but no further information has been found regarding his death.[260]

White, Elizabeth; Wife of Mike White.
Elizabeth White was born in Illinois around 1854. She was described as a beautiful and worthy woman. In 1880, she lived with her mother, Emma Huffman, and an Annie Huffman, presumed to be her sister.[261] According to court records, the life insurance company that insured Mike White was in litigation with Worley White and Elizabeth regarding the details of Mike White's death. Elizabeth eventually collected $7,500 from the policy.

White, Michael; Lynched.
Mike White was born in Rochester, New York. He came to Huntsville in 1860.[262] The newspaper reported that even though there was no room to doubt his guilt, he was a good Confederate Soldier, and was well thought of for many years after the war. He enlisted on September 5, 1862, in Captain Gaston's Company during a campaign for recruitment at the Big Spring in Huntsville. He was with Company F, of Russell's Fourth Alabama Cavalry. After his enlistment, he worked as the regimental butcher. Notes show that his horse was valued at $190 and the saddle at $30. Mike was captured

---

[259] *Maple Hill Cemetery, Phase One*, Robey, Johnson, Jones, & Roberts, 1995, page 104.
[260] *Maple Hill Cemetery, Phase One*, Robey, Johnson, Jones, & Roberts, 1995, page 40.
[261] 1880 United States Federal Census, Madison County, Alabama, Page 375.
[262] Interview of Mike White by the newspaper, *The Independent* (April 18, 1878).

many times during his service. Once, he was captured at Parker's Cross Roads on December 31, 1862, and taken to Camp Direction at Chattanooga, Tennessee. He was captured again at the Battle of Atlanta, July 21, 1864. White remained at Camp Chase until he swore his Oath of Allegiance to the United States, on May 19, 1865. After a diligent search a photograph of Mike White could not be found. However, a description was given of White during his Oath of Allegiance that described him as being 5' 8" tall, with blue eyes, fair skin and light hair.[263] In 1870, White was thirty-one years old, and worked as a butcher. He estimated net worth was $10,000 on the Census of 1870.[264] Between 1870 and 1878, he married Elizabeth Huffman, who was born in Illinois.

Whitman, William Felo; Citizens Meeting.
William Felo Whitman came to Alabama. In 1850, he was forty-one years old. His wife, Ann B. Whitman, was born May 11, 1811. In 1850, the couple had eleven children. Children at home were: Thomas, sixteen years old; Rebecca fourteen years old; Robert, twelve years old; James, ten years old, Mary, eight years old; Texanna, six years old; and Albert, four years old.[265] Daughter, Mary, died February 26, 1850. On March 2, 1859, William married Deidamia Spain, who had been born in North Carolina.[266] There is no information as to when his first wife, Ann, died. Pricilla Whitman forty-eight years old, and Alvadora, twenty-seven years old, lived with the Whitman's.[267] Twenty-seven people lived in the W. F. Whitman residence. Son, W. R. [Robert] Whitman, his wife and five children, lived in the home.[268] William Felo Whitman was buried in the Whitman Cemetery, in the NE corner, of Township 2 Range 2 East, Section 5 of the County. The tombstone reads, *"Born in Halifax County Virginia March 27, 1809, died at New Market, Alabama March 10, 1888. He was a earnest Christian, a kind and devoted husband and father and no appeal to his charity was ever in vain, he loved his neighbor as himself."* Dorothy Jones Whitman, W. F. Whitman's wife, was born 1815, died January 31, 1890.

---

[263] Military Service Records for the Confederate Company F of the Fourth Alabama Cavalry, microfilm copy.
[264] 1870 United States Federal Census, Madison County, Alabama,
[265] 1850 United States Federal Census, Madison County, Alabama
[266] Madison County, Alabama Marriage Records, Book No. 1 Page 140.
[267] 1870 United States Federal Census, Madison County, Alabama, Range 2T. 2E.
[268] 1880 United States Federal Census, Madison County, Alabama, Page 195.

Chapter Two
Wesley Brown
1883

The Huntsville Weekly Democrat.

VOLUME XVIII NUMBER ...

HUNTSVILLE, ALA., WEDNESDAY, OCTOBER 10, 1883

... CLAY, Editor and Proprietor.

The People Must be Heard, and Their Rights Vindicated.

POLICEMAN MURDERED
Negro Hung by a Mob.

On Monday last our community was startled by the news that Wm. J. Street, one of the most fearless and faithful policemen Huntsville ever had, had been murdered. It is difficult to get the exact facts. As near as we can get them, they are as follows: Two negro men (whose names we have been unable to learn), said to be from Birmingham, were guilty of some violation of law in a negro house of bad repute in the suburbs of Huntsville, known as Pin Hook. Complaint was made and Policeman Street went to arrest the offenders. He went in the front door and arrested one of them, and had him outside of the front door, when the other negro, who had gone out of the back door, came around to the front, and struck Street on the back of his head with the edge of an axe, laying open his skull with an awful gash. One of the negroes seized Street's pistol, and both negroes ran down the railroad towards Decatur. Street died in about half an hour. So soon as the murder became known, 20 or 30 armed men went in pursuit of the negroes, and came up with them about five miles from town. We understand that Alderman Stegall and Policeman Hutchens were the first to get up with them, that they arrested one, who had Street's pistol, and the other escaped into a brier thicket, next to a mountain on County Treasurer Wynn's farm. He was hunted Monday evening, and Sheriff Cooper with a posse hunted for him nearly all day Tuesday, without getting any knowledge of his whereabouts. The captured negro was brought to town by J. R. Stegall and Geo. B. Gill, who protected him from threatened violence, and lodged him in the county jail, Monday afternoon. Monday night some men assembled at the jail to administer lynch law, but refrained from doing so, on account of protests of law-abiding citizens. Last night between 10 and 11 o'clock, information reached Hon. Wm. Rich...

1883

From the years 1878-1883, many interesting historical events happened in the World, the United States, the State of Alabama and locally in Madison County, Alabama.[269]

World

President Garfield was assassinated.... Rodin exhibited his sculpture, *"The Thinker"*.... The game of Bingo was imported from Italy...Robert Louis Stevenson authored *"Treasure Island"*... First run of the Paris to Istanbul Orient Express... In Britain, women now had the right to own property... First volume of the Oxford English Dictionary was authored ... Frederic Auguste Bartholdi, French sculptor, designed the "Statue of Liberty"... French physiologist Etienne-Jules Marey, made the first motion picture...The United States Supreme Court declared the Civil Rights Act of 1875 unconstitutional, saying that the Federal government protected political, not social rights.

United States

James A. Garfield was elected President, but was assassinated a year later. Chester A. Arthur took office as the twenty-first President... The gunfight at the OK-Corral in Arizona made the Earp family famous... First Labor Day was celebrated in New York...Four "time zones" were proposed by developer William Frederick Allen. It would standardize time.... Maxim invented the machine gun... Women lawyers were permitted to argue cases before the Supreme Court... The first color photographs were invented...Clara Barton founded the Red Cross... United States Census showed that the population was at the fifty million mark... Mark Twain authored, *"Life on the Mississippi"*... Jessie James was killed... Edison pioneered the radio tube... The *Ladies Home Journal* began publication... Buffalo Bill's Wild West Show opened in Nebraska...Arlington National Cemetery was created... The first lighted Christmas tree was displayed.

---

[269] Information was gathered from local and state history books and local newspapers. Information was also obtained from, *A Dream Come True Vol. II*, James Record, 1978, John Hicklin Printing Co. Huntsville, Alabama, Library of Congress Card Number:76-11880.

State

Dr. Peter Bryce was superintendent of the insane hospital, later named *The Bryce Hospital*... Attorney Asbury O'Neal replaced Governor Rufus W. Cobb... The State Agriculture Department was formed.... Edward C. Betts of Madison County was the first Commissioner of the State Department of Agriculture... The Federal Census showed 1,262,505 people in the State of Alabama.... The first blast furnace started operation in Birmingham... The State Board of Health was created... Birmingham became the largest city in the State... "Honest Ike" (Isaah H.) Vinson, State Treasurer stole $250,000... The movement to erect the Confederate monument beside the State Capital was inaugurated... The *Birmingham News* was founded...Helen Keller was born in Tuscumbia... The Board of Dental Examiners was created.

Local

Maysville was incorporated... The Plevna Post Office was established... The Huntsville Electric Company was organized... A circus elephant died and was buried in the 500 block of Clinton Street.... J. W. Skinner's Carriage Factory opened across the street from the jail... The Huntsville Police Department had eight patrolmen...Huntsville hired its first black policemen: Joe Scales and Robert Brandon... The son of Nicholas Davis, (the Jr.) stabbed Howard Pleasants in the right breast, near the collar bone with a pocket knife, both boys were about seventeen years old. Davis was tried before Mayor Mastin and fined $50 and court cost... The first telephones were installed... Over 40 people subscribed to the rapidly growing telephone company... Sallie Leddy was the first "Hello Girl" and Robert Hay (see Chapter 6) was the first night operator... There were 36 Saloons in the county, eleven of them in Huntsville... The Huntsville Fair and Races commenced on October 9, 1883 and continued for five days... Judge William Richardson received warrants from the State Treasurer to pay off claims of disabled Confederate soldiers... Marbles were the new past time...Michael O'Shaughnessy opened a cottonseed factory on Jefferson Street, employing 80 people and delighting everyone with the sweet aroma it produced... The first public school was constructed on East Clinton Street.... There were 375 marriages and 22 divorce proceedings this year... The Dement building was under construction as was E. Campbell's two story brick building on Commercial Row.

Chapter Two
Wesley Brown-1883

Between two and three o'clock on Monday afternoon, October 8, 1883, two Negro men, Wesley Brown and Charlie Adams were enjoying themselves, at a house of bad repute owned by Ada Gaston. She was a Negro woman who came from Birmingham but now lived in a house across the common, north from the fair grounds. This area, known as Pin Hook, was located near the railroad.[270]

Brown and Adams were also from the Birmingham area and may have known Ada before she moved to Huntsville. The men began to assault her. They cut her and slashed her clothes, inflicting a few slight flesh wounds on her person. Things were getting out of hand. Ada was afraid of being killed, so she sent a hasty word into the city for the police.

When the messenger arrived at the police department with the complaint, William J. Street was present to answer the call. Officer Street mounted one of the horses kept at the station for this purpose, and rushed to the scene.

Upon arriving at Ada Gaston's home, Officer Street observed her injuries and felt they were sufficient enough to arrest the two men.[271] Using caution, he drew his pistol and headed for the front door. Street entered the house, arrested one man, and brought him out onto the front porch. The other man went out the back door. One of the women of the house, Euneline, supplied this man with an axe. He came around to the front where he knew the policeman was detaining his friend. He came up behind Officer Street and struck him with the sharp edge of the axe. The deadly blow landed above and behind Street's right ear and laid open his skull with an awful gash. Officer Street lay where he fell.[272] The blow also knocked Street's pistol to the ground as he fell. One of the Negroes

---

[270] It should be noted that the facts of this story were taken, for the most part, from the following Huntsville newspapers; *The Huntsville Weekly Democrat* (October 10, 1883), *The Weekly Mercury* (October 10, 1883), *The Huntsville Gazette* (October 10, 1883), *The Huntsville Gazette* (October 13, 1883), *The Independent* (October 18, 1883), *The Weekly Mercury* (October 17, 1883), *The Huntsville Gazette* (October 27, 1883), *The Democrat* (October 31, 1883), *The Independent* (November 1, 1883) *The Mercury* (May 25, 1887), *The Huntsville Times* (April 29, 1997), *The Weekly Mercury*, Lanier's fathers obituary, (September 1895).
[271] *The Huntsville Weekly Democrat* (October 10, 1883).
[272] The *Huntsville Gazette* (October 13, 1883).

reached down and picked it up as he fled the scene. Some witnesses said William Street lived thirty minutes, while others said he died instantly.

A hasty word was again sent into the city. The bearer of this information carried a much more serious message than the last dispatch. Officer William J. Street, one of Huntsville's most fearless and faithful policemen, had been murdered. The newspapers were quick to note that Street's murder was the first of an on duty policeman in Huntsville.[273]

The news of Officer Street's murder caused immediate action. Sheriff John W. Cooper and a posse of twenty or thirty armed men set out, as fast as they could, for Ada Gaston's home.

Upon their arrival, they received conflicting reports about the killing and the whereabouts of the two men. Some witnesses stated that the suspects had hidden in one of the many houses near by; others said that they ran down the railroad tracks toward Decatur.

All neighboring houses were closely inspected and then the search moved to the west of town. When the suspects were not found, the officers began to search the entire system of railroad tracks in the county. The posse continued to hunt for the criminals all Monday afternoon and early evening.

About dark, Alderman J. R. Stegall and Chief of Night Police, William T. Hutchens, came upon the criminals about five miles west of town. There was a confrontation. Stegall and Hutchens were able to capture Wesley Brown. The other man, Adams, escaped under the cover of darkness into the nearby woods. He was last seen going into a brier thicket next to a mountain on County Treasurer A. M. Wynn's farm.

While Chief Hutchens continued the search for Adams, Alderman Stegall and George B. Gill brought Brown to town. As members of the posse and officers of the law, they protected him from threatened violence. They lodged him in the county jail on Monday afternoon. Euneline, the Negro woman who supplied the killer with the axe, was also arrested and taken to jail for her part in the murder.[274]

The captured criminal provided the law with information about the other killer. Brown described Adams as a light colored brown, five feet eleven inches tall, with two or three of his upper teeth missing. He had on a pair of greasy brown pants and a black short tailcoat with side pockets.

---

[273] There are few crimes that pull a community together more than that of the killing of an on-duty policeman. Even in today's callused world, few people fail to show remorse and horror when told of such an action. Thus it was when Officer William J. Street was brutally murdered.

[274] No other information was found regarding Euneline.

He was wearing a red striped shirt, a blue navy vest and a narrow brim slouch hat with a piece out of the side. It was also reported that he had been wounded in the left shoulder about two weeks earlier. It was reported that Adams resided at Calera, which is south of Huntsville about 130 miles. It was believed that Adams was well armed.

When Brown was captured, he was carrying Officer Street's pistol. The recovery of the pistol placed Brown at the crime scene. There was no doubt that Brown was one of the suspects, but having the pistol did not identify him as the man who struck the blow with the axe.

Monday night, between ten and eleven o'clock, a group of men scaled the fence and surrounded the jail. The intent was to administer *Lynch Law* and hang Wesley Brown. The crowd refrained from completing their dreadful purpose because of the protest of law-abiding citizens.

Huntsville-Madison County Public Library

Huntsville Railroad Depot

Tuesday morning arrived bright and clear. Early morning found Sheriff Cooper and his men still searching for Adams. They searched all of that day but found no trace of him. Ex-policeman Smith[275] filled the vacancy left by Streets death.[276]

Tuesday afternoon, Policeman William J. Street was laid to rest. Services were held in the Presbyterian Church with the Reverend John H. Bryson performing the ceremony. Some of his remarks were:

"Mr. William Street was one of the bravest and most undaunted of officers, a useful and highly respected citizen commanding the friendship and esteem of all. His untimely end is universally and deeply regretted."[277]

Huntsville-Madison County Public Library

Presbyterian Church

---

[275] No first name was given.
[276] *The Huntsville Gazette* (October 13, 1883).
[277] *Ibid.*

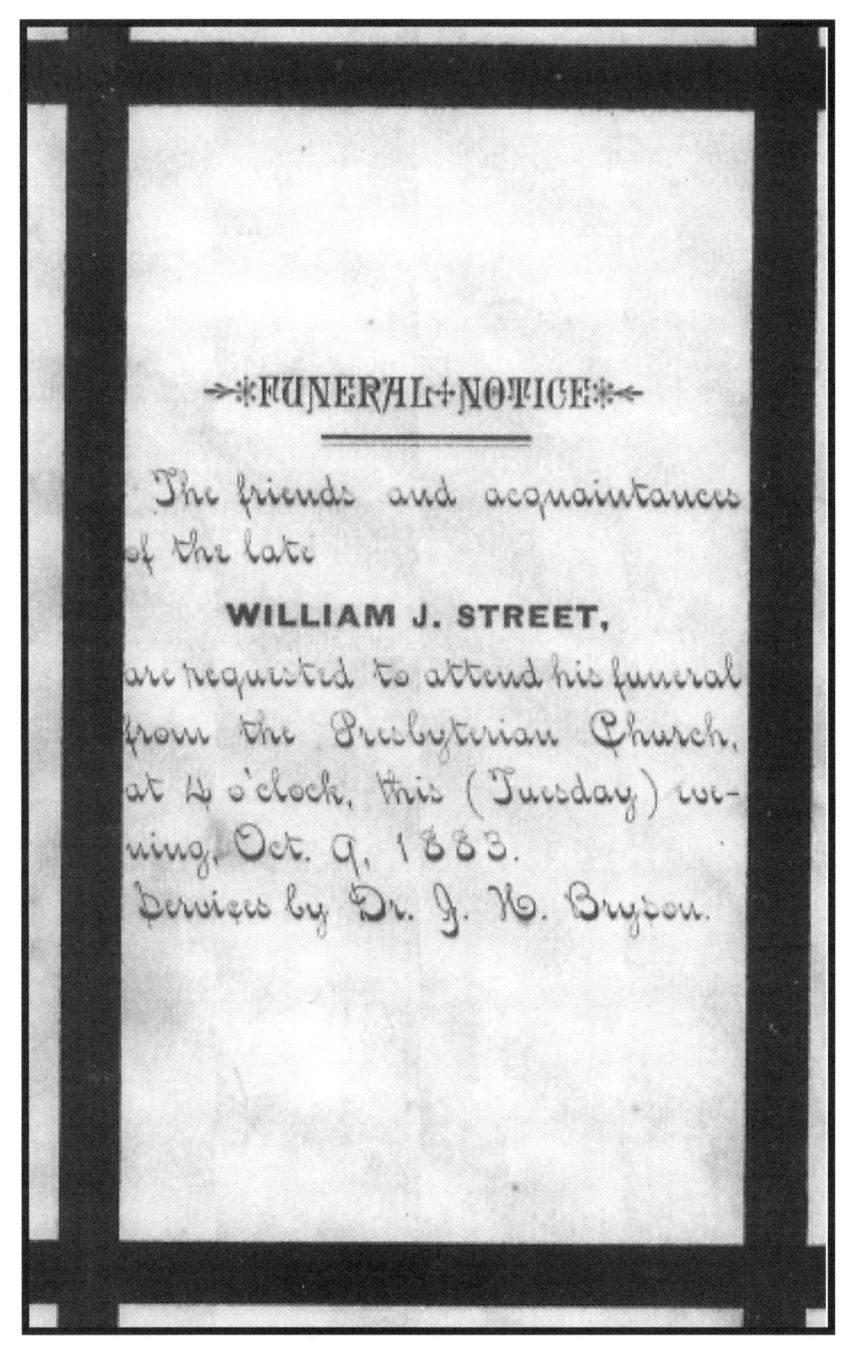

> **FUNERAL NOTICE**
>
> The friends and acquaintances of the late
>
> **WILLIAM J. STREET,**
>
> are requested to attend his funeral from the Presbyterian Church, at 4 o'clock, this (Tuesday) evening, Oct. 9, 1883.
>
> Services by Dr. J. H. Bryson.

This beautifully hand crafted announcement was distributed prior to the service for the slain officer.[278]

---

[278] A long time friend of the author, Huntsville Police Investigator Harold Hitchison, shares the original funeral notice with the readers, because of his interest in the case.

One friend of Officer Street was Detective Burwell Clinton Lanier, a fellow officer on the Huntsville Police force. Lanier, 29, was married to Mattie (Ashford) and the couple had one son, Alexander, at the time of Street's murder.

Lanier attended the funeral service at the Presbyterian Church and then went to the Huntsville jail to see Wesley Brown. Lanier believed Adams was the one who had dealt the final blow, and he knew it was his responsibility to prove it.

Clint Lanier used Brown's biggest fear, that of being lynched, to persuade Brown to help him catch Charlie Adams. In this manner he persuaded Brown to tell him what direction Adams had gone. Brown told Lanier that they had intended to go to Decatur, where Adams knew of a boat above the upper ferry. They were going to either cross the river in that boat, or walk over the Railroad Bridge.[279]

On Tuesday afternoon, Detective Lanier went to Decatur on a freight train. He then crossed back over the railroad bridge to the Huntsville side of the river and found the boat Brown had described. Since the boat was still there, Lanier thought it was unlikely that Adams had already crossed the river. He assigned an officer to watch the boat and the surrounding countryside in case Adams was still heading for the boat.

Lanier began to question the people who lived in the neighborhood around the boat. He then went to the railroad bridge where he and other officers stayed

Ferry docked at Decatur—Late 1800's

---

[279] *The Independent* (October 18, 1883).

94

until late that night. The detective decided that a watch should be kept at the bridge until daylight, Wednesday morning. Placing a guard there for the rest of the night, Lanier went into Decatur for a good night's sleep.

The lawless element continued with their plan to take Brown from the jail and lynch him. Their well-conceived plan involved removing all of the guards from the jail. A false rumor that a lynching mob was coming into town by way of Meridianville Pike was sent to the authorities.

In Huntsville that night, news reached the Honorable William Richardson, Judge of the County and Probate Courts,[280] that there was trouble brewing. Between ten and eleven o'clock, he heard the rumor that a party of men were coming into town, by way of Meridianville Pike, to take Wesley Brown out of jail and lynch him. Perhaps remembering the three hundred fifty horsemen that had ridden down Meridianville Pike in 1878, and lynched three men that were being held in the jail, the Judge became determined to see that history did not repeat itself.

Judge Richardson sent for Mayor Mastin in order to get the policemen together and send them to stop the mob. All the guards from the jail, along with the other police officers, left for Meridianville Pike. Of course, when they arrived, the Pike was empty and deserted. There were no men on the road. They were in town at the jail.

In the meantime, Judge Richardson hurried to the jail to warn the lone jailer of the impending danger. He rushed past several citizens on their way home from the Opera House, located on the corner of Jefferson Street and Clinton Avenue, where Miss Lizzie Evans had just performed in a play entitled, *A Farmer's Daughter*. At the play's conclusion, people were milling out onto the street, some no doubt heading across the street to McGee's Hotel Bar for a nightcap and to discuss the performance. Things seemed very normal. As the Judge approached the jail, a Negro told him some men were in the jail yard.

When Judge Richardson arrived at the jailyard fence, he knocked on the outer gate. Someone inside asked, *"Who is there?"*
The Judge replied, *"That is none of your business, let me in!"*
The voice for the other side cried; *"Is it you, Judge Richardson?"*
The Judge replied, *"It is."*
The voice continued; *"Well you can't come in. If you do, we'll have to hurt you."* At this point, the judge left saying; *"I'll try to see if I can't get some means to get in!"*[281]

---

[280] This was the Court of County Commissioners (Commissioners Court). This is now the position of the Chairman of the Madison County Commission.
[281] *The Huntsville Weekly Democrat* (October 10, 1883).

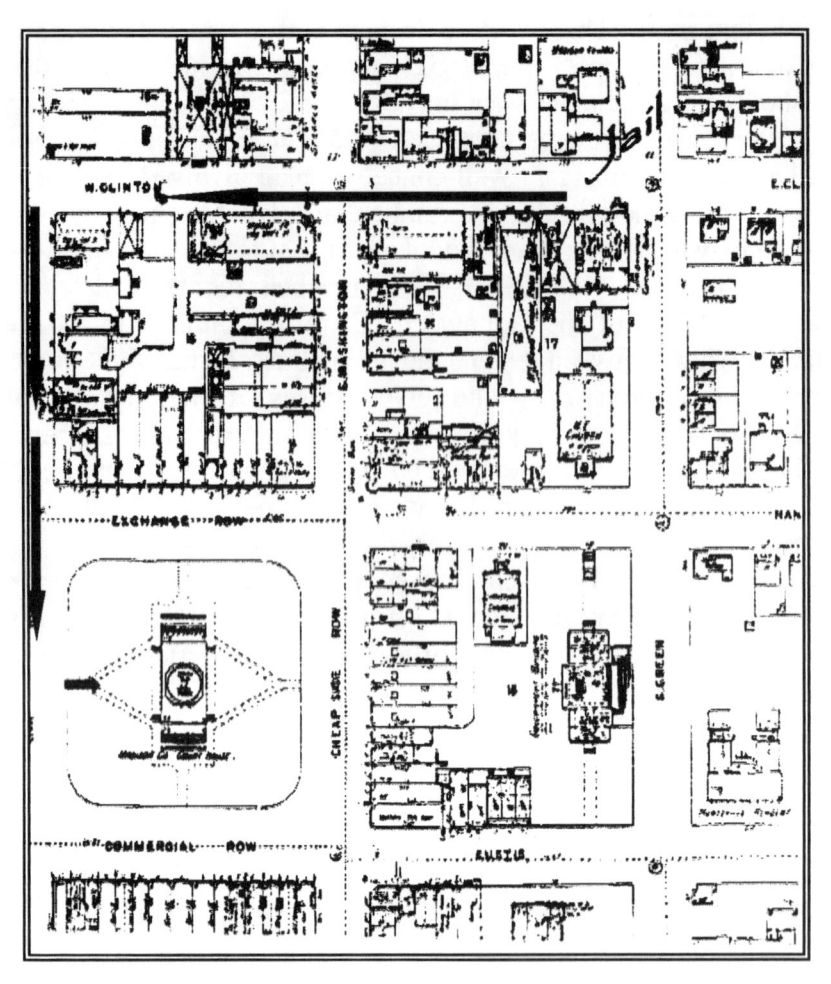

Drawing showing the route taken from the jail to the Courthouse Square to lynch Wesley Brown.

It appeared that Judge Richardson was too late. A group of men had already scaled the fence at the jail. They found the young jailer, Matt Weaver,[282] alone and asleep. About ten o'clock Matt was awakened and startled by the men. He later stated that there were perhaps sixty men inside the jail and at least a hundred in the jail yard.

The men demanded the jail keys. Weaver reported that he first refused to give them up, and the men proceeded to Brown's cell and threatened to batter down the door. To save injury to the jail, the jailer told them that the keys were on the mantelpiece.

---

[282] The 1880 United States Federal Census states that Matt's father was the jailer and the entire family lived on the jailhouse premises.

The men took the keys and opened Brown's cell. They took him and proceeded out of the jail. Seeing the Negro woman, Euneline, in the jail, threats were made to take her out and hang her along with Brown. But the men refrained from this disgraceful act and Euneline and the other prisoners remained locked in their cells.

Huntsville-Madison County Public Library
Madison County Courthouse Square-Northwest Corner

The group of men headed toward the Courthouse. They were reported to be quiet and orderly.[283] They did not call attention to themselves.

After leaving the jail, Judge Richardson set out to find the Mayor and the City Police that he had previously sent to stop the men coming down Meridianville Pike. At some point he passed a party of men coming quietly down the street. The Judge did not dream that the men had Brown and were moving him to the Courthouse yard for their own purpose.[284]

---

[283] *The Huntsville Weekly Democrat* (October 13, 1883).
[284] Or perhaps, his mind was full of the memories of the tragedy of events from five years past, and how to prevent this from happening.

It wasn't long after, to his great shock, he was told that Wesley Brown was hanging in the Courthouse yard on the west side of the Square. He would not believe it until he saw for himself.

The men had marched Brown to the very center of town and hanged him. They performed the lynching so quietly that the occupants of the stores on the public square, in which lights still burned, were not aware of what had happened. Everything was done quietly, with precision and regularity. When the Judge arrived at the Courthouse, Wesley Brown's lifeless body dangled from a limb of a walnut tree near the west gate.[285]

The City Police arrived back in town to find the prisoner taken from the jail and lynched. The plan of the lynchers had succeeded. Someone among the growing crowd insisted that the body be left hanging on the tree.

As ordered, Brown's body hung there for the remainder of the night. It was viewed by hundreds of people, white, Negro, men, women, and children. The ghastly sight horrified the passing law abiding citizens.[286] The body remained in the tree until seven o'clock the next morning when the body was taken down and buried.[287]

Local newspapers asked, *"Where were the police? How did it happen that after a previous attempt to do the same thing by a mob the night before, that the jail would be left without extra guard and in the sole custody of a single man who was unaccustomed to such duties?"*[288] [289]

The *Huntsville Weekly Democrat* stated that the police did not expect the mob to form and hang Brown, therefore they were not at the jail when the mob arrived. The police force was not prepared for an event of this magnitude.[290]

Sheriff Cooper had been in the saddle nearly two days looking for Charlie Adams and was home sleeping. Deputy Joe Cooper was at the

---

[285] At the time of 1883, there were 36 saloons in Madison County, eleven of which were in Huntsville. *"Probably many a pious soul blamed the devil of whiskey on both the Street murder and the Brown lynching."* Information was gathered from local and state history books and local newspapers. *A Dream Come True Vol. II*, James Record, 1978, John Hicklin Printing Co. Huntsville, Alabama, Library of Congress Card Number:76-11880.

[286] As reported by *The Huntsville Weekly Democrat* (October 13, 1883).

[287] It is unknown where the burial took place.

[288] Article by Charles Hendley, Jr., *"Brave and Timely Words,"* The Huntsville Gazette (October 13, 1883).

[289] *Weekly Mercury* (October 13, 1883), article by Rostan Betts entitled, *"Some Pertinent Question's."*

[290] *Huntsville Weekly Democrat* (October 13, 1883).

bedside of his very ill child, and it was reported in the local paper a couple of days afterwards that the child had died.[291]

The *Huntsville Gazette* published the following statement:[292]

"We think the weight of testimony is decidedly in favor of the prisoner Brown, as being innocent of striking the fatal blow, as far as the evidence in its crude and undeveloped state will permit a decided opinion. It is natural too, that the actively guilty party should make the more ardent effort to escape and be the criminal now at large."

Wednesday morning, after daybreak, Detective Lanier re-crossed the Decatur Railroad Bridge and found Adams' tracks.[293] While talking to people close to the bridge, a Negro woman told him that Adams had been there and asked for bread and coffee. Lanier found Adams' tracks leading from her house into the woods where he found a bed of leaves and grass where Adams had slept. He tracked Adams through a cornfield to the Railroad Bridge. Lanier then took the southbound mail train to Cullman, intending to get south of Adams and walk back on the railroad track, to meet him.[294]

At Cullman, about thirty miles south of Decatur, Lanier got off the train. By talking to all the people he met, he learned that Adams had been seen one mile north of Garden City. Lanier boarded a train heading for Warrior Station, and along with Marshall Butler, of Jefferson County, went across the Warrior River to watch the crossing until daylight that Thursday morning. After describing Adams to the bridge's watchman, Lanier returned to Warrior Station to get an area map and some sleep. About an hour and a half later he was awakened by the Section Boss and was told that Adams had passed him and was near the Warrior Bridge. Lanier hurried back to the bridge and saw two men pursuing Adams. The bridge watchman's wife told him that her husband had spoken to the suspect on the bridge and had recognized him from Lanier's description, but being unarmed had allowed him to pass.

Because there was no telegraph at Warrior, Lanier sent the bridge watchman ahead on horseback to notify the authorities at Morris, while he

---

[291] Eliza Cooper, Infant daughter of Mr. and Mrs. Joseph Cooper, died at the residence of John W. Cooper on Monday, October 15, 1883. She was about eight months old.
[292] The *Huntsville Gazette* (October 13, 1883).
[293] Postcard sent from B. C. Lanier, Jr. to the city officials notifying them of progress, (Oct. 10, 1883) Published in the *Mercury*.
[294] Printed by the *Independent* (October 18, 1883) interview by *The Age*, [a Birmingham newspaper] of Detective Clint Lanier in Birmingham, Alabama.

continued down the track on foot. As he neared Morris, he saw Adams leave the track and turn into the woods.

At Morris, Lanier tried to get a horse but was unsuccessful. He sent men out to watch the nearest roads while he continued down the track on foot. Two men, armed with shotguns, were on the east side of the railroad tracks and saw Adams. They got within fifty yards of him but failed to hit him so he escaped once more into the bushes.

Upon arriving at Cunningham Switch just below Morris, Lanier learned from Supervisor Ansley that the Section Boss, Duaney, had seen Adams and had given chase with all the section hands. A short quick fight ensued with Adams escaping. Adams lost his hat in the fight and it was taken to New Castle to keep for evidence.[295] Frank Gifford, of New Castle, along with some bloodhounds, went to the place where the murderer was last seen, but no further trace of him could be found.

Early History of Calera, Alabama[296]

Caboose at the crossing in Calera

---

[295] New Castle is about a mile or two south of the Cunningham switch or rail station. Both locations are north of Birmingham. (See map on the next page).

[296] *Early History of Calera, Alabama*, Barbara Baker Roberts, Published by Times Printing Company, Montevallo, Alabama.

Fred B. Simpson

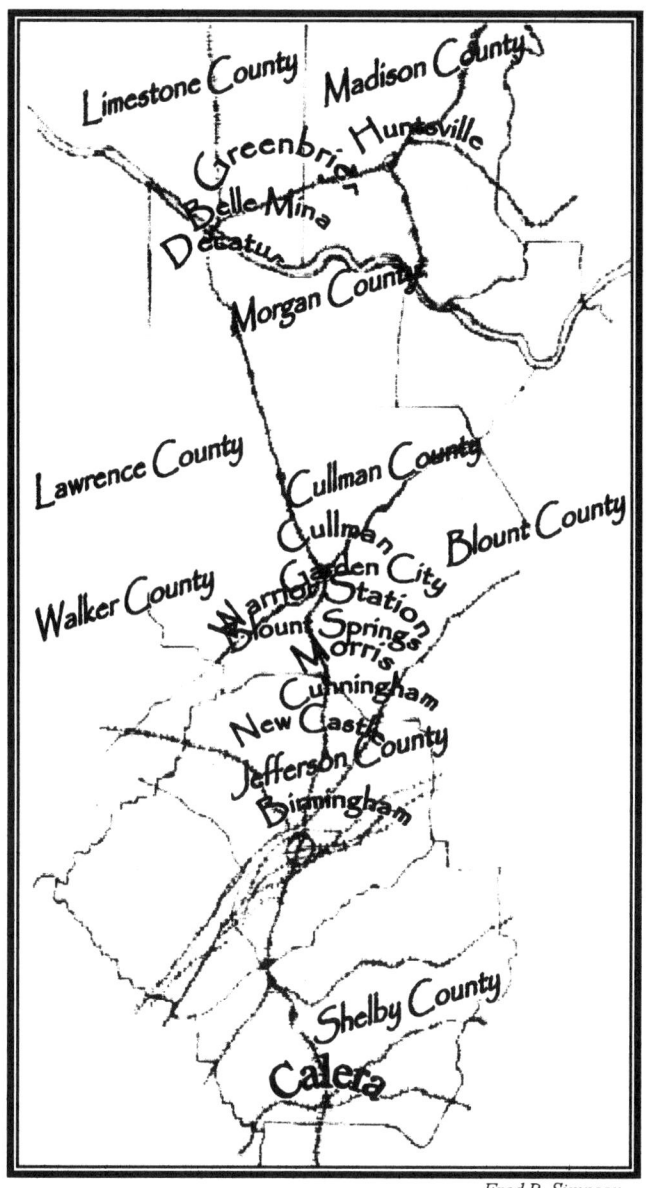

Detective Lanier rode the train on to Birmingham that Thursday night, still looking for the killer. About twelve o'clock midnight, a Negro man answering Adam's description was seen near one of the iron furnaces.[297] Captain Lewis and the Birmingham police force were notified to be on the lookout for Adams. Everyone was confident that he would be captured. Lanier had been chasing Adams since before the hanging of his

---

[297] Birmingham was a well-known iron-producing town. Furnaces were used to melt down the ore into metal.

companion, had tracked him as far as Birmingham, and now could only wait for additional information as to the killer's whereabouts.

It was reported that Adams went back to Calera and was furnished a mule by his brother for his escape.

Back in Huntsville, Mayor Mastin assembled the Board of Aldermen. In council, they voted and passed an ordinance for a $100 reward for the capture and delivery of Charley Adams to the Madison County Sheriff. Judge Richardson telegraphed Governor Edward A. O'Neal[298] to obtain an additional reward of $300 from the State.[299]

The Mercury
October 10, 1883

$400 Reward

The Governor of the State of Alabama has offered a reward of
$300, and the Mayor and Aldermen of Huntsville have
Offered $100, for the arrest and delivery to the proper officers
of the County of Madison
A colored man, who is said to be named, Charles Adams or Anderson.
Numbers of men went in pursuit of Adams, who murdered Police Officer
William J. Street On the afternoon of the 8th instant.

The local newspaper, *The Mercury,* demanded an investigation of the mob action and suggested a meeting to denounce the lynching of Brown. *"Our community can not afford to let such an act go unpunished. If private individuals are to be instruments of justice it would be eminently more fitting that they do their work before they commit their prisoner to the representative of the law."*[300]

The newspaper, *The Gazette,* asked the question, how the men could take over the county jail and remove the prisoner. After an attempt by the mob to do the same thing the night before, why was the jail

---

[298] "Governor O'Neal was originally from Madison County. He was a lawyer, financial conservative and realist." Information was also obtained from, *A Dream Come True Vol. II*, James Record, 1978, John Hicklin Printing Co. Huntsville, Alabama, Library of Congress Card Number:76-11880. page 54-55,
[299] *The Mercury* (October 10, 1883).
[300] *Ibid.*

unguarded? The *Gazette* stated that the police force[301] should explain how a noticeable crowd of men could enter the jail, remove the prisoner to the Courthouse yard, and hang him all in close view of passers-by. *"The weight of testimony is decidedly in favor of the prisoner as being innocent of striking the fatal blow. According to the Gazette, the citizens had a right to know the answers to these questions."*[302]

Response to the questions posed by the newspapers brought at least one police officer to the defense of the situation. On October 17, 1883, *The Mercury* published a letter from the Chief of Night Police W. T. Hutchens It is as follows:

> *Mr. Editors,*
> *As to your inquiries in connection with the hanging of Brown by a mob on the night of the 9th., On behalf of the Night Force, I will say there were only four of us and a town full of people with whom to contend and having been present and assisting in the capture of Brown, delivered him safely to jail in charge of the Sheriff J. R. Stegall, an Alderman of the city and I as justice to duty agreed to occupy the cell with the prisoner and defend him with my life during the night on the eighth. But the mob dispersing and nothing being done that night gave ample time for the jail to be put in condition by the proper officers as to prevent any such violence. Besides when hearing of the gathering of the mob on Meridianville Pike, on the 8th inst., In company with Mayor Edmond Mastin and Tax Collector J. C. Bradley went out to the jail, only to find the outer gate broken open, the cell empty and the mob gone. This, I think and hope will excuse the city officials from any neglect on their part in trying to stop the Lyncher's from their intentions and let the law mete out justice to the violators.*
> *Very Respectfully,*
> *W. T. Hutchens, Chief of Night Police*

Lanier continued his pursuit of Adams. He sent a telegraph to Mayor Mastin that a man fitting the description of Adams had been arrested and was at Fawnville, a small village on the R. R. & D. Railroad eleven miles below Calera. The Mayor took a friend of Adams, Sam

---

[301] The Huntsville Police Chief, in 1883, had eight employees; William Hutchens was the Night Chief, others included William J. Street, B. C. Lanier, James O'Riely, Sidney Pentecost, John Stegall, and William Blakemore. *A Dream Come True Vol. II*, James Record, 1978, John Hicklin Printing Co. Huntsville, Alabama, Library of Congress Card Number:76-11880.

[302] *The Gazette* (October 13, 1883).

Burgess,[303] along with him for identification. The person under arrest did not fit the description of Adams and the officials returned to Huntsville disappointed, but firm in their resolve to locate the policeman's killer.[304]

The community was still disturbed about the murder of their beloved policeman, William J. Street. They were anxious to have the murderer arrested and suffer the penalty for his crime.

Lanier later telegraphed Mayor Mastin from Selma, Alabama, and informed him that another Negro fitting the description of Adams had been arrested at Faunsdale, in Marengo County, Alabama. The Mayor telegraphed back asking if the Negro arrested had a wound in the right shoulder, and received an answer that he did. Mayor Mastin again took Charlie Adams's friend, Sam Burgess, with him to identify Adams.[305] The Mayor left Huntsville on the Thursday morning train on the 25th of October 1883, for Faunsdale.[306]

Arriving in Faunsdale, the Mayor hurried to see the prisoner. He found a man 5 feet 11 inches tall, weighing 136 pounds and having copper colored skin. He had two teeth out and a scar on his right shoulder. Mastin thought he had the killer at last!

He told Sam Burgess to look at the prisoner. Sam looked at the prisoner steadily two or three minutes without speaking. The Mayor asked if he could identify the prisoner. Sam replied that he was not the man. Charlie Adams had higher cheekbones.

The Mayor did not believe Sam and decided to have the law hold the man anyway. Later that day, the prisoner's wife appeared with a letter from her husband dated October 11th from Brierfield, Bibb County, saying that he would be home about October 18th, and would bring her some money. She was proven to the prisoner's wife and a credible person by local witnesses.

This did not satisfy the Mayor, and he decided that the prisoner would be brought to Huntsville for further investigation. The prisoner said he was unwilling to go to Huntsville because he felt he would be hung, but he was perfectly willing to go to the Brierfield Works, where he could prove he was working when Street was killed.

Mayor Mastin then telegraphed Robert L. McCalley, one of the owners of Brierfield Iron Works. He asked him if any Negro, with the prisoner's name, had worked there, and if so, the date he began and the date he ended his work. McCalley replied that the person described had

---

[303] Information could not be found on how Adams knew Sam Burgess.
[304] *The Huntsville Gazette* (October 27, 1883).
[305] *The Democrat* (October 31, 1883).
[306] *The Huntsville Gazette* (October 27, 1883).

worked there, continuously, from some time in September until October 18th. Street was killed October 8th. A detective from Brierfield knew Adams and said this prisoner was not the man.

This final piece of evidence finally satisfied Mayor Mastin that he indeed had the wrong man. He released the prisoner with the admonition that he was so much like the murderer he had better stay where he was well known.[307]

The Mayor got back to Huntsville on Sunday, October 31, 1883. The *Huntsville Democrat* printed a few comments learned from the developments of the trip:

The Democrat

November 1, 1883

"These facts ought to satisfy any reasonable mind of the grossing prosperity of mob law. He was a Negro, arrested as the perpetrator of a diabolical murder, justly deserving death under trial and sentencing of a legal tribunal. If found guilty. He so closely resembled the really guilty man, that it was difficult to distinguish them apart. Both were copper color, about five feet eleven inches and almost the same weight. Charlie Adams had lost three front teeth- the arrested man, two. Each had received a wound in the right shoulder. Would any excited mob have stopped to sift the evidence with the good sound judgment exercised by Mayor Mastin? No. It is probable, almost certain, that a mob would have hung the innocent Negro and had the guilt of murder on their souls. Things are not always as they seem! Therefore and for other waiting persons, we say give the accused a fair impartial, legal trial."

Detective Lanier eventually gave up the chase and returned to Huntsville. Lanier still adhered to the view that he was on the right track and thought that Adams was staying somewhere near Calera.[308] [309] [310]

Four years later, in 1887, Mayor Mastin received information from the Sheriff of Bolivar County, Mississippi, that he had captured the famous Charlie Adams. A photograph was taken of the prisoner in Mississippi and sent to Mayor Mastin. The Mayor sent it to Calera where

---

[307] *The Independent* (November 1, 1883).
[308] *The Independent* (November 1, 1883) *"Still at Large."*
[309] Calera was at one time a booming town. Known for its hotels and health resorts, people traveled from far and wide to visit Calera. *Early History of Calera, Alabama.* Barbara Baker Roberts, Times Printing Company, Montevallo, Alabama.
[310] *The Democrat* (October 31, 1883).

it was identified as being Adams.[311] The *Weekly Mercury* published a notice that:

"Charlie Adams, colored, the murderer of William Street, (was) in the clutches of the law. Mayor Mastin informed a reporter of the Mercury last night that he had received information from the Sheriff of Bolivar County, Mississippi, which indicates almost conclusively, that he had captured the famous Charlie Adams, colored, the murderer of policeman William J. Street, in October of '83. Adams was reared in Calera, Alabama, where he is well known. A photograph was taken of Adams in Mississippi and sent to Mayor Mastin, who sent it to Calera, and it was there identified and the fact communicated to Mayor Mastin as being the picture of Charlie Adams. The Mayor has telegraphed the Sheriff that an offer of $400 reward is offered for Adams, and if he will bring him here and he is proved to be the Charlie Adams that is wanted, he will get the money. To this the Mayor had not received a reply last night. Connecting all the circumstances together with conclusion seems established that the iron hand of the law has at last been laid on the right Charlie, and that justice is not to be robbed of its dues. Justice sometimes sleeps, but never dies."[312]

Sheriff Oscar Fulgham went to Mississippi to bring home the suspect, but the identification was wrong, and the person who had been arrested was not Charlie Adams. The Sheriff returned to Huntsville empty handed and defeated again.

The Huntsville Independent published an article stating that:

"Mr. Oscar Fulgham returned Sunday from Mississippi where he had been after the man arrested for murdering Mr. William Street, a policeman of this city, several years ago. Quite a handsome reward was offered for the capture of the murdering man, which occasioned quite a number of arrest at various times, but each time a case of mistaken identity was proved."[313]

Life went on. Both Adams and Street would be forgotten. There were other affairs of everyday life to interest the living.

Perhaps Charlie Adams stood on a hillside in later years, looking north toward Huntsville, thinking about the murder. Did he commit the alleged killing and escape his just punishment, or was he innocent of any actual killing and mercifully saved from an untimely death? We will never know.

---

[311] *The Weekly Mercury* (May 26, 1887).
[312] *Ibid.*
[313] *The Independent* (June 23, 1887).

Epilogue

Charlie Adams was never found or convicted for the murder of William Street. On several occasions, men would be arrested but later released when they supplied alibis or identification proving that they were not Adams. The $400 reward was never collected. Charlie Adams was never heard from again.

Ada Gaston was listed in the 1911 Huntsville City Directory as a cook in a home on Oak Avenue. No further information could be found regarding her.

Burwell Clinton Lanier returned to his family and the police force. At some point, he and his family moved to Decatur. He died of Yellow Fever on October 23, 1888 in Decatur. A grave for him has not been found.

Judge William Richardson remained the Madison County Probate Judge until 1886. In 1890, he ran for Governor as a Democratic. He carried all counties north of Birmingham, but withdrew his name in order to stop the dissension in the Democratic Party. In 1900, Judge Richardson was appointed to represent the people of the Eighth Congressional District after General Wheeler resigned. Judge Richardson died on May 31, 1914 and was buried in Maple Hill Cemetery. <See full biography in Chapter One>

William J. Street's funeral was one of the largest attended funerals in Huntsville history. However, a marker was never erected at his grave in Maple Hill. Over one hundred years after his death, William J. Street was finally memorialized for his act of bravery. For being the first Huntsville Police Officer killed in the line of duty, his name was selected to be included on the National Law Enforcement Memorial Wall in Washington D. C., on April 29, 1997.

On April 29, 1997, the following article appeared in the *Huntsville Times*:

"*William J. Street was axed in the back of the head on October 8, 1883, while trying to apprehend two rowdy men from Birmingham. He was the first Huntsville Police officer killed in the line of duty, and his name has been selected to be carved into the National Law Enforcement Memorial Wall in Washington D. C., which honors police officers who died in the line of duty.*"[314]

---

[314] *The Huntsville Times* (April 29, 1997), Section A-1.

Officer William J. Street's name is also inscribed on a monument on the Madison County Courthouse lawn, dedicated to those brave men who have given their lives in the line of duty protecting the citizens of Huntsville-Madison County, Alabama.

Fred B. Simpson

WILLIAM J. STREET
HUNTSVILLE
POLICE DEPT.
1883

Biographies–Chapter Two

The following short biographies are of the people involved in the preceding story. Every effort was made to find information on individuals no matter how small or large a part they played in the story. [315]

Adams, Charlie; Accused Murderer.
Charlie Adams escaped the law of Madison County. The $400 reward remained unclaimed. No further information was found.

Baldridge, Felix Edward; Doctor.
Felix Baldridge was born in December 1866, in Madison County Alabama, the son of Dr. Milton C. and N. C. Baldridge. Felix attended public school in Huntsville then received his Doctor of Medicine degree from Tulane University in New Orleans in 1894. Because of his outstanding medical skills, Dr. Baldridge received many scholarships from some of the greatest colleges. He married Alice Boarman from New Orleans, in 1895, and they had two children, Mrs. Vira B. Davis, who resided on St. Simons Island Georgia, and Milton Baldridge. Mrs. Baldridge kept her husband's books. Many times, with her husband's approval, they took produce and livestock in payment for a bill. Dr. Baldridge was the assistant company surgeon for the Nashville, Chattanooga and St. Louis Railway Company. He was one of the most trusted and respected men in the community. Dr. and Mrs. Baldridge lived in a white bungalow at 703 Adams Ave. in front of the famous "Old Oak Tree." Dr. Baldridge practiced medicine until a week before his death June 16, 1917.[316]

Brickell, Robert C.; Attorney.
Robert C. Brickell, Sr., was born in South Carolina in April of 1824. His wife of twenty-three years, Mary J., was born in Alabama. Robert was an attorney. Their son, Robert C., Jr., was born in September of 1877. Robert Jr. also became a lawyer. Robert Sr.'s sister, Eliza M., born December 1829, lived in the home in 1900. An eighteen-year-old servant, Mattie

---

[315] A search was conducted using the Huntsville City Directories; 1900-1910 United States Federal Census; *Madison County Cemeteries*, Vol. 1 & 2; *Maple Hill Cemetery, Phase One;* and private manuscripts regarding the cemetery; Dorothy Scott Johnson; *Merrimack Cemetery*, Ann Maulsby; Confederate *Veterans Census*, Dorothy Scott Johnson; various military records; Madison County Probate and Civil Court Records.
[316] *Medicine Bags and Bumpy Roads*, Goldsmith & Fulton, 1985, Valley Publications, Huntsville, Alabama.

Bailey, who was black, lived in the home.[317] A son, Benjamin Fitzpatrick Brickell, was born March 18, 1883, and died May 4, 1886. He was buried in Maple Hill, in Section 12. Robert Brickell died in 1935.[318]

Bryson, John H.; Minister.
Reverend John H Bryson was a Presbyterian minister and a native of Tennessee. He was born about 1832,[319] and was a Chaplain for the C.S.A. Army of Tennessee.[320] He came to Huntsville in January of 1880 as minister of the First Presbyterian Church located at 213 Gates Street.[321] Upon arriving at the church, he noted the church's high debt and stated he would not be Pastor in a church of that condition. The church pulled together and within six months had erased the debt. He was installed as Pastor with due ceremony in October 1882. During his service there, he revived a failing church by re-establishing its women's organizations, missionary and benevolent groups. Dr. Bryson was unmarried. The women of the church made sure that his home was clean and that there was food in the pantry. Since money was scarce, Dr. Bryson canceled his claim to unpaid portions of his salary. On April 5, 1896, Dr. Bryson asked for relief from some of his duties and thus semi-retired from the ministry. Reverend Bryson died February 1, 1897 in Shelbyville, Tennessee.[322] He was buried in Maple Hill Cemetery with Confederate marker #145. A house of worship was erected in Merrimack Village January 3, 1901, and named, *Bryson Chapel,* in his honor.[323]

Cooper, Joseph W; Deputy Sheriff.
Joseph W. Cooper was born in 1849, the son of John W. Cooper. The Huntsville City Directories for 1911 and 1916 listed Joseph as employed in the fire insurance and bond business whose office was located in the Struve Building. His home was at Shiffman Flats. By 1916, Joe had moved his home to 203 North Lincoln Street.

---

[317] 1900 United States Federal Census, Madison County, Alabama; Vol.38, Enumeration District 100, Sheet 6, line 46.
[318] *Maple Hill Cemetery, Phase One*, Robey, Johnson, Jones, & Roberts, 1995, page 98.
[319] Maple Hill Sexton's Records.
[320] *The Valiant Survivors: the United Confederate Veterans of Madison County—A Record of Their Services 1861—1865*; 2nd Edition, page 86, Charles Wells.
[321] 1896 Huntsville, Alabama City Directory, page 24.
[322] Maple Hill Cemetery Sexton's Records.
[323] *History of the First Presbyterian Church*, Charlotte Forgey Shenk and Donald Hugh Shenk, 1968, Paragon Press.

Cooper, John W.; Sheriff.
John W. Cooper was the Sheriff from 1880-1888. He was born on July 1, 1826, in Alabama. He married Eliza H. Thomas on March 12, 1848.[324] Their home was on Wells Avenue. In 1850, John was a thirty-three-year-old merchant, his wife, Eliza, was seventeen years old, and their daughter was, Henrietta, nine-months-old. John's father, Allen Cooper, a North Carolina native, also lived in the home. During the next ten years, John added money to his bank account and children to his home. His children were: Lawrence, born 1852; Lou T., born 1854; and Joseph E., born 1859.[325] In 1870, he lived in Ward 2 of Huntsville and had continued to add children to the home: William, born 1863; Carol [male], born 1866; and Cornelia, born 1868.[326] John and Eliza lived at 313 Randolph Avenue.[327] John's Father, Allen Cooper, died on September 16, 1869, and was buried in Maple Hill Cemetery. John and Eliza are buried in the family section, Section 7, Row 2. John died February 9; 1893; Eliza died March 28, 1905.[328]

Euneline ; woman arrested for participating in killing.
A search was conducted using court records, but her case was not located. No further information was found.

Gaston, Ada; woman, at whose house Street was killed.
In 1911, Addie Gaston was a cook in a home at 310 Oak Avenue.[329] No further information was found.

Gill, George B.; Protected Brown.
A complete biography may be found in Chapter One Biographies.

Hutchens, William Thomas; Policeman.
William T. Hutchens was born December 24, 1859 in Huntsville. He married Willie Thomas Armstrong on September 30, 1886. They had seven children: William Jefferson, Mary Elizabeth, Maude Elise, Allen Vick, Morton McAllister, Willard Coxey, and Vernon Fisher Hutchens. William was well known to friends and family as Will. He became a very

---

[324] Madison County, Alabama Marriage Records, Book 1.
[325] 1860 United States Federal Census Madison County, Alabama, page 204.
[326] 1870 United States Federal Census Madison County, Alabama, page 377.
[327] 1896 Huntsville, Alabama City Directory, page 28.
[328] *Maple Hill Cemetery, Phase One*, Robey, Johnson, Jones, & Roberts, 1995, page 46.
[329] 1911 Huntsville City Directory, page 152.

successful businessman and politician. In 1879, Will was twenty years old. He was appointed by the Huntsville Town Council to be the Chief of Night Police. The 1896 Huntsville City Directory listed Hutchens as, Hon. W. T. Hutchens of the Hutchens and Murdock Company. His home was at 228 Mills Street. In 1889, he was elected to the Town Council and in 1893 he was elected to his first term as Mayor of Huntsville. He was subsequently re-elected Mayor in 1895 and 1920. Hutchens was a life-long Republican. In 1898, President William McKinley appointed him Postmaster of Huntsville. In 1900, W. T. Hutchens and Henry A. Murdock were plumbers, gas fitters and steamfitters whose store was at 210 W. Clinton Street. He was re-appointed Postmaster by President Theodore Roosevelt in 1902 and 1906, and then again by President William Taft in 1910. He attended the 1903 Republican National Convention in Chicago as a delegate from Alabama and served on the Alabama State Republican Executive Committee in 1905 and 1907. He served on the Huntsville City School Board from 1907 to 1918, and the Huntsville Library Board from 1913 to 1921. He was President of the Library Board in 1915 when the Carnegie Library building was erected on the corner of Madison Street and Gates Avenue. He and a group of his friends organized the Byrd's Spring Rod & Gun Club in 1922. The club owned 800 acres of wetlands in Southeast Huntsville where members enjoyed fishing and hunting. By 1916, he was owner of the Enterprise Real Estate Company and listed his occupation as plumber, tinnier and electrician. His business was on South Jefferson and Clinton. He and Willie lived at 314 Mill Street [this change may have been the same house with reassignment of street numbers]. William Thomas Hutchens died February 24, 1940, and was buried in Maple Hill Cemetery.

Lanier, Burwell Clinton; Detective.
Burwell Clinton Lanier III was born on June 14, 1854, in Madison County. Clint grew up in the area of Madison County on which Redstone Arsenal is now located. He descended from one of the oldest and first families of Madison County. His name, Burwell Clinton, had been passed from father to son since the 1740's. His father was Burwell Clinton Lanier Jr. and his mother was Laura Prudence America Ford, also from one of the county's first families. The men in this family were reported to be tall, erect, splendid specimens of men with impeccable genial manners. Although his family lost much of the value of their property during the War Between the States, they continued to be prosperous merchants in the Madison Area. In 1870, Clint was sixteen years old and was working in the family business as a store clerk. Dr. George Harris and his family lived

with them. With eleven people in the house, it can be assumed they lived in a large home.[330] Between 1880 and 1883, Clinton obtained a job with the Huntsville Police Department as a detective. He married Miss Mattie C. Ashford on January 18, 1881.[331] Mattie was reported to have been a very cultivated, attractive, Christian woman. They had two children: Isaac Alexander Lanier, born in 1881 and Joseph B. Lanier, born in 1884. After an extensive search, the Lanier Cemetery was located in an inaccessible area of Redstone Arsenal. A tombstone was found that read, B. C. Lanier, 1820-1895. Close study led to the conclusion that this was the father of Detective Burwell Clinton Lanier. Detective B. C. Lanier died from Yellow Fever on October 23, 1888, in Decatur.[332]

Mastin, Edmund I.; Mayor.
Edmund I. Mastin served as Mayor of Huntsville from 1883-1885, 1885-1887, 1887-1889.

McCalley, Thomas Sanford; Neighbor.
A complete biography may be found in Chapter One.

O'Neal, Edward A.; Governor of Alabama.
Governor O'Neal was once a resident of Madison County. He was a lawyer and considered a financial conserative and realist. He succeeded Rufus W. Cobb as Governor. He ended his term as Governor with a $300,000 treasury surplus, in spite of State Treasurer Isaah H. Vincent's embezzlment of State funds.

Richardson, William; Judge of Probate Court.
A compete biography may be found in Chapter One.

Stegall, J. Rufus; Alderman.
Alderman Stegall was born in Tennessee on November 13, 1836. His wife was Mary E., born May 15, 1852. Before their deaths they lived at the Stegall Hotel that he owned. Mary died on February 19, 1883. Rufus died at fifty-nine years of age, on February 12, 1896. They are buried in the Lanier family plots of section twelve of Maple Hill Cemetery.[333]

---

[330] 1870 United States Federal Census, Madison County, Alabama, page 159.
[331] Madison County, Alabama Marriage Records..
[332] History of the Lanier Family, told by Felix Robertson Lanier, and written by John Fulton Lanier.
[333] *Maple Hill Cemetery, Phase One*, Robey, Johnson, Jones, & Roberts, 1995, page 95.

Street, William J.; Policeman
William Street descended from one of Madison County's first families. He served the C. S. A. in the Fourth Alabama Cavalry, Russell's Regiment, as did many of his friends from town. William was a twenty-eight-year old farmer in 1870. Next door was his grandfather, Reubin Street, and his neighbor and friend, George Shoenberger.[334] Ten years later, in 1880, William farmed, was single and thirty-eight years old. He lived with a brother-in-law, David Clark, on Spraggins Street.[335] William was killed on October 8, 1883. His funeral services were held at the First Presbyterian Church in downtown Huntsville. *The Weekly Democrat* reported that his funeral was one of the largest attended funerals in Huntsville history. William was buried in the family section of Maple Hill Cemetery in Block 8, Lot 186.[336] No tombstone was found for Officer Street. However, his name was placed on the National Law Enforcement Officers Memorial Wall in Washington D. C., honoring police officers that have died in the line of duty. The Wall is near the National Museum Building in downtown Washington D. C.[337] A monument on the south side of the Huntsville Courthouse Square displays his name as the first Madison County Law Enforcement Officer to die in the line of duty.

Weaver, Samuel Matt; Jailer.
Samuel Matt Weaver lived with his mother, Ann, and father, James, in 1870. Matt and his father were shoemakers and the jailer. He was nineteen years old.[338] An infant buried in Maple Hill Cemetery is listed as being the daughter of S. M. and Mary Weaver.[339] No other information was found.

Wynn, A. M.; County Treasurer.
A. M. Wynn was born in Virginia, in 1823. Wynn was the Madison County Treasurer. His wife was Martha C. Wynn. Their children were: Sallie, born in 1859; Mollie, born in 1861; Mattie, born in 1863; Lillie, born in 1865; John, born in 1867; and Alec, born in 1872. The family lived in Township 1 Range 1 West of the County.[340]

---

[334] 1870 United States Federal Census, Madison County, Alabama.
[335] 1880 United States Federal Census, Madison County,[Spraggins Street].
[336] Maple Hill Cemetery Office Records.
[337] *The Huntsville Times* (April 29, 1997).
[338] 1870 United States Federal Census, Madison County, Alabama, page 13.
[339] *Maple Hill Cemetery, Phase One*, Robey, Johnson, Jones, & Roberts, 1995, page 41.
[340] United States Federal Census, Madison County, Alabama, Enumeration District 204, Page 25, Line 28.

Chapter Three
Robert Mosley

WEEKLY MERCURY.
HUNTSVILLE, ALABAMA WEDNESDAY, MARCH 26, 1890.

HUNG!

Higher than Haman.

The Fate of Robert Mosely.

THE LECHEROUS NEGRO YOUTH.

Captured Near New Hope and Brought to the Scene

Of His Attempted Crime and Quietly Hanged.

Robert Mosely, the negro boy who assaulted Miss Ellie Austin, while on her way to school last Wednesday morning, rendered extreme expiation for his crime with his life at 4:35 p. m. last Friday. He died stoically, surrounded by about 300 people.

The capturing party was composed of citizens of Meridianville and Huntsville, who after a sleepless night ran down the fugitive at early sunrise last Friday on the place of Mr. Craft, about one mile north of New Hope. Mosely was not long in discovering that the mounted squad surrounding the house were after him, as the guilty conscience needs no accuser, and so he at once made a

BREAK FOR LIBERTY

1890

From 1887-1890, many interesting historical events happened in the World, the United States, the State of Alabama and locally in Madison County, Alabama.[341]

World

1883-1890: The Berlin conference of 14 nations discussed Free Trade in Africa...The Swiss introduced Social Insurance... Free elementary education was established in England... Japan held its first General Elections... Charles Babbage outlined the first computer... Richard Burton translated *Aladdin's Magic Lamp*... Sir James Dewar invented the first Thermos® Bottle... Robert L. Stevenson authored *Dr. Jekyll and Mr. Hyde*.... Queen Victoria celebrated her 50-year reign... William II became Germany's Emperor, called The Kaiser...Sir Arthur Conan Doyle introduced *Sherlock Holmes*... Vincent Van Gogh painted his *Self Portrait*... Sir Henry Stanley explored Africa... Peter Tchaikovsky composed *Sleeping Beauty*... Hansen described a "new yeast" that would revolutionize the Brewing Industry... Oscar Wilde wrote *The Portrait of Dorian Gray*.

United States

Benjamin Harrison replaced Grover Cleveland as President... Herman Hollerith developed a Calculating Machine... The United States population was 62,000,000...Idaho, Montana, Washington and Wyoming became states... United States troops massacred 200 Sioux Indian women and children at Wounded Knee, South Dakota... Child labor was widely used; 23,000 children worked in factories in thirteen states... Mark Twain authored *The Adventures of Huckleberry Finn*... Waterman patents the fountain pen...The capstone was placed on the Washington Monument...The Brooklyn Bridge was completed... The Haymarket Square riot occurred in Chicago... The Statue of Liberty was dedicated... John Phillip Sousa wrote "Semper Fidelis"... Eastman perfects the Kodak Land Camera... The first electric trolley line was built... New York began executing prisoners by electrocution... Singer marketed electric sewing machines... The Otis Brothers installed an electric elevator... Smoking by women was condemned... The coin operated telephone was introduced.

---

[341] Information was gathered from local and state history books and local newspapers. Information was also obtained from, *A Dream Come True Vol. II*, James Record, 1978, John Hicklin Printing Co. Huntsville, Alabama, Library of Congress Card Number:76-11880.

State

Thomas Seay was elected Governor... The first labor law, limited work to an eight-hour day... Society for Prevention of Cruelty to Animals was organized in Mobile... First electric street railway began operation in Montgomery... Jefferson Davis officiated at the laying of the cornerstone for the Confederate Monument beside the Capital... Isolated booths for voting were now in use... The first ocean going steamship arrived in Mobile... On a cold December day in 1889, Jefferson Davis died... Academy for the Blind was created at Talladega... Bessemer was founded...Convicts were leased to coal mines... Hawes Riot resulted in thirteen deaths in Birmingham... The 1890 United States Census showed 1,828,697 citizens in the State... First steel was produced in North Birmingham... The rise of the Populist Party began.

Local

The new post office was located at the corners of Eustis, Randolph and Greene Streets... Huntsville had one daily, five weekly and two monthly newspapers... Inducements were offered to bring the Dallas Mills to Huntsville... Madison County's population was 38,119... Huntsville's population was 7,995... The town government offices moved from the Courthouse to the White Building on Bank Row... The Monte Sano Turnpike was opened...Construction began on the Monte Sano Hotel... Horse-drawn streetcars moved from the depot to the cemetery... Wooden buildings on the Square were forbidden... Gas lamps lit the town but electric lights were powered from the electric plant on Miller Street... The first steam laundry was opened on West Clinton Street... Street names and house numbers were adopted... The first train arrived at New Market... H. C. Blake and T. T. Terry started their businesses... A "Dummy Line Railroad" up Monte Sano Mountain was completed... Harrison Brothers moved their business to the south side of the Square... G. W. Jones began a civil engineering firm... The city was now one and a half miles square... Construction began on a new Market House and City Hall... Herbert, Charles, Henry and Robert Chase opened a nursery... T. W. Pratt announced the opening of the Pratt Cotton Mill... An ordinance passed forbidding lewd women to ride through Huntsville on horseback... Dallas Mills Factory announced its opening... A sportsman of the day offered his services to the local Huntsville baseball team for a mere $75 per month, he was turned down; he is now remembered as was one of the all-time great players, Ty Cobb... Average pay for a teacher at one of the two public schools was $21.37 per month.

Chapter Three
Robert Mosley-1890

James Alexander Austin was born in Virginia about 1826. He married Mary Elizabeth Skeen in Virginia. The couple had five children: Mary Elizabeth, Eliza Virginia, Birdie (Byrdie), Johnson and Thomas. All were born in Lebanon, Russell County, Virginia.[342] James was a brick mason in Virginia in 1850.[343] Upon returning from the War Between the States, James found his house had been destroyed by the war, and his wife, Mary, and daughter, Birdie, had died of typhoid fever.

Absorbed in his grief, James abandoned his children and came south to find employment, ending up in Huntsville. He went to work rebuilding the Huntsville Depot.

James met Mildred J. Duryee, in Huntsville and on December 25, 1871, married her.[344] They settled on a farm northeast of Huntsville, on Winchester road, just west of Moore's Mill Road.[345] A step-granddaughter[346] reported that, *"God never made a better woman than Mildred Duryee Austin."*

James Austin and Mildred had only one child, Ellie Sando Austin, born 1871, in Madison County. She was a proud addition to the Austin Family.

James second daughter, Eliza Virginia, married Algernon L. Blunt in 1878. They purchased one hundred seventy-five acres of land about eight miles northeast of Huntsville, on Winchester road, just east of Moore's Mill Road, close to the Austin home. Their farm prospered and the family grew to include six children; James, William, Birdie, Susie, Maysie and Odelle.

---

[342] By 1858, Russell County had been reduced to an area of 483 square miles or 309, 120 acres. The crest of Clinch Mountain is currently the southern border. Sandy Ridge is the northern border. Clinch River meanders down near the center of the county from Mill Creek at the Tazwell County line to St. Paul in Wise County. The county seat is Lebanon.
[343] 1850 United States Federal Census, Russell County, Virginia, 54th District, family number 1776.
[344] Madison County Marriage Record, Book 6, page 32.
[345] It should be noted that the facts of this story were taken, for the most part, from the following Huntsville newspapers; *The Daily Mercury* (March 21-26-, 1890), *The Daily Age* (March 21-26, 1890), *The Weekly Mercury* (March 26,1890), *The Democrat* (March 26, 1890), *The Huntsville Gazette* (March 29, 1890).
[346] Nellie Snead Price, daughter of Mary E., first wife of James A. Austin. Account and personal history of the family as she remembered it and had written down in a letter of June 2, 1924.

After the death of her mother, in 1886, Ellie lived with her sister, Eliza, and Algernon on their farm. She became devoted to the children and enjoyed the stable life of the Blunt family. By 1890, Ellie was a young lady of nineteen. She was slightly above medium height, not frail in stature, with fair features and a bewitching form. She displayed a disposition that charmed all that met her. She had been an attentive student, above average in her schoolwork, and it was therefore not a surprise to her family and friends when she became a school teacher.

Her first teaching position was at Paul's Chapel, located not far from the Blunt farm. Ellie could walk to the school from her home. She would return in the afternoon to help with the many duties of a large farm.

To help with the work, A. L. Blunt hired Negro field hands. One of these workers was Robert Mosley. He was about five feet seven inches in height and was of slight built weighing no more than 140 pounds. He had a black complexion and a pimpled face. He had attended school and could read and write.[347]

Wednesday morning, March 19, 1890, at nine o'clock, Ellie left her sister's home and started walking to her teaching position at Paul's Chapel. About a half mile from the house near the edge of a lonely strip of woods, Robert Mosley lay in wait for his victim and attacked her.

Mosley sprang upon Ellie, pinning her arms and began forcing her into the woods. She fought and screamed, but Mosley was a boy accustomed to hard physical work, and he easily overpowered Ellie.

About seventy-five yards from the road, in the midst of a thick growth of underbrush, she saw the horror Mosley had prepared for her. Before her was an ominous looking pit that had been carefully and recently dug. Ellie could only imagine what waited in store for her.

Mosley had taken considerable time and effort in digging the pit and gathering logs and boards. He paid great attention to the detail of the construction of the framing boards for this pit. All of these fine points were lost on Ellie. She had only one thing on her mind at the moment—staying alive.

Mosley's pit was intended to become the girl's tomb, or at least her "keeping place." The pit was about seven feet long, three feet wide, and four feet deep. One end of the pit was located at a huge oak stump. The dirt was piled high as Mosley threw it from the pit. The sides had been neatly framed out with logs. The crosspieces were dovetailed together

---

[347] There is no record of what relationship Mosley had with the Blunt family other than as an employee. However, considering events, it would be reasonable to assume that Mosley either admired Ellie Austin from a distance or that he hated her for something done to him. Judging from the plans he laid, he must have thought about her often.

with the skill of a woodcrafter. At the head of the pit, was a short section of eight inch-stove pipe inserted through the top to admit light and air into the tomb.

Mosley forced the screaming girl down into the tomb he had so carefully constructed. To prevent anyone from chancing upon anything belonging to her, he threw her school books and slate into the pit with her. With his victim below ground, he shouted to her, *"Now, damn you, stay there and I'm coming back tonight and kill you."*[348] Her prison had become her tomb!

Mosley placed a number of poplar boards over the top of the pit. He nailed them down, and then placed old roots, stumps of trees and hastily shoveled dirt and rubbish over the top. He finished the concealment by adding leaves and twigs. The tomb and the entombment were now complete. He laid his pick on top of the tomb and covered it with dirt. There was nothing above ground that could be seen by anyone traveling on the road. He was confident that Ellie would never be found.

He left Ellie entombed, apparently intending to come back at a later time and carry out his threat.

Ellie lay in her tomb. We can only imagine the horror that passed through her mind. She must have cried out for help and thought her life was lost. However, she had the presence of mind to calm herself and fight for her life.

She examined her surroundings and with great determination began to plan a way out. She set to work to escape from her gloomy dark prison.

There was no way to get out of the grave through the logs around the sides, but she could see faint daylight through the cracks between the poplar boards above her. She knew the only way to free herself would be through those boards.

She pushed at the boards, but they would not give. She then used her fingers to dig out the dirt between the boards for a short time. Realizing this was futile, she felt around the pit for a stick or board, anything that would help her. She felt along the dampness of the ground, beneath her, until her fingers found the item that would save her.

It was the school slate Mosley had tossed into the pit with her!

---

[348] *The Daily Mercury* (March 26, 1890).

She held the slate in her hands and after some thought, she broke the slate into pieces. With a surge of strength, she began to scoop away the dirt between the boards above her with the fragments of the slate.

After working for some time, she began to see more daylight and was soon able to clear an opening large enough to pass her hand and arm through. She pushed and pulled at the boards with no success. Then, to her surprise, she touched the handle of the pick that Mosley placed on top of the pit. After several attempts, she got a firm grip on the pick and pulled it into the grave with her.

Her actions caused considerable quantities of dirt and rubbish to fall upon her. As she dug, more and more light surrounded her and she could see how best to proceed. She inserted the sharp point of the pick between the cracks of the poplar boards and pulled with all her might. After several tries, the board bent and finally broke. Using the pick, she cleared an opening large enough to crawl through.

She carefully pulled herself from the intended grave and not seeing Mosley about, hurried home. She had been in the pit for three hours.

A. L. Blunt went into Huntsville on the morning of the attack. When he returned home, he found the country aroused with search parties setting out in hot pursuit in all directions. Upon hearing what happened, Blunt immediately galloped back to the city to inform the authorities. As the news spread, many others joined the search looking for Mosley.

The Weekly Mercury reported the news:

"The City was startled on receipt of the news of a hell-conceived attempt made by a Negro to outrage the person of a young girl. The brutality connected with the savage attempt eclipses anything ever attempted by a devil in guise of human shape. In the broad light of day, in the glow of grateful sunshine, an innocent, merry hearted girl on her way to school is seized upon and a foul attempt made to rob her of that which is dearer than life itself, the priceless gem of virtue."[349]

The Telegraph's wires were tapping the description of Mosley to all points in the county. Police Officers were called and posted throughout the county to watch for Mosley. It was felt that his capture would be only a question of time and a short time at that. Newspapers around the State picked up the story from the telegraph and placed it on the front page. One paper's headline stated:

"A dead nigger, if caught. If caught, he will be hung without ceremony"[350]

---

[349] *The Weekly Mercury* (March 26, 1890). Apparently the Editors felt that it would have been better for the girl to die than to have been assaulted.

[350] A direct quote from, *The Daily Age Herald*, Birmingham Alabama (March 21, 1890).

Armed and determined men created search parties and set out to look for the Negro. One group of twenty-five men was ordered into Huntsville to determine if Mosley had sneaked into the city. The Chief of Night Police led this group. The group went to several suspected houses in the city and its suburbs and thoroughly searched each. The search parties were out all night but did not find the suspect. Mosley's elderly father was questioned but could only tell the direction his son had gone.

On Thursday morning, a newspaper reporter from *The Mercury* went out Winchester Road to the residence of A. L. Blunt. In the company of R. R. Pettus, several ladies from town proceeded to the woods where Miss Austin was assaulted.

They viewed the uprooted grass and the signs of a struggle where Mosley had forced Miss Austin into the woods. The group was led to the spot where the yawning pit that had been Ellie's prison for those awful three hours. Each could only imagine the horror if it had happened to them.

About sixty yards from Ellie's intended grave another pit was found. The signs indicated that it had been dug out some time in the past. Beside it lay a quantity of sage grass and pieces of burlap.[351]

The party was then invited into Blunt's home to talk with Ellie. Blunt's mother, Melvina Blunt, introduced the group to Ellie Austin. A few bruises were evident on her arms and there was a slight scratch on her neck. These were the only visible injuries received at the hands of Mosley.

Ellie was not reluctant to talk about her painful experience. In graphic details she related to the group how she fought and screamed as she was being forced through the woods. She was proud of her ability to get out alive, and stated she never once lost her presence of mind, not even when she was thrown into the tomb. She was asked about her escape from the grave and she remarked, *"Necessity is the mother of invention, and I found that my slate, when broken, was a good thing with which to scoop away the dirt and rubbish above me."*[352]

The group congratulated Miss Austin on escaping unharmed. They felt she was a true heroine of the Sunny South and a credit to her gender. They told her of the acclaim and congratulations she was receiving from the entire county. She stated that she felt grateful to the thousands of citizens who sprang to arms at the first whisper of trouble. As the group rose to go, she requested that the reporter from *The Mercury* express, in fitting terms, in the column of his paper, the gratitude she felt for all who had taken so deep an interest in the capture of her assailant.

---

[351] No explanation has been found to explain why this older pit was dug.
[352] Quote from the *Weekly Gazette* (March 22, 1890), Huntsville, Alabama.

Fred B. Simpson

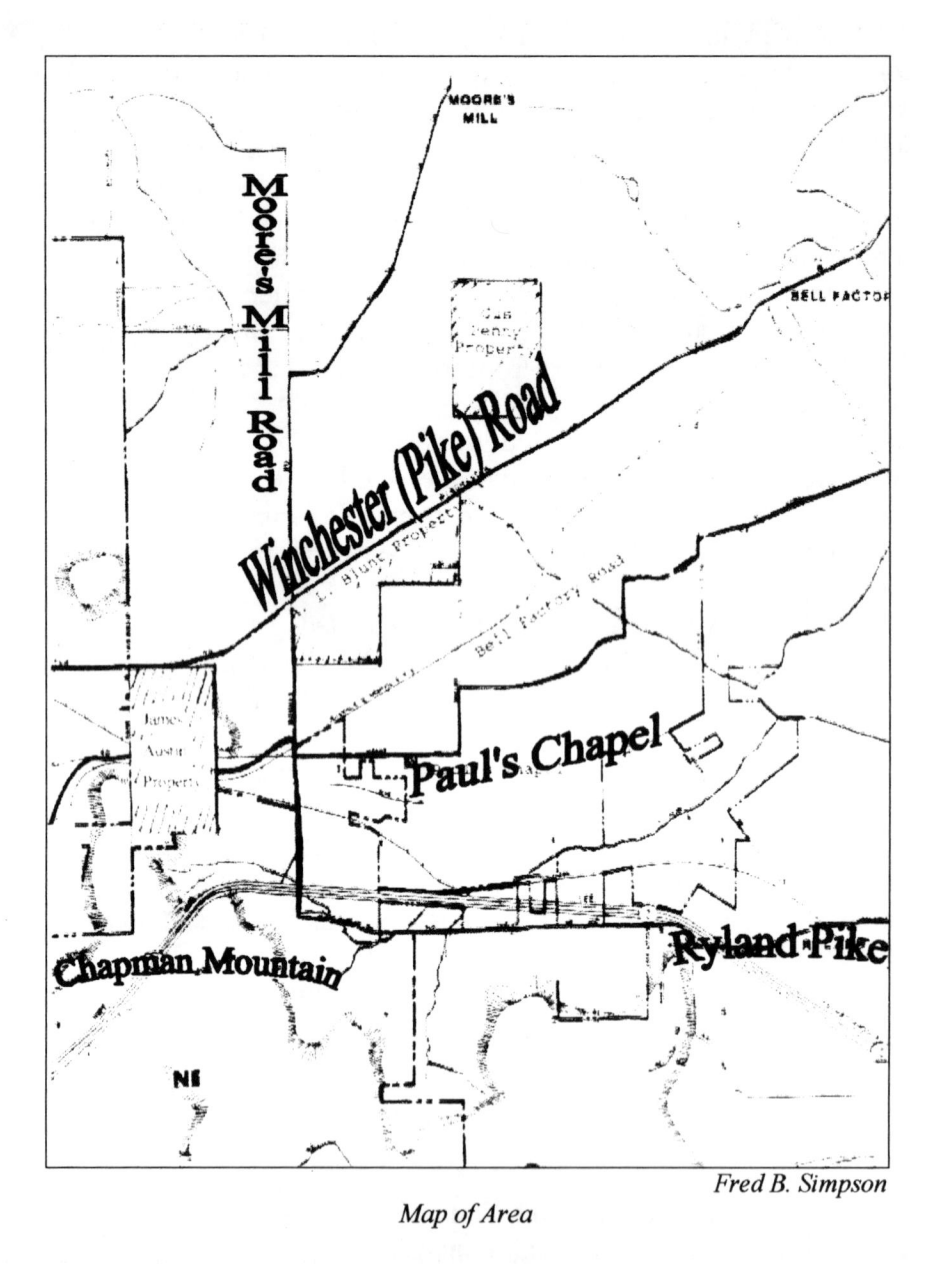

Map of Area

When Mosley discovered that Miss Ellie had escaped from the pit, he started for Huntsville by following the Elora railway track. He stopped at the house of his uncle, Frank Hamlet, who gave him supper and a dollar. Hamlett, knowing his nephew was in trouble, advised him to get out of the city. Mosley stayed all night in town and left at seven o'clock Thursday morning. Somewhere he secured a pistol.

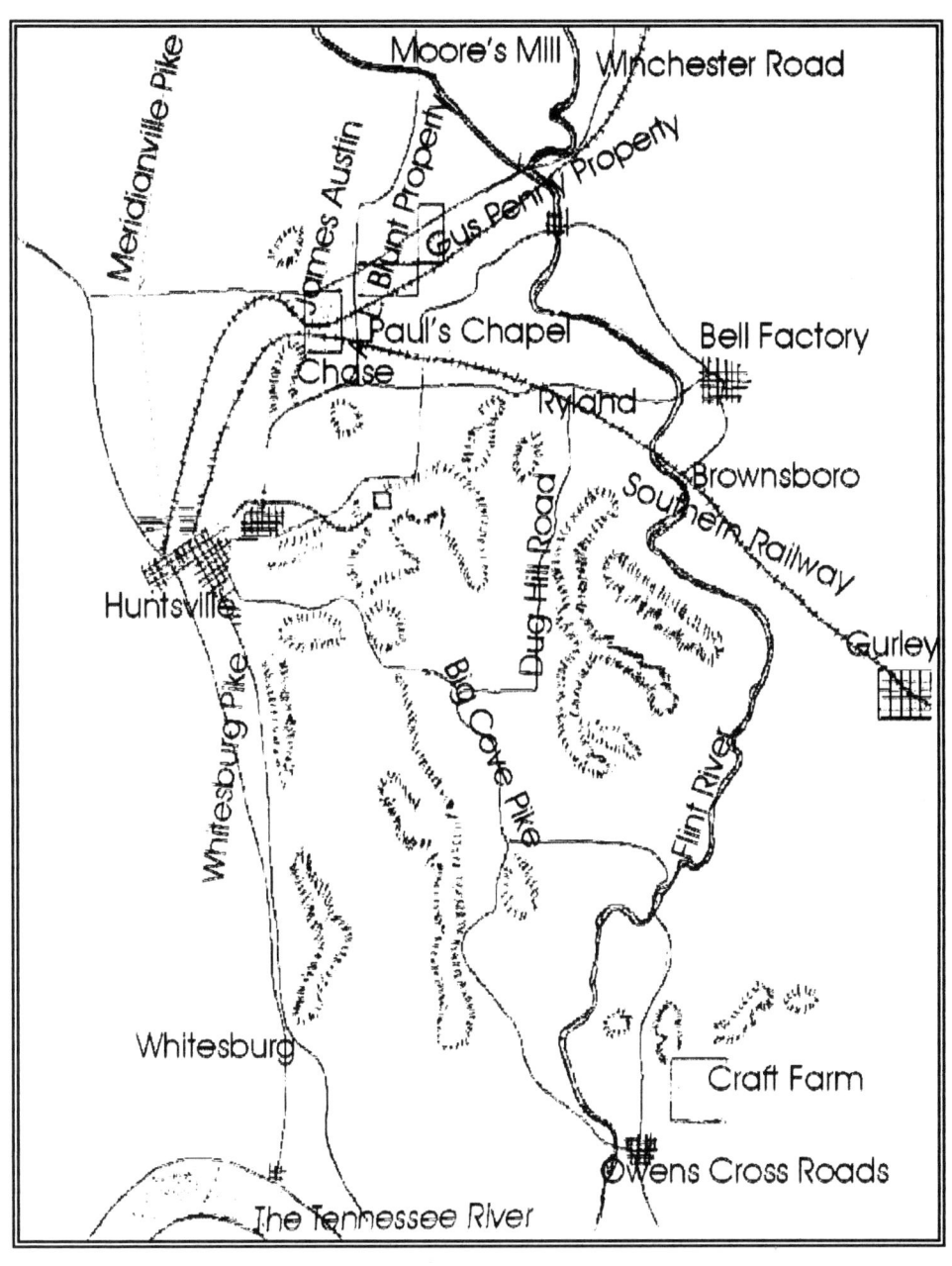

Fred B. Simpson
*Drawing showing the distance and location of the
Area covered by the search part for Mosley*

Mosley may have felt he was not in any danger because he had not harmed Ellie. However, he did leave the Blunt farm for parts unknown.

He traveled south over the mountains to the small community of Owens Cross Roads, about sixteen miles southeast of Huntsville. He walked north from Owens Cross Roads to the farm of W. N. Craft. He arrived about eleven o'clock in the morning, and hired out to Craft's son, Frank, as a farm hand for three months.

Later, he walked back to the Owens Cross Roads Post Office and mailed a letter to his father. Mosley's letter explained that he was working for Craft. He asked his father to use the name Willie Ward, on any letter addressed to him, to protect his identity.

The letter stated:

"dear father an mother an sister: i hired out to a man his name is frank craft 1 mile north of the cross roads the first mont *$ 9$ 10$ for monts if he like me i will stay all the year i left huntsville 7 o'clock in the morning an got to roads at 11 o'clock it was 10 an i walk around about a hour an then walk up the lain a piece and hired out you write my name back willie ward then no one will find it out an sen me word how things is thursday march 20 1890."[353]

The Mosley search party covered Madison County during a sleepless Thursday night. During the search, they received information, which lead them to the farm of Frank Craft, where Mosley was employed. The group grew as it traveled eastward and by sunup there were twenty or more men in the group.

At sunrise, Friday morning, Mosley was found in one of the out buildings that were reserved for field hands on the Craft farm. He was having breakfast when the mounted search party rode up, surrounded the house and called for Mosley to come out. He jumped from the house and ran off at a fast pace. A member of the group fired at the fleeing man. The ball grazed Mosley's head and knocked him down. He drew a pistol, but by then, the men were upon him and knocked the pistol from his hand. He was quickly bound and placed on a horse.

The group left the farm, but not for the county jail. 'Judge Lynch' was about to hold court and dispense justice. Runners were sent in all directions to inform all search parties that Mosley had been found. Everyone was told to assemble at the scene of Mosley's assault on the young lady.

---

[353] *Daily Mercury* (March 21, 1890), the letter is copied as written.

The trip on horseback and by wagon would have been a lengthy one. The route taken is not known but probably would have been from Craft's farm, to Owens Cross Roads, through Ryland and on to the Paul's Chapel area; a distance that would have taken several hours to cover.

There was sufficient time for people to be alerted and arrive even from some distance. On hearing of the capture and approaching lynching, at least one of Mosley's friends came to add comfort. A doctor and preacher from town came to assist. Many people dropped what they were doing and hurried to the place where they expected the hanging to occur.

The men brought Mosley back to the strip of woods where he had dug Ellie's pit. *Mosley was removed from a horse to face a group of about 500 determined men who had gathered to watch the hanging. Also present at the scene were about fifty Negroes who appeared to have endorsed the action of the white men.*[354]

The men took some time to get the rope into position and the mob turned its attention to Mosley. Through *"persistent questioning,"* the facts of the crime Mosley intended to commit were drawn out of him.

Mosley was told that his moments were numbered, but he knew that. One of the men told him that if he did not want to stand at the *"Bar of God"* with a lie on his lips, he had better tell the truth about why he had dug that pit. If anyone else helped him to do it, he had better name him. Then he was asked just what he had planned to do with Miss Austin.

A *Mercury* reporter was allowed to closely interrogate Mosley. He stated that he dug the hole Monday morning before nine o'clock. He had not intended to kill Miss Ellie, but just keep her there for a while. He first implicated Tom Burns[355] in the digging of the grave but later withdrew his statement about Burns.

Mosley requested that his body not be put in the pit he had dug, but that it be put in a coffin like other folks and buried.

After the questioning, Mosley called for his friend, Henry Cloyd, to come forward and take out of his pocket the few personal effects he had. There was only forty-five cents and a french harp. He appointed Henry his administrator and told him to give twenty-five cents to his mother, Emmy,[356] fifteen cents to his sister, Annie, and the new french harp and a nickel to his little brother, Willie.[357]

---

[354] *The Daily Age-Herald News* (March 22, 1890), Birmingham, Alabama.
[355] No information was found that would identify Tom Burns.
[356] 1880 United States Federal Census, Enumeration District 219, T3, R1E, page 12.
[357] Ibid. The census also listed another brother, Columbus, not mentioned here because he had possibly died before the lynching.

The men then got on with the business at hand. About twenty feet from the grave he had dug for Miss Austin stood a great white oak tree. A rope was thrown over an outstretched branch. Mosley's arms were tied behind him. He was placed on a horse and moved into position under the limb of the oak tree. A noose had already been made in the rope and this was slipped over his head and placed around his neck. Mosley was seemingly oblivious to his situation or the crime he had attempted.

He did not plead for his life. Even when the rope was placed around his neck, he seemed completely indifferent, and appeared to have accepted his position and was resigned to his fate.

Then, he said that he was ready to die.

One of the men took a handkerchief from Mosley's pocket and attempted to put it over his face. Mosley strongly objected. The last words he uttered were: "*Let me see one more time in this world.*"[358]

Elder Charley Woodson of Huntsville offered a prayer.

Everything was ready. The horse was drawn from under Mosley and he hung suspended between earth and heaven. For the first two minutes, he hung motionless, and then a slight twitching of the lower limbs proclaimed the death struggle. A doctor present pronounced him dead of strangulation eleven minutes after he was swung off. It was 35 minuets past four o'clock in the afternoon.

The body was cut down and in direct defiance to Mosley's request to be buried in a coffin, the men placed his body in the pit he himself had dug for Ellie.

On Monday, the body was taken out of the pit for a more decent interment, but all the nearby landowners refused to allow burial on their property. The body was hauled from place to place until that night when Gus Penny, a Negro farmer who lived north of Winchester Road, kindly consented for the burial to be on his farm. The body was left in an old abandoned house on the property until Tuesday morning, when Mosley's body was lowered into his final resting place.

Ellie lived another fifty-six years.

---

[358] *The Daily Mercury* (March 21, 1890).

Epilogue

Ellie's father, James Austin, died in December of that same year, at the home of his daughter, Eliza Blunt. They lived on Meridian Street in Huntsville.

A. L. Blunt's mother, Melvina Blunt, died in 1914 in Huntsville.

A. L. Blunt died in February 1899, at the age of forty-two, at his home on Monte Sano Pike. He left six children: James A., William, Birdie, Susie, Maysie and Odell.

Eliza Blunt died in November 1901 at age forty-nine. She was buried beside A. L. in Maple Hill Cemetery. Her sister, Ellie S. Austin, administered her estate.

Birdie Blunt married Lawrence Guinn and moved to Montgomery, Alabama.

A. L. and Elizabeth's daughter, Maysie, moved to Montgomery with Birdie and Lawrence.

Ellie Austin did not remain a teacher. She worked at the law firm of Newman and Schloss in Huntsville during 1911 and 1912. She never married. In the 1930's, Ellie moved to Montgomery, Alabama, where she died in 1938. Her body was brought back to be buried in Maple Hill Cemetery.

Ellie's Grave in Maple Hill Cemetery

Biographies—Chapter Three

The following short biographies are of the people involved in the preceding story. Every effort was made to find information on individuals no matter how small or large a part they played in the story. [359]

Austin, James A.; Father of Ellie S. Austin.
A short time after the marriage between, James and Mildred, they returned to Virginia get the children from his previous marriage. His oldest daughter, Mary Elizabeth (Austin) Snead, had married and moved to Kentucky. The two boys returned to Virginia, however one of the boys was killed and the other died of yellow fever. In the 1880's, Mary[360] broke her hip. Along with this news, she sent a photograph of herself with one son, Charlie and her three daughters. Before James could bring himself to go for her, she and her husband died. Upon reaching Kentucky, James sold their property and returned home with the two granddaughters, age six and three years old and the grandson, seven years old. He left the eight-month-old granddaughter, Bessie, to be reared by her Aunt Martha Franklin [paternal aunt] at Wheatly, Kentucky. James allowed others in the community to rear his grandchildren. Mr. and Mrs. Sidney Mayhew[361] took in the oldest grandchild, Nellie Sneed. Nellie married Walter Harp Price December 22, 1893, at the First Presbyterian Church in Madison County, Alabama. She died October 17, 1926. Bessie married John Devore June 1, 1933, in Carrollton, Kentucky.

An obituary notice appeared December 1, 1900, in a local newspaper; *"Mr. James A. Austin, age 76 years, died Wednesday morning at the residence of Mrs. A. L. Blunt on Meridianville Pike. He had been sick a number of months and his death was no surprise to his immediate relatives."* [362] Mildred J. Dupree died, March 11, 1886. She was buried in Section 6 Row 6 of Maple Hill Cemetery.

---

[359] A search was conducted using the Huntsville City Directories; 1900-1910 United States Federal Census; *Madison County Cemeteries*, Vol. 1 & 2; *Maple Hill Cemetery, Phase One;* and private manuscripts regarding the cemetery, Dorothy Scott Johnson; Merrimack *Cemetery*, Ann Maulsby; Confederate *Veterans Census*, Dorothy Scott Johnson; various military records; Madison County Probate and Civil Court Records.
[360] Mary was born August 4, 1849. She married William Thomas Sneed. This union produced four children; Nellie, born January 18, 1874, Charlie [no date is known but he died from the bite of a mad dog on his grandfather Austin's farm in Madison County]; Florence [birth date unknown, but she died at the age of eight at the Patton home on Green St. in Huntsville] and Bessie, born April 10, 1880.
[361] See the Maples Biographies in Chapter Six, for a complete review of Mayhew.
[362] *The Republican* (December 1. 1900).

Austin, Ellie Sando; Victim.
Ellie Austin never married. She worked in Huntsville during 1911 and 1912, for Newman and Schloss. In the 1930's, Ellie moved to Montgomery, Alabama. She lived on South Court Street with her niece, Maysie, until her death in 1938.[363] Her body was returned to Huntsville and was buried in Maple Hill Cemetery. She lies beside her two nieces, Birdie Guinn and Maysie Blunt. She was seventy-five years old at the time of her death.

Blunt, Eliza Virginia; Ellie's Sister and her family.
Eliza Virginia Blunt married Algernon L. Blunt on January 8, 1879.[364] Children from this marriage were: James A. Jr. born 1880; William, born 1882; Byrdie, born 1884; Susie, born 1886; Mazie, born 1892; and Odelle, born 1894. Algernon died February 18, 1899. Eliza died November 22, 1901, leaving Ellie to administer the estate and provide for the two remaining minor children. William died August 1905, in Tupelo, Mississippi at twenty-two years of age.

Cloyd, Henry; Friend of Mosley
Henry Cloyd lived in T3 R2W of Madison County. He was a mulatto male, born about 1845.[365] He and his parents were born in South Carolina. His wife's name was Julia. She, too, was mulatto, born in Alabama in 1853. She worked as a laundress. They had two daughters: Nannie L., born 1876, and Lula May, born 1878. Henry worked as a cook at a hotel.

Craft, Frank; Second Employer of Robert Mosley.
Frank Craft was born March 23, 1827. He died January 30, 1893 and was buried in the Moon Cemetery in Madison County. His wife, M. J., died May 22, 1845, and was buried beside him. The cemetery is located in the SW Quarter of Section 17, T5 South, Range 2E in Madison County.[366]

Guinn, Birdie (Byrdie) Blunt; Ellie's Niece.
Birdie, daughter of A. L. and Elizabeth Virginia Blunt, married Lawrence Guinn and moved to Montgomery, Alabama. Lawrence Guinn was a

---

[363] Montgomery Alabama City Directories, years 1916-1940. Alabama Department of Archives and History, Montgomery Alabama.
[364] Madison County, Alabama Marriage Records, Book #10, page 141.
[365] 1880 United States Federal Census, Madison County, Alabama, Enumeration District 202, Household #213.
[366] Madison County Cemetery Records (vol. 3), Page 116, manuscript, Dorothy Scott Johnson, Johnson Historical Publications.

shipping clerk with the Standard Oil Company. They lived at 416 N. Lawrence Street. Mazie Blunt, the daughter of Eliza Virginia, moved with them to Montgomery. Around 1917, Birdie went to work as a stenographer for Marshuetz & Co., Lawrence continued to work with Standard Oil. Both changed jobs. Birdie was a bookkeeper for People's Tire Company and Lawrence became a supervisor for Penick & Ford, Ltd.

Mosley, Robert; Lynched.
Robert Mosley was born in Alabama in 1876. He was the son of Bradford and Emmy Mosley, both black and born in Alabama. Bradford's parents were born in Virginia. Bradford was born in 1848, and Emmy was born in 1853. Robert had a twin brother, Columbus, born in 1876 and another brother, Willie, born in 1877. They lived in the Enumeration District 219 in T3, and R1E of Madison County.[367]

Penny, Gus [Augustus]; Mosley was buried on his property. In 1880, Gus Penny was forty-six years old. He was black, born in Georgia, widowed, and a farmer. Two children, both born in Alabama, lived with him: a daughter, Harriett, born 1876, and son, Jesse, born 1878. Also in the home was his brother-in-law, Thomas Woods, who was born in Tennessee, in 1860. Gus's mother, Seelie Penny, born 1805, in Virginia, lived next door with his sister, Harriet Tiller. Edmund, a brother, lived two doors up the road from him. The family of Robert Mosley lived next door.[368]

Woodson, Charley; Minister.
Charles and Mary J. Woodson's home was at 209 Steele Street. He was a minister and a drayman.[369]

---

[367] 1880 United States Federal Census, Madison County, Alabama, Enumeration District 219 T3, R1E, page 12.
[368] 1880 United States Federal Census, Madison County, Alabama Enumeration District, Beat 11, page 12.
[369] 1911 Huntsville City Directory.

Chapter Four
Mollie Smith
Amanda Franks

THEIR LIVES PAID THE AWFUL PENALTY.

The Death of Hon. Joshua O. Kelley Avenged by Farmer Friends.

NEGRO WOMEN DID THE POISONING.

The Principal Escaped but was Captured and Together With Her Accomplice was Hung by a Mob—The Full Confession—Other Arrests May be Made—Coroner's Jury Unable to Locate Responsibility for Lynching—The Community Perfectly Quiet After the Horrible Tragedy.

Swinging from ropes tied to a rail, supported by two trees, on the roadside a short distance from Jeff last Wednesday morning, were the cold and wet bodies of Mollie Smith and Mandy Franks, negro women. The awful sight was seen by a passing mail carrier who gave the alarm and had the neighbors cut the bodies down.

The hanging bodies gave indication that the Kelly poisoning mystery had at last been solved. The crimes which had killed Joshua O. Kelly and ruined the health of several of his family had been atoned by two of the guilty parties.

So far as can be learned the lynching was done by a mob of about twenty men early yesterday morning. So quietly was the work accomplished that the residents of the neighborhood knew of the affair until daylight when the passing mail rider gave the alarm.

A Bit of History—Suspicion Aroused

The first poisoning of the Kelly family occurred two months ago and it was then thought to have been accidental. Joshua O. Kelly died in intense agony. A party of friends and relatives sitting up with his remains on the following night became violently ill from another dose of poison.

The affair was then taken to be the work of conspirators.

to talk. Mandy made a full confession, telling all the details of the crime and implicating another person. She said she had been persuaded to do the deed. Mollie Smith she said, poisoned the family the first two times, and after being placed under close watch, was unable to do anything more. Mollie and then persuaded the confessor to place rat poison in flour from which biscuits were made Friday evening and eaten for breakfast.

Mandy said the poisoning had been carefully planned. She threw the poison in the flour while carrying it from the lockroom to the kitchen.

Having heard the confession, the lynchers proceeded in their gruesome work. A large rail was placed in the forks of two trees, giving the rail a vertical position. Ropes were tied around the women's necks, the ends thrown over the rail and willing hands jerked the bodies into the air. In this position the bodies were left in the cold wind and rain.

May Have Another Lynching.

The members of the mob which did the work are unknown. The story of the scenes at the hanging have leaked out and are public property.

Before another day passes, another party implicated in the crime may be summarily dealt with. It is understood

WEEKLY MERCURY.
HUNTSVILLE, ALABAMA, WEDNESDAY, MAY 19 1897

1897

Between the years 1890-1897, many interesting historical events happened in the World, the United States, the State of Alabama and locally in Madison County, Alabama.[369]

World

Basketball began to be played... Rudyard Kipling authored *The Road to Mandalay*... Peter Tchaikosky composed the *Nutcracker Suite*... Nicholas II became the Last Czar of Russia... Japan and Korea declared war on China... Beardsley produced *Hansel and Gretel*... Anthony Hope authored *The Prisoner of Zendal*... Cuba fought Spain for its Independence... Rudyard Kipling authored *The Jungle Book*... H. G. Wells authored *The Time Machine* and *The Invisible Man*... Rontgen discovered the X-Ray... Nobel Prizes were established for great achievements... Sienkiewicz authored *Quo Vadis*... Marconi received a patent for the Wireless Telegraph... Freud defined the Oedipus complex.

National

William McKinley was elected the President of the United States, replacing Grover Cleveland... Stanford White designed Madison Square Garden... Joel Chandler Harris authored *Uncle Remus*... The Boll Weevils entered the States from Mexico and infested most of the cotton fields in the South... Colorado adopted Women's Suffrage... Chlorine was first used to treat sewage... Henry Ford built the first successful gasoline engine... Utah became a state... The U. S. Supreme Court ruled that *Separate but Equal* facilities were constitutional, beginning what would be termed *Jim Crow* law in the South... Stephen Crane authored *The Red Badge of Courage*... Sousa composed *The Stars and Stripes Forever*... Sunday Comics first appear in the newspapers... Sears-Roebuck opened the Mail-Order Business... Rural free-mail delivery "RFD" was established... The first subway was completed in Boston... The Dalton Gang was broken up at Coffeeville, Kansas.

---

[369] Information was gathered from local and state history books and local newspapers. Information was also obtained from, *A Dream Come True Vol. II*, James Record, 1978, John Hicklin Printing Co. Huntsville, Alabama, Library of Congress Card Number:76-11880.

State

William C. Oates was the State's Governor from 1894-1896... Joseph Forney Johnson was the Governor of the State from 1896-1900... The University of Alabama and Auburn began their football programs... Electric streetcars arrived in Mobile... Mobile received a six-inch snowfall... The Normal School at Troy was opened... The State was divided into nine Congressional Districts... A Depression slowed business and farmers experienced hard times... There were labor strikes in Birmingham and Walker County... Alabama College at Montevallo was founded... The convict leasing system was reformed... Hydroelectric development on the Tallapoosa River began.

Local

Lilly Flagg, a local celebrity cow, was taken to the Chicago World Exposition Fair... Excavation started for the Dallas Mills building... The Town of Gurley was chartered... The argument continued regarding the hitching of livestock to the Courthouse fence.... The Donegan Block on Northside Square burned... The Tennessee River froze-over and could be walked across... The County announced plans to rework the Courthouse... The *Herald Tribune* and the *Gurley Herald* newspapers were started... There was a scarlet fever epidemic... A City ordinance outlawed the sale of indecent literature... There were over one hundred homes in Dallas Mill Village... Long distance telephone lines arrived in the city...Oakwood College was founded... There were thirty-one lawyers and twenty doctors... Madison County voted for William Jennings Bryan for President and Joseph J. Johnston for Governor... A Survey was started for the streetcar line... Huntsville experienced a four-foot flood in many areas of the City... The City bought its first rock crusher and powered road roller for $1,750!... The City installed a new sewer system... T. W. Pratt installed the State's first cotton bale press.... The City of Huntsville had nineteen teachers and 900 students... The County had reached a total of seventy schools and eighty-three teachers... The Monte Sano Railroad folded.[370]

---

[370] Information was gathered from local and state history books and local newspapers. Information was also obtained from, *A Dream Come True Vol. II*, James Record, 1978, John Hicklin Printing Co. Huntsville, Alabama, Library of Congress Card Number:76-11880.

Chapter Four
Mollie Smith and Amanda Franks-1897

Indian Creek flows southward through Madison County Alabama. Today it twists and turns before replenishing a reservoir in the wetlands of the Wheeler National Wildlife Refuge, and then empties into the Tennessee River.[371]

This beautiful stream is formed from a spring[372] located nine miles northwest of Huntsville. The spring was the hunting ground for the Cherokee Indians before the white man came. As Madison County was settled, the spring drew white settlers and eventually a small frontier settlement grew up around it. The crude houses of the settlement could not protect the early pioneers from the Indians and the center of the settlement was a blockade for protection.

After the land sales of 1809, various settlers owned land around the spring.

An early pioneer, Benjamin O. Wilburn, purchased the land around the spring sometime after 1828. He acquired additional nearby properties over the years as he formed his plantation and built his home. After Wilburn's death, his widow married Tom Graves, a much younger man. Mrs. Wilburn died a mysterious death and it was rumored that Graves killed her for her money. But that is another story.

The dreaded malaria fever was ever present in those early days. It was so severe that it caused the frontier colony around the spring to break up about 1845.

David E. Kelly came from Brunswick County, Virginia, and settled near Meridianville before 1820. He later moved to Pulaski Pike, northwest of Huntsville. In 1850, David's son, Joshua Oscar Kelly, married Sally Strong, whose family home overlooked the Meridianville Pike, about one mile south of Meridianville.

---

[371] It should be noted that most of the information for this book was found in the weekly newspapers; *Birmingham News* (May 12, 1897 and May 18, 1897); *The Weekly Tribune* (March 9-11-16, 1897); *The Huntsville Weekly Democrat (March 10, 1897); The Journal (March12-14, 1897), The Weekly Mercury, (March.12, & May 19, 1897)* and *True Tales of Old Madison County*, Virgil Carrington (Pat) Jones, Johnson Historical Publication, Huntsville, Alabama. Each fact or quote will not be repetitiously footnoted individually.
[372] An early deed in *True Tales of Madison County* gave the name as Price's Spring, but early maps show the name as Indian Spring. It is now known as Kelly Springs.

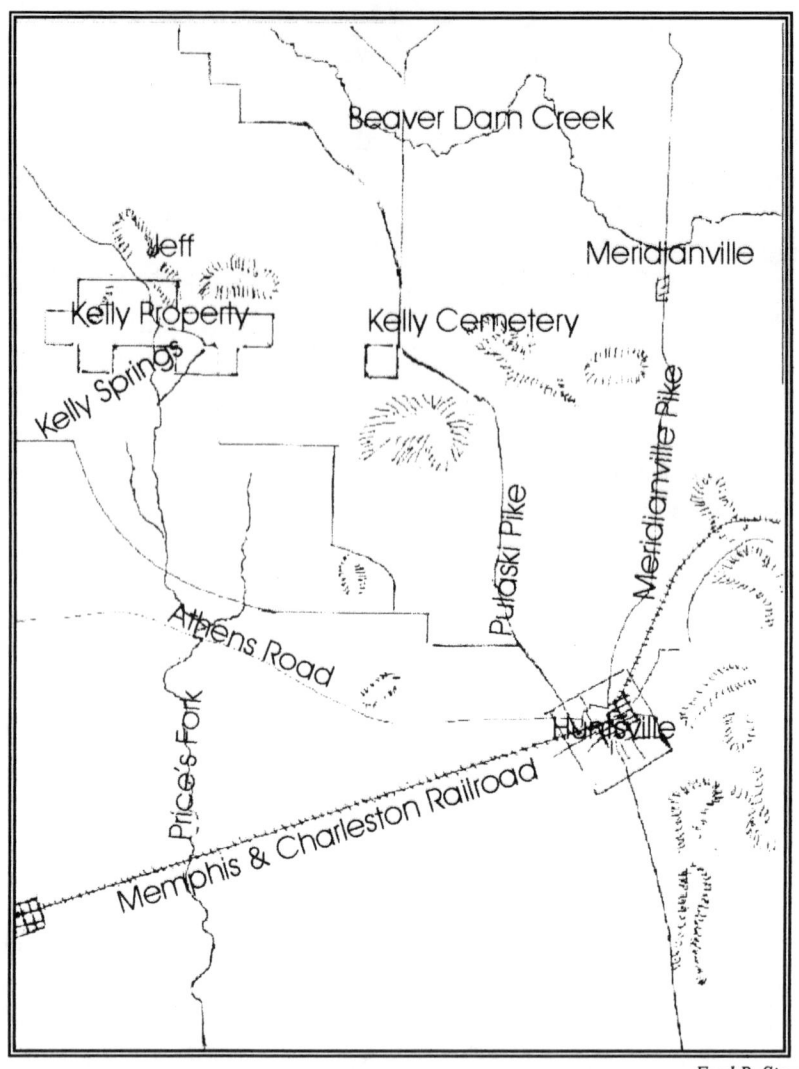

Fred B. Simpson
A section of Madison County, showing the location of the Kelly Farm

About 1853, J. O. Kelly purchased all the former holdings of Benjamin O. Wilburn from the Wilburn estate. There were more than six hundred acres encompassing over four quarter sections. The land was cultivated for cotton crops by the slaves who lived in a row of cabins located at the side of the main house.

The War Between the States caused Kelly to leave his family and join Russell's Fourth Alabama Cavalry of the Confederate States Army. He led one of the companies of the Fourth Alabama Cavalry Regiment and was elected Lieutenant Colonel (though newspapers state that he was called "Major") of Forrest's Regiment. He returned home without wounds, even though he participated in the battles of Shiloh and the campaign from Chattanooga, Tennessee to Atlanta, Georgia.[373]

While Kelly was away, Sally Kelly took charge of the plantation and slaves. It was necessary that she not only handle the normal duties, but also prevent the Yankees from making off with everything they owned. Even though the Union Army occupied the family home, it was not burned, as others in the area were, due the respect the soldiers had for Sally's courage and unyielding stubbornness.

Courtesy of the Kelly Family
Joshua and Sally Kelly and Sons at their home

Even after the war, sentiment was strong for southern independence, and during the following years, major landowner and faithful Confederate soldier, Major Kelly wanted to name the town, Jefferson Davis, honoring the first President of the Confederacy. The Federal Government would not allow the town to be named for the ex-president, so the name was shortened to "Jeff" and so it remains today.[374]

Major Kelly and his wife, Sally, produced a large family and amassed great wealth. Their two sons formed a partnership under the name of D. E. and J. O. Kelly. This business, located at Jeff, added to the growth

---

[373] Regimental Records of Russell's Fourth Alabama Cavalry of the Confederate States Army, Microfilm Copy, Huntsville-Madison County Public Library.
[374] A less romantic explanation is that the name was required to be short by government postal regulations.

of the settlement and provided black-smithing, cotton ginning, farming supplies and general merchandise to the surrounding area. They manufactured farming items like foot scrapers, and fireplace tongs, and they sharpened plow points for the farmers.[376] One brother, Lawson Kelly, was a horticulturist. He extended the Kelly operation by discovering the merits of watercress, which grew abundantly in the clear, cold spring-fed lake.[377]

The Kelly orchards were widely known. They grew Elbertas, Georgia Belles, and the Slappey variety apples. The store made the settlement into a self-contained village and it became a meeting place for those who lived for miles around.

Fred B. Simpson

*The Kelly Store at Jeff
which burned in 1999*

Jeff was really just one big family of Kellys and Burwells. What the Kellys did not own the Burwells did.[378]

After the war, several of the family's ex-slaves remained with the family as paid workers. They worked as field hands and as house servants.

---

[376] Information regarding the Kelly operation was from the personal recollections of Oliver W. Fraser.
[377] Madison County, Alabama would become known a few years later as the watercress capital of the world.
[378] An Article describing the estate of Alice Burwell; *Huntsville Times* (March 26, 1995).

The farm prospered and Major Kelly was noted as one of the leading farmers of north Alabama.

One of the Negroes, who had worked for a long time for the Kellys, was a woman by the name of Mollie Smith. She was from a bad family.[378] Many of her relatives were in prison, where they were leased out to the coal mines and were forced into a harsh life. Another younger house servant was named Amanda (Mandy) Franks. They were both good friends of another Negro woman, Jennie Burwell, who also lived on the farm.

On Saturday, March 6, 1897, a most serious case of poisoning occurred at the Kelly home. The poisoning produced the serious illness of Major Kelly,[379] his wife Sally, and Oakley Woodard, a man who resided with the Kelly family. Several of the Negro workers were also affected.

The poisoning of this old and worthy family was thought for a time to have been a deplorable accident. It was not. The circumstances surrounding the poisoning and the aftermath of those events created a most interesting and tragic story.

On Saturday evening, the Kellys had their evening meal after a day of overseeing operations on their large farm. During and after the meal, they sat drinking coffee and talking of the interesting items of current events. The home was a stopping place for travelers. As there were no eating places between Jeff and Huntsville, salesmen would frequent the home and stop off for a bite. There was also the unmarried clerk from the store to feed. That Saturday after the meal was served, the family and visitors took coffee as they sat and conversed about the hot topics of the day. The coffee apparently did not taste differently and during the evening's conversation, Major Kelly had several servings. The coffee was made in a large pot and several servants working on the farm were served from the same container.

In a short while, everyone became sick. Since the Major was in feeble health and possibly took a larger quantity of the coffee than the others, it affected him more violently. He was then almost seventy years old.

Dr. William Pettus was summoned and worked with his patients all night. Dr. Thomas Dryer, from Huntsville, was also summoned on Sunday, along with two other physicians from Madison. Everything that medical skill could do to save the poisoned was done. All of the doctors'

---

[378] *The Journal* (May 14, 1897), No. 20; Vol. III, page 2.
[379] Title referred to in the obituary notices, however it could not be verified from military records.

efforts proved unavailing for the Major. He died on Monday morning, the eighth day of March, in intense agony.

Mrs. Kelly remained in critical condition and the conditions of Oakly Woodard and the seven Negro servants were also serious. There were fears that they all might die.

Everyone was mystified about how the poisoning occurred. It was first believed that arsenic had been placed in the pantry and by some accident had become scattered and fell into the ground coffee. This was first thought to have been the result of Mrs. Kelly's carelessness in placing poison in the cupboard. Later it was thought that, through a mistake, the Negro cook of the family had spilled some of the coffee and when returning it to the container had mixed it with rat poison.

Since no one really knew how the family was poisoned, a large number of cooking utensils and everything that could possibly absorb or harbor the poison were destroyed.

The following Tuesday night, March 9th, the body of Major Kelly was laying in state at the residence. A group of eleven friends and relatives sat up with the family of the Major as they grieved and tried to understand what had happened. The attending physicians remained at the house to care for those still sick. During the night, those at the wake ate food prepared at the house. They all quickly showed the symptoms of poisoning and soon became violently ill.

Seven white people were poisoned: David and Eva Kelly, Joshua O. Kelly Jr., G. L. Kelly, Oakley Woodard, Percy Lewis and Irvine D. Patton of Cleveland, Tennessee. Eight Negro servants were also poisoned and it was felt that two of them might die. The doctors also were sick. Mercifully, this poisoning did not result in a fatality, and after a few days everyone recovered.

Julia, the Negro cook, was quite sick. David E. Kelly and G. L. Kelly seemed to have gotten a heavier dose than the others.[380] They had not fully recovered from the first poisoning and the second dose was almost fatal to both men.

The Major was taken to the family cemetery on his father's plantation on Pulaski Pike and in the presence of his family and friends, put to his final rest in the 71st year of his life.

The death of the Major was a shock and a great loss to Madison County. It was reported in a local paper:[381]

---

[380] *The Weekly Mercury (*May 12, 1897), Wednesday Vol. XII, No. 219, Page 6.
[381] *The Weekly Tribune* (May 9, 1897).

"Mr. Kelly was one of the most substantial citizens, best farmers, and staunch democrats in the county, and a brave Confederate soldier, without fear and without reproach. He was a Christian, kind, unselfish and true in his ties of blood and friendship. As a progressive and successful farmer, he had not a peer in this state. To his daughters and sons, and his noble wife he was a king among men, and his many friends loved and respected him. Our tears are mingled with those of his loved ones in their great grief."

Kelly had served with the Fourth Alabama Cavalry Regiment during the War Between the States with many of his friends and neighbors. He was remembered as a courageous Confederate soldier. His comrades in arms passed a resolution of respect at the time of his death.[383]

"Died, at his residence in Madison County on the 8th inst., Comrade Joshua O. Kelly, member of Egbert J. Jones Camp no. 357 United Confederate Veterans in the 71st year of his age. At a meeting of Egbert J. Jones Camp no. 357 United Confederate Veterans on the 12th inst., the following resolutions of respect to Comrade J. O. Kelly were unanimously passed: resolved, we have heard with great pain of the death of our Comrade Joshua O. Kelly. With pride and affection, we bear testimony to his patriotism and courage as a Confederate soldier, his purity, integrity and usefulness as a citizen, his charity and hospitality as a neighbor, his piety and good deeds as a Christian and his fidelity and devotion as a father, husband and friend; enterprising, progressive and successful as a farmer, his death is a great loss to the community in which he lived, as well as to the state and county. That we will always cherish his virtues and keep green in our hearts his memory. That a copy of this resolution be spread upon the minutes of this camp, and copy be furnished the city papers, and a copy be sent to the family of our deceased comrade." Signed: Daniel Coleman, William J. Mastin, John W. Wall and Ben Patterson, Adjutant.

Of course, the second poisoning aroused suspicions and the family set in motion an investigation to determine the cause of the problem. The circumstances led some members of the family to believe that this was not an accident but a conspiracy from outside the family. The younger members of the family began an attempt to solve the mysterious crime.

Detectives were quietly employed and neighbors set about visiting the home and watched for any unusual activity. Suspicion came to focus on the house girl, Mollie Smith. However, no evidence was found to

---

[383] Ibid.

indicate she was responsible for the incident. Though every effort was made to find the cause of the poisoning, there were no answers.

Precautions were taken to prevent such an incident in the future. All food was placed in a locked storage room in the kitchen. Family members and others watched the preparation of food closely. Life began to resume the normalcy that the family needed to get on with their lives.

Two months later, while the investigations were still ongoing, another shocking poisoning occurred.

The Kelly family, on Friday, May the 7th, arose at an early hour to begin work, as was the custom for all farm families. Sally Kelly was away visiting family in Athens and was not there for the morning gathering. I. D. Patton, a commercial traveler, had once again stopped off at the Kelly home.

In the kitchen, the household servants were at their table. Outside, the Negro field hands were also eating breakfast before beginning the day's work. Everyone was being fed from the same kitchen as the members of the Kelly household.

Shortly after breakfast, the family, household servants, and field hands all became violently ill, showing every symptom of being poisoned.

There were fourteen people affected: David E. Kelly and his wife Eva, Joshua O. Kelly Jr., G. L. Kelly, Oakley Woodard, Percy Lewis, and I. D. Patton.[383] There were also seven Negroes affected. Most became violently ill and it was thought that some might die.

A runner, (in fact, one of the victims of the former poisoning), was sent to Huntsville to bring Dr. Felix Baldridge. The doctor left immediately for the Kelly home at Jeff. He told those at his home that again several members of the Kelly family were ill, apparently induced by drinking coffee, containing poison.

Sally Kelly was notified about the poisoning and quickly returned home. She directed the treatment of those affected and once again set in motion an investigation as to the cause of this latest tragedy. The sick recovered slowly but remained in a dangerous condition for some while. I. D. Patton soon recovered and returned to his home in Tennessee.

At first it was believed that the coffee served at breakfast once again contained the poison. The family was not to be fooled this time. As they talked about the details, it became apparent that David E. Kelly drank no coffee but was as sick as the others. The investigation intensified and

---

[383] A commercial traveler from Cleveland, Tennessee; *The Weekly Mercury* (May12, 1897).

there now could not be the slightest doubt that someone was deliberately trying to kill the family.

Sheriff Oscar Fulgham went out to Jeff and assisted in the investigation. He stayed well into the night. He and the Kelly family set out to find the criminal who was obviously in the house.

Immediately after becoming aware that the family had been poisoned at breakfast, David's wife, Eva Kelly, preserved a bit of every article of food eaten during that meal. Her quick thinking would eventually solve the mystery. The articles of food saved by this brilliant woman were sent into Huntsville to be examined. From this examination, performed Tuesday morning, May 11th, it was learned that the flour used to make the biscuits contained the poison. The biscuits were impregnated with so much poison that the flour was changed from a normal snowy white to brown.

Physicians said that if the amount of poison placed in the flour had been put into the coffee, the entire family and all others who drank the liquid would have been killed. As it was, the dose in the biscuits was so strong that it acted as an emetic, causing the sick to vomit, which most likely saved their lives.

Suspicion centered on the cook, but she seemed to be cleared of all blame for she had also became dangerously ill from the effects of the poison. It was noticed that Mandy Franks and Molly Smith were not poisoned. Mollie Smith had, in fact, pretended to be sick, but the family was not fooled. The physicians decided that she was shamming.[384]

The investigation intensified. It was decided to make a thorough search of the kitchen. A discovery under the kitchen floor produced incriminating evidence. A box of poison called, *"Rough on Rats"* was found. On the box was the stamped trademark of D. E. & J. O. Kelly Grocery Store. Unbelievably, this was the family's grocery store at Jeff, across the road from the Kelly home.

It did not take long to learn that only two people had bought this brand of rat poison at the store during the entire past year. The clerks at the store knew who bought the poison from the account books. One box was sold to a white man and the other to a Negro woman, Molly Smith. It was decided to place a close watch over both Molly Smith and Mandy Franks.

Sometime during the day Tuesday, Mollie became aware that the white people knew she was involved in the poisoning. She became restless and decided to remove herself from the Kelly farm. She left and struck out

---

[384] Another term during that time for faking, or acting like.

north at a fast pace. She was being watched all the time but not closely enough to prevent her from slipping away. It was not long until her absence was noted.

A group of men set out to find her and bring her back. Tuesday night Mollie was captured while still making her way north towards Tennessee. She was still in Alabama, but was near the Tennessee line in Limestone County when stopped. She wore a pair of men's boots, and was taking herself from the neighborhood for good.

The men took her to the home of her partner in crime, Mandy Franks. They arrived as a rowdy group and quickly awakened Mandy and her family. The men took Mandy aside to talk to her. After some convincing, Mandy made a confession.[385]

Mandy said Mollie put the poison in the coffee the first time, but because of the close surveillance could not do it again. Through her contempt for the Kelly family and her cunning ways, she found an opportunity to poison the sausage on the night of the wake. She caught not only those watching, but also the attending physicians.

After the second poisoning, the close surveillance and the investigation prevented Molly from using the poison again for some time. Not being able to complete the business by herself, she persuaded Mandy Franks to do the work for her. Mandy confessed to the men that she had put the poison in the flour that was made into the lethal biscuits. The poison had been placed in the flour while it was being carried from the locked storage room to the kitchen.

The men took both women to the scene of their crime. The two women were locked in the basement of the Kelly store. It was a cold rainy night[386] and they warmed themselves as best they could. They must have listened to the wind whistle around the building and wondered what their destiny would be.

All during the days and nights after the Friday poisonings, the community talked of a lynching as soon as the guilty parties were found. They were eager to punish those who had done such a terrible thing and caused such tragedy to the Kelly family.

The community took advantage of the first opportunity to carry out this plan. Men of all ages gathered to form a lynch mob. They removed the women from the basement of the store and took them to their final

---

[385] *The Birmingham News* (May 18, 1897).
[386] *The Weekly Mercury* (May 19, 1897), Wednesday Vol. XII Page 5.

destination—*"the tree"*. They chose a stretch of forest along the edge of Cluttsville Pike for the execution.[388]

When they arrived, the women were informed that if they had anything to say, they had better say it quickly. Mollie Smith refused to talk. Mandy, again confessed to the crime, gave all the details, and implicated Mollie. The men did not stand in the freezing rain and ask any more questions.

Having heard the confession, the lynchers proceeded with their gruesome work. It was early in the morning hours, between midnight and daybreak when a large rail was placed in the forks of two, huge, white oak trees located just off the side of the road, at the site of an old home place.[389] Nooses were slipped around the women's necks and the ends of the ropes were thrown over the rail. Their feet were tied together and their hands were tied behind their backs. The women were then swung into the air and to their deaths. The bodies were left hanging among the branches of the trees in the bitter, windy weather.

Wednesday morning, a passing mail carrier saw this awful sight and raised the alarm. Just off the road, at the intersection of the Monrovia-Jeff road, were the bodies of the women gently swinging in the cold breeze. Mollie Smith and Mandy Franks paid the penalty of death for their sins. So quietly was the work accomplished that the residents of the neighborhood knew nothing of the affair until daylight. A crowd gathered and some of the on-lookers cut the bodies down.

The newspaper[390] stated:

"The Negro women were found suspended from an oak in the forest near the recently sadly bereft and once happy and prosperous home of the family of the lamented Joshua Kelly. The hanging bodies gave indication that the Kelly poisoning mystery had at last been solved and had been atoned for by the death of the two guilty parties."

The residents of the neighborhood, Negroes as well as whites were now satisfied that the right parties had paid for their misdeeds.

A Coroner's Jury was called and after an inquest reported:

"We the jury, after examining the bodies of Mollie Smith and Amanda Franks and hearing the evidence find that said Mollie Smith and Amanda Franks came to their death on the night of May 11, 1897, about

---

[388] Now Kelly Springs Road.
[389] Letter written by eyewitness of the scene after the hanging, Oliver W. Fraser, the son of John Fraser, (He was the owner of Huntsville Wholesale Nursery, located at Stringfield Road and west of Pulaski Pike).
[390] *The Journal*, (May 14. 1897), No. 20 Vol. III Page 2.

11 miles northwest of Huntsville on the Cluttsville Pike, by hanging by the neck, by parties unknown to the jury from the evidence given."[390]

Some people believed that other parties were involved in the poisoning. It was generally believed that the women did not act alone, but that the real instigator was a man.

Some suspicion fell on Jim Nance,[391] a Negro man that worked on the farm.[392] Nance was so afraid of being implicated in the crime that he quit his plow in the field and fled when he heard that Mollie Smith had been taken by the mob. There was a rumor that Nance was seized by the mob and injured, but the rumor was not true.

Jennie Burwell, another worker lived on the Kelly farm, confessed that she knew about the plot to poison the Kelly family. She admitted knowing that Mollie Smith was the person who put the poison in the coffee and knew she would repeat the effort. She claimed to know that Amanda Franks had a part in planning to poison the Kelly family but she did not care to tell on them. Due to the Christian sentiment of the Kelly family, this woman was given just three days to take herself out of the county. She left on a westbound train.

Rumors that others were involved were never substantiated. No information was ever found that anyone else participated in the crime. It was generally felt that if others were discovered, the rope would do its work. The motive that prompted the two women was never learned.

The members of the mob were neighbors who knew each other. They were church going, hard-working people who would withdraw in horror if asked to commit any sinful act, much less murder. They had to live with the memory of their actions. They had to stand in church with their families and think about the two women hanging in the trees.

The Negro newspaper, *The Journal*,[393] had this to say about the lynching:

---

[390] Signed by W. Y. Vaughn, J. P., acting Coroner; J. F. Smith, G. A. Johnson, W. L. Hilliard, T. J. Wall, J. W. Vaughn, G. W. Wall, jurymen. *The Weekly Mercury* (May 19, 1897), Vol. XII, page 5.

[391] Rubin Nance is listed as living with the Kelly family on the 1880 United States Federal Census (Page 135, line 150, Enumeration District 199), He was a black man, age 25, and a laborer. However, also in the neighborhood is found a black man, James Nance, age 71, widower, farmer, born in Virginia to Virginia born parents, with a son, James Leslie; page 117 line 131.

[392] *Inquest Over the Dead Girls, The Birmingham News* (May 18, 1897). The article states that Nance had been implicated in the Kelly poisonings, been caught and shot. All parties denied the rumor; however, Nance had not been seen and he was thought 'to have been put out of the way.'

[393] *The Journal* (May 14, 1897), No. 20 Vol. III Page 2.

"If these women were guilty, and we do not say they were not, why not give them a trial? What are our laws for? Are they to be set aside at any time, at the pleasure of those thirsting for human gore. To the noble Christian gentlemen of this town, we appeal for protection. If we have violated your laws, try us by them. But for the fair name of your county, for the sake of humanity, for all that is right and noble, stop these murders by mobs. Vengeance is mine and I will repay, saith the lord, and certainly He will heap this up for the time of harvest. Every man or boy that took part in that lynching is a murderer, and will wear the brand of Cain to his dying day."

The unknown men who took the women to the woods that night must have believed the paper. There was no pride in the action taken. The story of the hanging leaked out and became public knowledge, but the men spent the rest of their lives attempting to keep their identities from becoming public knowledge.

The small community of Jeff has kept the secret of the identities of the members of the mob to this day. Friends and members of the families will not talk about the details of the lynching that occurred on that dark and cold night so many years ago in a small community nine miles from Huntsville.

Courtesy of the Kelly Family

Photograph of the Kelly home during a snowfall of 1899

Courtesy of the Kelly Family

Joshua O. Kelly

Epilogue

A young lady named Debbie Johnson worked in my law office for years. She believed that her grandfather was in the lynching party. She asked her grandmother questions for me, and the only answer she received was that her grandfather would never talk about the event, not to his family, nor to anyone else; and she would not talk to her granddaughter about it.

Many were questioned, but few answers found.

The Kelly home is still at the same location in Jeff. It has been remodeled and brick veneered. Little of the old home can be found. However, the grounds still have some of the landscaping started by Sally Kelly after the War Between the States.

Fred B. Simpson

Kelly Home 1988

Many descendants of the Kelly family still live near the spring that gave life to the settlement. The family has contributed greatly to the growth of Madison County. None of the land bought by Kelly in 1853, or the more than 2,500 acres added since has ever been under a mortgage.

A descendant of Joshua O. Kelly's brother lives in Huntsville. He is an attorney, Joshua O. Kelly III.

Jennie Burwell was never heard from again.

Dr. Thomas E. Dryer continued to serve Madison County as the health officer from 1896-1907. He was remembered for his kindness and philanthropic ways, especially during the typhoid and smallpox epidemics. Dr. Dryer died in 1931, and is buried in Maple Hill Cemetery.

David and Eva Kelly remained on the family farm in Jeff for the remainder of their lives. Both are buried in the Kelly family cemetery on Pulaski Pike. George Lawson Kelly never married and was also buried in the family cemetery.

Sheriff Oscar Fulgham served as Sheriff until 1900.

Dr. William David Pettus served rural Madison County as a physician for only a few years before his untimely death of pneumonia in 1915. Dr. Pettus was buried in the Pettus Cemetery in Monrovia.

Fred B. Simpson

Tombstone of
Joshua O. Kelly and Sally Strong Kelly
At the Kelly Cemetery

Biographies–Chapter Four

The following short biographies are of the people involved in the preceding story. Every effort was made to find information on individuals no matter how small or large a part they played in the story. [395]

Baldridge, Felix; Doctor.
A complete biography may be found in Chapter Six.

Burwell, Jennie; Suspect.
Jennie Burwell was born in Alabama in 1858; she had no knowledge where her parents were born. She was married to David Burwell. David was born in Alabama in 1850 to Virginia born parents. They lived in the house next to the Kelly family. No further information was found.

Dryer, Thomas; Doctor.
Thomas Edmund Dryer was born October 5, 1856, in Tuskegee, Alabama. He was the son of James Edmund and Sara Caroline Dryer. James was a merchant and druggist, and his father, Edmund, was a physician in Tallassee, Alabama. Dr. Dryer also shared ancestors with President George Washington. He was the great-grandson of George's sister, Mrs. Betty Washington Lewis. Dr. Dryer received his formal education at Park High School in Tuskegee and later entered the University of Alabama Medical School in Mobile where he received his Doctor of Medicine Degree in 1886. He practiced one year in Tuskegee, then in Birmingham for seven years, and then came to Huntsville in 1894. His practice was general medicine, surgery, and obstetrics. Dr. Dryer married Mabelle Rose White of Huntsville, on January 1, 1892. During the typhoid epidemic and smallpox scare, Dr. Dryer was asked to serve as the Madison County Health Officer. He served on this board from 1896-1907 and was president of the County Medical Society from 1908-1914. Dr. and Mrs. Dryer lived at 111 Calhoun Street in a lovely home built in 1837. They were members of the Holmes Street Methodist Church. Dr. Dryer died at the age of seventy-two on May 28, 1931. His service was held at the Methodist

---

[395] A search was conducted using the Huntsville City Directories; 1900-1910 United States Federal Census; *Madison County Cemeteries*, Vol. 1 & 2; *Maple Hill Cemetery, Phase One;* and private manuscripts regarding the cemetery; Dorothy Scott Johnson; Merrimack *Cemetery*, Ann Maulsby; Confederate *Veterans Census*, Dorothy Scott Johnson; various military records; Madison County Probate and Civil Court Records.

Church and his burial was in Maple Hill Cemetery. Mrs. Dryer lived only thirteen months after the death of her husband.[395]

Franks, Amanda; Lynched.
Information on Amanda Franks could not be found.

The Kelly Family; Victims of Poisoning.
David E. Kelly, came from Brunswick County, Virginia with his brother, sometime before 1820, and settled near Meridianville.[396] Later he moved to a plantation on Pulaski Pike. David's son, Joshua O. Kelly was born March 17, 1826, in Madison County, Alabama. J. O. Kelly married Sally B. Strong of Meridianville. They were blessed with the following children: Sue (wife of James R. Burwell); David E. (husband of Eva Thompson); Joshua O. Kelly Jr. (who died in 1928); Lawson; Lena (wife of Judge George Malone); Lula (who died single); and Nanny (wife of Henry B. Malone of Limestone County). In September of 1853, Joshua O. Kelly bought a plantation in the area now known as Jeff. Kelly enjoyed an active and productive career as a cotton farmer, County Commissioner, and Director of the Memphis and Charleston Railroad that ran through Huntsville.

During the War Between the States, the Yankees occupied the family home at Jeff. On at least one occasion, the Yankees came from Huntsville to burn the home, but were talked out of it. When Kelly came home from the war, he was poor, but fortunate that he still had his home and family.

Mammy's log cabin at the Kelly Farm *Fred B. Simpson*

---

[395] *Medicine Bags and Bumpy Roads*, pages 179-180, Goldsmith and Fulton, 1985, Valley Publishing Company.
[396] *A Dream Come True Vol. II*, James Record, 1978, John Hicklin Printing Co. Huntsville, Alabama, Library of Congress Card Number:76-11880.

With the help of the ex-slaves that chose to stay, Joshua began to rebuild. One of these was Fanny Strong,[397] the old Negro Mammy. She had a substantial one-room log cabin with a large fireplace that still stands in the yard.

In 1885, two of J. O.'s sons, David E. and Joshua O. Jr., had reached manhood. They started a partnership in the mercantile, blacksmithing, ginning, and farming business under the name of D. E. and J. O. Kelly.

D. E. was appointed postmaster. He married Eva Thompson in 1888, and moved into a separate home on the farm. They had the following children: Thompson R., (married, Adelene Rhyne), Aurora (married Homer M. Rowe), Joshua O. (married, Eula Russell), Mary Lena (married Jeff Davis Luten).

After the death of the parents, J. O. and Sally, the single children, Joshua, Lawson and Lula continued to live in the family home. It was remodeled with a brick veneer in 1928. Twelve rooms, eight of which were original, were fitted with antiques and fine paintings (most of which were painted by daughter, Lula).

The settlement around the home included a post office, blacksmith shop, general merchandise store, a cotton gin, sweet potato curing house, and 2,500 acres were in cultivation, much of it as an orchard. The firm shipped more Transparent Apples and Keiffer Pears that any other firm south of Virginia. In addition, the firm had a large cattle business.

J. O. Kelly died March 8, 1897. His obituary told of a man that was tenderhearted and a friend to the needy. His wife, Sally, died May 19, 1915.

Patton, Irvine D.; visitor in the Kelly home.
Irvine D. Patton was the son of Olive B. and Billie Patton. He was born in 1872.[398]

Pettus, Dr. William David; Doctor.
William David Pettus was the son of William R. and Rebecca Love Pettus. He was born in Pettusville, Limestone County, Alabama, on April 12, 1843. At nineteen years of age William entered service to the Confederate Army, but because of ill health, was discharged. After recuperating, he re-entered the service and was assigned to Company D, of the Thirty-fifth

---

[397] Fanny Strong is listed living in the home with the Kelly's on the 1880 United States Federal Census (Enumeration District 199, page 145 line 150). She was fifty years of age, black, born in Alabama to Virginia born parents.
[398] United States Federal Census, Enumeration District 233 Ward 3, Page 89 Line 114.

Alabama Volunteer Infantry. He served with Co. J under V. Robinson until a musket ball in a battle near Decatur, Alabama, fractured his leg, on October 28, 1864. Dr. Pettus began his study of medicine at the close of the war. He graduated from the University Medical School, Nashville, Tennessee, in 1868. He began his practice in the community of Rep, which is near Jeff. Dr. Pettus married Ann Dew Brown on December 23, 1869. They had five children: William H.; Annie R. Pettus (Douglas); Ellen H. Pettus (Kelly); Mary B. Pettus (Phillips); and Miss Nora E. Pettus. Dr. and Mrs. Pettus built their home on Douglas Road. Dr. Pettus was said to be very devoted to his profession and never denied medical assistance to any man, rich or poor, Negro or White. In 1905, Dr. Pettus was attending a reunion for the Confederate Veterans in Louisville Kentucky when he became ill. He contracted pneumonia and died a few weeks later on August 13, 1905. It was reported that his funeral, held in Rep, attracted the largest crowd of people ever assembled for a funeral in Madison County. The mourners included the scores of his patients, black and white. He and Mrs. Pettus were buried in the Pettus Cemetery in Monrovia.[400]

Smith, Mollie; Lynched.
Mollie Smith was born in Alabama, in 1853. Her parents were born in Kentucky. She was married to Jessie Smith, black and was born in 1858, in Kentucky. They had a daughter, Ida, who was born in 1879. In the home with the Smiths was a sister-in-law, Malinda Lacky, born 1862, a mulatto. Mollie's older daughter by another marriage also lived in the home. She was Lizzie Drake, born in Alabama in 1873.[401]

---

[400] *Medicine Bags and Bumpy Roads*, pages 149-151, Goldsmith & Fulton, Valley Publishing Co., 1985.
[401] United States Federal Census, Madison County, Alabama, Enumeration District 198, Beat 9 & 11—page 86-line 87.

Chapter Five
Elijah Clark

THE WEEKLY MERCURY

HUNTSVILLE, ALABAMA, WEDNESDAY JULY 25 1900

VOL II

ELIJAH CLARK, NEGRO RAPIST, TAKEN FROM JAIL AND HANGED

Mob Surrounded the Jail in the Morning and Remained all Day.

TAR AND FEATHERS USED TO SMOKE DEFENDERS OUT

Sheriff Fulgham Was Rescued from Jail in Semi Unconscious Condition.

Mob Then Took Possession of the Building and Broke into the Negroes Cell—Clark Taken Out to Moore's Grove Where He Was Hanged.

Sheriff Oscar Fulgham.

At the hands of a quiet and orderly but determined mob of one thousand men, Elijah Clark a negro boy twenty years old, last evening paid the extreme penalty for a criminal assault Sunday afternoon upon a white girl. The negro was taken out of jail after the sheriff had been overcome by smoke, carried to the girl and identified and then taken to the Moore grove, near Dallas and swung to a limb, his body being riddled with bullets. The body is at a late hour tonight swinging to a limb in a deserted grove and stands as a warning to other negroes who may have an idea of committing this crime.

Clark was guilty of one of the most dastardly offenses of assault ever committed in North Alabama. He caught smoke was boiling through the upper windows, and Sheriff Fulgham could be seen by his friends close to a window gasping for breath, Chief D. D. Overton, by rare tact and good judgment, worked his way by the guards and up the steps to where the sheriff was standing. After convincing him of the hopelessness of further resistance Mr. Overton assisted the now weakened but determined officer down the steps and carried him to city police headquarters where he was placed in charge of several physicians.

The suffocating power of the fumes from the barrel were demonstrated on Chief Overton, who, while exposed to them only a few moments was nearly overcome and it took him some time to recover.

Sledge Hammers and Chisels.

1900

Between 1897-1900, many interesting historical events happened in the World, the United States, the State of Alabama and locally in Madison County, Alabama.[401]

World

1897-1900—United States Battleship, Maine, docked in the harbor of Havana Cuba was blown up...United States declared war on Spain... American forces defeated Spanish at the *Battle of San Juan Hill*... The War ended with the *Treaty of Paris*... Aspirin was introduced as a new modern medicine... China revolted against foreign domination in the Boxer Rebellion; however they failed to rid their country of the foreign devils... Monet began his famous series of paintings with *The Water-Lily*... Picasso exhibited his paintings for the first time... Potter authored *The Tale of Peter Rabbit*... Conrad authored *Lord Jim*... Rimsky-Korsakov composed *The Flight of the Bumblebee*... The first Browning revolvers were manufactured.

United States

William McKinley was re-elected President and Theodore Roosevelt was elected the vice-president... America was snatched away from *Isolationism* and established as a world power because of the Spanish-American War... What was called the *"Splendid Little War for the rich,"* ended in three months... A laboratory for the study of cancer opened... The first tuberculosis hospital opened... An Act by Congress established the Food and Drug Administration... United States annexed Hawaii and Wake Island... Congress enacted the Gold Standard... Charles Gibson painted the *Gibson Girl*... L. Frank Baum authored *The Wonderful Wizard of Oz*... Telephone lines across the United States exceeded one million miles of wire... The United States population was 76 million... The first Gideon Bible was placed in hotels...Casey Jones died at the throttle of his *Cannonball Express*... The vacuum cleaner was invented... Ten-thousand people were killed in Galveston, Texas during the nation's most violent hurricane, called the "Hurricane of the Century."

---

[401] Information was gathered from local and state history books and local newspapers. Information was also obtained from, *A Dream Come True Vol. II*, James Record, 1978, John Hicklin Printing Co. Huntsville, Alabama, Library of Congress Card Number:76-11880.

State

Joseph F. Johnston of Jefferson County was the Governor for two terms... The place where Jefferson Davis was inaugurated at the Capital was identified with a gold star... Camps were set up with the supplies needed for the Spanish American War... A law was passed prohibiting children under fourteen and women from working at dangerous jobs... Eight out of ten Alabamians still lived in rural areas... The years from 1890-1900 were called the *Decade of the Cotton Mills*... Most farmers were sharecroppers; they mortgaged their crops to the landowner... Railroad competition slowly drove the steamboats out of business... Locks were built to tame the Coosa River...Improvements were made on the Tennessee River, including the construction of canals, locks, dams... Barbecues, box suppers, fish fry's and watermelon cuttings were popular... Concerts, stage plays, lectures, black-faced minstrel shows and grand operas were the rage.... A popular name for lectures was Chautauquas.

Local

The public demanded that no jail be built near the Big Spring Branch; it was decided that the new jail would be built on the Old East Clinton lot... The Huntsville Rifles became the local Company K of the National Guard; Robert L. Hay was elected the Captain... 12,000 Spanish-American soldiers were stationed all over the town of Huntsville... The Second Brigade Hospital was stationed in Moore's Grove... At the end of the War 10,000 Madison Countians gathered on the South side of the Square, December 1, 1898 to donate a horse to General Joseph Wheeler... The electric car line called a *streetcar* was started; rails were laid around the Courthouse... A town ordinance was passed to prevent hitching livestock to the Courthouse fence... There was flooding for five miles below the Big Spring... Ground was broken for the Merrimack Mill... Women were not allowed to enter a swimming pool or a billiard room... The temperature fell to 17 degrees below zero during the winter... 500 houses were under construction in Huntsville in 1899... A destructive fire spread through the downtown district, apparently started in the livery stable on Clinton Street... Dallas Mills was constructed.

Chapter Five
Elijah Clark-1900

There was widespread poverty in Huntsville and throughout the South, during the period of reconstruction. Leaders began pursuing northern investors and industry. The South had an abundance of cotton just waiting to be manufactured into finished goods. The cotton mill was the answer. Whether the mills saved the South or simply exploited an underpaid workforce has still not been decided.[402]

The Dallas Mills, Huntsville, Ala.

In 1881, the Huntsville Cotton Mill, a cotton-spinning mill, was constructed near the Memphis & Charleston depot.

Michael and James O'Shaughnessy organized prominent Huntsville citizens into a company that eventually constructed Dallas Mills with a work force of over two thousand.

---

[402] It should be noted that most of the information for this book was found in the weekly newspapers that were published during July and August of 1900. They were; *The Weekly Mercury, The Weekly Tribune, The Evening Tribune, The Journal* and *The Weekly Democrat*. Each fact will not be repetitiously footnoted individually. Other facts were gathered from legal and personal records, and they will be noted in the footnotes.

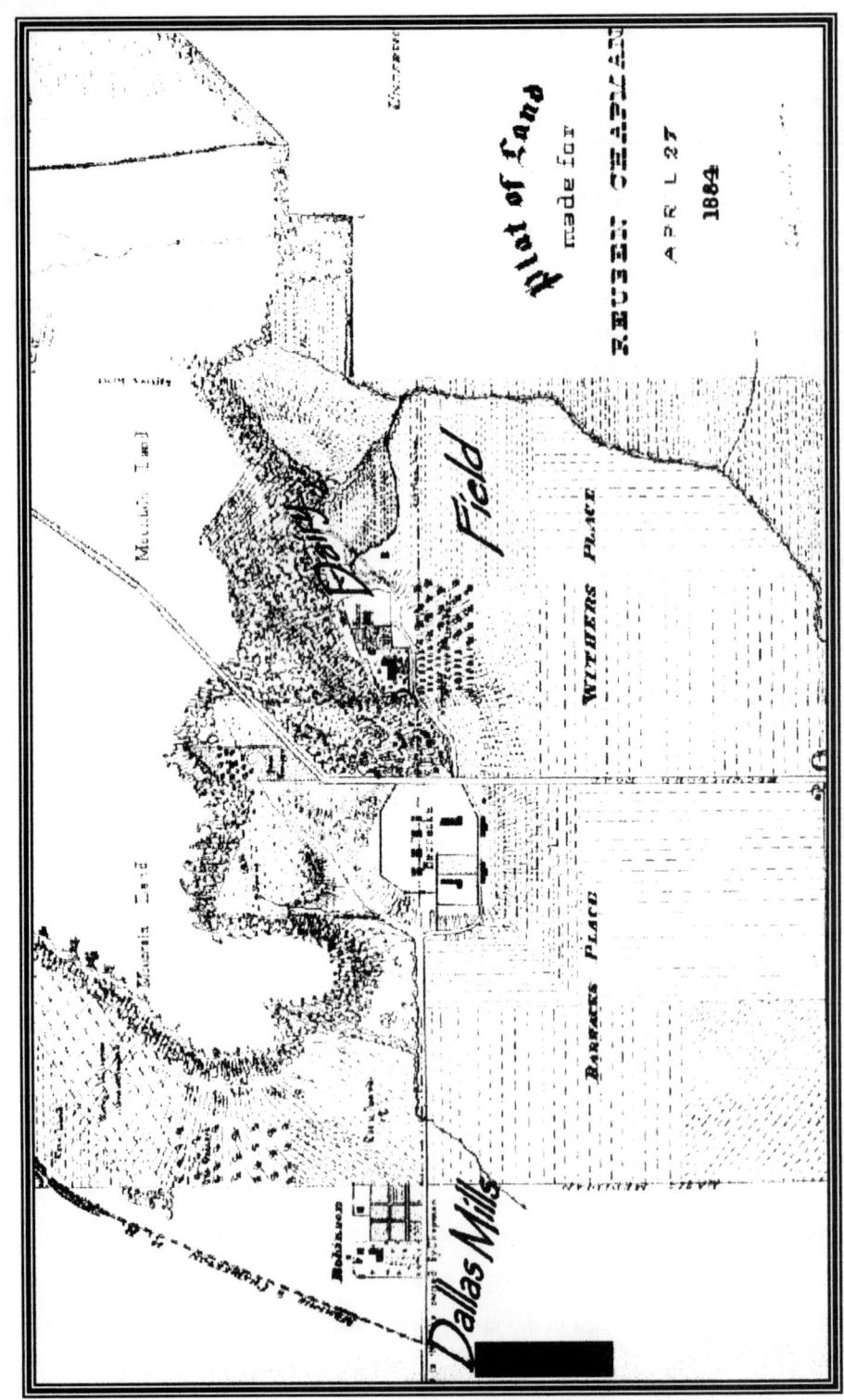

Huntsville-Madison County Public Library

Dallas Mill was chartered to manufacture cotton and woolen goods and fabrics instead of cotton yarn. Construction on the building began in 1891. Operations began in 1892. By 1894, 516 employees ran 25,000 spindles and 704 looms. The building was doubled in size in 1899.

New workers were needed and they arrived from the county and from out of state. The city's population increased in a steady stream. The majority included semiskilled or unskilled workers willing to work long hours for low wages. Long-time residents viewed the mill workers as non-residents.

The mill owners constructed cheap company housing in rows of identical duplexes. The mill villages were self-contained entities where the owners of the mills controlled the lives of the workers from the cradle to the grave.

Dallas Mill was located northeast of Huntsville, with a Company community[403] surrounding it. This community had churches, a store, a post office, and the later Rison School, all built in Moore Grove. The mill was named after, Trev B. Dallas, one of its major investors and the first general manager.[404]

Tracy W. Pratt arrived in Huntsville from South Dakota to construct the West Huntsville Cotton Mill just outside the city limits, near Triana Boulevard. Merrimack Mill was Huntsville's third mill. Because the mills were constructed outside the city limits, it was necessary to plan a streetcar system that would link Dallas Mill Village and Merrimack. The streetcar created the suburbs.

In 1900, Pratt secured five cotton mills for Huntsville. They were: Lowe Mill, Rowe Knitting Mill; Rowe Mill joined with and became West Huntsville Cotton Mill and Eastern Mills and Dallas Mill. This was Huntsville's turn of the century development.

Negroes had always been resented, but mill workers were resented, also. They represented a new group of lower class workers, ones not born in Huntsville. However, their lower class money was not resented. The signs of expansion and improvement in the town could be seen everywhere. There were new stores, hotels, churches and schools. The living conditions of the upper class improved because of the wages of the mill workers. Huntsville had mansions on Echols Hill and Adams Avenue that were within a mile of the mills, but separated by much more than distance. The mills seemed to bring

---

[403] It was first called Lawrence Village.
[404] This area is now part of the city of Huntsville.

them closer in some ways, because the upper and middle class Huntsvillians depended on the mills for their livelihood.

The men's boring work at the mills sometimes was relieved by acts of violence. Assaults or shootings were not uncommon, and on weekends, drinking in the local bars was considered a normal pastime. Carrying a concealed weapon was considered a natural freedom. Mill workers were sensitive and easy to take offense. Women had no standing in the villages except that given them by dominating men.[405] [406] [407]

Fred B. Simpson

Mill house on Humes looking toward Dallas Mill

---

[405] *Northern Dollars for Huntsville Spindles*, Patricia H. Ryan, Huntsville Planning Department, 1983.
[406] *Mine, Mill and Microchip*; Wayne Flynt, Windsor Publication, Inc., Northridge, California, 1987.
[407] Changing Huntsville, 1890—1899, Elizabeth Humes Chapman.

It was a hot day, but it was always hot in July and besides, everyone was used to the heat. People would talk about how bad it was while they sat in the shade and fanned themselves. Cultured Southerners have always known not to be outside during the noonday heat. Only the poor and foolish worked at midday. The land would be quiet and still as if it were midnight. People could sometimes catch a cool breeze to cool off. They would remember the cold of the winters, when they would sit by the fire and roast on one side and freeze on the other. It helped remind them that the heat wasn't so bad.

The brick building that housed Dallas Mill could be seen by looking from the porch of mill village homes. Indeed, the building could be seen from just about anywhere in the mill village and even beyond, almost to downtown Huntsville.[408] The village consisted of homes that could hardly be identified one from the other.[409]

Children playing on the wooden floors of the house caused a hollow sound that echoed back from the ceiling and across the porch. It was Sunday afternoon, July 24, 1900, in Dallas Mill Village.

Huntsville-Madison County Public Library

Children who worked at Dallas Mill

---

[408] The view remained the same until the Dallas Mill building burned in 1991.
[409] There are some streets where the old mill houses still remain, that still look the same. With renovation and construction, they are fast disappearing.

Mrs. Helen Priest lived on Humes Avenue, a street that stretched for almost a mile through the village. Helen's husband had died and she was left with several children: sons, Will, Greenberry, Marion, Richard, and Woodard; and daughters, Susan and Nellie. Helen Priest had moved from Bedford County, Tennessee, to Huntsville looking for work, and had lived in Huntsville for about a year. All her children worked in the Dallas Mill except for her ten-year-old daughter, Nellie.

Susan, age thirteen, worked at the mill, as did most of the children of the village. It was Sunday, and she was not working. She left home with her little ten-year-old sister, Nellie, to pick strawberries near the base of Chapman Mountain. They went through the fields, past the Huntsville Brick Company almost to the Monte Sano Dairy.[410]

After picking strawberries, the girls started home. On the return trip, they passed by the Huntsville Brick Company and entered a wheat field when Elijah Clark, and another Negro youth, approached them near a plumb thicket.

Elijah Clark, age twenty, lived and worked with his father, Peter Clark, on a farm near the dairy. Elijah was also a driver of one of the wagons at the Monte Sano Dairy.[411] He was not a big boy, standing 5' 6" and weighing only 140 pounds. He had always been regarded as a peaceful citizen. He was dressed in a dark calico shirt, dark pants with yellow stripes, tan shoes and a white straw hat.

The girls were not afraid; Negroes were not to be feared, in fact they were part of the community and everyday life. They passed them every day. Clark lived in this part of town. The girls knew him. However, this time was not to be like any other chance encounter.

As Clark came near the girls, they saw that he had a knife in his hand. Both girls screamed. The other Negro youth,[412] having no evil purpose, fled quickly and was soon out of sight. The younger girl, Nellie, ran screaming toward home. There was no attempt by Clark to stop the little girl.

Left alone with Suzie, Clark showed no fear and grabbed Susie Priest by the neck straight away, saying he would kill her and cut her heart out, "*if she made any further noise or alarm.*" Though

---

[410] The foundations of the dairy are all that remain of the once thriving business. The ruins are located off Dairy Lane in the Chapman Heights Subdivision of Northeast Huntsville.

[411] *The Birmingham News* (July 23, 1900) reported that he worked for the Huntsville Brick Company.

[412] This person was never questioned or identified.

she struggled, he overpowered her and threw her to the ground. She screamed and he began choking her. As he choked her near death he told her he would cut her throat if she did not hush.[413]

Clark made a few slashes at the girl with his knife and cut a hole in her sleeve but did not cause any flesh wound. He dragged the frightened girl up a ditch and while she was almost unconscious, to use the terms of the times, *"ravished or outraged"* her. After he had accomplished *"his fiendish and vile purpose,"*[414] he told her to go home or he would kill her. He then set off in the direction of the dairy and fled into the mountains.[415]

"If captured, it was very unlikely that he would ever reach the jail."[416]

This was reported, at the time, as one of the most horrendous or revolting offenses of assault ever committed in North Alabama and was heinous and most repulsive.

Nellie ran home as fast as her little legs would carry her. When she reached Dallas, she told her mother and those men present what had happened to her sister. The men started at a run for the wheat field. In a few minutes the men reached their destination, but by this time the assault was over and Clark was gone. Some of the men made arrangements to take Susan to her mother's home. She was found in an unconscious state where Clark left her, and was taken home on a stretcher.

Arriving at her mother's home, she told the story of the assault. When she recovered sufficiently to do so, she gave the name of her assailant[417] and a perfect description of him. Later, in a timid and feeble way, she also told her story to a reporter for *The Weekly Tribune*.

Dr. McKelby and Dr. E. D. Burwell were called in to dress Susan's wounds. They found Clark's fingerprints on her throat. Medical treatment was given and the doctors' pronounced the injuries serious but said that the young lady would recover. She spent the night comfortably, considering the nature of her injuries.[418]

The men did not wait for the doctors' medical report, nor did they wait for officers of the law to be informed. A group of more than a hundred men was formed and swiftly started in pursuit of Clark.

---

[413] *The Birmingham News* (July 23, 1900).
[414] Ibid.
[415] *The Weekly Tribune* (July 25, 1900).
[416] *Birmingham News* (July 23, 1900).
[417] She must have been acquainted with him to have known his name.
[418] There is no statement that she was raped.

Within a short period of time the entire male population of the Mill Village had taken up arms and surrounded the mountains in the direction Clark had taken. However, they were almost an hour behind Clark and were quickly losing any chance of finding the assailant.

Night fell and the armed men were still searching through the mountain and surrounding countryside. Most southern men owned a variety of guns and understood how to use them. They shouted to one another and gathered in groups to plan, drink whiskey, and talk about where to look next. Many had torches to light the way. The suspect would have had little chance for justice if found by this angry group of hunters in the darkness.

Sheriff Fulgham was notified and arrived upon the scene. He offered a reward of fifty dollars for the arrest and safe delivery of Clark to the county jail. The law officers joined the search for Clark but it was their intent to make Clark their prisoner and deliver him to the courts for justice to be carried out.

Some men went to Clark's home, near the dairy, and questioned Peter Clark, the boy's father. They asked him if his son had been there and he said, no. Men were then stationed around his home all night in case Elijah returned home.

Sheriff Fulgham and his deputies searched through the mountains, but returned to the city by nine o'clock. When Clark was not found, they knew he had escaped and would be a long way from the area. Being experienced law officers, they knew that the best way to locate Clark was by asking others where he might be, and by looking for him at the home of his relatives. They separated and started on the trail, each with plans to search locations where Clark might be hiding with family. Sheriff Fulgham was so sure that Clark would be captured that he returned to the city to make arrangements to receive his prisoner at the jail.

Deputies Jack Jamar and Robert Phillips were selected to search for Clark at his uncle's home in the north part of the county. One officer took a buggy to be used by the soon-to-be prisoner, while Deputy Jamar rode his horse. They made their way to the Meridianville neighborhood, north of Huntsville and eight miles from the wheat field at Dallas. The two deputies followed Clark's trail another two miles northwest to Walter Otey's farm. They made a few inquires there and after crossing Beaver Dam Creek[419] soon arrived at the home of Will Jasper, Clark's uncle. They had been out all night.

---

[419] See the map in Chapter Four.

Huntsville-Madison County Public Library
Dallas Mill can be seen in the background behind the wheat field

At daybreak, they parked their buggy and horses away from the house. They watched for some time but nothing moved in or about the small place. They knocked on the door and announced themselves as officers of the law. The family denied that Clark was there. The officers decided they would search the home anyway. In one of the rooms, they saw two boys in bed that appeared to be in a very strange posture. When the officers investigated, they found Clark concealed in the covers under the boys. Clark had gone to the home during the night and asked his cousins to hide him. The cousins made an attempt to conceal Clark by laying on him and covering themselves with bed covers. The officers unceremoniously pulled Clark out of bed and hustled him out of the house.

He did not give any resistance as he was questioned. He acknowledged that he was Elijah Clark, and that he was expecting the officers as he had been in a little fight, in town, during the day with two little white girls and had to knock one of them in the head. This was an admission that he had committed an assault on Susan Priest.

He came along with the officers, peaceably enough, and the group left for Huntsville at about six o'clock that morning. Clark was placed in the buggy while Deputy Jamar went ahead to Huntsville. He notified the Sheriff that Clark had been found and was coming into town with Deputy Phillips through the western part of the county. They were expected to come into Pulaski Pike at Nance's store.

Sheriff Fulgham met Deputy Phillips a few miles out from the city. The Sheriff along with Deputy Jamar and others moved down Church Street and turning on Arm Street reached the jail in a round about way. Clark was placed in a cell on the third floor at about eight o'clock that morning. There was hope that the "mill boys" would not learn of the jailing. Deputy Phillips reported to the Sheriff that Clark had been alone in the buggy with him on the drive from town. They had talked and Clark had confessed to the crime. The Deputy said that while confessing Clark gave the excuse, with an expression of pride, that he knew his victim was a poor cotton mill girl. He thought the crime would be insignificant and nothing would be done about it.[420]

A newspaper reporter was waiting for Sheriff Fulgham when he arrived at the jail. The Sheriff told him that he hoped there would be no trouble, but prospects were gloomy. The officers believed that the mill village men would try to harm the prisoner. The prospects became gloomier when the Sheriff or his deputy told the press and others about the prisoner's statement that cast such disrespect on the mill village people.

The Sheriff, recognizing the gravity of the situation, placed a strong guard at the jail. Several citizens were deputized, armed and placed on watch about the jail premises. The guards would soon be needed and were placed in line just in time to meet the first of the small crowd that was beginning to gather at the jail. The news of the prisoner's capture had spread through the community to many of the mill workers.

By nine o'clock Monday morning, as the rays of the sun beat down upon the east side of the jail at the corner of Clinton and Green Street, the lawless element made their presence felt. Just as soon as it became known that Clark had been put in jail, a crowd of people gathered on the corner of Washington and Clinton Streets, just one block from the jail. Some wild talk occurred and the prevailing sentiment was that Clark should be taken out of the jail and lynched in the presence of his victim. The crowd stood around, apparently waiting for a leader to appear. No leader appeared and no action was taken, but the crowd did not leave all day.

As the town began to wake up, news spread and the townspeople went to watch the excitement and see what would happen next. The presence of all these people gave courage to those who would eagerly take the law into their own hands.

The crowd grew.

---

[420] The two were alone and we have only the word of the officer that such a statement was made. The confession could have been tested in a court of law.

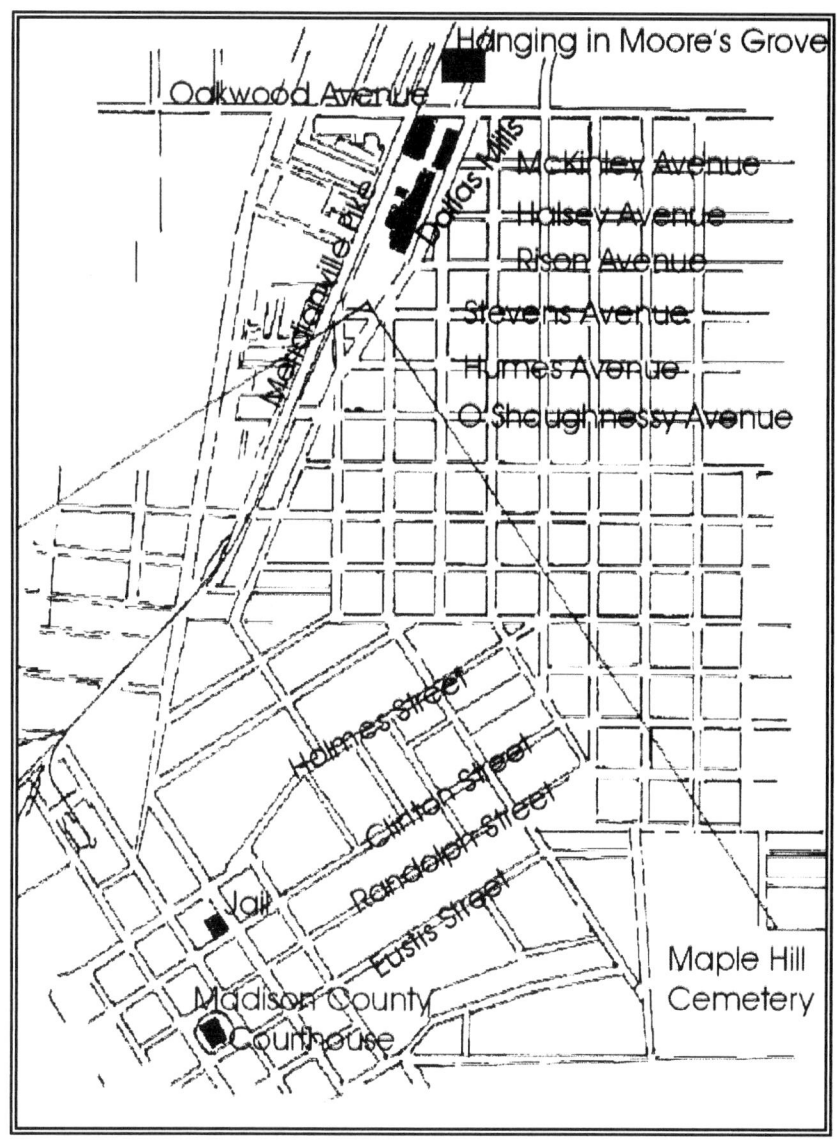

Fred B. Simpson
1900 Cross-section of a map of downtown Huntsville

One Negro on the outskirts of the crowd made the remark that he had six pistols that would be shot empty before the crowd could take the prisoner. Some white men heard this and made a rush for him. He lost no time in getting away and was not seen afterwards.

Sheriff Fulgham saw that he had a mean crowd on his hands and placed guards in the jail armed with Winchester shot guns. The scatter-guns would fire small shot, but in a wide pattern. The intent was not to kill anyone, but to discourage any violence by the crowd.

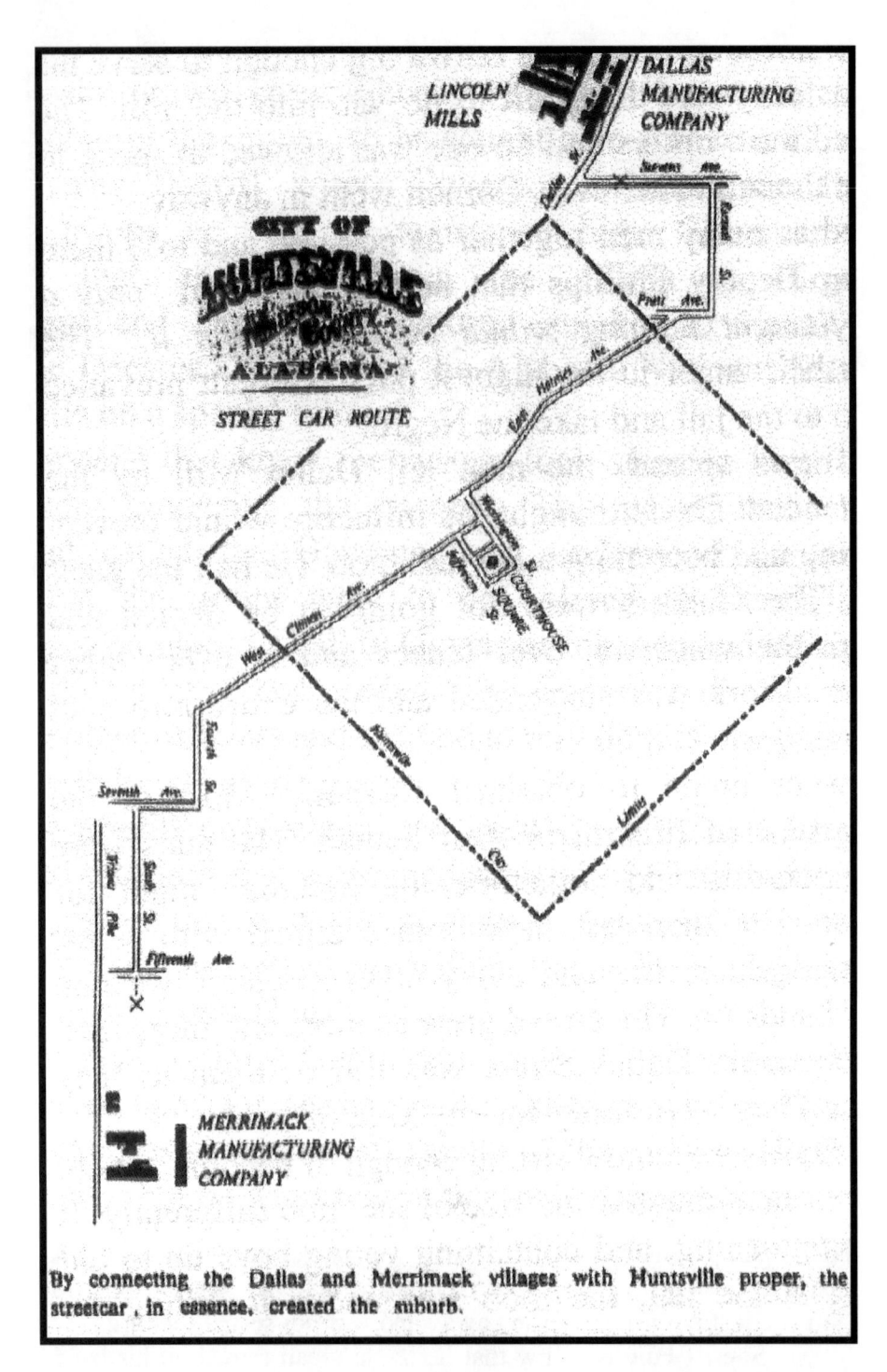

Permission granted from the Huntsville Planning Department

(Map of the streetcar system that connected the two mill villages)

As the crowd grew, Sheriff Fulgham knew that his force could not control the crowd, so he sought help from the Governor of Alabama. The Sheriff wired Governor Johnson the facts and requested troops be sent to assistance him. Governor Johnson responded that he had ordered the militia at Birmingham, Montgomery and Decatur to proceed quickly to Huntsville. He ordered the Decatur Company of the Alabama National Guard to go to Huntsville on a special train.

Someone who knew the system took steps to keep the State soldiers from protecting the prisoner. This person knew that the Sheriff had called the Governor and understood the procedure necessary for troops to be ordered to Huntsville. This unknown person placed a call to Governor Johnson and informed him that the soldiers were not needed. The Governor did not bother to check with other officials, and seemed to rely on this one phone call to order the withdrawal of the troops.

The Sheriff next telephoned local Circuit Court Judge S. M. Stewart and told him that an immediate trial of Clark was necessary. The judge replied that he would arrange for a special session of court at three o'clock that afternoon before Judge H. C. Speake in the Madison County Court House.

The local National Guard unit, under the command of Captain Hay, was called upon for assistance, but failed to appear. There would be several excuses given for this failure of the military to perform its duty to the city, but no good reason was ever forthcoming.

The mob grew to alarming proportions. The Sheriff appeared at an upstairs window of the jail overlooking Clinton Avenue and made an attempt to stop the crowd. He announced that a special trial had been scheduled for the prisoner and he would be placed before the court at three o'clock that afternoon. The crowd greeted this statement with jeers. Someone in the crowd hollered up to the Sheriff to hand over the keys. He refused saying that the mob would have to kill him to get them. The crowd grew larger and became angrier.

James Cornatt, a well-known local contractor who resided at Dallas, seemed to have become the leader of the crowd at the jail. He demanded that the prisoner be given over to the men of the mill village. The Sheriff again refused. Cornatt realized he did not have the men necessary to take the jail. He walked through the crowd and made his way out to the Dallas Mill.

He began to stop men on the street and tell them about the situation at the jail, but there was not a crowd big enough to serve his purpose. There was only one thing left to do. Go into the mill. The overseers controlled the workers and no one was allowed to speak to any workers inside the mill. However, Cornatt went in anyway. These men had had very little sleep because of their long nights search, but most had reported for duty that morning at the mill to work their shift.

He gathered as many men together as possible and told them about Clark telling Deputy Phillips that he had assaulted *"only a factory girl and thought nothing would be done about it."* The statement aroused their anger to the highest pitch. Cornatt prevailed upon the men to go to the jail and take the Negro.

When the news spread, the men left Dallas Mill by the hundreds. Superintendent Davis thought his influence would prevent the men from leaving and becoming a lawless mob. He had the gates and doors locked. However, the workers were not going to be denied and they simply left through the windows, over fences and in every other conceivable manner. Work was suspended and the entire mill shut down.

The men went home to obtain weapons. Most of the workers kept some type of firearm in their house. The guns were used for hunting, contests and sometimes, on Saturday night, for shooting each other. The men left their homes armed with rifles, shotguns, pistols, sledgehammers and every other available weapon they could lay their hands upon. The crowd grew as more and more men ran to join the excitement. Dallas Street was full of them as they headed toward town. They were ready for any kind of trouble.

The men of Dallas were now strong enough to become a mob. Those who were present estimated the size of the mob differently. It was continually strengthening, and containing young boys and old men. Upon arriving at the jail, the mob surrounded it, filling the streets, even around to the corner of Clinton Avenue and Washington Street. Every street leading to the jail was lined with people watching the action. The street was impassable for a block each way. Huntsville Police Chief David Overton was seen in the crowd.

While there were grave fears and apprehensions expressed among the citizens, that did not stop them from rushing from their homes or business to watch the action. News of the mob spread throughout the town and business completely stopped. Most business houses closed and everyone went to watch the goings on down at the jail. Thousands of people witnessed the first mob trouble that had been in Huntsville for years. A great excitement prevailed. Guns, pistols, and other weapons were seen everywhere. It was feared that blood would flow freely.[421]

Drawing that appeared in the *Birmingham News* (July 25, 1900).
Caption under the drawing reads:
The Madison county Jail—Scene at Monday's Lynching at Huntsville. The Crowd Drawing Back From an Expected Explosion of Dynamite.

Either Chief Overton or Mayor Moore had every saloon in town closed that morning to minimize the number of drunks and they remained closed until the trouble ended. A great deal of drinking had been done privately and was still going on as the men passed their bottles around. The mob pushed and shoved their way to and from the jail. There was constant shouting and the noise was loud enough to be heard all over town. The men chewed tobacco, cussed, bragged and waved their guns![422]

---

[421] *Birmingham News* (July 23, 1900).
[422] *Birmingham News* (July 25, 1900).

Judge S. M. Stewart met with the leader of the mob about half past ten o'clock and attempted to work out a plan to prevent violence to the jail. Immediate action of the court was pledged. Cornatt still seemed to be the leader and confronted the Sheriff. With the men of the mill village behind him, he became more confident and demanding. Cornatt and other members of the mob demanded several times that the Sheriff hand over the keys to the jail. The Sheriff refused, saying that he could do no such thing under his oath and they would have to kill him to get the keys.

Being refused the keys, the mob began to make preparations to break into the jail. With encouragement from the onlookers, some of the men put a sledgehammer into use against the wooden door to the first floor. The front door did not last long and the mob cheered as the door burst open.

Jailer Connally and his wife kept their stand in the jail until the first floor door was battered down. Members of the mob who intended to remove them from the jail surrounded Mrs. Connally. She pled with the enraged men to let the law take its course and allow the prisoner to be tried in court. They ignored her. Members of the mob carried Mrs. Connally away.

As the door was broken down, the Sheriff and his deputies retreated to the stairs leading to the second floor. After milling around inside the first floor for some time, the mob made a rush for the iron bars and the line of deputies on the steps.

William Vining, an employee of the Streetcar Railway Company as an electric trimmer, was at the front of the mob when he attempted to rush up the steps. The deputies opened fire with their Winchester shotguns. The small shot came downward, peppering Vining's flesh in the shoulder and side, inflicting a painful wound. He was brought out of the mob, and taken to the Stegall Hotel where he received medical treatment from Dr. Frank May and Dr. Benton Hall. The physicians said the young man was not fatally hurt, but the wounds were serious. He came back out on the street as soon as his shoulder wounds were dressed, receiving cheers from the mob, and was later carried home. Vining was a well-known young man, being the brother to Miss Lillie Vining, one of the employees of a local newspaper, *The Evening Tribune*.

Another man was peppered with small shot but his name was not known.[423] The shooting by the officers checked the mob for a while but they did not leave the jail and continued to shout and

---

[423] *Birmingham News* (July 23, 1900).

display their weapons. Even the shotguns did not stop the mob for long and the Sheriff knew he had no real means to stop them.

Sheriff Fulgham was compelled to vacate the second floor and take refuge on the third floor of the new jail. He moved his prisoner with him. Clark was locked into one of the new steel cells. The Sheriff then locked himself in with his prisoner by locking the door to the stairway leading to that floor.

Huntsville-Madison County Public Library

Huntsville Fire Department in front of Fire Department

The mob made plans to smoke the Sheriff and his deputies out of the jail. Barrels of oil and tar were brought to the jail. The mob also found a large amount of sulfur and several bushels of feathers. All these items were placed in the barrels and set on the cement ground floor. A match was applied. A suffocating smoke arose and quickly spread through out the jail.

Sheriff Fulgham retreated to the corner farthest from the fire, taking his prisoner with him. More tar and feathers were brought in and added to the fire. The mob was in full possession of the ground floor and was seeking to gain control of the entire building. The community seemed to succumb to the power of the mob and stood around on the streets watching the action.

Seeing that the Sheriff would not, under any circumstances, allow them to get into the jail, the leaders of the mob decided to carry out their purpose in a different way. Several pounds of dynamite were brought to the jail. The mob began to burrow holes and lay dynamite under the walls. The leaders of the mob again hollered up to Sheriff Fulgham. They told him to surrender the keys or they would blow up the jail. Fulgham again, refused to turn over the keys. He and his deputies were warned to get out and bring the prisoner with them. The mob intended to blow up the jail or have Clark.

Ministers and prominent citizens opposed to violence, addressed the crowd and begged them to await the action of the law. The speakers might as well have been speaking to the wind. Captain Milton Humes attempted to speak from the front steps of the jail, but was frequently interrupted. Former Solicitor, Daniel Coleman also attempted to make a speech and was cried down. George T. Miller, W. R. Rison and John H Wallace Jr., made speeches in an endeavor to pacify the mob and prevent bloodshed but they also were hooted down. The mob would hear no more even though immediate action of the court was pledged. Mayor Moore also advised the crowd to disburse.

Judge Henry Clay Speake appeared on the jail steps and attempted to make a speech but was interrupted continuously. He begged the mob to follow the law and go home. He stated that he had received a telegram from Governor Johnston directing him to give Clark a speedy trial. He read the telegram to the crowd that promised a special term of court and ordered a jury impaneled immediately to try the prisoner. A member of the mob asked him when the trial could be held. The Judge stated that the trial would be that very afternoon. This had the effect of quieting the mob for half an hour.

After that time, James Cornatt, who had been with the mob all day, got on the steps and

Courtesy of the Speake Family
Judge Henry Clay Speake

stated that he had come to town with the full intention of getting Clark out of jail, but since an immediate trial was promised the mob

180

should disburse. He was frequently interrupted by cries of, *"Give us another leader!"*

Judge Speake stood on the jail steps surrounded by the crowd that stretched for blocks and continued to plead with the mob. The mob jeered at the judge, reminding him of past cases that had not gone as they felt they should. They named the Thompson case[424] [425] and the Decatur case,[426] and again returned to their tar barrel and dynamite.

About eleven o'clock a partial compromise was made between Judge Stewart and the leaders of the mob for a speedy trial for Clark, no later than three o'clock that afternoon in the Courthouse before Judge Speake. A promise was received from the leaders of the mob that they would not take any further action until after three o'clock, but the leaders of the mob swore that if the authorities did nothing by that time, the jail would be blown up by dynamite. The mob quieted down and seemed willing to await a trial of Clark at the appointed hour. The mob, however, did not leave the jail or move outside.

About noon, Mayor Moore received a telegram from Governor Jos. F. Johnston, that if danger no longer existed he was to

---

[424] Albert Thompson was a black member of the Tenth United States Cavalry, who was charged with the outrage of a white woman. The evidence indicated that the black soldier was at the home of Callie King, (not Miss or Mrs.) between 9 and 10 at night. After the *"commission of the deed,"* her husband, a hack driver, told a neighbor about the crime. He was advised to wait until the next day to report the offense. The next day the neighbor looked out the window of the woman's home and saw Thompson. He asked Callie if that was the man and she replied that she thought he was the man. That testimony was considered in error and caused a retrial. He was sentenced to life imprisonment after the conviction. He appealed and the case was sent back for a new trial. The outraged woman would not testify and Thompson plead to ten years imprisonment. 26 So. 141, 122 Ala. 12, Thompson v. State, (Ala. 1899)

[425] Solicitor Tancred Betts explained in a letter to *The Mercury*, that he paid for the victim expenses for trial and sent a hack to get her. She refused to testify. A member of the jury said, the case required a stretch of the evidence to convict at all and the Judge was doubtful of conviction. (*The Mercury*, 1900)

[426] The Decatur case involved three Negroes who detained a small white girl at their home several days. They were arrested and lodged in the Huntsville jail for safekeeping. A big mob gathered around the jail but was persuaded to let the law take its course. The Negroes were convicted and sentenced to death. Appeals were taken and no punishment had been inflicted on the date the mob came to get Clark. The Alabama Supreme Court later dismissed the appeal and the death sentence was ordered to continue. 23 SO. 1005, 118 ALA. 657, BUFORD V. STATE, (ALA. 1898)

wire Capt. Wallace in Decatur that he need not send his company of soldiers to Huntsville.

When the Mayor received the above telegram, he went to the Southern Depot and called Captain Wallace, to urge him to rush the troops to Huntsville, as there was imminent danger. He told him that Sheriff Fulgham was besieged in the jail and the town seemed to have succumbed to the will of the mob. Mayor Moore even went so far as to stand personally responsible for a special train to convey the troops from Decatur to Huntsville. Captain McAllister of the Southern Railway had all trains clear the track between Decatur and Huntsville to make way for a special train bringing the troops. The soldiers were ready to get on board at the Decatur depot and the engine and cars were ready.

Captain Wallace told Mayor Moore that the Governor had countermanded his orders. There was information received from someone in Huntsville that all excitement had ended. He could not move his troops without official orders from the Governor. When the facts became known, it was too late for the Governor to act.

The mob milled around and waited, but did not, as promised, wait until three o'clock. The dynamite *fiend* [sic] was to make its presence known.[427]

Shortly after noon, the first stick of dynamite was thrown up the main stairs of the jail. It exploded in the southwest corner of the entrance. The explosion did considerable damage to the stairs. Smoke and dust poured out of the doors and windows from the explosion. The sound of glass breaking and falling and breaking again as it hit the ground could be heard as every windowpane on the first and second floor was shattered. Every window in front of the building was blown out into the street. The explosion hurt no one but did renew the excitement for the onlookers. A great crowd was standing around the jail at the time and no one, of course, knew who threw the dynamite.

The mob took up the cry again and warned Sheriff Fulgham to come out with his deputies and prisoners. The Sheriff again firmly refused to come out but he knew he could not defend the jail against the mob. After considering the dangers, the Sheriff felt that he could not endanger the lives of his deputies. He gathered his men around him and told them that they could be dismissed and to leave the jail. All of the deputies put up their shotguns and left the jail, leaving the

---

[427] Called *fiend* in the *Weekly Mercury* (July 25, 1900).

Sheriff alone with the prisoners. Screams from prisoners could be heard for blocks, even over the noise of the crowd.

Judge Speake went to the Courthouse at two o'clock that afternoon, to organize a Grand Jury under the special term of court ordered by Governor Johnston. He summoned eighteen persons for a Grand Jury. He charged the Grand Jury that a rape had been committed and the accused person was in jail and that they were to consider his case.

The Grand Jury was impaneled at half past two o'clock.[428] Judge Speake charged the jury as to their duties under the law and by three o'clock that afternoon the Grand Jury began their investigation.

At half past three o'clock, Judge Speake left the Courthouse and hurried to the jail. Poisonous smoke was boiling through the upper windows. The Judge again mounted the steps and stated that he had impaneled a special Grand Jury and that Clark would be tried on Wednesday. Judge Speake stated that he would be forced to wait until four o'clock when the Grand Jury was expected to make a report and return an indictment. It would take an hour for the system to follow the law. This was unsatisfactory to the mob and more oil was placed in the jail and another fire started.

The mob from Dallas was not interested in the law or the system.

Sheriff Fulgham could be seen close to a window gasping for breath. The mob kept the fire going and did not take note of the cries coming from the cells. Repeated appeals were made to the Sheriff to come out of the jail. His friends had gone to the jail and begged him to get out of the building. To all these appeals, he answered *"Dispense the mob and I will come out like a man."*

More tar and feathers had been ignited and the smoke was enough to stifle any human being. They did not pay attention to the pitiful cries of the prisoners who felt they would be burned alive.

After an hour of deliberation, the Grand Jury made a report at a few minutes past four o'clock returning an indictment against Elijah Clark, charging him with rape. A *petit jury* would have to be drawn, the prisoner arraigned, and given one day's notice before trial. It was Monday and the trial was set for Wednesday.

The system was too slow. The mob would not wait. It was too late.

---

[428] The jury was composed of the following well known citizens: George C. Patterson, John McCalley, S. S. Darwin, H. P. Turner, E. R. Matthews, Christ McDonald, W. T. Rolf, W. D. Steger, John Stoner, C. C. Anderson, James Vaughan, E. M. Gives, L. R. Wellman and Bob Wade.

At four o'clock, Huntsville Police Chief, David D. Overton seemed, at last, to realize the serious situation in which Sheriff Fulgham was placed. He begged the leaders of the mob to allow him to go up the stairs and rescue the Sheriff. He told the mob that the Sheriff was by this time most likely suffocated. The Sheriff's absence from the third floor window indicated that he might be smothered. The members of the mob reluctantly agreed to allow the Sheriff to be brought down.

Overton worked his way through the crowd of men and dashed though the dense volume of smoke and gas. Once inside the jail he made his way up the steps leading to the upper floors. He found the Sheriff in a state of semi-consciousness overcome with the heat and gases and almost unable to speak.

Chief Overton had considerable trouble in getting the Sheriff to leave his prisoners and the jail. The Sheriff said that he preferred to die rather than desert his post.

"Oscar, you must get out of here," said the Chief, *"or you will die." "Go back, Dave, I must stay here and protect this man. I am willing to die by my duty!"*[429] said the plucky Sheriff.

Overton convinced the Sheriff of the helplessness of further resistance and the Sheriff finally consented to leave the jail. Chief Overton forced the Sheriff to come out with him. The heat was intense and the Sheriff's condition was quite serious. The two men unlocked the cells holding women prisoners and brought all of them out with them. The women were overcome and in serious condition when they arrived on the street. The male prisoners were left alone with their suffering. The Sheriff did all he could to protect the remainder of the prisoners when he locked every cell and took every key and threw them away.

Overton assisted the now weakened officer down the steps, carried him through the mob and up Clinton Street one block to the corner of Washington where City Hall and the police headquarters were located. There the Sheriff was placed in the care of Doctors Lowry and Darwin.

The suffocating powers of the fumes from the barrels were devastating. Chief Overton was exposed to the fumes only a few moments but was nearly overcome. It took him some time to recover. He was burned about the face and eyes and suffered considerably from the effect of the smoke and heat.

---

[429] *The Age-Herald* (July 24, 1900) Birmingham, Alabama.

After the Sheriff was taken out there was no opposition left. The mob was in complete control and took possession of the jail. They battered down every door that obstructed the search for their victim. The men arrived on the third floor but could not find a key to any of the cells.

Clark was in a modern steel cage and there was no way to get him out except by breaking the lock. This would be a hard job but the mob was determined to open the door. Men went outside to search for a chisel. There were plenty of sledgehammers among the mob. The work was done in a confined space, as there was only the narrow hallway in front of the cell that could be used. The hall was crowded but the men soon organized the work. One man held the chisel while other men took turns with the sledgehammer. The noise vibrated up and down the hall and through the steel cells. The sound of the sledgehammer hitting the chisel against the steel of the lock could be heard up and down the streets in front of the jail.

As the men neared the end of their task, Jailer Connelly offered the key to the cell, hoping to save the new cage, but the men refused and continued with their work. The lock of the fine steel cage was broken after an hour of hard labor.

While the men were at work, Clark crouched in a corner at the back of the cell, in plain view, watching the men work on the lock.

The mob entered the cell just minutes before five o'clock. Several men brought Clark out of the cell and took him down stairs to the first floor. Before coming out of the jail with Clark a member of the mob mounted the jail steps and said: *"Now gentlemen you must put up your guns; We don't want anyone to fire a shot because we don't want any blood spilled. We are going to hang this man in Dallas and if no one interferes, none will be hurt."*[430]

This request was carried out, and the work was done in a very orderly manner. Clark was brought out of the door and appeared on the front steps of the jail behind about twenty men armed with rifles, followed by an equal number men in the rear. A plow line was around his neck and the members of the mob dragged him along. They dragged him out of the jail yard and into the street. The crowd parted to let them pass.

He attempted to walk but was repeatedly pulled off his feet. Clark was dragged down the street by the shouting mob. Hundreds of

---

[430] *The Weekly Mercury* (July 25, 1900).

people who wanted to witness the killing followed them. The crowd soon grew to at least two thousand people and began the march out to Dallas, a distance of one-mile. By the time the village was reached, the crowd exceeded six thousand. Ladies and children of Dallas and the town thronged about the scene.

Clark was taken down Humes Avenue to the home of Mrs. Priest. He was carried before Susie Priest and she identified him. The girl was asked if this was the Negro. She said, *"That's the man; I can prove it by Nellie."* Little sister, Nellie, also identified Clark as the guilty person who attacked her sister. The crowed filled the streets.

The identification complete, the victim was again taken into the street. He walked unaided for some distance and was dragged part of the way. The trembling young man lost all control of his legs and members of the mob were compelled to carry him. The mob took him up and carried him on their shoulders.

Their destination was a tree-filled-farm across Oak Avenue,[432] just north of the mill. This old grove of trees was part of the Moore family farm that had been made into a park for the mill employees. Moore's Grove had been decided upon as the place for the hanging. In the old grove the large trees shaded the grounds and it looked peaceful and quiet. It was not far from the spot where Clark was accused of attacking the girl. Clark arrived at the place of his soon-to-be untimely and violent death.

Among the estimated six thousand people surrounding the Grove were women and children who crowded in to watch the show. Some people pushed and shoved to get closer for a better look. Many hurried from town, afraid they would miss the action. Buggies lined the street.

One of the many horses from the crowd was borrowed and Clark was placed on the animal's back. The horse was led to an immense oak tree where Clark would end his life. Will Priest, the brother of the outraged girl, took one end of the rope around Clark's neck and threw it over a limb of the great oak and tied it securely.

After all the details had been taken care of, one of the leaders of the mob asked Clark if he had anything to say. Clark replied; *"I do not."* Some in the crowd checked their watches to remember that precisely at six minutes of six the horse was whipped and sprang out from under Clark. He dropped about three feet and began to die of strangulation. It took ten minutes for him to die. As he dangled and

---

[432] Known as Oakwood Avenue today.

danced, his body was riddled with bullets from half a hundred rifles, pistols and shotguns.

Clark had paid the extreme penalty for his alleged criminal assault upon a white girl. After the hanging, the crowd dispersed and seemed comparatively happy. Work at the Dallas mill was suspended for the day.[432]

The Decatur militia arrived, but was too late and returned home. It was believed that the Decatur militia went to Huntsville without any ball cartridges[433] intending to bluff the crowd. The company officers received censure for their lack of planning.[434]

The body was left hanging all that evening and throughout the night in the deserted grove to stand as a warning to other Negroes who might have an idea about committing this type of crime.

Large crowds thronged the grove during the night and the next morning to view the body.

The next morning at nine o'clock, the undertaker cut Clark's body down. The boy's father refused to have anything to do with his son's remains. The county authorities disposed of Clark's body.

Sheriff Oscar Fulgham was out on the street by sun-up the next morning. He was telling those interested that he held the jail against the mob, expecting every moment to be relieved by the arrival of troops from Decatur.

A notice in the *Birmingham News,* bearing the date July 24th, stated that an interview was had with Governor Johnston in which he said: *"I was in communication with the Mayor of Huntsville all along during the day; and I was under the opinion from information given me by that official, that nothing rash would be done."*

By noon, Mayor Moore had denounced the call to the Governor, stating that there was no eminent danger of Clark being hanged, as false. He gave the following statement to the press:

"I desire to state that I was in communication with the Governor several times during the day of the 23rd and in every instance implored him to furnish us troops, either from Scottsboro, Decatur, or Florence, and at no time during the day did I intimate there was no danger. I, at my own personal responsibility, had the agent of the Southern Railroad Road Co., send a telegraph to Capt. Pegriun at Memphis, and had a special train at Decatur to convey

---

[432] Details of the lynching from *American*, Baltimore, Md.(July 24, 1900); and *Herald,* New York, (July 24, 1900).
[433] Ammunition.
[434] *Birmingham News* (July 25, 1900).

the troops here from ten minutes after 2 o'clock till after 4 o'clock. And urged Capt. Wallace as late as half past 3 o'clock or nearly four to hurry up and come, when he informed me that his order to report here had been countermanded. If anyone informed the Governor that troops were not needed at any time during the day in my name, it was without my knowledge or sanction. I can prove my position in the matter by, R. A. Moore, Mgr. of the Bell Telephone Co., J. M. Samford, Agt., Southern R.R., and Capt. Wallace of Decatur. [Signed] Alfred Moore, Mayor."

The sentiment of those at Dallas over the lynching was reflected in the words of a citizen of that community.

"The human fiend has reaped his reward, and today while his body is dangling between heaven and earth the citizens of Dallas with light hearts and clear consciences are playing their different vocations in life. The people of Dallas showed the utmost gratification at the way in which the beastly crime was expiated. If such a performance could be deemed orderly, this lynching could be styled as such dating from the time Sheriff Fulgham was taken out of the jail."[435]

The fine new jail was badly wrecked by the mob and it was estimated that it would cost nearly two thousand dollars to pay for the damage. The doors, iron cage, locks and walls suffered heavy damage. The dynamite showed its handiwork in the defaced walls of the jail. However, the damage was much less than first reported.

A later report stated that, *"The county plays about even in the affair. The damage to the jail is just about the same amount in money as a special term of the Circuit Court would cost."*[436]

Reports were circulated by the *Mercury* that the Dallas Manufacturing Company would pay for all the damages. Members of the Dallas Manufacturing Company stated to the *Tribune* that any such report stating that the company would pay for the loss was not true. Trev Dallas was not even in the city and of course nothing could be done unless Trev Dallas was present.

Will Vining, the man shot while trying to enter the jail with the mob, was reported to be improving at the home of his mother in East Huntsville. His physician, Dr. Benton Hall, stated to a reporter that one hundred and sixty squirrel shot entered Vining from the right

---

[435] *The Weekly Mercury* (July 25, 1900).
[436] *Birmingham Age-Herald* (July 25, 1900).

thigh to the right shoulder and the good doctor was attempting to remove the shot. Vining had some fever, but his condition was not considered serious. Everyone was relieved.

Captain Robert Hay, of the Monte Sano Guards[437] said: *"The reason the Company did not materialize was that they had no orders."* He further remarked that the boys were all on hand ready for service. It is true, he said, *"we were short on ammunition and had only about one hundred cartridges. We did however, make two efforts to get cartridges."*

The editor of a local paper, *The Weekly Mercury*, thought this was reason enough. *"We think this statement exonerates Captain Hay and the Company, they could not act without orders. Having no orders, they were blameless."*

The same paper felt that the local community was not at fault—those living out of town were the cause of the problem. *"There was something radically wrong. Governor Johnston is wholly to blame for not getting the military here, or else Governor Johnston was duped."*

The *Evening Tribune* took the position that the local officials should have controlled the situation and prevented the lynching. *"Where were our police, by what sanction did they remain invective? Was there nothing occurring to invoke their interference."*

Fred B. Simpson
View of Dallas Mill from "The Tree" in Moore's Grove

---

[437] The local National Guard unit.

The *Mercury* resounded, "*Nothing occurred which called for interference by the city police. But something might have occurred if the hysterical editor of the Tribune had not scampered out of the crowd so rapidly at one period.*"

The *Mercury* stated that Clark deserved death, but not at the hands of a mob. Had the mob taken him before he was taken to jail no particular complaint would have been raised. Had the mob been more considerate they would not have dynamited the jail.

The *Weekly Democrat*[438] took the position that the city police "*had a grand opportunity of displaying their courage but they didn't take advantage of it. The people think well of the Sheriff for his actions. The crime of the Negro fiend was terrible, but when the wretch was in the hands of the Sheriff, in jail, under the control of the courts, the vile criminal should have been executed by law.*"

The *Journal* stated, "*The lawlessness will be handed down to posterity. The jail could have been protected. Huntsville should hang her head in shame. A precedent was established and a weakness was demonstrated.*"[439]

The *Birmingham News* stated, "*Huntsville's disgrace was enacted in a city claiming 10,000 inhabitants and setting itself up as one of the most progressive cultured in the South.*"[440]

Governor Johnson, in his statement, said that he felt sure the solicitor and the Grand Jury would make a careful investigation and take steps to apprehend the members of the mob.

An investigation would be needed to find out who sent the fake message to Governor Johnston causing him to countermand the order for State troops. A Grand Jury would convene the next Monday and make a full investigation of the lynching and return indictments against members of the mob. It was not believed that any indictments or convictions could be secured.

---

[438] The Weekly Mercury (August 1, 1900).
[439] *The Journal* (July 27, 1900), H. C. Binford and Sons; Editor; (a local black newspaper).
[440] *Birmingham News* (July 24, 1900).

Epilogue

William "Ed" Vining was an escaped felon from Texas when he was shot in Huntsville. He had served a term in the Texas penitentiary and was released only to commit a burglary within a few days. He was indicted and his extradition was requested from Alabama. In 1905, Thomas C. McLellan, a relative of a member of the Alabama Supreme Court, was sent from Texas to return Vining to that State. He was boarding the train with his prisoner when a Huntsville Justice of the Peace issued a Writ of Habeas Corpus to free Vining; then McLellan was arrested on a charge of kidnapping. The Law firm of Grayson and Grayson represented McLellan. After the District Attorney intervened, McLellan was freed, but Vining had skipped out on his bond and was not located. It seemed that Vining and his mother were friends of Sheriff A. D. Rodgers.[441]

It was reported that:

"There is no record of more daring, more manly, more self-sacrificing, or nobler or braver courage than that so dauntlessly and so heroically displayed by Oscar Fulgham, the Sheriff of Madison County, who yesterday placed his own noble life between the life of one infamous ruffian and the insane lawlessness of a mob, lustful of a man's blood!" [442]

However, at the next election, Sheriff Fulgham lost the Sheriff's race to A. D. Rodgers. He moved away from Huntsville and was only in the city as a visitor thereafter.

The cotton mill business declined and eventually Dallas Mills closed its doors, and was abandoned. A local real estate investor bought the property and attempted to turn it into a high tech shopping mall. However, before the plans could be finalized, the mill burned to the ground. The cause of the 1991 fire has never been determined.

Judge Samuel Morgan Stewart continued as Probate Judge until his retirement in November of 1904. He died, June 18, 1924, and was buried in Maple Hill Cemetery.

---

[441] Alabama Governor's Papers, Governor Jelks Correspondence, 1905; Letter from J. H. Arnold, District Attorney, Coryell County, Texas, regarding extradition of Vining's back to Texas to face charges. (The State of Alabama Department of Archives and History; Montgomery, Alabama)

[442] *The Birmingham News* (July 24, 1900).

Judge Henry C. Speake died December 8, 1900; his wife, Carrie, died March 20, 1906. They are buried in Maple Hill Cemetery.

Mayor Alfred Moore lost the next mayor's race, in 1903, to Thomas W. Smith.

Chief of Police David Overton was the Huntsville Police Chief from 1898 until 1907, when he resigned. He was elected to the position of Circuit Court Clerk in 1911, and served until 1916, when he was charged with killing Probate Judge W. T. Lawler. He was tried and sentenced to hang. While in the Birmingham jail for safekeeping, he escaped and was shot and killed where the present-day gate to Birmingham Southern College stands.

A few of the old trees were still standing in the Old Moore's Grove until I-565 Interstate Highway took most of them out. Those passing over the elevated highway have no way of knowing they are passing over the place where Clark was lynched.

Fred B. Simpson

Historical Marker located on Oakwood Avenue

Fred B. Simpson

Door into the abandoned Dallas Mill

The Priest family continued to live in Huntsville. While the girls could not be traced, Will married and continued to work for the mills for many years. However, he did change from millwork later in life and began to work as a traveling salesman.

Huntsville-Madison County Public Library

Streetcar heading north on Washington Street

Biographies–Chapter Five

The following short biographies are of the people involved in the preceding story. Every effort was made to find information on individuals no matter how small or large a part they played in the story. [443]

Anderson, Charles C.; Member of the Grand Jury.
Charles C. Anderson was the son of John B. Anderson. He was born around 1861. In 1896, Charles was a druggist whose store was in the Huntsville Hotel Block. His home was at 329 Eustis Street.[444] Charles was married around 1893, to Lila (Lelia[445]) C., who had been born in Alabama in December of 1875. Their child was Lucille C., born May 1894. During 1900, Charles' brother lived with the couple. By 1916, Charles was the proprietor of the Anderson Drug Store located in the Milligan Building, on East Side Square.[446]

Burwell, Edwin Dudley; Doctor.
Dr. Edwin Dudley Burwell, Sr. was born in 1848, at Jeff, Alabama. He was the son of James William and Ann (Walker) Burwell. His parents were natives of Virginia, settling in Madison County around 1840. He received his medical degree from Louisville, Kentucky Medical College on February 25, 1875. He returned to Jeff and began his medical practice. He married Carrie Davis in 1879. She was eighteen years of age at the time of her wedding. Their children were: Howard Beirne and Edwin Dudley, Jr. Dr. Burwell, became quite a trader for his services. It was often heard, *"Doc, we'll pay you when we can."* To which he would reply, *"Well, let's strike a bargain."*[447] In 1896, Dr. Burwell moved his practice to 535 Holmes Street. Dr.

---

[443] A search was conducted using the Huntsville City Directories; 1900-1910 United States Federal Census; *Madison County Cemeteries*, Vol. 1 & 2; *Maple Hill Cemetery, Phase One;* and private manuscripts regarding the cemetery; Dorothy Scott Johnson; Merrimack *Cemetery*, Ann Maulsby; *Confederate Veterans Census*, Dorothy Scott Johnson; various military records; Madison County Probate and Civil Court Records.
[444] 1896-97 Huntsville City Directory, Page 19.
[445] 1911-Huntsville City Directory.
[446] 1916-Huntsville City Directory, Page 108.
[447] *Medicine Bags and Bumpy Roads,* Page 161, Goldsmith & Fulton, 1985, Valley Publications, Huntsville, Alabama.

Burwell died November 6, 1910.[448] Mrs. Burwell died nineteen years later in 1929. His son, Edwin, continued to live with his mother, until her death. Edwin Jr. worked as a planter and cotton broker. His office was first located at 101 Northside Square, but he later changed it to the Dement Building. Dr. Burwell's son, Howard Beirne followed him in the medical profession.[449]

Clark, Elijah; Lynched.
Clark, Peter; Father of Elijah Clark.
Nothing could be found regarding these two individuals.

Coleman, Daniel; Attorney.
A complete biography of Daniel Coleman may be found in Chapter One.

Connally, John W.; Jailer.
John W. Connally was born May 25, 1843. He served in the Confederate Army, Company K, of the Forty-Ninth Alabama Infantry.[450] The Reverend Peter Maples married John to Mary T. Wright, January 15, 1870. John and Mary lived at the City Jail and he was employed as the jailer. He and Mary are buried in the Gurley Cemetery, however there is no information on the tombstone to show the dates of death.[451]

Connutt, James; Leader of the Mob.
James M. Connutt was born June 28, 1845, at Lafayette, Walker County, Georgia. He entered service in the Confederacy as a private, March 15, 1862, at Chattanooga, Tennessee. He was in Company C, of Morgan's Brigade. He continued his service until May 12, 1865, with his surrender in Kingston, Georgia. Nothing further was found regarding James Connutt.

---

[448] Madison County, Alabama Birth and Death Records, 1881-1911. Huntsville-Madison County Public Library Archives.
[449] *Medicine Bags and Bumpy Roads*, Page 199, Goldsmith & Fulton, 1985, Valley Publications, Huntsville, Alabama.
[450] *The Valiant Survivors: the United Confederate Veterans of Madison County—A Record of Their Services 1861—1865*; 2nd Edition, page 90, Charles Wells.
[451] *Cemeteries of Madison County, Alabama*, Vol. III, page 11, Dorothy Scott Johnson, Johnson Historical Publications.

Darwin, James L.; Doctor.
James L. Darwin was born July 8, 1859, in Madison County, Alabama. He was the eldest son of Mary Lanier and Sidney Sledge Darwin. Sidney Sledge Darwin was a pioneer businessman in the mercantile business on Huntsville's Cotton Row. James received his education in private and public schools in the county. Later he attended the Agriculture and Mechanical College in Auburn, Alabama. Afterwards he was educated in New York and abroad in the science of medicine and surgery. He further prepared for his medical profession at Bellevue Medical College in New York, receiving his Doctor of Medicine degree in 1888. He was the head resident surgeon at Bellevue for five years. He was on the staff of the Harlem Hospital until resigning to accept a position on the resident staff of the New York Cancer Hospital, where he served for one year. Physicians who knew Dr. Darwin said he was one of the best diagnosticians in the South. He built a large practice, representing his profession very well. He served as the President of the Madison County Medical Society in 1909, and was jail physician in 1912. One night Dr. Darwin left the house on crutches to attend a difficult birth. He slipped on ice, bruising his shin, a very difficult place to heal. He never recovered from the fall. His death on March 3, 1916 was listed as "*Overwork*." The couple lived in the home built by Leroy Pope in 1827, at 350 McClung St. Dr. Darwin's practice was located at 101 ½ Northside Square. He and Mrs. Darwin are buried in Maple Hill Cemetery.[452]

Darwin, Sidney Sledge; Member of the Grand Jury.
Sidney Sledge Darwin was born in 1831. He is the father of Dr. James Darwin (above). He was known as a pioneer businessman in the Mercantile Business on Huntsville's Cotton Row in the late 1800's. His home was on Randolph Avenue and First Street. He served with the Fourth Alabama Infantry, Company I of the Confederate Army. Sidney was married to Mary Lanier. She was born February 8, 1836. She died May 28, 1897. Sidney died March 19, 1911. C.S.A. marker (number unknown) was placed on his grave. They are buried in Maple Hill Cemetery.

---

[452] *Medicine Bags and Bumpy Roads*, Pages 185-186, Goldsmith & Fulton, 1985, Valley Publications, Huntsville, Alabama.

Fulgham, Oscar; Sheriff.
Oscar Fulgham served as Sheriff of Madison County from 1896-1900. A. D. Rodgers replaced him as sheriff in 1900. Further information on Oscar Fulgham could not be found.

Hall, Benton; Doctor.
Benton McMillian Hall was born in Huntsville, October 28, 1876. He entered Tulane University Medical School, in New Orleans, Louisiana, and earned his Doctor of Medicine degree in 1900. Dr. Benton was a member of the First Alabama Volunteer Regiment during the Spanish-American War in 1898. After returning to Huntsville, Dr. Hall established his private practice and was regarded as one of the area's most promising young physicians. Very shortly afterwards his career was interrupted when he contracted tuberculosis. He and his bride, Mary Susan (Wallace), moved west to Texas and then to Colorado in pursuit of a more healthful climate. The search failed and the couple moved back home where Dr. Benton died May 17, 1911. He was only thirty-five years old. The grief-stricken widow became a recluse during her fifty-eight remaining years. Their home was at 608 Adams Street, which was the home of his father, Dr. Cicero Hall. Dr. and Mrs. Hall are buried in Maple Hill Cemetery.[453]

Hay, Robert; Captain of the Monte Sano Guard.
A complete biography of Robert Hay may be found in Chapter Six.

Humes, Milton; Attorney.
A complete biography of Milton Humes may be found in Chapter One.

Lowry, Samuel Hickman; Doctor.
A complete biography of Samuel H. Lowry may be found in Chapter One.

Matthews, E. R.; Member of the Grand Jury.
A complete biography of Elliott R. Matthews may be found in Chapter Six.

---

[453] *Medicine Bags and Bumpy Roads*, Page 235-236, Goldsmith & Fulton, 1985, Valley Publications, Huntsville, Alabama.

May, Frank H.; Doctor.
A search was made, but nothing could be found regarding Dr. Frank May.

McCalley, John; Member of the Grand Jury.
John McCalley was a Civil Engineer and a Surveyor. His home was at 101 Williams Street. He lived with his brother, Charles,[454] and sisters Kate T. and Connie L., in Huntsville. They were the children of Thomas S. and Caroline M. (Lanford) McCalley.[455] John C. McCalley never married and died on May 22, 1902. He was buried with his family in Maple Hill Cemetery, Section 8-Row 7.[456]

McDonald, Christopher; Member of the Grand Jury.
Christopher McDonald was born August 15, 1849. He was employed as the saloonkeeper at the McGee Hotel, located at the corner of Jefferson and Clinton Street. Christopher died on March 23, 1908. He was buried in Maple Hill Cemetery, Section 15. A Confederate Cross of Military Service (#61) is on his grave. Christopher's widow, Mary L., lived at the hotel after his death. Information regarding Mary's death was not recorded.[457]

McKelby (McKelvey), William.; Doctor.
Dr. William McKelvey worked on Dallas Avenue as a physician for the Dallas Mill workers. Further information could not be found regarding him.[458]

Miller, George T.; Made Speech.
George T. Miller was born April 6, 1848, near Whitesburg in Madison County, Alabama. He entered service for the Confederacy as a private in the Fourth Alabama Cavalry and continued until he was paroled in Huntsville, Alabama in May 1865.[459] George resided at 320 Humes Avenue and worked for the Dallas Manufacturing Company. In 1911, George and his wife, Lillie, were working for the Merrimack Mills Their home was in the Merrimack Mill Village.

---

[454] See Chapter Six.
[455] See Chapter One.
[456] *Maple Hill Cemetery, Phase One*, Page 58, Robey-Johnson-Jones-Roberts; The Huntsville-Madison County Historical Society. 1995.
[457] *Maple Hill Cemetery, Phase One*, Page 138, Robey-Johnson-Jones-Roberts; The Huntsville-Madison County Historical Society. 1995.
[458] 1896 Huntsville City Directory, Page 53.
[459] Confederate Service Records, Huntsville-Madison County Public Library.

Moore, Alfred; Mayor.
Alfred Moore was born December 23, 1844, in Limestone County, Alabama. He entered service for the Confederacy as a private in September of 1864, enlisting in Huntsville with Company E, of the Fourth Alabama, Russell's Regiment. He continued until his release from prison at Camp Chase, June 1, 1865.[460] Alfred worked at a teller for the First National Bank of Huntsville. He served as Mayor of Huntsville from 1899-1903. He resided at the corner of Lincoln and Williams Streets.[461]

Overton, David D; Chief of Police.
David D. Overton was born in March of 1868. His wife, Sallie H., was born in 1872. They were both born in Tennessee. They married in 1898, and had a daughter, Nora, and a son, David V.[462] The family resided at 217 North Grove Street. Overton had been employed with his brother, Ambrose, in the Overton Transfer Company and also worked as a clerk for the Madison County Circuit Court.[463] Overton served as Huntsville Police Chief from 1898 until 1907, when he resigned. He was elected to the position of Circuit Court Clerk in 1911, and served until 1916,[464] when he was charged with killing Probate Judge W. T. Lawler. He was tried, convicted, and sentenced to hang in 1917. While in the Birmingham jail for safekeeping, he escaped and was shot and killed where the gate to Birmingham Southern College now stands.[465] Sallie later lived at 204 Walker Street with her son, David V. who worked at the West Huntsville Cotton Mill. David D. Overton is buried in Maple Hill Cemetery in Section 23, Row 17. His tombstone reads, 1868-1917. Sallie Overton died in 1964 and is buried in Maple Hill.[466] [467]

Patterson, George; Member of the Grand Jury.
George C. Patterson was born August 19, 1870. He was married to Pearle around 1906, and they lived on East Clinton Street. Both had

---

[460] *1907 Confederate Census, Limestone, Morgan & Madison Counties Alabama*, Johnson Historical Press, Page 17.
[461] 1896 Huntsville City Directory, page 57.
[462] 1900 United States Federal Census, Madison County, Alabama.
[463] 1911 Huntsville City Directory, Page 61.
[464] 1920 Huntsville City Directory, Page 268.
[465] Accumulated Madison County Records regarding the case of *The State of Alabama vs D. D. Overton*.
[466] 1920 Huntsville City Directory, Page 268.
[467] Maple Hill Cemetery Office Records.

been born in Kentucky. George was the assistant foreman at the Huntsville Daily Times, located on East Holmes Avenue. The couple married around 1906. They had two children: Mary, born 1908, and George Jr., born in 1910. In 1916, George began working as an insurance agent, with his office located at 224 Washington Street. He and Pearle lived at 201 Lincoln Street. George died on September 7, 1929. He is buried in Maple Hill Cemetery. His tombstone reads, *"His toils are past, his work is done, he fought the fight, the victory won—Papa."*[468]

Phillips, Robert [Bob] L.; Deputy Sheriff.
Robert L. Phillips was a grocer at 302 Madison Street in 1896. His wife was Nancy. Their home was at 406 Walker Street.[469] Robert was a Deputy Sheriff in 1900.[470] He later became the Sheriff, where he served Madison County from 1915 until 1916.[471] He became involved in the killing of Judge William Lawler and committed suicide in 1916.

Priest, Nellie; Sister of Victim.
Priest, Susan; Victim.
Priest, Will; Brother.
The family was from Bedford Co., Tennessee, and moved to Huntsville to seek employment with the Dallas Cotton Mill. Further information on Nellie and Susan was not found. Will Priest married a woman named, Daisy. Their home was at #4 Davidson Street in the Abington Mill District.[472] In 1917, Will was employed as a traveling salesman and they lived at 423 W. Homes Street.[473]

Rolf, W. T.; Member of the Grand Jury.
William T. Rolf was born in Alabama in 1850. He worked as a carpenter and lived on Pulaski Pike.[474] He was widowed with children: Estelle, born 1873; William, born 1878 (also worked as a carpenter); Meghew, born 1879 (worked as a nurseryman); Garth, Meghew's twin, (worked as a nurseryman); Charlie, born, 1886

---

[468] *Maple Hill Cemetery, Phase One*, Page 83, Robey-Johnson-Jones-Roberts; The Huntsville-Madison County Historical Society. 1995.
[469] 1896 Huntsville City Directory, page 62.
[470] 1911 Huntsville City Directory.
[471] 1916 Huntsville City Directory, page 207.
[472] 1911 Huntsville City Directory.
[473] 1917 Huntsville City Directory, page 211.
[474] 1896 Huntsville City Directory, page 66.

(worked as a foreman); and twins Katie and Alecia, born 1884.[475] [476] William T Rolf died January 10, 1935, at the age of eighty-four.[477]

Speake, Henry Clay; Judge.
Henry Clay Speake was born in Lawrence County, Alabama, June 17, 1834. He was the son of James B. and Susan B. (Lindsey) Speake. The family came to Lawrence County, near Oakville, two years before the birth of Henry. Henry was raised on a farm and received a public school education. At the age of 20, he taught school to procure money to attend the Cumberland University Law School. He graduated in January 1857. He moved to Decatur, but served six months in the Texas war. He was married January 27, 1860, to Carrie O. Mayhew. The couple had three children: Kate M., Henry C. Jr., and Paul M. (see chapter six). Henry Speake lived in Decatur until he entered the army of the Confederacy as a private. Henry joined the Fourth Alabama Cavalry Regiment (Russell's), Company D, and was soon promoted to sergeant major and later to adjutant of the regiment. In January of 1864, he was appointed quartermaster of the regiment. He was captured with a part of Forrest's command, near Columbus, Georgia. After the war, he settled near Moulton and in 1874, he was elected Chancellor of the Northern Division of Alabama. In December 1876, Judge Speake moved his family to Huntsville. In August of 1880, he was elected Judge of the Eighth Judicial Circuit of the State. Judge Speake was a Mason and practiced the Campbellite faith; his wife was a Presbyterian. Judge Speake died suddenly, on December 8, 1900. An obituary reported, *"His cheery words were always ready to make us feel that the world was better for his living in it, and when the hand of affliction came to rend our hearts, he was always the first to offer sweet sympathy and consolation."*[478] His wife, Carrie, died March 20, 1906. They are buried in Maple Hill Cemetery, Section 11 Row 17.[479]

Steger, W. D.; Member of the Grand Jury.
William D. Steger was born in Buckingham County, Virginia, May 7, 1846. He entered service for the Confederacy as a Private, March of 1864, at Kingston, North Carolina. He enlisted in Company C, of the

---

[475] 1900 United States Federal Census, Madison County, Alabama.
[476] Madison County, Alabama Poll Tax Records.
[477] Maple Hill Records, Main Office.
[478] *The Huntsville Weekly Democrat.*
[479] *Maple Hill Cemetery Book Phase One,* Page 93, Robey, Johnson, Jones, Roberts; Huntsville-Madison County Historical Society.

38th C.S.A. Artillery, Reed's Battalion. He continued serving until the surrender in 1865.[480] By 1904, William was fifty-eight years old, and had been married to Margaret, (who was forty-six years old), for twenty-eight years. They were the parents of six children. Margaret was the librarian for the W. R. Rison Library. Their home was on Humes Avenue.[481]

Stewart, Samuel Morgan; Judge.
A complete biography may be found in Chapter Six.

Stoner, John; Member of the Grand Jury.
John C. Stoner was a clerk of the Dallas Mill. His wife's name was Amanda. They lived on Meridian Street.

Turner, Henry P.; Member of the Grand Jury.
Henry P. Turner was born August 22, 1844, in Madison County, Alabama. He entered service in the Confederate Army as a private in the spring of 1862, in Company I of the Fourth Alabama Infantry. He was paroled at Appomattox in April of 1865.[482] Henry married Fannie L. Ailed, on October 27, 1869. Magistrate R. K. Brown performed the ceremony.[483] The Turner home was at 307 Randolph Avenue. Henry worked for the Tax Collector for Madison County. His death came on February 12, 1911. Fannie and Henry P. are buried in Maple Hill Cemetery.[484]

Vaughn, James B.; Member of the Grand Jury.
James B. Vaughn was born about 1860. His mother was Mavalina Vaughn. He worked as a clerk at the W. I. & J. R Thompson's Hardware. He married Ellaree about 1897. Ellaree was born in 1874. They had four children: William Buford, born in 1900; James Robert, born in 1903; Mable Evelyn, born in 1906; and Martha Louise, born 1907.[485]

---

[480] *1907 Confederate Census, Limestone, Morgan & Madison Counties Alabama*, Johnson Historical Press, Page 24.
[481] 1900 United States Federal Census, Madison County, Alabama.
[482] The Rooster for Confederate Soldiers, 1861-1865, Page 368, Edited by Jeanette B. Hewlett, Broadfoot Publishing Company.
[483] Madison County, Alabama Marriage Records.
[484] Maple Hill Cemetery Office Records.
[485] 1910 United States Federal Census, Madison County, Alabama.

Vining, Will; Shot in the Siege.
Will Vining was a fugitive from Coryell County, Texas, who came to Huntsville and the safety of his mother and sister. District Attorney, J. H. Arnold, of the 52nd Judicial District of Texas, wrote the Governor of Alabama a letter in 1905, regarding his fugitive. A portion of that letter is as follows; *"You will recall that in the latter part of the last March or the first of April, you honored a requisition from the Governor of Texas for one Ed Vining, who is indicted in Coryell County, Texas, for the offense of burglary. Your warrant of rendition was issued to one A. D. Rodgers, Sheriff of Madison County, Alabama. Ed Vining was in Huntsville, Alabama at the time and was well known to the Sheriff there. W. C. McClellan, our representative of this State, visited there for the purpose of receiving Vining and conveying him back to Texas for trial. Sheriff Rogers was absent, but a deputy delivered him to McClellan and he made an application to the local Justice of the Peace for a writ of Habeas corpus, which was granted and bond was allowed securing his escape from the agent of this State. The agent, McClellan was held on kidnapping charges. The Sheriff admits his friendship for this party. It seems the officers there are harbouring [sic] this man and refuse to render out officers to apprehend him."*[486] Vining remained at large.

Wade, Bob; Member of the Grand Jury.
Robert B. Wade married Mary P. Boggs on April 23, 1851.[487] They are buried at the Wade Cemetery in Madison County, Alabama.[488]

Wallace, John H, Jr.; Made Speech.
John H Wallace was born in June of 1835 in Alabama. He and his wife, Mary C., had four children: John H. Wallace, Jr., born 1873, and working as a lawyer; William J., born 1876; a son (unreadable); a daughter (unreadable).[489] In 1911, John Wallace worked as a game commissioner and lived at 316 Locust Street.[490] In 1916, the family's residence was 512 Adams Avenue. John Wallace died January 16, 1922, and is buried in Maple Hill.[491]

---

[486] Correspondence Files of the Adjunct General, 1889-1907: Alabama Department of Archives and History.
[487] Madison County, Alabama Marriage Records.
[488] Madison County Cemeteries, Dorothy Scott Johnson, Johnson Historical Publications.
[489] 1900 United States Federal Census, Madison County, Alabama.
[490] 1911-1916 Huntsville City Directory.
[491] Maple Hill Cemetery Office Records.

Chapter Six

Horace Maples

1904

Huntsville Herald.

HUNTSVILLE, ALABAMA, FRIDAY SEPTEMBER 9, 1904.   NO. 47

PROMPTLY INDICTED

By Grand Jury For Horrible Crime

JURY COMPOSED OF PROMINENT MEN

Verdict of Murder in The First Degree Found by The Grand Jury

As stated in yesterday's News, the special grand jury was empaneled with the following members:
A. J. Mudrick, J R Jones, A.

THE NEGRO MURDERER HORACE MAPLES HANGED BY A MOB LAST NIGHT ABOUT ELEVEN O'CLOCK.

DENNIS SMITH INDICTED

For Murder in The First Degree and

His Trial is S... For Next Wednesday. Killed a Negro Woman About Three Weeks Ago.

The grand jury that found a

Sheriff and Guards Were Forced To Give Him up After Being Nearly Suffocated by Fire and Fumes of Burning Pepper and Sulphur

MURDERERS JUMPED FROM SECOND STORY.

Is Caught By the Mob and Hung in the Court House Yard. The Body Was Not Cut Down Until About Nine O'clock This Morning. A Gruesome Sight Viewed by Curious Crowd.

LEADERS OF MOB

Will be Punished Says Judge Speake

ANOTHER GRAND JURY HAS BEEN DRAWN

They will Sift the Matter to Bottom and if Possible Find Guilty Parties

Judge Speake and Solicitor Pettus are determined to punish the leaders of last night's mob if such a thing is possible.
To this end another grand jury

Glossary of Laws and Legal Terms

This glossary is to help the reader understand the terminology of the legal proceedings described in this chapter.

We are governed by three sets of laws, Federal laws are established by acts of Congress, States laws are established by the State Legislature, City laws are established by the City Council.

WARRANT OF ARREST- A court ordered document that allows law enforcement officers to arrest and jail a person suspected of having committed a crime.

GRAND JURY- Qualified people randomly selected from the community to hear evidence presented by the District Attorney. The Grand Jury may be summoned to serve one term or several short terms. All votes are taken in secret. The District Attorney is in charge of the Grand Jury. The Grand Jury can report an indictment, which orders a person to a jury trial.

INDICTMENT- A grand jury's written accusation, (true bill), charging a person (the defendant) with having committed a crime against the people.

SUMMONS– A court order for a person to attend court.

ARRAIGNMENT- A procedure where an accused must appear in court and plead guilty or not guilty to an indictment.

VENIRE- The group of sworn jurors called to serve during the term of court.

VOIR DIRE EXAMINATION-The preliminary questioning of jurors (the venire) to establish their qualifications.

STRIKING A JURY- Attorneys "strike" or excuse jurors until twelve remain. These twelve become the trial jury.

OPENING STATEMENT- Outline of expected evidence of their case presented to the jury by the attorneys at the beginning of a trial.

STATE'S CASE- Presented in the form of evidence and witnesses intended to prove the accusation made against the defendant.

DIRECT EXAMINATION- The questioning of witnesses by the attorney of the party on whose behalf they are called.

CROSS EXAMINATION- Questioning of a witness by the attorney of the opposing party.

OBJECTION- A statement by an attorney opposing specific testimony or the admission of evidence.

OVERRULE- When the court overrules an objection to evidence, the jury may consider the evidence in reaching their verdict.

SUSTAIN- When the court sustains an objection to evidence, the jury may not consider the evidence in reaching their verdict.

DEFENDANT'S CASE- Presented in the form of evidence and witnesses that is intended to prove the innocence of the defendant.

EVIDENCE- Any legally presented proof established by witnesses testimony, or documents.

CLOSING ARGUMENT- A summary of the evidence to the jury by the attorneys. Presented first by the defense and then the State, which is allowed the last argument.

JUDGE'S CHARGE TO THE JURY- Instruction to the jury on the issues to be decided and rules of law that apply to the case.

JURY DELIBERATIONS- After listening to the judge's oral charge, the jury retires to discuss the case. Selection of a foreperson is the jury's first duty. The foreperson presides over the discussion of the case and acts as spokesperson for the jury.

VERDICT- Decision made by a jury, read before the court and accepted by the judge.

SENTENCING- If the accused is found guilty or pleads guilty, the judge or jury sets the punishment.

HUNG JURY- A term used when a jury cannot reach a verdict, resulting in a mistrial.

APPEAL- The accused can ask the Alabama Supreme Court to review his case to determine if there was a fair trial.

Trial Participants

JUDGE- An elected or appointed official who conducts the trial, rules on questions of law raised by attorneys and, at the close of the trial, instructs the jury on the law that applies to the case.

PROSECUTING ATTORNEY- An elected or appointed official who represents the State in criminal cases.

DEFENDANT- The person charged with or accused of a crime.

DEFENSE ATTORNEYS- Employed by the parties (or if the defendant is unable to pay for an attorney, is appointed by the court at the State's expense).

WITNESSES- Present testimony under oath about what they have seen or know about the facts of the case.

SHERIFF- An elected official who is the county's chief law enforcement officer. The Sheriff serves summonses on witnesses, jurors and defendants; provides court security; and is in charge of the jail.

COURT REPORTER- Records a word-for-word account of all court testimony and proceedings and, in the event of an appeal and upon request will transcribe the record into a written document (transcript).

Huntsville-Madison County Public Library

Washington Street looking north

Introduction to Chapter Six

Alabama is divided into numbered Judicial Circuits in order to manage the business of court cases and law enforcement. Each county has its own courthouse in which to conduct the county's business, but a Judicial Circuit might encompass several counties. As the population increases additional circuits are carved from the larger circuits.[492]

At the turn of the century, the Eighth Judicial Circuit was composed of Cullman, Lawrence, Limestone, Madison and Morgan Counties. In 1903, the Alabama Legislature passed an act named the "Lusk Bill." This act created a new Sixteenth Judicial Circuit that included only Madison and Limestone Counties.

A political agreement was approved to appoint the judge for the new circuit from Madison County and the Solicitor from Limestone County.

In October 1903, Paul Mayhew Speake was appointed to the new position of Judge of the Sixteenth Judicial Circuit. Judge Speake was born in Moulton, Alabama, the son of Judge Henry C. Speake, the Judge of the Eighth Judicial Circuit. After completing law school, Judge Speake practiced law in Huntsville and was active in political and civic affairs. He was greatly devoted to his wife and children. In 1904, he was thirty-one.

Erle Pettus was appointed Solicitor from Limestone County. He attended the University of Alabama. He served in the State Legislature, and was the youngest member, being elected prior to his graduation from Cumberland Law School. He began the practice of law in Athens, in 1899. In 1904, he was twenty-seven.

These two attorneys became leaders in a legal system that has always taken every precaution to prevent a miscarriage of justice. Rules of common sense are followed, and are set forth in an intelligent method that has been used for centuries. The system will not allow the government to punish a citizen without the consent of the people. A randomly selected jury represents the people. The jury determines the facts and returns a verdict of guilty or not guilty. The people, through the jury system, have the power to convict on very little evidence or they may disregard the evidence altogether and show mercy. The people decide when the State is allowed to put a citizen to death.

---

[492] Madison County was created from a larger circuit and is now the Twenty-third Judicial Circuit.

There is no way to know how many people have been charged with capital murder during the past two hundred years.[493] There are no records to indicate how many of those charged actually went to trial. It is known that from 1800 to 1900, twenty-two citizens were sentenced to hang. Some of these were pardoned. There have been few executions from Madison County in the Twentieth Century. From 1900-2000, only twelve citizens were sentenced to die by the verdict of a unanimous jury. Only two were actually executed.[494] The people have exercised the privilege to put a citizen to death on very few occasions.

One of the twelve men sentenced to die was Dennis Smith. During the mob violence of 1904, Smith was tried and convicted of murder and given the death penalty. His death sentence was rendered only because of the emotional state of the population surrounding the lynching. The lawlessness of the mob was allowed to spill over into the very foundation of our judicial system. The mob had moved from the street into the jury box.

---

[493] Very few records have been kept of the exact number of murder cases in Madison County. District Attorney Fred Simpson (the author), during the decade of the seventies, tried 64 murder cases. Computerized records began to be kept in 1883 and show that Madison County had 215 murder cases, 45 of which were capital murder cases.

[494] In 1936, Walter Miller was executed for the rape and murder of Vivian Woodward. In 1965, William Bowen was electrocuted for the murder of Janice Thomas.

1904

Between 1900-1904, many interesting historical events happened in the World, the United States, the State of Alabama and locally in Madison County, Alabama.[495]

World

Queen Victoria of England died and was succeeded by her son, Edward VII...Elgar composed, *Pomp and Circumstance March*... Landsteiner demonstrated that blood had three types, A, B, and O... Robert Bosch invented the spark plug... First Tour déFrance bicycle race...Panama proclaims itself an independent republic... Butler authored *The Way of All Flesh*.... Barrie authored *Peter Pan*... Puccini composed *Madame Butterfly*... First motor taxi service began in London... Korn transmitted a photograph by telegraph... The London Symphony Orchestra gave its first performance... The Rolls-Royce Company was founded in England.

United States

President McKinley was shot and Theodore Roosevelt became President... Orville Wright and Wilbur Wright launched the first motorized airplane at Kitty Hawk, N. C... Walter Reed discovered that yellow fever was spread by mosquitoes... Maryland passed the first state workmen's compensation law... Congress authorized the building of the Panama Canal... Jack London authored, *Call of the Wild*... Kate Douglas Wiggin authored *Rebecca of Sunnybrook Farm*... Telegraph cable was laid from California to Hawaii... The first Tournament of Roses football game was played... Electricity powered by overhead wires was installed... First annual World Series... Richard Stieff designed the first "*Teddy Bears*," named after President Roosevelt...New York subway began service... Booker T. Washington was refused admission to three Springfield, Massachusetts hotels.

---

[495] Information was gathered from local and state history books and local newspapers. Information was also obtained from, *A Dream Come True Vol. II*, James Record, 1978, John Hicklin Printing Co. Huntsville, Alabama, Library of Congress Card Number:76-11880.

State

William J. Samford was the Governor 1900-1901. He was a lawyer and a Confederate veteran... A convention was called to adopt Alabama's present State Constitution... The new constitution was used to disfranchise Negro voters with residence requirements and the poll tax, limited time for registration, and written test... William D. Jelks became the Governor in 1901, taking over when Governor Samford died... Jelks became ill during 1904, and Russell M. Cunningham became the acting Governor... The State Department of Archives and History was established ... The State Capital was enlarged.... Houston County was the last county to be created... Laws were enacted for the regulation of child labor in factories, for the better treatment of convicts, and for larger appropriations for schools ... The office of Lieutenant Governor was created.

Local

Madison County's total population was 43,000—8000 lived in Huntsville... The streetcars ran from six o'clock in the morning until midnight, passing every fifteen minutes... Lowe Cotton Mill was dedicated, it was Huntsville's seventh mill... The Struve building was constructed at Washington and Clinton... Trolley parties were popular along with concerts on the Courthouse lawn... The Market House bell tolled for the opening and closing of business... An ordinance prohibiting the sale of cocaine was passed due to the rapid growth of the habit... Newspapers warned young men to quit smoking... President McKinley's train stopped in Huntsville in 1901... Congressman William Richardson introduced McKinley... The first paved street was made of vitrified brick; it was from Randolph to Clinton on Washington... First Elks Lodge was organized...Harrison Brothers building on South Side Square burned... Huntsville Bar Association was organized...Carrie Nation visited Huntsville... Tallulah Bankhead was born on Eastside Square... Motion pictures were shown... In 1904, people could walk across the dried up Tennessee River... First high school football game played... J. B. Fisk brought his load of watermelons into town; each one weighing an average of 49 lbs... W. L. Halsey bought a building on Jefferson Street, near the railroad depot, for his grocery business; it is still there today... The County Board of Education system began in 1904, and consisted of the Superintendent and four elected trustees.

Chapter Six
Horace Maples-1904

It was 1904 in Madison County, Alabama.[496]

Charles Holder and J. W. Webster whipped up the horses and shifted their position on the hard wagon seat as they traveled along the New Market Pike northeast of Huntsville near Bell Factory. It had been a long eight miles from town and near seven o'clock. It was still warm, and in some places would be called hot, on this September evening.

As they approached the first bridge across the Three Forks of the Flint River, they saw a team and wagon standing loose in the road in a spot overhung with trees. As they moved closer, they saw the body of Elias D. Waldrop laying on the side of the road about ten feet from his wagon and fifty yards east of the bridge. They could see that his head had been beaten into an almost shapeless bloody mass. It did not take the men long, nor require that they be master detectives, to see that the victim had been murdered.

Holder and Webster returned to the hard seat of their wagon for the trip to give the alarm.

The Coroner,[497] Colonel E. B. Stewart was called to the murder scene by telephone. It was an hour later that Tuesday night, on September 6, 1904, when he arrived. The body had not been moved and the Coroner had no problem determining the cause of

---

[496] It should be noted that most of the information for this book was found in the weekly newspapers of 1904; *The Daily Mercury* (September 8, 1904); *The Huntsville Weekly Democrat* (September 14, 1904); *The Huntsville Weekly Democrat* (September 24, 1904); *The Huntsville Weekly Democrat* (September 28, 1904); *The Weekly Mercury* (September 8, 1904); *The Weekly Mercury* (September 14, 1904); *The Weekly Mercury* (September 21, 1904); *The Weekly Mercury* (September 28, 1904); *The Weekly Mercury* (October 5, 1904); *The Weekly Mercury* (October 19, 1904); *The Weekly Mercury* (November 2, 1904); *The Weekly Mercury* (November 22, 1904); *The Weekly Mercury* (December 6, 1904); *The Birmingham News* (September 8, 1904); *The Birmingham News* (September 15, 1904); *The Birmingham News* (September 19, 1904); *The Birmingham News* (September 20, 1904); *The Birmingham News* (September 24, 1904); *The Birmingham News* (September 30, 1904); *The Birmingham News* (October 5, 1904); *The Montgomery Advisor* (September 14, 1904); *The Huntsville Herald* (September 9, 1904); *The Huntsville Herald* (September 30, 1904); *The Huntsville Herald* (October 7, 1904); *The New York Sun* (September 20, 1904); *The Journal* (October 27, 1904); Footnotes will be provided where necessary.

[497] An elected official who must determine the cause of death not due to natural causes.

death. The ground around the body indicated that a struggle had taken place and that Waldrop had fought bravely to save his money and his life. It appeared that a bloody axe found beside the road was used to do the killing. Every pocket in the dead man's clothing had been turned wrong side out. It was not hard to see that robbery was the apparent motive for the act that culminated in the homicide.

Coroner E. B. Stewart impaneled a jury at the scene and held an inquest over Waldrop's body. This inquest consisted of conversations between Stewart and other selected members of the curious crowd. The jury could only find that a person, or persons unknown, had committed the homicide.

It was left to Waldrop's friends in the crowd to rush forward with the bad news, to prepare the Waldrop family for the shock, and to take the remains home.

It would be a long night for the Waldrop family. It would be a long month for Madison County.

Elias Waldrop lived on the Lawler place, about two miles from Bell Factory, with his wife and three children. He had two sons, Jack, twenty-four, and Charley, sixteen. His daughter, Cara, was about thirteen. His neighbors held him in high esteem. He was engaged in the peddling business; the selling of chickens and country produce to customers in Huntsville. He had gone to Huntsville that morning with a load of produce and had the profits made from his work with him when he was returning home. He had been robbed a year before at almost the identical spot where he was murdered.

Coroner Stewart telegraphed to Chattanooga for bloodhounds even though he knew that the dogs could not reach the scene before nine o'clock the next morning. He knew that the trail would likely be too cold by that time.

Many calls had been made during the night and the murder was the main topic of conversation in Huntsville and throughout the County by Wednesday morning. The *Weekly Mercury* gave all the details, which were read with interest by everyone. Feelings of anger spread over the county when the murder of Waldrop became known.

Wednesday, September 7, 1904, would be an eventful day for Huntsville and Madison County.

The bloodhounds from Chattanooga arrived and were taken to the scene of the crime. As anticipated, the trail was too cold to be followed. Morning light found a large crowd of people standing around looking at the empty road where the murder had occurred, talking about the killing.

The authorities asked questions, and the investigation focused on a Negro man named Horace Maples who quickly became the prime suspect. That morning Sheriff Rodgers saw Maples in town, but at the time, did not know of his involvement in Waldrop's death.

The Officers of the law found a gentleman, who said that while driving in to Huntsville from Meridianville, late Tuesday evening, he had met Waldrop's wagon and Horace Maples was with Waldrop. Good police work always dictates that the last person with the victim be found and questioned. Investigators located a man who identified Maples as the man that passed him on the road coming towards Huntsville from the Bell Factory area. Another peddler was found who said that the day before, Maples had asked Waldrop for a ride home in his wagon with him.

Detectives learned that in the past few days, Maples had tried, unsuccessfully, to borrow a pistol from two different people. It was also discovered that he returned to the City on the nine o'clock train from Mercury,[499] Tuesday night. This morning he had been spending money freely, having approached several creditors and began paying his debts, using nickels and dimes. His action had aroused the suspicion of several townspeople. Unbelievably, he had not changed his clothes and they were covered with mud and briars. He might as well have carried a sign of his guilt printed on his back.

It was apparent that Elias Waldrop had been kind enough to allow the killer to ride with him. Maples had planned for the robbery to take place in the loneliest and the darkest place on the road to Bell Factory. When the intended victim resisted, he was murdered for the small amount of money in his pocket.

Maples was a well-known person around Huntsville. He once operated a café on Jefferson Street and was later employed at the Owl Restaurant. At the time of the murder, Maples was out on bond, on an old unsettled charge of robbing another Negro man. His reputation was generally bad.

---

[499] The present area known as Chase.

The suspect seemed to go about his daily routine without a care or worry regarding his action in taking a human life. Had there not been an investigation, he would have lived out his life without paying for his deed.

Coroner Stewart impaneled a more formal jury to look further into Waldrop's death. The jury finished its investigation that morning and returned a verdict that the deceased came to his death by having his brains beaten out with a blunt instrument in the hands of Horace Maples.

Sheriff A. D. Rodgers, Huntsville police and others were ordered to make an arrest. Officer H. P. Wilson and Constable[500] W. L. Phillips set out in a buggy to find Maples. Within a few minutes they saw him going down West Holmes riding as a passenger in a delivery wagon. The officers whipped up their horses. Maples and the driver looked back, and seeing that they were being pursued, made off as fast as they could. There ensued an exciting and lively chase down Holmes Avenue to the North Carolina and St. Louis Railway crossing, where Maples jumped from the wagon and set out for the coal yard near the depot.[501] Officer Wilson was on foot, just behind him.

Maples ran out of the coal yard and across the Southern Railway tracks just in front of a moving train. The train was then between Maples and the officer. This allowed the fugitive to gain a hundred-yard lead. Maples ran through some of the lots fronting Pulaski Pike while several shots were fired at him. In trying to double back toward the railroad tracks, he ran right into Officer Wilson's arms. He gave up quietly when the officer "*got the drop on him with a big pistol.*" Maples was brought back into town, and placed in the city jail.[502]

Maples capture occurred just prior to the departure of the 11:15 Southern Railroad Company westbound train. The Sheriff knew he could have taken the prisoner to Decatur for safe keeping, but felt that since a rape charge was not involved there was no need to take that precaution. He did not anticipate mob violence.[503]

---

[500] A constable was an elected official whose duties were similar to those of a Sheriff, though his powers were less and his jurisdiction smaller.

[501] Holmes and the Railroad tracks were then located where Memorial Parkway crosses Holmes Avenue today. Neither Holmes nor the tracks have moved.

[502] Then located at the northwest corner of Clinton and Green Streets.

[503] Sheriff Rodgers report to Governor Cunningham, Administrative Files, Governors Papers, 1904 (Jelks), Alabama Department of Archives and History.

During the day, news of Maples' arrest spread like wild fire. The community was horrified at the news of the killing but relieved that an arrest had been made. There was great indignation throughout the city and county and a general feeling that something would have to be done. There then began talk of a lynching.

The last time an event of this nature occurred, involving a Negro man, the law-abiding citizens of Huntsville had allowed the Negro prisoner to be taken from the Huntsville jail and lynched at Dallas. Nothing was done to punish the men who had taken part in that lawless act. The 1900 Clark lynching, would be a guideline for the tragedy that was about to begin.

People gathered in large crowds about the city to discuss the details of the events. The largest gathered at the jail. Threats were made about attacking the jail and taking the prisoner.

As the day passed, the crowd around the jail grew larger. Wells' Livery was located directly across Clinton Avenue from the jail and those arriving from the county placed their horses in the livery stable, and merged into the swelling crowd. There were rumors circulating that people residing in the area around the Bell Factory area (where the murdered man and his family lived) had started toward the city, to take Maples out of the jail and hang him.

Mayor Thomas W. Smith, fifty-four years of age, assisted by the City police mingled with the crowd and advised them to disperse. However, neither city officials nor the Sheriff's Department made any efforts to disperse the crowd or arrest those who were becoming leaders of the crowd

Solicitor Erle Pettus, twenty-seven years of age, arrived in Huntsville from Athens about eleven o'clock that morning to attend a murder trial during the September term of court. The Grand Jury was not in session.[504] William B. Bankhead, a local attorney, informed Pettus about the death of Elias Waldrop and the arrest of Maples.

---

[504] During the next two weeks Huntsville would see a flurry of legal activities. There would be three grand juries and a military court of inquiry. A Grand Jury had already been impaneled to hear the normally scheduled criminal cases of the circuit. The first special Grand Jury was impaneled to handle the indictment of Maples and Smith. The second special Grand Jury was impaneled to investigate the lynching of Horace Maples. The fourth proceeding, the Military Court of Inquiry, was ordered to investigate the inaction of the Huntsville National Guard at the time of the Maples lynching. To complicate matters, while all of these legal proceedings were ongoing there would also be seven jury trials taking place.

Pettus then went to the jail and talked to members of the crowd, who seemed good-natured and agreeable to the law taking its course.

Near the middle of the day, Pettus suggested to the Sheriff that he move the prisoner to another city. The Sheriff felt such a move would not be necessary, and he might not be able to move the prisoner safely. The Sheriff felt that while the crowd seemed somewhat excited, it was good humored with no ugly temper being displayed.

Local citizens watched the crowd with growing apprehension. A committee of gentlemen from the crowd at the jail went to the courthouse to see Judge Paul Mayhew Speake, one of the state's most prominent jurists, who was conducting a jury trial in a term of the Circuit Court. They conferred with him about the mob that was approaching from the Bell Factory area, and the crowd around the jail. Judge Speake gave assurance that a special Grand Jury would be impaneled and, following an indictment, Maples would be given an immediate trial. This was satisfactory to the members of the committee. They returned to the street and informed the crowd of the Judge's statement. The assurance of Judge Speake had a temporary quieting effect on the crowd that was gathered downtown, but they did not disperse.

Judge Speake impaneled the special Grand Jury at three o'clock that afternoon. He delivered a brief charge urging the importance of a prompt investigation into the killing of Waldrop.

The Grand Jury was chosen from men who were in the Courthouse serving as jurors on the trials set for that week. Some originally summoned to serve on trial jury duty, now found themselves selected for a Grand Jury.

Another Negro man, Dennis Smith, was in the County Jail charged with the murder of his paramour, Mrs. Mollie Watkins. He was waiting for the next session of the Grand Jury that would consider an indictment against him. Smith would become a victim of the excitement of the Maples investigation.

Judge Speake decided not to wait on the normal Grand Jury to indict Smith. He instructed this special Grand Jury to also investigate the case of murder by Dennis Smith and return an early indictment.

The men, selected to serve on the special Grand Jury, began their investigation by taking testimony from witnesses presented by the Solicitor.[504] The Sheriff stated he would attend to the Grand Jury personally.

While a big crowd milled around the Courthouse in Huntsville, there was another big crowd gathered around a freshly dug hole in the ground out on Winchester Road at the Locust Grove burying ground. At about four o'clock on a warm September day, in the seventy-first year of his life, Elias Waldrop was being laid to rest in the presence of his wife, his children, and his many friends.

Back in Huntsville, curiosity and word of mouth about the events enlarged the crowd at the jail. The crowd soon became threatening and would not disperse. Men stood around waiting for a leader to help them attack the jail.

The committee of gentlemen went back to see Judge Speake with a new message that the crowd was growing and becoming angry. Judge Speake left the Courthouse and made his way down Washington Street to the jail. He gave a short address to the crowd. He cautioned everyone to observe the law and begged them to let the law take its course. He told them a Grand Jury had already been ordered, Circuit Court was in session, there would be no delays, and a trial would be held for Maples at once.

Reverend Frank P. Culver, Pastor of the First Methodist Church, also made a speech to the crowd, begging them to go home and let the law take its course. James Mitchell, a sixty-five year old

Fred B. Simpson

---

[504] The Grand Jury was composed of the following members: M. M. Cantrell (Foreman) A. J. Murdock, J. R. Jones, A. E. Overton, J. R. Thompson, L. D. Ford, J. C. Webster, J. N. Williams, H. J. Lowenthal, Oscar Goldsmith, A. E. Matthews, W. L. Halsey, R. A. Givens, S. R. Lewis, R. L. Hughes, J. D. Dennis and J. Ed Gardner, S. S. Darwin had been selected, but was excused. C. A. Potts was appointed bailiff.

mill worker, came through the crowd, approached Reverend Culver and quoted a passage of scripture, *"Whosoever sheddeth man's blood, by man shall his blood be shed."*[505]

Other men also spoke up urging that no violence be employed against the jail. This appeal by prominent citizens seemed to have had some quieting effect on the crowd. However, later that afternoon the crowd still grew larger. No forcible attempt was made on the jail, only violent threats and shouts for the release or the prisoner were made. The crowd still seemed to remain good-humored, but a few people thought that an attack on the jail was imminent. *The Mercury* reported that the better and law-abiding class of citizens favored the use of the court system and not illegally hanging the prisoner.

Judge Speake issued an order closing the saloons and places selling firearms. These prompt actions by the Judge were highly praised.

During all this time, the Grand Jury continued holding its deliberations in a closed courtroom. Three hours were spent examining thirteen witnesses. About dark, the jury reported a true bill,[506] in open court, against Horace Maples, charging him with murder in the first degree.

The Grand Jury also investigated the charge against Dennis Smith. There was not enough time to complete their deliberations, so they planned to meet the next day to consider an indictment against him.

A special jury for the Maples trial was drawn. The trial was set for Wednesday, September 14th. One week would be needed to set the legal system in motion. This was not quick enough for the crowd. They had something a little quicker in mind.

Several United States prisoners were in the jail, since it was the practice then, as now, to house Federal prisoners in the County jail.

Federal Judge Shelly was notified about the disturbance around the jail. He telephoned the Deputy Federal Marshalls and notified them that their duty required them to look out for the safety of the Federal prisoners and take the names of those who endangered any prisoner's life. Taking names seems to be the only duty or responsibility the Federal Marshalls had.[507] The officials were confident that there would be no trouble.

---

[505] *The Weekly Mercury* (October 5, 1904).
[506] An indictment or charge against the defendant.
[507] These incidents set the stage for a later investigation before the United States Grand Jury. *The Weekly Mercury* (October 5, 1904).

Chief of Police David Overton, thirty-six, and his brother, policeman James Overton, forty-five, came upon a citizen they knew from the Cotton Mills. James Mitchell was standing in a wagon making a speech to the crowd. The officers ordered the crowd to disperse. They also told Mitchell to move along. Mitchell replied, *"All right, but we are coming back at eight o'clock tonight."* Loud enough for all to hear, he then said, *"Wait till Dallas turns out and then we'll get the nigger."*[508]

The crowd grew. Law enforcement officers realized that the crowd meant business. Word was sent to the Courthouse about the situation. Mr. Lane and Captain Humes[509] advised Judge Speake that the militia would be needed.

Judge Speake talked to Sheriff Rodgers about the problems of protecting the prisoner at the jail. The Sheriff felt that there was no problem with the crowd but concurred with the Judge's opinion that more help might be needed. Permission was asked, and received from Governor Cunningham, to call out the local National Guard.[510]

Judge Speake and Solicitor Pettus also suggested to the Governor that other units be dispatched to Huntsville to prevent another lynching. The Governor wired back that the man must be protected at all costs and promised to send troops.

About four o'clock in the afternoon, the Judge had the Sheriff call out Company F of the local Guard.

Thomas Hay worked at the Huntsville Hotel and was a Lieutenant in the guard. He was on the corner of Clinton Avenue and Jefferson Street with George P. Brock, the company's first sergeant, when he received orders for the company to report to the jail. He went up Randolph Street to find the Company commander, his older brother.

Robert L. Hay, thirty-seven of age, had been elected commander of the National Guard in 1898, holding the rank of Captain. Hay's younger brother, Thomas, was second in command. This was a civilian army unit and the men were part-time soldiers. Because he had not prepared a roll call in some time, the Captain was not sure how many men he commanded. The company drilled only once each week and all the men did not appear at each drill.

Captain Hay was in his office on Randolph Street when his brother came in and told him to report to the Sheriff on the orders of

---

[508] *The Weekly Mercury* (October 5, 1904).
[509] Apparently members of the committee.
[510] Locally it was called the militia but statewide it was called the National Guard.

Judge Speake. The Captain went to the jail and was informed by the Sheriff that his command had been ordered to protect the prisoner. He set out to find the men of his command to order them to report to the armory.

Lieutenant Thomas Hay, along with Lieutenant S. Morgan Stewart[511] set out to round up the men and have them report to the armory. Only twenty-five men could be mustered. A full company was not present because most of the troops had gone to camp at Manassas Virginia.

At the armory on Dallas Street,[512] the soldiers changed into their uniforms. They opened boxes of riot cartridges and loaded their Kragg-Jaugerson rifles. For about ten minutes, they practiced loading and unloading their rifles. The officers strapped on their swords. The Captain ordered bayonets fixed before leaving the armory. However, the men were ordered not to load their rifles. About twenty-five soldiers fell into line and marched down Clinton Street to the jail where the entire area was covered with people.

At half past five the company arrived at the jail, and reported to the Sheriff, who was sitting in front of the jail under a tree in his shirtsleeves. The orders that were given, and who gave what orders, would later be the subject of much controversy. It can be said, with surety, that Sheriff Rodgers and Captain Robert L. Hay discussed the events, and what to do about them.

Lieutenant Stewart arrived at the armory with some of the men he had located but the unit had left for the jail. He took his men with him and followed. When the Company was assembled, the Captain ordered the streets cleared and the soldiers performed their duty. The crowd offered no resistance and moved away as the soldiers directed.

Lieutenant Stewart helped Sgt. William A. Giles post fifteen men inside the jail and the remainder outside. Two soldiers were posted as sentinels on Clinton Avenue, nearly as far as Washington Street.[513] Ropes were stretched across Clinton Avenue, in front of the crowd. Sentinels were posted at the opening between the jail and Washington Street, one in front of the jail, one at the south end of

---

[511] S. Morgan Stewart was the Probate Judge for Madison County. He retired in November of 1904. No reason was given for his retirement. The new probate judge would be W. T. Lawler who was killed by D. D. Overton in 1916.

[512] The present day (1999) location of Eastside Community Center.

[513] This was also called Stegall's Corner. The location of the Stegall Livery Stable, Hotel, Bar and Lunch Room. It was located on the northwest corner of Washington and Clinton Streets; the present day location of Bubba's Restaurant.

Green Street, below the jail and one on Clinton Street East. The soldiers were ordered to hold the crowd back from the ropes. The men took their places behind the ropes and waited for orders to load and fire, but the orders were never given. There were no arrangements made to support the sentinels. The men were not informed that there would be no backup and they believed they would be supported if attacked. The sentinels marched up and down in front of the crowd with their unloaded rifles at the ready.

While the soldiers were containing the crowd, the Sheriff went to the Windsor Restaurant on Jefferson Street to have supper. Capt. Hay went looking for the Sheriff, and joined him at the restaurant. Lt. Hay found them there, after seven o'clock in the evening and gave them a telegraph from the Governor ordering the guard to protect the jail.[514]

Capt. Hay stopped off at the telegraph office at 7:30 o'clock, and wired Governor Cunningham that Company F had charge of the jail but that they needed help.[515]

In response to the Governor's orders, a company of Birmingham Militia was placed on the northbound train. However, they would not arrive in Huntsville until two o'clock in the morning. A Scottsboro Company of soldiers was ordered to board the train that would arrive in Huntsville at ten o'clock that night. As it happened, they could not gather their men and board the train by that time. An effort was made to bring troops from Decatur, but the railroad did not have equipment available.

Major John Elliott, commanding officer of the Birmingham National Guard, wired the Governor that he had thirty-five men from Birmingham and Woodlawn, ready to move.[516]

The shift change at the cotton mills began at eight o'clock. The mill villages of Merrimack and Dallas emptied. The men from the cotton mills poured into town, much as they had four years earlier, when they felt the courts were not moving fast enough against Elijah Clark. They felt they could better decide justice themselves.

---

[514] The Sheriff later stated he had left to seek Mayor Smith's assistance from the city police, and then he returned to the jail.
[515] Telegraph from Captain Hay to Governor Cunningham, Administrative Files, Governors Papers, 1904 (Jelks), Alabama Department of Archives and History. Montgomery, Alabama.
[516] Telegraph from Major John Elliott to Governor Cunningham, Administrative Files, Governors Papers, 1904 (Jelks), Alabama Department of Archives and History.

The excitement grew as the mill village men and young boys arrived in front of the jail.

They spread into the crowd between City Hall and the jail. The threatening talk increased. The men hollered and shouted at the troops and guards in the jail. Cussing one and all they demanded action. Many men were armed. Torches were carried by men throughout the crowd casting shadows on the surrounding buildings and the faces of the angry men.

The mob grew and the atmosphere changed to a more dangerous tone.

Lt. Stewart was watching the crowd when Capt. Hay said, *"Notify the men of the guard lines that Sheriff Rodgers has ordered that, when assembly sounds, all the men outside of the jail are to get inside."*[517] [518] The Lieutenant walked down the line of men and was talking to a guard when the lines on Clinton Street were rushed.

All at once there was a sudden charge and, with the swiftness of a mad dog, the crowd turned into a raging mob and rushed the lines at several places, at the same time.

The mob attacked the soldiers at the corner of Clinton and Washington. They cut the ropes and wrestled the rifles from the soldiers as the mob surged toward the jail. There was mass confusion. Threats filled the air as the men shoved and pushed against each other. Men were swearing and shouting obscenities.

All this could be heard at a great distance. More men arrived to investigate the noise. Shots were fired from the mob as the soldiers were outwitted and overpowered.

Private Thomas E. McClain and Private J. S. Carter had the post at the ropes on Clinton. As McClain made a turn at the end of his post, the mob rushed over the ropes and grabbed him. Private Adams, with the Recruiting Office, went to the corner where the mob first broke through. As he arrived, he saw the line run over Private McClain.

McClain would not have had time to fire, even if his rifle had been loaded. He shoved one man against the wall of Skinners's Carriage Factory on the corner. Another man grabbed him from behind and began choking him. He fell backwards and dragged the three men, who held his rifle, down with him.

---

[517] *The Daily Mercury* (September 8, 1904).
[518] *The Huntsville Weekly Democrat* (September 24, 1904).

Huntsville-Madison County Public Library

Skinner's Carriage Factory-Across from Jail

Sergeant W. T. Giles ran to the place where the lines were rushed and found Private McClain on the ground badly beaten by the crowd.

Sergeant Giles was joined by Private Adams and Sergeant Gooch. Sgt. Giles held the mob back at the point of his bayonet for several minutes while they got McClain on his feet and took him from the mob. The mob hesitated when Sgt. Giles ordered them to do so. Adams took a pistol away from one of the men in the mob, but in the fight they took it back. The two carried McClain to the jail where he regained consciousness. He never lost his rifle.

The other soldiers were disarmed without firing a shot. After the mob took the rifles away from the soldiers, they told them to move on and did not allow them to join the other soldiers at the jail. The company's fighting force was considerably reduced. A squad of only fifteen men would have been available to be inside the jail to repel a very large mob.

Sergeant Brock ordered Private N. T. Rafford to sound assembly as the mob rushed the lines. The distance from the jail to the place attacked by the mob was only about 100 yards.

The attack found ten of the men sitting around on the curbstones having supper. Lt. Hay commanded the men to fall in. The company was formed in front of the jail. They were ordered by someone to go inside the jail.[519]

The Sheriff returned from supper just in time to go into the jail with the soldiers. The Sheriff's son went into the jail with his father.

Over the noise of the crowd, Lt. Stewart heard assembly called and returned to the jail, saw the men going into the jail and followed. Inside, Lt. Stewart set to work issuing ball and cartridges and said, *"Fill your magazines and then your belts."*[520] He expected the order to fire would be given and wanted everyone to have enough ammunition. As the men finished loading, he told them to station themselves on the steps. The Sheriff shut the door and followed them. As the mob approached the jail, Captain Hay asked if he should fire. Sheriff Rodgers said, *"Not now"* or *"Not yet."*[521] [522]

A number of shots were fired by the mob. This commotion aroused the citizens in their homes. They rushed from their residences and went downtown to see what was gong on. They found the jail surrounded by violent men, shouting for the release of the prisoner. Rocks were thrown through the windows. The mob broke out every window in the first floor and began to pound on the lower floor doors.

The ordinary, thin paneled, ground floor door was battered down and the mob poured into the first floor hallway. No effort was made to hold the lower floor. The Sheriff insisted that Capt. Hay stated, *"We can't stay here, we will have to go upstairs."*[523] The soldiers took up a new position at the end of a hall or corridor, on the winding stairway to the portion of the jail where the jailer and his family lived. Sheriff Rodgers shouted, *"Don't let anyone come up here."*[524] He was seen standing on the stairs, unarmed, motioning his hand as if to stop any further advance. He informed the mob below

---

[519] Who gave what order would be the subject of much controversy and testimony later.
[520] *The Weekly Mercury* (September 21, 1904), *The Huntsville Weekly Democrat* (September 14, 1904).
[521] *The Weekly Mercury* (September 28, 1904).
[522] Military Court of Inquiry Transcript, Adjunct General's File, 1904, Department of Archives and History.
[523] *The Birmingham News* (September 20, 1904).
[524] *The Daily Mercury* (September 8, 1904).

that he would kill anyone starting up the steps. Members of the mob shouted that they wanted the prisoner.

Huntsville-Madison County Public Library

Madison County Jail

Deputy Ward had been sent to hurry the city police to the jail. He reported back to the Sheriff and was asked to go down and talk to the mob and prevail upon them to stop their actions. The other two regular deputies, Potts and Ferrell, were present but did not defend the jail.

After taking over the first floor, the mob grew bolder. They started a fire of tar and Cayenne pepper. This created an almost unbearable smoke. The fence around the jail was broken up and pieces were used for the fire. Tables were added to the fire in the lobby of the jail in full view of the Sheriff and Militia. The back part of the jail burned fiercely.

When the fire started, the soldiers began asking about firing at the mob. Capt. Hay said, "*Don't shoot without an order from the*

Sheriff."[525] The men began to kick and wanted to do something. One said "*For God's sake Lieutenant, let's shoot or do something*". Lt. Stewart turned and said, *"Captain, the men want to do something and not just stand here."* Capt. Hay replied, *"I can't do anything without Sheriff Rodgers's orders. Go see him."*[526]

The Sheriff attempted to put out the fire by throwing a bucket of water down the stairs. A member of the mob called to him, "*Mr. Rodgers, go back, if you give us the nigger we will put out the fire!*"[527] No orders were given to fire. Another fire was started in the dining room, downstairs, and a rear hall, not commanded by the guns of the soldiers. The fire was behind them and could not be seen or reached without abandoning the stairway. The Sheriff hollered down stairs, *"If you will put out the fire we'll give you the nigger."*[528] The mob answered that they would not put out the fire until the prisoner was turned over to them.

For an hour or more, the fire spread and the woodwork started to burn. The fire soon spread throughout the first floor and the heat was overwhelming. Dense smoke spread through the upper floors of the jail. The City police officers were not to be seen downtown. Chief of Police Overton was in the crowd but neither he nor the nine men in the Huntsville Police Department took part in controlling the mob. After all, it was the Sheriff's problem! While one police officer was interested in rescuing two prisoners who were friends, the other officer mingled with the mob in the hallway and hollered to the Sheriff on the stairs.[529]

Reuben A. Gulley, a Baptist preacher, was a prisoner in the jail and cried out, *"For God's sake, don't burn us men, we are white men and gentlemen and you are killing us and we can't get out."*[530] The prisoner's pleas were answered by the heartless jeers of the mob, none of them being familiar faces or known property owners.

When the fire died down, more fuel was added and the flames flashed higher and smoke began to pour out the windows upstairs. Reverend Gulley was on the top floor. The smoke flowed through his cell as through a chimney and he continued to call out, "*Boys, for*

---

[525] *The Birmingham News* (September 20, 1904).
[526] *The Weekly Mercury* (September 21, 1904).
[527] *The Daily Mercury* (September 8, 1904).
[528] *The Birmingham News* (September 20, 1904).
[529] Some of the men had apparently been present at the last lynching. The methods used were much like those used in 1900. Four years before, the mob had dynamited the steps and set fires that gave off suffocating fumes.
[530] *The Daily Mercury* (September 8, 1904).

God's sake let them put the fire out."[531] His frantic appeals were again answered by the callous hoots of the mob.

While some of the mob gave orders, others piled wood on the fire and many more just stood around doing nothing. One member of the mob said, *"Burn her down, let's have him."*[532]

Citizens prevailed upon the Mayor to order out the Fire Company. The City fire engine, the chemical engine, and the hose carriage responded to the fire alarm and came at once but were not allowed to connect to a fireplug or lay a hose. They were met by cries of, *"Don't stop!"* and *"Cut the hose!"*[533] Curses and stones were hurtled at the Engine Hook and Ladder Company. When someone fired a pistol at the engine, the horse became frightened and unmanageable, could not be held, and ran wildly down the street. The firemen took the engine back to Washington Street and Clinton Avenue and let the fire burn. It was apparent that the jail would burn to the ground unless the firemen were allowed to fight the blaze. When there was a cry to allow the firemen to fight the blaze, some of the mob shouted, *"Wait until they give us the nigger and then we will put the fire out for them."*[534]

Telegram from Solicitor Pettus to Governor Cunningham

---

[531] *The Daily Mercury* (September 8, 1904).
[532] *The Weekly Mercury* (September 28, 1904).
[533] *The Huntsville Weekly Democrat* (September 14, 1904).
[534] *The Daily Mercury* (September 8, 1904).

The regular deputies of the Sheriff, except Thomas W. Ward, were not seen in, or about the jail. Deputy Ward went to the Sheriff on several occasions during the siege, and was sent to get aid from the city police. He was never ordered to summon other deputies to aid the Sheriff in the situation. The Sheriff did not summon a posse or special deputies to defend the jail. The Sheriff appeared to have relied on the city police, the militia and his influence with the mob.

No member of the mob came up the stairs. Some of the soldiers asked if they should fire through a door on which the mob was hammering. The Sheriff said, *"No, don't shoot to try to scare this mob."*[535]

From the steps of the jail, Reverend Culver made another address to the crowd while the fire was going full blaze. He begged them to let the fire department come, extinguish the flames, and save the prisoners who appeared to be in danger of perishing. James Mitchell said, *"Damn the jail, we will burn the damn jail and every man in it unless they give us the nigger. We are going to hang him."*[536] [537] Silas Worley told the crowd *"Burn her down, let's have him."*[538] Several members of the mob seized hold of Reverend Culver and pushed him down the steps by force. James Mitchell's son, Will, struck him with a piece of iron pipe and cursing him said, *"You are a preacher and you have no business in the crowd."*[539] James Mitchell shouted at the Sheriff, *"Shoot if you want to and this crowd will fix you."*[540]

Finally, the Sheriff, his son, and his guards, almost stifled with smoke, heat and the suffocating fumes of burning red pepper and sulfur, had to make a decision to fire on the mob or surrender the jail. The Sheriff made a decision to abandon his duties and ordered Jailer Giles to release the prisoner. The Sheriff, in a decision that he would live with the reminder of his life, gave up his keys to the jailer and then he walked out. The Militia followed him.

The Sheriff had failed to clear the streets during the day and evening. He had failed to summon a posse to assist him and he had

---

[535] *The Weekly Mercury* (September 28, 1904).
[536] *The Weekly Mercury* (October 5, 1904).
[537] Military Court of Inquiry Transcripts, Adjunct General's File, 1904 (Jelks), Alabama Department of Archives and History.
[538] *The Weekly Mercury* (October 5, 1904).
[539] *Ibid.*
[540] *The Birmingham News* (September 30, 1904), *The Weekly Mercury* (October 5, 1904).

failed to give the militia an order to fire. It was impossible to escape the conclusion that he had neglected his duty.[541]

Maples, in a cell on the second floor, was then turned out of his cell by the jailer, taken to the head of the stairway and released to his destination with *"the tree."*

After looking into the faces of the mob, Maples ran back through the jailer's room and jumped, or was pushed, from the upper window on the west side of the jail. When Maples leaped from the window, he was not seen by most of the mob, who stood around watching the fire. When a few did see him, they attracted the attention of the rest of the mob. Maples was seized, promptly knocked down and led off, with a plow line around his neck. Someone hollowed *"Here he is, boys!"*[542]

As Maples jumped from the window, the soldiers who had given up to the mob, marched down the stairs, and out of the jail. They were assaulted, cursed, separated, and lost their identity as a military unit. The company could not preserve its formation within the mob and was scattered into the crowd.

The Sheriff and Sergeant Giles walked down the stairs together. On the bottom step, Worley and two or three others tried to take the rifle from Sergeant Giles. Deputy Ward went to his assistance and prevented the mob from taking the weapon.

As the men forced Maples up Clinton Avenue and Washington Street, toward the Courthouse, Fire Chief Abe Wise and his fireman were allowed to return to the jail and extinguish the blaze. Many did not believe that Maples had left the building. They remained, watching the fire department fight the blaze in the jail. Quiet returned to the jail and the calmer of the mob stayed there. The Sheriff stayed at the jail watching the fire.

Maples was lead up Clinton Avenue by the mob. Many would later state that they were not members of the mob, but rather watched from the sidewalks as the parade went by. R. L. Stephens, overseer of the carding room[543] in the Dallas Mill, was standing near the Van Valkenburg and Matthew's Hardware Store. He walked to the corner of Washington and Clinton and stood in front of the Stegall Hotel.

---

[541] Letter from Judge Speake to Governor Cunningham, Administrative Files, Governor's Papers, 1904 (Jelks), Alabama Department of Archives and History.

[542] *The Daily Mercury* (September 8, 1904). The Military Court of Inquiry Transcripts, Adjunct General File, 1904, Alabama Department of Archives and History.

[543] A carding room is where the raw cotton is separated and processed to send to the spinning room to be processed into threads.

Stephens saw the men who had hold of Maples. They were walking in the middle of the pavement on Clinton Avenue and he watched as they turned onto Washington Street. W. L. Brigham, a Dallas Mill worker, was on his way to the post office. He was in the street leading up toward the Courthouse yard and saw Maples with the men as they went by. Tom Kirk, an overseer in the spinning room[544] of the Dallas Mill, was at the Stegall Hotel. He had also started to the post office and was walking in that direction when the crowd passed him with Maples in tow. It seemed that there were many men going to check their mailbox at the post office that night.

On the east side of the Courthouse yard, a lawn fete was in progress. The Daughters of America were holding an ice cream festival with brilliant colored Japanese lanterns lighting the event. Women and children were playing and generally enjoying the festival. The mob went through and scattered the festival until it was also part of the crowd. [545]

With the plow line around his neck, Maples was led around to the south side of the Courthouse Square to the intersection of Commercial Row and Cheap Side Row.[546] He was taken into the yard surrounding the Courthouse, and stopped at an elm tree nearest the Courthouse on the southeast side. He was surrounded by thousands of people shouting and milling about.[547] One of the leaders of the mob told Maples that he would soon die and that he should confess.

The victim's son, Jack Waldrop, was pushed forward and asked Maples, "*Horace, did you kill my old dad?*"[548] Waldrop made a motion as if he would draw a gun or knife from his pocket. Members of the mob restrained him. Jack Waldrop was unable to control his emotions and was forced to leave the crowd.

Maples said, "*Gentlemen, before God, I am innocent. I did not kill Mr. Waldrop. I rode out of town with him then got out at Newsom's Nursery and came back to town.*"[549] While the mob stood around, Maples was questioned further and tripped up by several of his statements. He finally admitted that he had gone the entire

---

[544] A spinning room is the room where the cotton is spun into thread and onto cones.

[545] No mention was made of why a quiet party was going on at that hour of the night when a fire, shooting, and loud noises from a mob of thousands were easily seen and heard just down the street.

[546] Today this would be at the intersection of Southside Square and Eastside Square; across the street from Harrison Brothers Store.

[547] *The Birmingham News* (September 8, 1904)

[548] *The Daily Mercury* (September 8, 1904).

[549] *The Daily Mercury* (September 8, 1904).

distance with Waldrop, but then gave a new story and said that two Negroes held them up.

Little by little, the details of the killing were forced from him. He was made to admit that he had killed Waldrop with a small club that he later threw into the river. He stated that he had three accomplices, two Negroes and a white man. He gave the names of the three men to some of the mob standing nearby.[550]

While the men in the yard were forcing a confession from Maples, Attorney John H Wallace Jr. was spotted on the steps of the Courthouse and asked by the law-abiding citizens to say something. They were looking for a leader to calm the mob and prevent what was fast becoming evident. Wallace responded and made an eloquent appeal for the upholding of the law. Attorney Robert C. Brickell also gave an address to the mob and asked the men to honor the authority of the courts. Other men were on different parts of the Courthouse lawn and gave speeches for the respect of the law. W. B. Bankhead spoke in favor of upholding the law. The speakers were interrupted by frequent cries to *"hang the nigger."*[551]

Judge William Richardson spoke on behalf of law and order. That portion of the mob within hearing of the speakers' voices was greatly impressed, but the majority hooted down each speaker in turn. Nothing the speakers could say was of any avail after Maples confessed. While it was evident that not everyone present was in favor of the lynching, no one lifted a hand to stop it.

Solicitor Pettus gave an address, asking the mob to obey the law and called upon all that were in favor of law and order to raise their hats. There was a sea of hats, as half of the mob did so. They were called upon to return Maples to the jail, but after hearing his confession, the mob was beyond argument and meant to kill him. The paper reported that any attempt to save the prisoner could have resulted in an insurrection that would have proven fatal to many innocent people, or possibly injuring someone or damaging property.

A crowd of between one thousand to five thousand people witnessed the event.[552] Many commented on the politeness of the crowd around the Courthouse that night. There was no shoving or swearing. The crowd became quiet and orderly. Some said that not more than twenty-five people actively participated in the lynching.

---

[550] There is no indication that anyone investigated the three men named.
[551] *The Daily Mercury* (September 8, 1904).
[552] There were several estimates of the numbers in the mob from different witnesses and all the newspapers. A reliable figure cannot be obtained.

Most of the citizens opposed the lynching, but the thousands chose not to control those twenty-five men. The silence of the spectators gave approval to the public murder.

The Sheriff did not attend the hanging. He had not attempted to form a posse or appoint special deputies to appear at the Courthouse to save the prisoner from the mob. The city police may have been in the crowd, but they did not make their presence known. No member of the National Guard attempted to re-form the soldiers into a unit, to prevent the murder.

As the crowd watched, the gruesome work was carried out in a business-like manner. The end of the plow line was attached to Maples' neck and was thrown over a convenient limb of the elm tree. Maples was pulled up, and held dangling from the limb. A man climbed the tree and asked that the weight of the man be taken from the rope while he tied it around a limb. Several men lifted Maples from the ground. A member of the mob held the end of the rope until it was securely fastened. In a manner calm and deliberate, the Negro was swung up.

Maples watched all this with the knowledge that he was about to die. For a short moment, he turned his face upward and saw the great cross on the spire of the Church of the Nativity just down the street. The sign of the cross and the symbol of Christianity were the background for this most sinful act.

Maples was allowed to swing free. The body swung, twisted, and humped. While he was in the last moments of life, the leaders of the mob cleared the crowd away from the tree. As Maples died a slow death by strangulation, several pistol shots were fired into his body. Then his kicking ceased and he was dead. The great clock in the tower, of the Courthouse, struck eleven.

The crowd watched the lynching with morbid curiosity. Some made way so women and children could get a better view of the victim. That night, each person in the crowd had to choose between staying and watching, or walking away. The thousands present indicated that there were not many that turned away. Many "bona-fide" ladies were present and indulged in the morbid taste for the horrible sight.

Attorney Robert H. Lowe watched from the edge of the crowd, helpless to stop the injustice. Tom Kirk, Reverend Frank P. Culver and farmer Tom Talley were in the yard. Reuben Clutts and Silas Worley were seen near the east gate of the fence. James B. Pollard, a bartender; Archie Hawking, foreman at the Lowe Mills; John Billingsley, Jim Couch, Tom Mason, Jr., and Dr. W. P. Hooper were near the tree. Ex-Senator Ed. L. Pulley was very close to the tree. The man who climbed the tree to tie the rope bumped against him.

Souvenir hunters cut the trouser legs of Maples' pants away above the knees. One man cut off Maples' little finger as a souvenir. The crowd that remained for several hours around the body during the night forcibly discouraged further attempts at mutilation. There is no information on who put them in charge. They were self-appointed leaders of the protection committee to save the body from the mob. *"One cheery fact in connection with the horrors, is that the souvenir hunters, after cutting away part of the negro's clothing, were not allowed to cut off any more fingers or his ears!"*[553]

The Sheriff remained at the jail until one o'clock in the morning to make sure the fire was thoroughly extinguished. Then he went home.

A few members of the crowd would stay on the court house lawn all night.

The Birmingham provisional Company arrived at half past three o'clock, in the morning. Majors Elliott, Yeatman, and Captains Brown and Smith commanded the company. Sentries were placed around the jail, setting up barricades and blocking off the area as ordered, but the streets were now quiet. Only those standing around the body in the Courthouse yard could be found. Major Elliott reported to the Sheriff at his residence. The Sheriff told him that the prisoner had been taken from his jail and lynched and he had no orders for the company. There was no report that the Sheriff ordered the body of the prisoner to be taken from the tree. Major Elliott did not take it upon himself to visit the lynched prisoner and, after four hours, the soldiers returned to Birmingham, leaving the body still hanging from the tree downtown. Maples was allowed to swing all night under the watchful eyes of the small crowd protecting the body.

---

[553] *The Birmingham News* (September 8, 1904).

Huntsville-Madison County Public Library

In November 1905, a crowd of several thousand gathered on the south side of Madison Counties Courthouse to dedicate the Confederate monument. "The tree" can be seen just to the left of the monument. This must have looked like the scene at the lynching, fourteen months earlier, except that it was night and the only light was the torches carried by the mob.

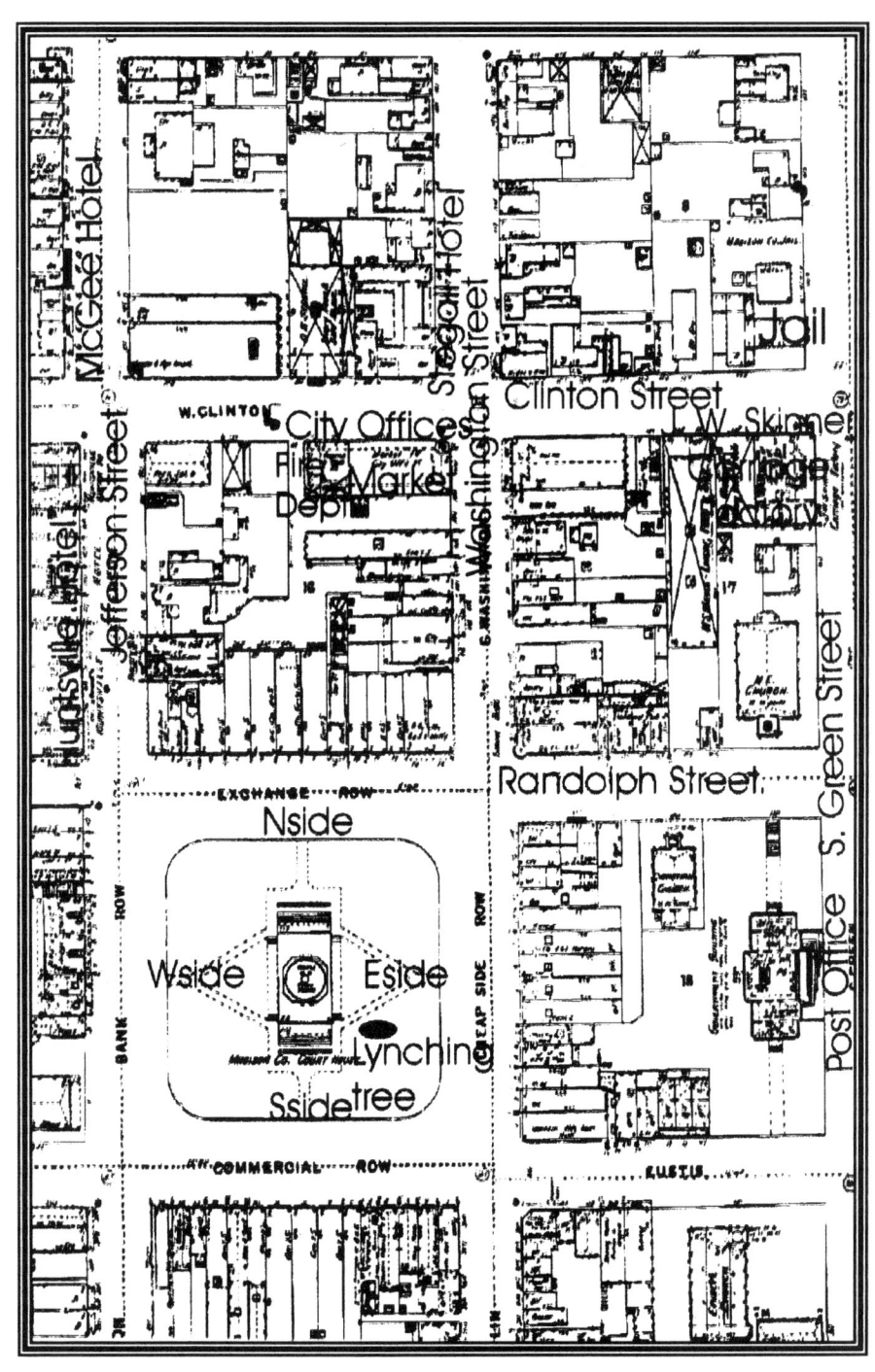

Downtown Huntsville

Courtesy of Attorney Patrick W. Richardson

Photograph of Maples lynching

Wednesday September 7, 1904

A gruesome sight met the gaze of the citizens of Huntsville the next morning. As the September sun rose over Monte Sano Mountain, the first rays filtered through the trees and crept slowly down Eustis Street as if not wanting to touch the sight at the corner of the Courthouse. Dangling from a limb of a large elm tree at the southeast corner of the Courthouse, the body of Horace Maples turned in the morning breeze. Were he alive he could almost have reached out and touched the house of justice that was built to insure a fair trial for every citizen.

A streetcar rounded the square making a screaming noise on the rails that were set in the brick streets. People went about their normal morning routine. There was a great deal of downtown traffic. Circuit Court opened that morning and many men reported for jury duty. Some reported to work while others came to see Maples' body. A crowd stood all around the Courthouse, along Commercial Row and Cheap Side Row. As the crowd watched the body slowly turn, the dead man twisted to one side, allowing his face to be seen. It was grotesque with eyes bulging out and his tongue protruding. Blood had run down his body from the gunshot wounds, through his clothes, and dropped onto the ground.

Horace Maples had paid the price for killing E. D. Waldrop.

A white sheet had been placed around the body during the night, but the shiny black head protruded from the top. The gruesome spectacle of the body hanging there, with a bloody sheet flapping in the breeze, did not prevent several hundred men and women from standing around, watching the dead man sway to-and-fro. Cameras were produced and photographs were taken. Men posed in front of and around the body. As photographs were taken, the men placed their hand on the corpse as if it were their trophy. The rope was cut up and given to those who collected such items.

After swinging for ten hours, Maples' body was cut down, at nine o'clock in the morning, by the Coroner. It was taken to Laughlin's undertaking establishment on West Clinton Street. Maples' burial was expected to be carried out that day but details, unfortunately, were incomplete.

Judge Speake and Solicitor Pettus discussed the situation while the body still hung in the tree outside. What these two had to say to one another throughout that day could only be guessed. It is certain that they were determined to punish the leaders of the mob. Both felt that to take any action against the lynchers could mean the end of their political careers, but courageously started the necessary action to stop any further lynching in Madison County. They discussed what action to take and decided they would attempt to indict and try every leader of the mob.

Curious crowds visited the empty tree throughout the day.

With the opening of Circuit Court that morning, Judge Speake ordered another special Grand Jury,[554] to convene on Friday. Their job would be to investigate the lynching, the fire in the jail, and any violation of the duties imposed upon any public officer. Mob violence, according to Judge Speake, could not *"go unpunished."*[555]

The authorities viewed the serious damages to the jail. They found that the steps leading up from the hall were burned away and the dining room and kitchen were in a wrecked condition. The intense heat had injured the walls. Hundreds of rocks had been thrown into the building and there was not a whole windowpane in the jail. The fence around the premises, used in the fire, would have to be replaced. There was more destruction to the jail, this time than four years earlier when dynamite was used.

Coroner E. B. Stewart, who had been near the lynching tree Tuesday night, summoned a Coroner's Jury and an inquest was held at two o'clock in the afternoon. The usual verdict of *"Hung By Persons Unknown"* was returned. *"We find that he came to his death by hanging from a tree in the Courthouse yard on the night of September 7, 1904, by parties unknown to the jury."* Signed by A. E. Overton; J. L. Orgain; S. B. Stewart Jr. and H. P. Turner.[556]

J. T. Cooper refused to sign the verdict and produced his own version that praised the defenders of the jail for protecting the thirty prisoners still in the jail and allowing Maples an opportunity to escape through the window.[557]

---

[554] This is the third Grand Jury called into session. This Special Grand Jury would investigate the lynching of Horace Maples.
[555] *The Birmingham News* (September 8, 1904).
[556] *The Weekly Mercury* (September 14, 1904). Coroner Stewart was named as being at the scene of the hanging but is now instrumental in returning a verdict of *"Hung by persons unknown."*
[557] Ibid.

The first special Grand Jury returned to finish their work from the day before when they had been in a hurry to appease the crowd and indict Maples for murder. In the rush of excitement they did not have time to consider the case of Dennis Smith.

Twenty-four hours later, after hearing witnesses, they returned an indictment against Smith charging him with murder in the first degree. Smith was arraigned in the Circuit Court during the day and pled, '*not guilty.*' His trial was set for Wednesday, September 14th. Attorney's Shelby Pleasant and Robert Brickell were appointed to defend him.

Governor William D. Jelks was absent from the State during all of 1904, due to bad health. In his absence, Dr. Russell McWhorter Cunningham, of Birmingham, a successful doctor and businessman, filled the office. He had served Lawrence County in the legislature until he was elected Lieutenant Governor, under Governor Jelks.[558]

Governor Cunningham was neither slow nor timid in starting an investigation. He asked for all of the details of the lynching. Letters were written to the principal players in the drama. The Governor's private secretary, J. Kirk Jackson, wrote the Sheriff and Captain Hay for detailed information about the affair.

Governor Cunningham questioned the soldiers who traveled from Birmingham to Huntsville, but had arrived too late to prevent the lynching. They supplied him with considerable information concerning the lynching, which could be used in an investigation, military or civil, as well as in criminal proceedings.

One member of the Birmingham military unit declared that the Huntsville soldiers laughed at the matter and that the description of how the Negro got through the window and out of the burning jail was just simply ludicrous.

The Governor had a conference with the Adjutant General and by his command, an order was promulgated, for a Military Court of Inquiry to assemble and investigate the actions taken by the local military on the night of the lynching. The Governor's instructions were that the Court was to investigate and report the facts together with their recommendations in reference to the conduct of the officers and men composing Company F, 3rd Regiment, Alabama National Guard. The Military Court of Inquiry was ordered, even though Captain Hay, the commanding officer of the unit, had sent a report of

---

[558] After leaving office in 1907, Governor Jelks organized the Protective Life Insurance Company in Birmingham and served as its first president.

the affair to the Governor. The Court of Inquiry was ordered to convene at Huntsville, Monday, September 19th.[559]

One newspaper did not agree with the violence and lawlessness and immediately stated an opinion in forceful words:

"Today, we are forced to admit in shame that we live in a country where law, peace, and dignity are a myth. The actions of last night prove our statement. There was an absence of generalship by Sheriff Rodgers, like Sheriff Fulgham who suffered a similar disaster four years ago. The jail cannot be held from the second floor. They should shoot from the front steps and shoot to kill. Otherwise, a howling mob of irresponsible men with torch in one hand and rope in the other can expect no violence from the military or the law. In the future, before the court acts, before the guilt or innocence of a prisoner is passed upon, the cotton mill boys must be consulted, their pleasure ascertained. Twice they have defied the laws and twice participated in firing our jail. What are we going to do about it? The Huntsville Police are a farce. They stated they were guarding dynamite and the fight was Rodgers', not theirs. They failed to defend the fire department. Any man who dared cut a hose used to put out a dangerous blaze should be killed dead in his track. A city of eighteen thousand inhabitants should have brave police. Twice our sheriffs have failed and twice our city police have refused to act. The Tribune is disgusted."[560]

Friday, September 9, 1904

The Governor called a press conference, the morning of Friday, September 9th. He began by saying that at the time of his first notification, he had taken every action allowed him by the law and could only await reports, which he hoped to have in a few days. He continued by saying he greatly deplored the tragedy and considered it very unfortunate for the State.

---

[559] This information is from a statement issued in Montgomery, by way of a special report to the *Birmingham Age* newspaper.
[560] *The Weekly Mercury* (September 8, 1904) copied article from *The Tribune* (no date given).

Huntsville-Madison County Public Library
Southeast corner of the Madison County Courthouse.
This is one of a series of photographs taken of the scene of the lynching.
"The tree" is the one closest to the courthouse, behind the wagon.

At ten o'clock that Friday, the special Grand Jury, called into session by Judge Speake, convened and began their investigation into the lynching of Horace Maples, the fire in the jail, and any violation of public duty. The jurymen were composed of E. R. Matthews (foreman), R. E. Pettus, J. P. Watts, E. T. Bailes, J. G. Grayson, C. S. McCalley, F. P. Culver, J. W. Battle, W. W. Esslinger, R. L. O'Neal, and S. S. Fletcher. The brave men would listen to the Judge as he charged them with the instructions that public welfare demanded an investigation of the mob violence and that the law must be returned to the system set up to defend all people justly.

While the Circuit Court Judge is charged with the responsibility of convening a Grand Jury, the Solicitor would be the person presenting witnesses to the jurymen. His duty would require him to subpoena witnesses and guide their testimony in order to seek an indictment against those suspected of participating in the lynching. Solicitor Pettus knew he would be criticized and attacked for performing his duty, but he took the action anyway and accepted the consequences.

In answer to the order of the Governor, Sheriff Rodgers sent a telegraph on Saturday, September 10th, stating that he would not mail a report until the following Monday, as he was using all the department's time for the Special Grand Jury.[561] Captain Hay wired that he was preparing his report and would mail it on the Fourteenth.[562] The Governor would not make public the two reports and ask the public to suspend judgment until an investigation was complete.

From Athens, Solicitor Pettus sent an account of the mob's actions. He wrote the Governor on Monday, September 12th, from the Hotel Bismark in Decatur, that he felt the Grand Jury would return indictments for capital offenses, but knew it would be difficult to secure convictions.[563]

The Governor took a strong stand against lynching by stating, *"If it is permitted, you and I could be easily arrested and accused of a bad offense, and without trial could be lynched by our enemies. It must be stopped."*[564]

During that week, there was much discussion, among several groups, as to what could best be done to stamp out forever the lawless spirit, which permitted the taking of prisoners from the jail. It was not just Maples, but Elijah Clark, who also had been taken from the same jail in 1900 and lynched.

It was decided that the better plan would be to hold a citizen's meeting at the Courthouse where there could be a full discussion and plans made to ensure that never again would this type of disgrace be allowed.

It was stated in one of the local papers:

"Through the wild passions of the mob, shame and disgrace were brought upon our community. Justice was violated and the very temple of justice was insulted at her door. We ask if the law-abiding citizens are going to allow this type of lawlessness to dominate them? If lawlessness combined to break and destroy the law, the good

---

[561] Telegraph from Sheriff Rodgers to Governor Cunningham, Administrative Files, Governor's Papers, 1904 (Jelks), Alabama Department of Archives and History.
[562] Telegraph from Captain Hay to Governor Cunningham, Administrative Files, Governor's Papers, 1904 (Jelks), Alabama Department of Archives and History.
[563] Letter from Solicitor Pettus to Governor Cunningham, Administrative files, Governor's Papers, 1904 (Jelks), Alabama Department of Archives and History.
[564] *The Birmingham News* (September 19, 1904).

citizens must combine to protest the law and to see that the law is not trampled under foot."[565]

The papers asked the community if it would be necessary in the future to '*consult the cotton mill boys*' before the law could take its course. They pointed out that twice the *"lint-heads"*[566] had succeeded in over-riding the law and killing a prisoner.

Wednesday, September 14, 1904

The meeting took place at the Madison County Courthouse, on Wednesday September 14, 1904, and was called to order by Robert C. Brickell, an attorney. He moved that S. J. Mayhew, be made chairman.

Mayhew delivered a speech in which he said:

"Huntsville is arraigned before the world, by the acts of a few, as a lawless community. The law-abiding citizens must prepare to prevent any further scenes like the one we have just passed through."[567]

Attorney Brickell then moved that a committee of five be appointed to draft resolutions on the matter. They were; himself, R. E. Pettus, R. W. T. Hutchens, O. R. Hundley and Dr. F. E. Baldridge.

C. P. Lang, John Burke, Erle Pettus, Postmaster W. T. Hutchens, Reverend Frank. P. Culver, John Young, and Oscar R. Hundley made excellent speeches. There was a great deal of criticism and condemnation of the local law enforcement agencies.

A resolution was passed which denounced and condemned the lawless conduct. The committee pledged the aid and assistance of the members to restore law and order. They demanded that the officers of the law exercise the power vested in them, to uphold the law regardless of any hazard. Hutchens offered a resolution to purchase seventy-five riot guns for arming citizens to prevent another mob from braking into the jail.

---

[565] *The Weekly Mercury* (September 14, 1904).
[566] Name often used to describe the mill workers, due to the cotton dust that would settle in their hair during the day's work.
[567] *The Weekly Mercury* (September 14, 1904).

Thursday, September 15, 1904

Judge Speake discussed the mob violence with United States District Judge, Thomas G. Jones. He encouraged the Federal government to review the actions of the mob when the Federal Grand Jury met in October. He further hoped that United States Marshalls would be allowed to arrest those indicted.[568] Judge Jones forwarded a report to Governor Cunningham, of the United States Marshall's action, regarding the mob and the military guard at Huntsville. He indicated he was working with Judge Speake and Solicitor Pettus but wished the report not be given to any other person.[569]

Although the special Grand Jury would continue its investigation for days, it rendered a partial report to Judge Speake about nine o'clock Thursday night. Eight indictments against alleged lynchers, for capital murder, were returned. The names of the indicted were not made public in order to prevent the men from leaving the county before their arrest. There was much interest in learning who was to be charged and arrested. It was rumored that the class of men who were to be arrested would be a surprise. There would be not only men of the cotton mill community but also several prominent Huntsville citizens. While the Grand Jury's report was made in open court, the deliberations and indictments were secret. The newspapers had to wait for information, as did the public.

The press around the State took a strong stand against the lynchers.

"The young men who belong to our National Guard are not generally cowards. Who is responsible for the humiliating part they played at Huntsville? Didn't the Sheriff know that it was his duty to fire on the mob if necessary to save his prisoner? Didn't the military officer know that it was his duty to fire when he and his command were being smoked out and his sentinels rushed? It is time to quit the farce of calling out the military to guard a jail if they are not to fight. They are put on guard to kill persons who assault the jail. That is their business. If the first man who struck a match to smoke out the soldiers had been shot, that would have ended the mob. A volley fired into the crowd, which came within the forbidden limits, would have settled the lynchers. If our military are to stand with folded hands

---

[568] Letter from Judge Speakes to Governor Cunningham, Administrative Files, Governors Papers, 1904 (Jelks), Alabama Department of Archives and History.

[569] Letter from Judge Jones to Governor Cunningham, Administrative Files, Governors Papers, 1904 (Jelks), Alabama Department of Archives and History.

when such devilishness is enacted as took place around the Huntsville jail, the sooner the military is disbanded the better."[570]

Solicitor Pettus contacted the Governor by letter discussing the prosecution of those indicted. He requested that a local attorney be appointed to assist with the coming trials. He was from Limestone County and needed an attorney from Huntsville who knew the local people and could assist in the selection of a jury. He suggested the Governor contact D. A. Grayson, a Huntsville attorney to see if he would fearlessly serve his people and his state in this emergency.[571]

David A. Grayson practiced law in Huntsville with his brother Claude A. Grayson. He was well known by the community and in turn he was very knowledgeable about the people of Huntsville.[572]

Grayson was contacted by the Governor and replied that if there were only one case, he would gladly lend his best efforts to secure a conviction without pay, but he would leave setting the fee for his services, to the Governor. Grayson went on to say that he was convinced the lynchers should be punished and he preferred to prosecute rather than defend.

Grayson was appointed by the Governor as an Assistant Solicitor to help in the prosecution of the coming cases. For the sum of $250, the attorney was, as he stated himself:

"Prompted by the best motives, I trust, that swell within the bosom of a patriotic citizen. I am going to engage in the service hoping that I can be a great benefit in the loyal efforts being made to vindicate the majesty of the law." [573]

Ben Hill, a worker at the Lowe Cotton Mill, was the first to be arrested upon an indictment for murder. The arrest took place shortly before noon at his home in Lowe Mill Village. He was placed in the same jail that he was accused of burning on the night of the lynching.

Deputy Sheriff H. N. Strong arrested Tom Winkle, who worked at the Huntsville Cotton Mill on a charge of arson of the jail. Walter Solway, a day laborer, was arrested on a misdemeanor charge of throwing rocks into the jail.

---

[570] *Montgomery Advisor* (September 14, 1904).
[571] Letter from Solicitor Pettus to Governor Cunningham, 1904 (Jelks), Administrative Files, Governors Papers, Alabama Department of Archives and History.
[572] It was the practice then, as it is now, to retain a local attorney to assist an out of town attorney to try a case. The local attorney knows the people and the rules of the local courts.
[573] Letter from Prosecutor David Grayson to Governor Cunningham, Administrative Files, Governors Papers, 1904 (Jelks), Alabama Department of Archives and History.

Solicitor Pettus left his Athens home for a very long stay in Huntsville. His new home would be the Huntsville Hotel on the northwest corner of the Square. Pettus had no illusions, he knew several prominent citizens of the county would be indicted and jailed. He had heard rumors that when certain men were arrested, their friends would free the prisoners by storming the jail and burning it to the ground. To prevent this he called Governor Cunningham and requested that National Guard troops be sent to Huntsville to protect the courts. The Governor agreed and ordered troops from the Birmingham National Guard to stand ready to move to Huntsville when ordered.

Judge Speake did not want the troops sent to Huntsville because of the rumors that a Negro regiment was going to be sent by the United States government. He thought the troops would be adding fuel to the fire. Their presence would be misconstrued and magnified so as to cause more trouble.[574]

A Provisional Company commanded by Captain Lucien E. Brown left Birmingham shortly after noon that Thursday, on the regular northbound Louisville and Nashville train. This Company was composed of forty members of the Birmingham Rifles and twenty-three members from the Jefferson Volunteers of the Third Alabama Infantry, Alabama National Guard. Arriving in Decatur, Captain Brown did not care to wait two hours for the regular train to leave, so he ordered a special train dispatched and they arrived in Huntsville about five o'clock in the afternoon.

The public did not know that the troops were coming until the soldiers arrived at the depot. The soldiers marched up Jefferson Street, around the Courthouse Square, and down Washington Street to the jail on Clinton and Green Streets. Crowds began to line the streets. There was great excitement and wild rumors were circulated.

The troops surrounded the jail and threw out picket on Washington Street, Clinton Avenue, Green Street and Holmes Avenue. The entire area around the jail was placed under Marshall Law No one was allowed to approach within a block of the jail, unless they could prove that they had business there. The company came with all manner of camp equipment and apparently was prepared to stay several weeks if necessary.

Judge Speake, on authority of the Governor, issued an order to Captain Brown placing him in command of the situation. This gave

---

[574] Letter from Judge Speake to Governor Cunningham, Administrative Files, Governor's Papers, 1904 (Jelks), Alabama Department of Archives and History.

him permission to use any means necessary to defend the jail and the courts. Captain Brown moved the arms and munitions from the armory, headquarters of Company F, to the jail to prevent them from falling into the hands of any mob.

As the troops marched around the outside of the Courthouse, the trial of Dennis Smith started inside. He had been in jail since August 8th. He was tried for what was called *"one of the county's most cold blooded murders that had ever been committed."*[575]

The evidence was presented before Judge Speake and an all-white jury. Attorneys Foster and Cooper represented Smith. Smith testified that he told Mollie Watkins, his live in girl friend, not to come up town or he would kill her. She decided to come anyway and as she walked up the street with another woman, Smith began to openly beat her. He finally pulled a knife and began to fiercely cut and stab her, driving the knife into her neck, which nearly severed her head. She staggered home, with the knife sticking out of her neck and fell dead. Smith fled and escaped capture for several days but was apprehended on the Matthew's place about nine miles from town. Deputy Sheriff Ward and Police Officer Wilson arrested him. The trial was still in progress late that night and the judge adjourned court until the next day.

That night Solicitor Pettus brought the Grand Jury to Judge Speake's courtroom to make another partial report of the indictments. The Grand Jury inquired about methods of impeachment and this caused a great deal of talk among those in the courtroom. Juror Charles P. Lane addressed the court.

"If your honor please, if the Grand Jury, in their wisdom and discretion, see fit to impeach the high Sheriff of Madison County and his honor, the Mayor of the City of Huntsville for failure to discharge their duty in executing the law, we desire to do it legally. Therefore we ask your honor for a full and complete instruction as to all formalities and specifications, so that we may avoid errors, irregularities or technicalities."[576]

That night a crowd of spectators gathered at the City Hall on the corner of Clinton Avenue and Washington Street. It did not look as if the crowd meant any harm, but neither had the crowd around the jail on the night Maples was lynched.

Captain Brown addressed the crowd:

---

[575] *The Huntsville Herald* (September 9, 1904); *Huntsville Weekly Democrat* (September 28, 1904).
[576] *The Birmingham News* (September 15, 1904).

"Gentlemen, I hope you will disperse and go to your homes where all good citizens should be at a time like this. We cannot receive visitors now and do not care to have crowds gathering on the street. We are here for business. You must not cross this line, (indicating the picket line) and if you do, I will not hesitate to order my men to fire on you."[577]

The crowd quickly dispersed. John Fullington resisted the soldiers who were dispersing crowds near City Hall on Clinton Avenue and Washington Street. He was arrested, but released later in the evening.

The night was a quiet one around the jail. Those soldiers in the jail wrapped army blankets around themselves and slept on the cold floor. Their comrades patrolled the streets all night to prevent any crowd from forming.

Huntsville-Madison County Public Library

Westside Square looking north

---

[577] *Huntsville Weekly Democrat* (September 28, 1904).

Friday, September 16, 1904

Early that morning, Thomas W. Riggins, one of the most popular men in the county, was arrested on a charge of murder in the first degree for his part in the hanging and shooting of Maples. Riggins was the proprietor of the Stegall Hotel, located at the corner of Clinton Avenue and Washington Street. He retained for his defense, two of the best attorneys in town, Lawrence Cooper and Ephraim H. Foster.

The Judge, Jury, and Attorneys left home before daylight because Dennis Smith's trial was resuming early. They all took their assigned places and the trial was resumed. Witnesses were called and the last details of the story unfolded. There were few witnesses left to testify. Closing arguments were concluded during the morning hours.

Judge Speake finished his charge before noon and the case was given to the jury. They would be out all afternoon.

Friday afternoon, arraignments started in Judge Speake's courtroom. Those arrested were forced to appear and plea, guilty or not guilty. At two o'clock, Thomas Riggins and Ben Hill appeared in court on their charges of murder. The Courthouse was filled to capacity. Every seat was taken and many people were outside trying to get into the courtroom. The two men were seated and surrounded by armed squad of soldiers, with loaded rifles and fixed bayonets. Other soldiers stood around the inside of the courtroom with rifle at ready.

The blood ran cold in the veins of the old timers. The people were witnessing an event that had not been seen in Huntsville since the days of the War Between the States. Some thirty-nine years prior to this event, the Union Army had occupied Huntsville and the memory flashed fresh to the present. It did not take long for local people to resent the show of military strength within the old Courthouse. Most of the resentment would be directed against Solicitor Pettus.

William B. Bankhead Esq., Ben Hill's attorney, asked the Court to delay the trial until public feelings was not at a high pitch and he needed time to bring back several witnesses who had left town. Solicitor Pettus argued against delay. Judge Speake denied the motions stating that the public demanded a speedy trial of the lynching cases.

One of the most important legal points made that morning was when Attorney Bankhead filed a motion to void the indictment against his client. The grounds for his motion was: that the Lusk Bill, an act passed by the legislature, which made Madison County a separate circuit, the Sixteenth circuit, was unconstitutional. This motion was to have wide ranging consequences later.

The Solicitor read the indictment. *"For the Murder of Horace Maples by hanging him in a tree and shooting him with a pistol."*[578]

Ben Hill pled not guilty. Trial was set for Monday, September the 26th.

Hill sat down and Thomas Riggins took his place before the Court. His attorney, Lawrence Cooper, began to speak, and his remarks created instant excitement:

"Thirty years ago this Courthouse was invaded by the Militia and it has taken thirty years to wipe out that stain cast upon our government. I desire to enter protest against the entrance of the Militia into the Courthouse." He looked at the soldiers that ringed the courtroom and continued, *"Noble fellows as they are, they are out of place here and as a citizen of the State of Alabama, I protest. It is not right nor is it justice to intimidate the people in this manner. This defendant does not need their protection and does not desire it. He needs no protection besides his own innocence of the crime against him."*[579]

The statement was delivered with impassioned eloquence and was well received by the crowd in the courtroom.

Solicitor Pettus replied:

"The Militia eluded to of thirty years ago, consisted of alien soldiers. These men are boys from the hills and valleys of Alabama who go where they are ordered by their State to preserve and uphold the laws. They are not here to intimidate, but because

Photograph Courtesy of Erle Pettus Jr.

Erle Pettus Sr.

---

[578] *The Huntsville Weekly Democrat* (September 28, 1904); and *The Weekly Mercury* (September 21, 1904).
[579] *The Weekly Mercury* (September 21, 1904).

open threats have been made to remove these defendants from the jail. If they had reached here at six o'clock on the evening of September the 7th, the laws of this State would not have been violated and arson would not have been committed in the shadow of this temple of justice."[580]

Judge Speake did not know of Captain Brown's intention to bring the soldiers into the courtroom until he sat upon the bench. However, he did not place blame on others but spoke with some feeling:

"The militia has been brought here on my suggestion after consulting with the Sheriff, and on his suggestion that ordinary authorities would be unable to maintain order. Your speech, Sir, is incendiary and liable to arouse slumbering passions of the people."

After the speech making was over, Thomas Riggins and Ben Hill plead not guilty. Trial for Thomas Riggins was set for Thursday, September 22, 1904. He would be the first lyncher tried.

Judge Speake felt that Riggins would certainly be acquitted, and wished to try Ben Hill first. However, acting impartially and true to his duty, he allowed Hill to be tried later, based upon Riggins's attorney's statement that he could not gather his evidence in time for an immediate trial. While the Judge knew that not all of those charged could be tried during the two-week present term

Photograph Courtesy of the Speake Family

Judge Paul Mayhew Speake

---

[580] Ibid.

of court, he was determined to try as many as possible.[581]

Judge Speake knew it would be difficult, if not impossible, to convict any of the lynchers, but he believed that, notwithstanding the expense, the trials would have a positive effect in deterring mob violence and in encouraging law enforcement officers to do their duty in the future. Speake knew that almost all of the town was against him but looked to the future when lynching would be stopped forever in Madison County.[582]

Night arrived and the jury in the Smith case had still not reported it verdict. The jury deliberated all afternoon. After almost ten hours, at half past nine o'clock, the jury filed into the courtroom. The foreman read the verdict aloud. *"We, the Jury, find the defendant guilty of murder in the first degree, and fix his punishment at death."*[583]

The condemned man was calm as the verdict was rendered and his expression did not change. His sentencing was set for the next day. His attorneys gave notice of an appeal to the Supreme Court.

Saturday, September 17, 1904

The next morning, Dennis Smith appeared in court before Judge Speake and received his death sentence. His attorneys, Foster and Cooper, made a motion to stop the sentencing but were overruled by the Court. When asked if he had anything to say, Smith said, *"Nothing, except that I acted in self-defense."*[584] The date of execution was set for October 21, but an appeal to the Supreme Court would force a stay of the execution.

Sunday, September 18, 1904

Sunday, September 18th, was a quiet and normal day. The churches overflowed and, before and after the services, the Grand Jury report and the pending trials were the topic of all the conversations.

---

[581] Letter from Judge Speake to Governor Cunningham, Administrative Files, Governor's Papers, 1904 (Jelks), Alabama Department of Archives and History.
[582] Letter from Judge Speake to Governor Cunningham, Administrative Files, Governor's Papers, 1904 (Jelks), Alabama Department of Archives and History.
[583] *The Weekly Mercury* (September 21, 1904).
[584] Ibid.

Grand Jury indictments of the lynchers were placed in the hands of the Sheriff's Department. The deputies were less than diligent and seemed to be in sympathy with the mob element. It seemed evident that someone had given warning to those indicted because many of the men sought, had learned of their indictment, and departed Huntsville for safer places. It was rumored that the main leaders had crossed the line into Tennessee while others had gone to Texas. The factory hands scattered to the "*four winds.*"[585]

Deputy Ward, with the assistance of Captain Brown, had arrested only four men. Judge Speake advised the Sheriff that he had the authority to summon special deputies to help in the arrests. The Sheriff stated he was busy serving summons, on those who were to appear before the special Grand Jury.[586]

Captain Brown complained to the Governor about the slowness of the men being arrested. The Governor called Judge Speake, who suggested that Sheriff Rodgers deputize the Captain to assist in making arrests. Captain Brown and Captain Northington were deputized to expedite the arrests.

Monday, September 19, 1904

The first Military Court of Inquiry ever held in Alabama convened in Huntsville. Its purpose was to improve the service of the National Guard by determining the competency of the officers of Company F, Third Regiment and to inquire into their conduct of September Seventh.

Selected, as President of the Court was, Colonel Thomas Sydney Frazer, a resident of Union Springs and a well-known young attorney. He had graduated from the University of Alabama Law School in 1896. He was a member of the State Senate and a Colonel on the Governor's staff. Other members of the Court were Captain Edward D. Smith, Commander of the Brandon Light Artillery. Smith, although young, was regarded as one of the most promising attorneys of the State and was the City Attorney for Birmingham. Captain W. D. Vaiden, Company Commander, First Regiment at Union Town. He had commanded a company in the Spanish American War and he had served in the regular army in the Philippines. He had been private

---

[585] Judge Speakes letter to Governor Cunningham, Administrative Files, Governor's Papers, 1904 (Jelks), Alabama Department of Archives and History.
[586] Judge Speakes letter to Governor Cunningham, Administrative Files, Governor's Papers, 1904 (Jelks), Alabama Department of Archives and History.

secretary to Governor William Oates and had a wide number of acquaintances throughout the State.

The court convened at two o'clock in the afternoon and spent the rest of the day hearing evidence relating to the conduct of Company F., while it had been on guard in the Madison County jail on the night Horace Maples was lynched. Captain Hay was the first witness.[587]

Captain Hay related that he reported to the jail with his men at half past five. The Captain testified that the Sheriff gave him no orders. Sentinels were posted with fixed bayonets, but their rifles were not loaded. He received a telegram from the Governor with orders to protect the jail. He sent back a telegram asking for help. He presented both telegrams to the court. He also gave the court the roll listing the twenty-five soldiers serving with him that night.[588] He further stated that after he had sent the telegrams, when he returned to the jail, the Sheriff was sitting on the steps and the Sheriff told him "*I want you to stay here.*"[589] He said, if he were in command, he would have fired upon the mob. He denied that the Sheriff gave him any orders to fire at the mob.

He stated that the Sheriff's son came to him and stated, "*If Papa gives you the command to shoot, don't you do it.*"[590] The Captain stated he received wounds on his hand and in his eye from falling glass from pistols being fired into the jail. He asked those in the mob to let the law take its course and was cursed soundly. He did not attempt to form his men after they left the jail and did not go to the square and see Maples hanged.[591]

Lieutenant T. P. Hay was the next witness. He was very evasive about what he did and seemed not to remember much about the facts. To over half of the questions, he stated he did not remember, he did not know, or could not swear to the facts. He stated

---

[587] Much of the testimony of Captain Hay and Sheriff Rodgers have not been placed in the story because it in direct conflict with other witnesses. When the transcript of the hearing and the newspaper were not the same, the transcript has been accepted as the most reliable.

[588] The telegraphs and list were made exhibits of the hearing. Transcripts of Court of Inquiry, Adjunct General's Files, 1904, Alabama Department of Archives and History.

[589] *The Weekly Mercury* (September 28, 1904).

[590] Military Court of Inquiry, Transcripts, Adjunct General's Files, 1904, Alabama Department of Archives and History.

[591] Ibid.

that he reported to his brother, found some men and told them to report to the armory.

He did not see Sheriff Rodgers when the soldiers arrived at the jail. He did not know whether the Captain or the Sheriff were away from the jail. He did not know if the soldiers' rifles were loaded or not. In fact, it was difficult to know just what he did, and where he was that night. He related that there were about three thousand men in the mob and he was only armed with a pistol. He made no effort to reform the men after they left the jail.[592]

Sergeant George P. Brock was examined next. He was the Company First Sergeant and received his orders at the corner of Jefferson Street and Clinton Avenue from Lieutenant Hay to round up the men and report to the armory.

He did not receive specific orders, but understood that if the mob rushed the lines, the men were to assemble in front of the jail and hold it. He therefore told the musician to sound assembly. Captain Hay ordered the men to fall in, at the front of the jail. According to Brock, there were about two or three hundred people in the mob. No orders were ever given to load the guns. The Sheriff gave the order to go inside the jail and go upstairs. Three shots were fired from the back steps. After Maples was turned out of his cell he was standing in the hall. Maples recognized Brock and spoke. Brock did not know his name, but he recognized Maples.

The testimony extended on into the night, before it was decided, to break for the night. Court adjourned until the next morning.

Tuesday, September 20, 1904

The morning session started with Second Lieutenant Stewart as the first witness. He received orders about half past three from Lt. Hay to report to the armory and did so, but no one was there. He met Captain Hay on the street and was told to find as many men as possible. He returned to the armory about half past five o'clock. Captain Hay had already marched the men down to the jail. Stewart stated that he took his men with him and followed.

He placed two sentinels at the corner of Clinton and Washington. One half way up and down the block on Green Street, one halfway down the block on Clinton. He remembered a crowd of

---

[592] Ibid.

one or two thousand people that was at Clinton and Washington between city hall and the jail. Lt. Stewart went to Green Street and that's where he was when the line was rushed by the mob. He went in the front door of the jail. Captain Hay was in the jail when the line was rushed. Lt. Hay was outside.

He heard the bugler sound assembly and returned to the jail where he issued ball cartridges and gave orders for the men to fill the magazines of their rifles and their belts. He expected an order to fire. As the men loaded, they were stationed on the steps, as ordered by the Sheriff, to prevent anyone from coming up the stairs. The Sheriff said *"Do not allow the men to come up stairs."* [593] He hollered that he was there to protect the Negro and they could not come up there. We wanted to shoot when the fire started, but the Captain said, *"I can't do anything without Sheriff Rodgers's orders, Go see him."* [594] [595]

He removed his drill sword to get a better weapon. He left the sword in the jail. He next saw it at Sinskey's store. After Maples was taken uptown, he stood on the street and watched the fire department put out the fire. He then went up town.

He did not know whether he would have given the order to shoot that night, if he had been in command. It would have been his duty to take charge if the Sheriff had put his soldiers in danger. He felt the Sheriff's conduct was satisfactory, but that Captain Hay did not do all that could have been done. They could not have kept the mob back for long even if they had been given an order to fire and certainly not until three o'clock in the morning when the troops from Birmingham arrived.

Stewart was asked if he knew Douglas Stewart.[596] He said he did, but he did not see him that night. He did not know anyone in the mob. The company had elected him in the usual way.[597] His commission had expired on the Seventh of September, the day Horace Maples was lynched, but a successor had not been elected.

When the Articles of War, allowing an officer to take charge when his superior officers were proven incompetent, were read to him, he said that the incompetence of his superiors had not been proven to him. When asked what he would have done if in command,

---

[593] *The Weekly Mercury* (September 21, 1904).
[594] Ibid.
[595] Military Court of Inquiry, Transcripts, Adjunct General's Files, 1904, Alabama Department of Archives and History.
[596] Unknown person. He could have been a leader of the mob.
[597] In those days, the men picked their leaders by an election.

he said he would have *"Obeyed the orders of the Sheriff, and would not give orders to fire until told to do so."*[598]

Sergeant W.T. Giles was the next witness. He stated that he received his orders about five o'clock. He was to post sentinels around the jail. He went with Sgt. Gooch to Clinton and Washington where he found Private McClain on the ground and helped take him to the jail. He held the mob back at the point of his bayonet. Private McClain was badly beaten by the mob but did not give up his rifle. Giles believed that if all the soldiers had been in the jail and ordered to shoot, the jail could have been held. His memory was that there were five hundred men at the jail, but only two hundred fifty[599] were taking an active part in the violence. He was never given an order to fire. He was still on the steps when told the prisoner had been turned out.

Private Radford testified that he was the company musician. He sounded assembly with his bugle, on orders of Sergeant Brock. He had not been issued a weapon.

Court adjourned until three o'clock.

When court reconvened, Attorney Robert C. Brickell testified that he saw the crowd at seven o'clock in the evening, but did not see them again until he went to City Hall at eight o'clock. There were two or three hundred men present but only thirty or forty taking an active part. He saw two or three members of the mob armed.

Private Daniel A. Adams, with the recruiting office, stated that, he was at the corner of Washington Street and Clinton Avenue where the mob broke through. He saw them run over a sentinel, choke and throw him to the ground, and take his weapon.

Jailer Giles was the next witness. He stated that the military came to the jail about five o'clock that afternoon. The Sheriff told them not let anyone come up the stairs. He stated that when the troops arrived the men seemed quiet, not excited, but extremely frightened. The soldiers did not fire a shot nor resist the mob.

The soldiers put out the lights. Captain Hay was in the parlor. They did not resist the mob. Soldiers were in his room. Some of the soldiers were sitting on the floor smoking. There were two or three under his bed. On cross-examination, he said he could not see the men under the bed, but he could feel them. His story was discounted.

---

[598] *The Weekly Mercury* (September 21, 1904).
[599] The numbers of the crowd differ with each witness.

Sheriff A. D. Rodgers appeared in Court but his counsel objected to his testifying, as the evidence might tend to convict him in later proceedings. The Court overruled the request but gave the Sheriff the right to refuse to answer any questions.

Rodgers saw Captain Hay about three o'clock and told him there had been talk of a mob. Judge Speake told him to order out the Militia.[600] About fifteen soldiers arrived about five. *"I said to Leonard (R. L.) Hay in the presence of Captain Hay and where the latter could have heard, had he wanted to that they must take care of the jail and protect the prisoner."*[601]

He gave the order for the soldiers to come into the jail. The soldiers went up the stairs; he shut the door and followed them. Capt. Hay said, *"We can't stay here, we will have to go upstairs. I told Captain Hay to shoot any man who came up the stairs. Someone knocked on the back door. One of the soldiers wanted to shoot at the door. I said, No! Lieutenant Steward suggested to me to give up and said, 'We can not stand this,' I urged them not to weaken, that we could keep the mob back."*[602]

Sheriff Rodgers said that he heard some shots fired outside. He found no bullet marks on the walls of the jail, but saw three men with guns and military rifles taken from the soldiers in the crowd. He stated none of the men had attempted to come up the stairs because he told them he would shoot them. He recognized John Jamar, John H Lehman, Sam Russell, Rube Street and John Bayless in the mob, which was trying to take the jail and get the prisoner.

He stated the twenty-five soldiers could have protected the jail. On advice of council, he refused to answer whether Captain Hay did his job, but stated that the military did not give him the assistance that he expected. He gave up the prisoner only when it seemed certain the destruction of the jail along with the other prisoners was imminent.

Private T. E. McClain testified that Sgt. Gooch placed him on sentinel duty. He was to keep the mob behind the rope that was stretched across Clinton Avenue. He was there with J. S. Carter. He was not instructed to load or to fire. At about eight o'clock, he turned at the end of his post, when the mob ran over the rope and grabbed

---

[600] The Sheriff stated in his report to the Governor that he notified Captain Hay, about noon, that he would need his company to guard the jail. (Sheriff's report to Governor Cunningham, Administrative Files, Governor's Papers, 1904 (Jelks), Alabama Department of Archives and History.
[601] *The Weekly Mercury* (September 21, 1904).
[602] The Weekly Mercury (September 21, 1904).

him. His rifle was not loaded, but he had no time to fire anyway. He shoved one man against the wall of a store with his rifle and three others grabbed it. A man choked him from behind and he fell, dragging the three men down on top of him. He lost consciousness and his rifle when he fell. He recovered consciousness at the jail, in the jailer's room.

First Sergeant Victor Gooch posted the sentinels and then remained at the corner until the crowd broke through. He instructed his men not to load until given orders by Captain Hay but to keep the crowd behind the rope. He did not hear any orders from the Sheriff to the officers but he heard Captain Hay order the soldiers not to fire unless the Sheriff ordered them to do so. The mob could not have been held even if the soldiers had fired. He did not see Maples until he was hanged.

The testimony was finished. There had been two long and tiring days of questions and answers. The attorneys for the officers and Company F had no further evidence to offer. It was time for closing arguments, but the attorneys did not wish to make any closing remarks so the trial was over.

After Court was adjourned that afternoon, the three officers serving as court judges, left for Birmingham to finish their reports to Governor Cunningham.[603] It was widely reported that Company F had not done their duty. It was believed that they had been disgraced and would be mustered out of the Service.

In 1878, Congressman William Richardson stood in Meridianville Pike and urged, unsuccessfully, over 300 horsemen not to lynch three men then in the county jail. He was considered influential in local community affairs. He was urged to intervene on behalf of the local Huntsville Guards. Their reputation and their unit's existence was in jeopardy. Congressman Richardson wrote Governor Cunningham that he had heard of the possible deactivation of Company F, Third Regiment, Alabama National Guard. He stated that he was personally acquainted with the members of the company and expressed his sentiment that the men not be mustered out of service.[604]

---

[603] Letter from Tom S. Frazier, (President of the Court of Inquiry) to Governor Cunningham, Administrative Files, Governor's Papers, 1904 (Jelks), Alabama Department of Archives and History.
[604] Congressman William Richardson's letter to Governor Cunningham, Administrative Files, Governor's Papers, 1904 (Jelks), Alabama Department of Archives and History.

The Grand Jury had been in session for eight workdays. They had examined many witnesses daily. The jury was reconvened that Monday night in Judge Speake's courtroom and gave a final report that would bring much excitement to the county. Seven indictments were returned making a total of twenty-six in all.[605] Most of the indictments were for the capital offense of murder. They confirmed the rumors (that were all over town) by recommending that various city and county officials be impeached. The Grand Jury did not fail to censure every person in authority who did not stop the mob violence. The Grand Jury recommended the following:

- That Sheriff Rodgers be impeached for incompetence or willful neglect of duty because he did not order the mob to be fired upon. That he permitted the lives of prisoners under his care to be jeopardized and that he allowed the lynching of a prisoner in his care.
- That Thomas W. Smith, Mayor of the city, be impeached for incompetence and willful neglect of duty for failing to send city police protection for the fire department and that he failed to send aid to the Sheriff while there was a riot in the streets of Huntsville.
- That David Overton, City Chief of Police, be impeached for incompetence or willful neglect of duty, for failing to aid the Sheriff and failing to disperse a mob in the streets of Huntsville.
- That the city police force be reorganized.[606]

The Governor was commended for ordering an investigation of the National Guard, as it appeared that the commanding officer was either incompetent or ignorant of the law.

Judge Speake commended the Grand Jury saying: *"Gentlemen, the county is to be congratulated upon having men to have the courage of their convictions and the backbone to do their duty. It will take years for us to remove the stain and stigma, which recent occurrences have thrown upon our community, yet I am sure this material report and your faithful and courageous actions will go very far to that end."*[607]

The editor of the *Weekly Mercury* later stated in an editorial: *"That rarely has a Grand Jury been called on to perform duties more unpleasant. The brave men fearlessly and bravely met the emergency*

---

[605] Names of all those indicted were not disclosed and have not been found.
[606] *The Weekly Mercury* (September 21, 1904).
[607] Ibid.

and performed their duty. All good citizens will endorse their action. The censure placed upon the Sheriff, Mayor, and other officials was well placed. In this trying affair, Judge Speake conducted himself in an admirable spirit and displayed those qualities, which mark the honest man. Whatever may be the opinions entertained now by some people, in years to come, the actions of Judge Speake and this Grand Jury will be pointed to with pride and their names remembered for the honor they bring to Madison County. If the Maples lynching had occurred in New York or Massachusetts, instead of in Alabama, a Grand Jury investigating the affair could not have discharged its duty with a higher sense of its obligation to the State than the Grand Jury at Huntsville has done." [608]

That afternoon and into the night arrests were being made. Silas Worley and Tom Winkle were arrested for arson. James (Jim) H. Mitchell, George Frame, a merchant of Dallas Village, and James Armstrong were arrested for murder. They were placed in the same jail they had attacked.[609]

That Monday night, Judge Speake sat in his second floor Courthouse office and typed a letter to Governor Cunningham answering his telephone request for information about the affair.

The Judge's opinion was that the Sheriff neglected to perform his duty and he had only one deputy, Thomas W. Ward, who was brave, conscientious, and fearless in the discharge of his duties. The other deputies were, he felt, political trimmers, heartily in sympathy with the mob element. He wrote that the best people thought the officers did not do their duty, but these same good citizens were also, really, in sympathy with the mob. Speake wrote;

"I fear it will be very difficult, if not impossible, to secure convictions; but at the same time believe, notwithstanding the heavy expense to the State and County, the proceedings will have a good effect in deterring mobs in (the) future and in making officers do their duty."[610]

---

[608] A clipping that appeared in, *The Weekly Mercury* (September 21, 1904), excerpt from the newspaper, *The New York Evening Sun*, September 20, 1904. This item forwarded to Governor Cunningham by the Southern Immigration Society of New York. Administrative Files, Governor's Papers, 1904 (Jelks), Alabama Department of Archives and History.

[609] No other men were found in the Sheriff's Bond Book except those listed.

[610] Paul Speakes letter to Governor Cunningham, Administrative Files, Governor's Papers, 1904 (Jelks), Alabama Department of Archives and History.

He stated that the members of the Grand Jury were deserving of special praise and honor because of their trying responsibilities, although they were greatly criticized by the so-called *good citizens*.[611]

The present term of court ended that week, so Judge Speake called a Special Term of Court. The trials would continue without interruption.[612]

Silas Worley and James Mitchell appeared at the Courthouse for their arraignment on Wednesday, September 21, but the key to the jury room was not found and their appearance was put off until the next day.

Thursday, September 22, 1904

The trials started at ten o'clock Thursday morning. There would be long hours for all involved. Judge Speake started court at an earlier than normal hour and continued taking testimony late into the night.

The general feeling in the county was that the men should not be tried. Clearly, most of the residents were opposed to the prosecution of any of the man who took part in the lynching. Fortunately, the court system would not be ran by the wishes of the people, who no doubt felt the lynching was justified. The trials would begin.

The Stegall Hotel was a popular gathering place of people from the county. Thomas Riggins was the proprietor of the hotel and one of the most popular men in the city and county. Riggins arrived at the Courthouse with his attorneys that morning. The streets of the town and the corridors of the Courthouse were crowded with hundreds of curious out-of-towners, who joined town residents to see the trial. He met and greeted many of his friends. Everyone wanted to see the drama unfold and many hoped to get into the courtroom to find a seat for the main event. The courtroom was crowded with standing room only, and very little of that. The crowd milled about the square and overflowed into the streets beyond. They talked and waited for the latest news of the events inside.

The jury was chosen from a special venire[613] of fifty men. From this number, the two sides would strike off names until only twelve men remained. This twelve would be the jury. Many hours

---

[611] See Judge Speake's complete letter at the end of this chapter.
[612] Terms or sessions of court, at that time, would normally be four times each year. If more court time were needed, a special term or session would be scheduled.
[613] See legal terms at the beginning of this chapter.

were spent in selecting the jury. Every man, of the jury, was asked the question, if he would hold a man guilty of murder that composed the mob that lynched Maples. Many men stated they could not convict anyone charged in the lynching.

Selection of the jury resulted in twelve white males being seated as jurors. It would be so in all the trials, Negroes and women were not allowed to serve on a jury at that time.

Many of the States witnesses had disappeared, which caused delays while the authorities, looked for them. There was much speculation that they had left town in order to avoid testifying. The trial finally began at two o'clock that afternoon without the State's desired witnesses; much to the delight of the defense

Jailer Giles testified, for the State, that he thought the jail was going to burn or that the Negro would certainly be lynched. He unlocked Maples cell and told him to get away if could. After Maples jumped from the window, Riggins and several other men demanded his keys. He told them he had no keys, but they searched him, found the keys and went through the jail.

Douglas Yancey testified that he heard Riggins say that he had taken the keys from the jailer.

In an attempt to get the trial going, a night session was called and the Court recessed until seven o'clock Thursday night. The State had presented their evidence and stopped. It was time for the defense to present their case. Riggins's lawyers called Dr. Wheeler, the county health officer, as their first witness. He testified he was with Riggins during the riot. Wheeler said that Riggins told him that it was a shame and an outrage for the mob to hang the Negro and set fire to the jail.

The defense rested and the testimony was over. Judge Speake removed the jury while the attorneys presented arguments for both sides. Lawrence Cooper, attorney for the defense, moved to dismiss the case, as the State had failed to make out a case against Riggins. He said that his client was innocent. Everybody knew he was not guilty, but a hung jury might cause him to spend more time in jail. Solicitor Pettus objected and urged that the jury be allowed to decide the case.

Judge Speake knew the State had failed to make a case against the defendant and the trial could not go on. After the argument, Judge Speake called the jury back and charged them that if they believed the evidence, to return a verdict of not guilty. The jury did so without leaving the box.

His many friends warmly congratulated Riggins. The crowd surrounded him and escorted him out of the Courthouse where the rest of the people cheered his acquittal. The first of their own had stood trial and had been found not guilty.

James Armstrong, a well-known young farmer was arrested that night. He was charged with murder in the first degree. Armstrong had returned to the city from New Orleans, where he had gone during the investigation.

Friday September 23, 1904

Silas Worley was the second alleged lyncher to be placed on trial. His trial for murder started Friday morning. The usual large crowds attended the trial. Spectators and reporters crowded in, wherever they could. In fact, the crowds attended every session, of every court and heard every word of the evidence and arguments with great interest until they became bored with the monotony of the trials.

Attorney's F. Turner Petty and E. H. Foster defended Worley.

The entire morning was spent in jury selection. It was not quite as difficult a selection as in the Riggins' case.[614]

Sheriff A. D. Rodgers was the first witness for the State. He testified that he had seen members of the mob making a fire on the floor of the jail, but did not see Worley.

Sergeant William Giles stated that when ordered out of the jail, he walked down the stairs with the Sheriff, where Worley and two or three others tried to take his rifle. Giles stated that he recognized Worley as one of the several men throwing oil and wood on the fire. Attorney Petty attempted to prove that Giles was a professional witness and that he sold his testimony to anyone. The Court sustained the objection of Solicitor Pettus, to the questions and did not allow an answer.

The questioning of Deputy Sheriff Ward brought out the ugly side of the defendant. Ward identified Worley's involvement in trying to take Sergeant Giles's gun away from him. Ward stated that Worley had told the crowd at the jail to *"Burn her down, let's have him!"*[615] Ward told the jury that he had warned Worley to get out of

---

[614] The jurymen selected was J. R. Thrift, W. J. Sibly, A. D. Sharpe, J. E. Popejoy, R. L. Lyne, J. B. Whitworth, L.C. Blair, D. C. Tumlinson, F. L. Mitchell, R. A. Manning, T. A. Newby, and H. N. Strong.

[615] *The Weekly Mercury* (September 28, 1904).

the jail. Other witnesses for the state testified that Worley stood in the jail and said, *"Let her burn, let's get the nigger."*[616]

John Jones, an important witness for the State, was sworn in as a witness during the morning, but could not be found in the afternoon. Court was recessed until half past seven o'clock that night to allow the State time to find their witnesses. The Court was informed at that time that the deputy spent all afternoon looking for Jones and had found that he had enlisted in the United States Army and was sent to St. Louis. Judge Speake ordered a fine of $100 assessed against Jones and ordered the matter investigated.

William B. Bankhead, Esq., attorney for some of the men who were accused of the lynching, was the last witness for the State. He stated that he was at the fire and heard the prisoners calling for help, but could not say Worley was present. The witness recalled the events of that night in all their detail, but he did not identify any leaders of the mob. His testimony only revealed that the defendant was at the jail and in the Courthouse yard, but not that he had participated in any part of the lynching.

On this note, the State was forced to rest its case.

The defense opened its case with Attorney Petty placing on the stand, Count Berryhill, W. F. Worley, Jim Worley, brothers of Silas Worley, and Miss Kate Glassford. All these witnesses sought to prove an alibi by testifying that Worley was with them until nine o'clock that evening.

Archie Cleveland testified that he was with the men placing planks on the fire at the jail, but he did not see Worley.

Dr. T. F. Madden saw Worley near the jail and they discussed whether the crowd was burning the jail or tearing it down.

Reuben A. Gulley, the jailed Baptist preacher, said he watched from the third floor, in the tower, as the mob broke over the guard line and broke down the door. He stated that he did not see Worley until later in the evening when the fire department arrived and he was not part of the mob and was only a spectator.

A bit of a sensation was created by the question, put to this witness during the cross-examination, by the Solicitor, as to whether he knew any other member of the mob.[617] Objections were made, overruled and the witness was allowed to answer the question. He said he recognized Nunnally, a former prisoner, and Thomas Johnson. They were carrying wood to the jail to be placed on the fire.

---

[616] *The Birmingham News* (September 24, 1904).
[617] No explanation was given why this caused such a sensation.

On cross-examination it was brought out that the preacher was placed in the jail in August, because of a Grand Jury indictment charging him with carrying a concealed pistol.

Another witness, Wade O'Neal was introduced and testified that, he had seen the defendant at the jail. He testified that at the time he saw Worley, he was not part of the violence and in fact, he was not doing anything but watching the excitement.

The hour was late and the Judge stopped the trial for the night. The crowd left, but prepared to return to the Courthouse early the next day.

Saturday, September 24, 1904

The next morning a rare Saturday session of court was held. William Mitchell, Night Chief of Police of the City of Huntsville, was the first witness. He, along with Edward Glassford, J. W. B. Hawkins, Saxe Simmons, Ex-Sheriff J. P. Powell, and J. E. Gardiner all testified that the character and reputation of Worley was good.

The Defendant, Silas Worley was the last witness. He stated that he drove into town on his wagon at seven o'clock. Arriving home he fed his team of horses, had supper, and then walked uptown. He saw the large crowd and went to see what the trouble was about. He did not see the fire in the jail until he went around on Green Street. He was standing in front of the jail when the fire department made its run and saw several rocks thrown at the firemen. He heard two or three pistol shots. He saw people pile wood on the fire at a window of the jail. He was at the front entrance when soldiers were coming down and saw members of the mob grab the rifle of a soldier. Assisting Deputy Sheriff Ward, he pulled the hand of one of the men from the soldier's throat. He went to the Courthouse, heard the speeches, and went home. He denied that he encouraged the mob to burn down the jail and he did not see Maples brought from the jail.

Sergeant Giles was used as a rebuttal witness by the State. He said that Worley pulled at his rifle on the steps, but said nothing. Deputy Ward was behind them and saw Worley.

The evidence presented by both sides came to an end before lunch. After the evidence was completed, a short break was allowed and then the closing arguments began.

The defense lawyers, F. Turner Petty and E. H. Foster argued that the legal principal of equal responsibility should not be used, but that there should be a reasonable doubt in the minds of each of the jurors.

Solicitor Pettus summed up for the prosecution. He said that the Defendant was as guilty as any member of the mob who had actually piled fuel onto the fire and that the jury should return a verdict of guilty, as charged, in the indictment. He argued that the people who planned, participated in or encouraged the lynching should be held responsible, the same as anyone who held the rope. They were all equally responsible under the law, if they took an active role in any part of the shameful episode. He argued that the accused would not just be the person who played the most prominent part, or was the most outspoken leader. The acts and words of several men and all of them caused the death, including the accused on trial and he should be held accountable and equally responsible for the murder.

The argument of the attorneys occupied several hours. It was agreed that the attorneys were the best speechmakers in the county. Their voices would lower as they stood next to the jury box. Then they would step back and their voices could be heard outside the Courthouse and across the Square.

Their arguments were presented as directions down a highway to the destination of the attorney's thinking. A story would be told that sought to convince the members of the jury, that no other conclusion could be drawn from the evidence. They were allowed to say whatever was in their mind.

There was a break for supper for which everyone must have been grateful. The lawyers and spectators went their separate ways. Some went home while others went across the street to a café or to a bar. Some lawyers went back to their office and got ready for the trial to resume. Then it was back at it again in the hot, smelly courtroom.

After supper, Judge Speake charged the jury, reading passages from the law freely. The charge took nearly two hours. The jury filed out at nine o'clock that night. The crowd stood around talking about the trial. Some felt that there would be no verdict that night, but when the jury did come back, it would be an acquittal. One hour later, the jury returned to the crowded courtroom. When the jury filed into court, the buzzing noise of conversation ceased. At ten o'clock, the verdict was read.

"We, the jury, find the Defendant, not guilty,"[618] was the decision reached by the jury on this late Saturday night. When the clerk read the verdict, the crowd applauded. Judge Speake stopped this display and discharged the jury.

---

[618] *The Weekly Mercury* (September 28, 1904)

Judge Speake had ordered the removal of the troops from the streets in the daytime, but as a precaution against any trouble in the event of a verdict of guilty, Captain Brown had a squad of men stationed in the courtyard to provide a safe escort of the defendant, back to jail. Worley did not go back to jail, but left the Courthouse with his friends, a free man. The crowd waited until they were outside the Courthouse before they renewed their celebration for the accused.

Sunday, September 25, 1904

Boys standing on street corners that Sunday morning were selling the papers that screamed in big bold headlines that another lyncher was found not guilty.

"Silas Worley is found 'Not Guilty' Second of Alleged Lynchers Was Acquitted by Jury Last Night. Verdict Was Found Sooner than Was Expected."[619]

The talk at every meal and over every cup of coffee was about the trials that had been concluded and the trials set for the next week.

Captain Brown and the Birmingham Company of soldiers departed for home that morning, leaving the jail guarded by civil authorities. Judge Speake had contacted Governor Cunningham, and told him there was no further need for keeping the military in Huntsville. He felt the presence of troops allowed the lawless element to arouse public sentiment in order to secure acquittals. When the company received their orders, they were ready to departure in four hours. It was estimated that the cost of guarding the jail from Thursday afternoon, September 15th, through Sunday noon, September 25th, amounted to $1,300. Ironically, many of the soldiers found, upon their return to Birmingham, that they had lost their jobs.

Monday September 26, 1904

The trial of Ben Hill, an employee of the Lowe Cotton Mill, started on Monday. Attorney William Bankhead[620] represented the Defendant. The lawyers began questioning members of the jury panel and it went on for hours. Seventy-seven men were questioned for jury duty before a jury of twelve was selected for the trial. About half of

---

[619] *The Weekly Mercury* (September 28, 1904)
[620] Father of Tullula Bankhead, the actress.

the men swore that they would not convict a man for murder who had taken part in the lynching. The solicitor had an impossible task. A jury could not be selected that would be fair to the State.[621]

All the witnesses for the State had to be subpoenaed, or forced, to attend court and testify. Witnesses for the accused were waiting in line to testify. The State's witnesses swore that Hill was one of the three men who climbed the tree during the hanging. Others testified that he was not.

Coroner E. B. Stewart stated that he saw three men go up the tree to tie the rope that was around Maples' neck. Two of them were in the tree at the same time and one man went up later to tighten the rope. There were more than a thousand people in the Courthouse yard but only a few took an active part in the hanging.

James B. Pollard, another worker at the Lowe Mills, saw only one man in the tree wearing dark clothes and a slouch hat; he saw Archie Hill go up the tree and drop his hat. The electric lights, near by, were burning brightly. He knew it was Hill, he saw his features and that he was bareheaded when he came down. There was no mistake, he saw Hill at the Lowe Mill everyday. Hill told Will Brigham that he started up the tree but lost his hat and climbed down.

Sheriff Rodgers was the last witness. He testified that he did not see Hill at the jail or at the hanging.

The State had finished their case, then it was the defendant's turn. The defense witness testified positively that Hill was not part of the hanging. The witnesses recalled the events of the night but not a one of them could positively identify any of the mob leaders. They could place the men in the crowd, at the jail or the Courthouse, but their testimony was that the defendants were observers and did not take part in the lynching.

Tom Talley saw the hanging but could not say Hill was one of the men involved. Cleave Howard, a fourteen-year-old boy, testified that he held Hill's hand during the lynching and that Hill did not take any part in the crime. John Billingsley saw two men climb the tree, not ten feet from where he was standing and he watched as they tied the rope around a limb. He stated that he knew Hill and he was not one of the men and, in fact, he was not there at all. When questioned further, he admitted that he did not know any man there.

---

[621] The jury was composed of: J. J. Crowson, R. H. Parm, S. L. Cobb, E. A. Bailey, Stanfield Buford, John Mitchell, Alex Steger, R. H. Cantrell, K. W. Fisk, V. H. Wells, J. M. Steger and W. D. Buckner.

Jim Couch saw two men he did not know in the tree. He saw Hill near the tree after the hanging, but Hill did not lose his hat.

Ex-Senator Ed L. Pulley bumped against the man who climbed the tree to tie the rope and he did not think Hill was the man.

Dr. W. P. Hooper was at the hanging and saw a man go up the tree, but it was not Hill.

Tom Mason Jr. saw two men climb the tree and saw another go up to tighten the rope. He did not believe Hill was one of the men but would not swear positively.

Reuben Clutts saw the hanging but did not see Hill. He testified that the character of Hill was good.

John Billingsly, Jim Couch, Tom Mason, Jr., G.T. Bragg, Dr. Hatcher and other witnesses also testified as to Hill's good character.

The trial continued until ten o'clock in another night session. William Bankhead gave closing arguments for the defense.

Tuesday September 27, 1904

The next morning, Solicitor Pettus gave a closing argument for the State using the same argument he had used in the other trials. Finally, the Judge charged the jury. During the delivery of the charge, the spectators were silence. The jury retired to consider their verdict and spent two hours in deliberation before returning a verdict of not guilty.

Hill was the third alleged lyncher to be tried and acquitted. A pattern was now obvious. Each trial would bring an acquittal and with the verdict of not guilty, there would be a celebration for the accused. The State officers were discouraged with the verdicts of the first three trials, but would not admit defeat, and pressed on with the next trial.

Events moved right along. As soon as the Hill trial was over, the George Frame trial began. Frame, a merchant in Dallas, was charged with murder. He had been in jail eleven days. E. H. Foster and F. Turner Petty were his defense attorneys. David A. Grayson assisted Solicitor Pettus.

The same problems in securing a jury were experienced as in the other cases. Seventy-five men were examined before twelve jurors were seated in the box.[622]

---

[622] Jurymen were: W.F. Hall, W.R. Beadle, C. B. Christian, Albert Carrager, J. P. Faulknerberg, John Slaton, Pryor Farley, W. I. Spiver, John W. Giles, Joe Bridges and J. R. Barclay.

The State contended that Frame helped break in the doors of the jail, and lead Maples, with a firm grip on his coat collar, to the Courthouse.

Sheriff Rodgers and Jailer Giles told of the fire, but did not admit seeing Frame in the crowd. W. L. Brigman saw Frame holding Maples, leading him up toward the Courthouse yard. The Baptist preacher, Gully, who was a prisoner in the jail, saw Frame holding a sledgehammer at the front door of the jail. On cross-examination, Gully gave a minute description of Frame and stated he was well acquainted with him. At this point the State had to rest its case because two important witnesses had disappeared.

Then it was the Defendant's turn.

R. L. Stephens, overseer in the carding room of the Dallas Mill, testified he saw Frame near the Van Valkenburg and Matthews Hardware Store and walked with him to the Stegall Hotel. Frame appeared to be taking no interest in the events around the jail. Frame was on the sidewalk while those with Maples were in the middle of the street. Stephens said that he and Frame were with an old man, at that time, having an innocent conversation.

Courtesy Huntsville-Madison County Public Library
1904 Post Office

Tom Kirk, an overseer in the spinning room of the Dallas Mill, talked to Frame at the Stegall Hotel while the jail was on fire. Kirk started toward the post office, up Green Street, as the crowd passed him. He was in the crowd at the Courthouse but did not see Frame take any part in the activities.

The witness jumped behind a tree when the mob fired at the hanging prisoner.

Silas Worley, who had been tried and acquitted on Saturday, testified that he saw Frame near the east gate of the Courthouse fence and they both walked down the street with him before any of the shots were fired. Lowe saw Frame but said that he was not part of the mob.

Closing arguments begun at seven thirty and ended at nine thirty. It was too late to go on and Court was adjourned until the next morning.

That night it was reported that James Lee Carter, rural mail carrier and one of the soldiers at the jail on the night of the lynching had died. Sulphur fumes from the fire made him very sick and he never recovered. He died at his home in Meridianville.

Wednesday, September 28, 1904

The next morning Judge Speake charged the jury at the early hour of eight fifteen. For forty-five minutes, he explained the law to the jury. The jury filed out of the courtroom at nine o'clock. They were out for five hours, returning to the Courthouse shortly after the dinner hour.

The verdict, *"We, the jury, find the Defendant, not guilty,"*[623] came as no surprise to anybody in and around the Courthouse. Spectators joined in a now familiar scene with well-wishers crowding into the courtroom and onto the Courthouse grounds to offer their congratulations to Frame.

During the dinner hour, the crowd around the Courthouse had other news to talk about. The report of the Military Court of Inquiry was released which caused much interest. The report had been delivered to the Governor the past Friday, but had not been released to the public until now. The Court found that a life had been taken unlawfully by a mob, under circumstances, which could have been prevented. That Company F, Third Infantry, Alabama National Guard was ineffective and worthless. It was recommended that the Company be disbanded and the soldiers mustered out of the service immediately.[624]

The Military Court commended Second Lt. Stewart for his conduct, but had nothing good to say about any of the other

---

[623] *The Huntsville Herald* (September 30, 1904).
[624] *The Weekly Mercury* (October 5, 1904)

commissioned officers. After reviewing the report with William W. Brandon, the Adjutant General, Governor Cunningham ordered that the recommendations of the Board be carried out at once. October 4, 1904 was set as the date the Company would cease to exist. The Governor seemed to think that the best course of action was to get rid of the Company and put an end to a bad situation.[625]

The murder trial of James H. Mitchell began as soon as the Frame trial had ended. The attorneys for Mitchell were Zack Drake and William B. Bankhead. Solicitor Erle Pettus and David A. Grayson were the attorneys for the State. Jury selection was again a problem and took a great deal of time.

The State believed Mitchell to be the leader of the mob as evidence showed him to be around the jail nearly all day and up to the time of the hanging and that he encouraged and advised the mob in many ways. The press considered the upcoming testimony some of the most interesting evidence heard in any of the series of cases.

Rev. Frank P. Culver, Pastor of the First Methodist Church was the principal witness for the State. He stated that he was speaking to the crowd about law and order when Mitchell interrupted him, and Mitchell's son struck him. Rev. Culver gave testimony that Mitchell took an active party in inciting the riot.

Chief of Police Overton was next and told of seeing Mitchell in a wagon making a speech to the crowd about "*getting the nigger.*"[626]

Will Brigman heard Mitchell tell the Sheriff to go on and shoot and the crowd would "fix" him.

D. C. Finney heard Will Mitchell, one of Mitchell's sons, bragging about his part in the riot and that he took a gun from a soldier.

Many of the same witnesses testified as they had in the other trials, but it was necessary that this new jury hear this evidence. The testimony took many hours making it s necessary to continue into another night session. The State had not rested their case at the close of court that night.

---

[625] Report of the Military Court of Inquiry, Adjunct General's Files, 1904, Alabama Department of Archives and History.
[626] *The Weekly Mercury* (October 5, 1904).

Thursday, September 29, 1904

The next morning the State rested their case. The first witness for the defense was James H. Mitchell. From the witness box he revealed a great deal of contempt and distaste for the legal system. His testimony, on his own behalf, would be unusual:

"I was born in Lincoln County, Tennessee. I am an ex-confederate soldier, age 65 years and I live in Dallas. (Tom) Ward and a squad of soldiers arrested me. I was asleep when they came. I went by the jail about three o'clock in the evening and that was the first I had heard of my old friend Waldrop's murder, and it flew all over me. That made me mad and I said that his murderer ought to be hung. The Judge made a pretty speech and made us a fair promise, I thought, and he said the law would hang the negro, and if the law did not, the judge would help the mob get him out of jail and hang him. I advised the men to let the law take its course and if they (the law) did not hang him, then we should hang the Judge. I just considered this a joke but it now looks like the gentlemen want to make a crime out of a little fun. I have a son named Will, who is in Texas, having gone there several weeks before the hanging. I never told anybody that I was willing to lead the mob nor did I tell Jeff Terry that I would help hang the negro." [627]

"I never had my hand on a soldier. I did quote a passage of scripture to Culver and thought he was a fool. Somebody told me he was a preacher and I said that all preachers like him, if they go to heaven, are hitched outside at the gate." [628]

Solicitor Pettus said, *"Since the Court has been reflected upon by the witness, in charging that your Honor would participate in the lynching of Horace Maples, in the event the jury acquitted him, I think it well, that you should make a statement to the jury."* [629]

Mitchell had implicated the Judge in the lynching but the Judge would not be drawn into the testimony. Judge Speake said, *"It is against public policy for a Judge to testify in his own Court."* [630]

Grayson called the attention of the Court to a case in which a Justice of the Peace had testified in a case before him. Judge Speake created considerable merriment by remarking that a Justice of the Peace has more power than the Supreme Court.

---

[627] *The Weekly Mercury* (October 5, 1904).
[628] Ibid.
[629] Ibid.
[630] Ibid.

Mitchell talked as he pleased during the cross examination and showed his contempt for Pettus when he stated that Solicitor Pettus should have a rope placed around his neck because he was trying to convict an innocent man.

The defense team felt so sure of an acquittal that they used only one other witness, a family member, to establish an alibi. Mitchell's daughter testified that her father was home on the night of the lynching.

David A. Grayson began closing arguments for the State. Zack Drake and William B. Bankhead closed for the defense. Solicitor Pettus finished for the State. Judge Speake gave the charges of law and the Jury got the case before the dinner hour just after five o'clock in the afternoon.

During another night session, the jury filed into the courtroom and handed a slip of paper to the clerk who read it.

"We the jury find that we are unable to agree"[631] [632]

The crowd had been prepared to hear a not guilty verdict so this statement created considerable surprise. The jury was sent back to the jury room to try again. They again reported no verdict could be agreed upon. The Judge sent the jury to bed overnight to try again the next day.

Friday, September 30, 1904

The next morning, the jury again announced that eleven of the men voted *"not guilty"* but that one jury would not change his vote. A mistrial was declared and the jury discharged. Mitchell was returned to jail until the February term of court.

After the jury was discharged it was learned, that it was S. M. Blair that would not agree to a *"not guilty"* verdict. He refused to vote not guilty and hung the jury. So bitter were the mill workers toward him that they threatened to boycott his employer.[633]

With each trial the disappointment and frustration of the State Attorney and the Judge increased. While the State Attorney was discouraged by the acquittals, it was still his obligation to continue. It became clear that the public and the government believed that no one would be punished for the lynching.

The next trial was for Tom Winkle, an operative in the Huntsville Cotton Mill. He was charged with arson. His trial began

---

[631] *The Weekly Mercury* (October 5, 1904).
[632] *The Birmingham News* (October 1, 1904).
[633] *McClure Magazine*, "What is a Lynching," page 312, Ray Stannard Baker, December 1904.

that afternoon. The usual difficulty was experienced in impaneling a jury. Eighty-five men were examined before a jury could be settled. The jury was selected during a break in the Mitchell trial and Winkle's trial started just after the Mitchell jury went out to deliberate.

C. W. Freeman, Superintendent of the Plumbers Planning Mill, was the principle witness for the State. He testified that Winkle told him that he had helped keep the fire burning in the jail, but he did not hang the Negro. The State had no other witnesses and was forced to allow the Defense to take over questioning.

Harness maker John Fullington was a witness for Winkle. He testified that Winkle was with him during the riots and they were only spectators to what was being done. An interesting exchange occurred when Solicitor Pettus asked Fullington if he had been convicted of a crime. Fullington replied, *"I have not and I will kill any man who said I have."*[634] The Solicitor called for the records and they showed that in 1894, Fullington had been tried for murder, convicted of manslaughter, and sentenced to a term of four years in the penitentiary.

The witnesses had completed their testimony by nine o'clock that evening. Attorneys were allowed an hour on each side to make their closing arguments. The arguments were finished at eleven that night. Court adjourned until morning.

Saturday, October 1, 1904

Court reconvened the next morning with little interest on anyone's part. They were all tired and the outcome was certain. Judge Speake charged the Jury at an early hour. The jury did not deliberate long. The verdict was *"not guilty."* No large crowd was present. The courtroom was almost empty and only the families and friends of the defendant were present. The town had lost interest.

The sixth and last trial started the same day.[635]

The trial of James Armstrong, who was charged with arson, started just after the Winkle trial. Armstrong was the last of the alleged lynchers in jail. This last trial began rather unceremoniously

---

[634] *The Weekly Mercury* (October 5, 1904).
[635] There is not as much information about the last trials as there was the first. The press had reported the same testimony many times and everyone felt that Armstrong would be found *"not guilty."* There was just no more interest in what remained of the cases.

with only a few spectators present. William B. Bankhead and Zack Drake represented Armstrong.

Witnesses could not be located and the State was forced to seek a continuance. The Judge granted the motion and continued the case until the next session of court in February. Armstrong was returned to jail. The few people in the courtroom gave no indications of interest nor were there celebrations. The court proceedings had become mundane and routine.

Tuesday, October 4, 1904

The State's Adjutant General came to Huntsville to carry out the recommendation of the Military Court of Inquiry and the order of the Governor. He disbanded Company F, Third Regiment and mustered the soldiers out of the service. It was not felt that any of the soldiers would be allowed to enter the service again.[637]

The next day, on Wednesday, October 5th, Judge S. M. Stewart (recently Lieutenant Stewart) of the Probate Court released James Mitchell and James Armstrong from jail on a writ of *habeas corpus*.[638]

The term of Circuit Court in September was historic, and very expensive, It was the longest every held in Huntsville. The court convened in August and was in session nine weeks. There were three grand juries, the one that sat for three weeks at the beginning of the term, the one that sat for two days and indicted Horace Maples and Dennis Smith for murder and the famous Grand Jury that returned twenty-six indictments against alleged lynchers.

The estimated cost was staggering. The regular Grand Jury had its normal expenses. It was estimated that the special Grand Jury that indicted Maples and Smith was in session two days and cost $68. The special Grand Jury and its lynching investigation cost $288. The trial of each alleged lynchers cost between three to four hundred dollars. Other court costs would total about $400. Then, there was the damage to the jail. The State paid over $3,000 for soldiers to be sent

---

[637] Madison County would not have a National Guard Unit again until 1922. (*A Dream Come True*, Vol. II, 1878, John Hicklin Printing Co. Huntsville, Alabama, Library of Congress Number: 76-11880.)

[638] Habeas corpus, The name given to a variety of writs having for their object to bring a party before a court or judge. The primary function of the writ is to release from unlawful imprisonment. The office of the writ is not to determine prisoner's guilt or innocence, and only issue, which it presents, is whether prisoner is restrained of his liberty by due process. (*Black's Law Dictionary*, Centennial Edition (1891-1991) Sixth Edition, West Publishing Company, 1990.

to Huntsville, and more for the Court of Inquiry. It was safely estimated that the State and County would pay at least $6,500 for mob violence in September 1904.[638]

None of the men arrested and charged, with leadership in the lynching, had been found guilty. Dennis Smith would be the only person found guilty of all those tried that month, and his case had nothing to do with the lynching. He was the only person sentenced to death and of course, he was a Negro.

Later that Month

Federal Judge Jones took up the case, charged his jury vigorously, and some members of the mob were indicted in the Federal Courts.[639]

The action of the Federal Courts surprised the community. Some believed the Federal government would interfere with a case of assault between a white man and a Negro, if race prejudice were shown as the real problem. The courts might go so far as to interfere with a contract between whites and their Negro servants. This would even force the same wages for Negroes to be the same as a white mans.

Governor Cunningham directed the Adjutant General to take the necessary steps to start the impeachment procedure and remove Sheriff August D. Rodgers from office. The State's Attorney General filed charges against the Sheriff, in the Supreme Court on October 18th. In a petition consisting of three charges, including 10 specifications, the Sheriff was accused of the impeachable conduct of willful neglect of duty, incompetence, and negligently permitting a prisoner to be taken from the jail and put to death. The State asked that Rodgers be removed from office and be disqualified from holding public office ever again.[640]

The Sheriff was ordered to appear before the Supreme Court on the 24th of November 1904, to answer the charges. The Sheriff's attorneys, Walker and Spraggins, filed a motion to end the

---

[638] *The Weekly Mercury* (October 5, 1904).

[639] After the vigorous charge to the Federal Grand Jury nothing was done. No action was ever taken against the lynchers by the Federal Government.

[640] Correspondence files of the Adjunct General, 1889-1907; Alabama Department of Archives and History.

impeachment. After hearing arguments of counsel on the motion, the Supreme Court took the matter under consideration.[641]

The Sheriff and counsel returned to Huntsville where public, sentiment was greatly in favor of the dismissal of the proceedings. No one was surprised when word was received that the Supreme Court had granted the motion and the impeachment proceedings came to an end.

A hotel proprietor, a merchant, four-day laborers, and their friends in the cotton mills had made Huntsville safe again. The citizens of Huntsville allowed these men to be the judge, jury and executor.

People wanted to forget that the lynching had occurred. The newspapers stopped running headline stories about the lynching. The press turned to people pleasing matters and the memory of the lynching faded.

After all, tomorrow was another day and the mills needed to open on time.[642]

Sunday, October 23, 1904

Rev. Frank P. Culver's, sermon to the First Methodist Church, spoke about the jurymen who acquitted the alleged lynchers in the Circuit Court. Culver said, *"Men are afraid, they dare not speak out."* He continued with, *"I refer to the spirit which defies the law, tramples down authority, disrespects civil magistrates, and intrigues against justice."* He said, *"I had rather be Paul Speake than a thousand of those who would slander him for trying to do what he considered to be conscientiously doing his duty. If it is a lawyer's sworn duty to try to set free every client, whether innocent or guilty, then before I would practice law, I would pick rags, sweep the streets, or do anything rather than lose my self respect and honor."*[643]

---

[641] The *Weekly Mercury* (October 19, 1904).
[642] Phrase associated with Margaret Mitchell's *"Gone With the Wind."* (New York, New York, The MacMillan Co., 1936.
[643] *The Journal* (October 27, 1904).

The names of Judge Paul Speake, and Solicitor Erie Pettus are not displayed in any public place of honor in Madison County.

Epilogue

Judge Speake was unpopular with segments of the community after his court actions against the lynchers. However, he was popular enough to be nominated by the Democratic Party from Madison and Limestone counties to run for the judgeship again.

The mill workers and others attempted to defeat the Judge in the coming election. They went to Shelby Pleasants, an attorney who was a Republican, and asked him to run against Judge Speake. "*I will not be a mob's candidate,*" he said. "*I endorse every action of Judge Speake.*"[645]

Several other lawyers were approached but none could be found to run against the Judge.

However, before the election a decision of the Supreme Court, reversal of the Lusk Bill, removed him from his office and returned him to private practice.

On September 16th, in the arraignment of Thomas Riggins and Ben Hill, William B. Bankhead, attorney for Hill, filed an exception to the indictment, on the grounds that—an act passed by the legislature, the Lusk Bill, making Madison County a separate Circuit, the Sixteenth Circuit, was unconstitutional.[646]

In early October, the Alabama Supreme Court ruled that the House and Senate had not constitutionally passed the Lusk Bill, which did not become law, and was therefore, unconstitutional.[647] Therefore, Madison County reverted back to the Eighth Circuit with Limestone, Morgan, Cullman, and Lawrence Counties. The court official's were now D. W. Speake (Uncle of Paul Speake) of Decatur and Solicitor David Almon of Moulton. The passage of the Lusk Bill, in effect, simply cut off two counties from the Eighth Circuit and the decision of the Supreme Court put them back in.

All the legal authorities agreed that the decision of the Supreme Court affected the validity of the indictments against the lynchers. The State was entirely without authority during the trials. The impeachment of Sheriff A. C. Rodgers, Mayor Thomas W. Smith and Chief of Police Overton was now the same as if any sixteen men had censored them. They also agreed that Judge Speake and Solicitor

---

[645] McClure's Magazine (January 1905).

[646] The first test of the Lusk Act was in the conviction of Ralph Armstrong. Before the Supreme Court ruled on the case Armstrong hung himself in his cell. It was believed that he would have been given a new trial. (The Birmingham News, (September 10, 1904).

[647] *The Huntsville Herald* (October 7, 1904).

Pettus were not then officials of the State. Dennis Smith, sentenced to hang on October 21st, would have a new trial.

During November 1904, the Huntsville Fire Department went on strike, spurred by the events surrounding the mob overtaking the jail. The problems centered on the lack of action taken by the Police Department, to secure their safety.[648]

Election time was approaching and nominees had to be selected for the office of Judge and Solicitor, in the Eighth Judicial Circuit.

The Democratic Executive Committee met to decide who would represent the Democratic Party in the Eighth Circuit. Three North Alabama Counties, Morgan, Lawrence and Cullman, nominated D. W. Speake for Judge and David Almon for Solicitor. Madison and Limestone Counties nominated Paul Speake for Judge and Erle Pettus for Solicitor.

At the meeting, Erle Pettus stated he would not claim the nomination and asked that D. C. Almon be declared the nominee for Solicitor. Judge Speake did not attend the meeting but forwarded a letter expressing his decision to give up the judgeship in favor of the nominee, his uncle, D. W. Speake. The decisions of both men were accepted with a vote of thanks.

Paul Speake returned to private practice for the next twenty-three years. He was noted as one of the best attorneys in the State. He was so highly regarded that in 1911, he was elected President of the State Bar Association.

In 1927, Madison County was made a separate Circuit, the Twenty-Third Judicial Circuit,[649] and on August 17 of that year, Governor Bibb Graves appointed Paul Speake to the Judgeship of this new Circuit. A large and representative delegation of citizens from Madison County had visited the Capital asking for the appointment. Governor Graves said that there is was no doubt about the people of Madison County wanting Judge Speake for their judge, and that he took a great pleasure in giving him the appointment.

In 1928, the voters elected Judge Speake to a full term. In 1934, he was re-elected and became known throughout the State for his fairness and clear interpretation of the law.

Speake was an unsuccessful candidate for Associate Justice of the Alabama Supreme Court, but had the admiration of lawyers

---

[648] *The Weekly Mercury* (November 2, 1904).
[649] Madison County is still designated as the Twenty-third Judicial Circuit.

throughout the State. He held office until his death. He died at his home on Eustis Street on December 6, 1937 at the age of sixty-six. Though sick he had presided over a term of court the last week of his life against the advice of his friends. Pallbearers were M. U. Griffin, Walter Price, Elbert Parsons, Charles Stewart, Thomas W. Jones, Hugh Doak, W. B. Whitfield and Henry M. Hughes. He left his wife, Florence H. Speake, three daughters and one son.[650]

Solicitor Pettus was never accepted in the Huntsville community again. He had made too many statements in court against the popular leaders of mob violence. The people never forgave him for his stand against the white citizens of Madison County

He continued as District Attorney until he gave up the nomination as candidate for the Democratic Party. He returned to private practice in Athens. He soon learned that he could not continue to live in North Alabama and that it would be better to seek his fortune in another city. In 1906, he formed a partnership with Judge Zell Gaston in Birmingham and became an outstanding advocate in the courts of that city.

He gained something from his days as solicitor in Huntsville. He met a young lady while in Huntsville and returned to marry her. His marriage to Eellelle Chapman, granddaughter of Ex-Governor Reuben Chapman, took place in November 1907.

He served as U. S. District Attorney in Birmingham for some time but returned to private practice where he became a great lawyer. His closing arguments to juries were considered masterpieces. He later practiced with his son, and never retired. He died July 5, 1960.[651]

In March of 1905, Dennis Smith was retried. The trial lasted two days. After deliberating thirty minutes, the jury found him guilty of murder in the second degree and fixed his punishment at twenty years imprisonment.

Mayor Thomas Smith was re-elected in 1908. The indictment had no affect of his career.

Sheriff A. D. Rodgers lost the next election in 1907 and reverted to his previous occupation as a horse trader.

Lieutenant Morgan Stewart of the National Guard resigned his position as probate judge in 1904 with no reason given.

---

[650] Obituary Notice, *The Weekly Mercury* (December 6, 1927).
[651] Interview with Erle Pettus Jr., by Fred B. Simpson, Mary Daniel and Gay Campbell (1999).

Murders would continue throughout the years but there would never be another lynching in Madison County.[651]

The actions of Judge Speake and Solicitor Pettus had forever stopped the sin of murder by a mob. There would be crowds and much talk of lynching at other times and places, but in the future, all officials would do their duty and prevent a lynching.[652] [653]

---

[651] In 1915, Herman Neely, a Negro field hand, shot at a black boy on a mule; he missed the boy and the mule, but wounded a white man, Arthur Craft, in the knee. Deputy Sheriff Silas Hunt arrested Neely and was at the Whitesburg Railroad Depot when six men took his prisoner and shot him to death. This is not classified as a lynching, but as a cruel murder committed by a small group of men. See foreword at the front of this book for classification of lynching.

[652] In September 1930, H. E. Ross was killed in his home. His wife did not get a good look at the person, but thought he might be black. When a suspect was placed in the Madison County Jail a large crowd gathered, carrying ropes and guns. Sheriff Frank Riddick told the mob that the man was not the killer. Some of the mob threw rocks at the jail and attempted to force entry. Some went in search of dynamite. The sheriff armed every deputy with shotguns and expected to fire. Judge Paul Speake notified the Governor and Company A, of the National Guard, commanded by Capt. Edwin Jones was ordered to move around the jail. Thrown objects injured two soldiers, shots were fired over the heads of the mob and six men were arrested. The crowd left and the suspect was sent home. All the officials carried out their duties and prevented mob violence. *(A Time for Justice*, Fred Simpson, "*Old Huntsville*" Magazine, Number 62, Huntsville 1996)

[653] In March of 1936, nineteen year old, Vivian Woodward went to a movie in downtown Huntsville. She was walking towards home, and almost reached her house on Walker Ave. when she was raped and killed. Bloodhounds tracked the killer to a house occupied by several black men. A mob surrounded the house and four black men were taken outside. A wire was placed around the neck of each man, and it appeared that a lynching would take place. However, the police arrived and took the men to jail. That night, a large crowd gathered around the jail. Law enforcement officers stood firm and the crowd was dispersed. The prisoners were taken to Birmingham for safekeeping. After several days, the real killer, Walter Miller, was arrested. The family of the deceased girl pled with the community to let the law take its course. Judge Speake knew he could not trust the citizens to maintain order without the presents of armed guards. One hundred-twenty-five Alabama National Guardsmen escorted Miller from Birmingham to Huntsville for his arraignment. With mounted machine guns on every entrance to the courthouse uniformed guardsmen patrolled the Courthouse Square. All spectators and newspapermen were searched before being allowed to enter, and then only by the South door. The crowd gathered on the east and south side of the Square, generally harassing the guardsmen. The thrill came when a few men and the National Guardsmen got into a fight, but the Guardsmen quickly dispersed them with a barrage of tear gas bombs. Some people were indignant at the use of tear gas and what they termed the "hard-boiled attitude of the troops." Many protested the use of tear gas as, "unjustified and unwarranted." Solicitor John E. McEachin asked Governor Bibb Graves not to send National Guardsmen to Huntsville when Miller was returned to Huntsville for his trial, saying, "the Sheriff and local officials can

After Paul Speake returned to the judgeship his resolve to prevent the lawlessness of a lynching was tested and he used the power of his office to prevent a lynching in Madison County.[654]

One year later, in November of 1905, there was a crowd of several thousand people at the same site of the lynching. They were not there to take action against mob violence. The occasion was the dedication of the Confederate monument on the Courthouse lawn. Governor Jelks was present, sitting on a platform erected on the lawn, within the shade of the *"tree."* The Governor accepted the monument on behalf of the State of Alabama. He stated, *"The monument will commemorate the deed of the brave..."*[655]

Race relations continue to provide fuel to the problems of today, much as they did when Norah Davis authored her novel, *The Northerner*, in 1905. The novel's setting was Huntsville, Alabama, and it was an indictment of race relations in the South. Her central character was Gregory Falls, believed to be Tracey Pratt, who came south to educate the *"sinful southerners."* He was not a bigot and brought progress through fairness to the *"small sleepy town."* He saved a Negro man from a mob lynching and made the *"south safe again."*

---

handle the situation." Madison County's prior history with mob violence could leave little doubt that drastic action was needed to protect prisoners. Judge Paul Speake had the foresight to know the potential problems that could arise. Judge Speake ordered National Guardsmen to protect the prisoner and to insure an orderly trial. (*The Mercury*, May 7, 1936). On the morning of the trial, Monday, May 11, 1936, Miller and four companies of National Guardsmen arrived at dawn, by train. The soldiers were armed with bayonet rifles, side arms, machine guns, grenades and gas equipment. A white line was drawn on the pavement around the Courthouse and the crowd was not allowed to enter the Courthouse lawn. By ten o'clock, when court opened, the crowd was standing behind the white line and the streets were crowded around the Courthouse. Only those having business in the streets were allowed into the building. The south door was again, the only entrance. Everyone was questioned and searched. Even pocket knives were taken from the spectators. (*The Mercury*, May 14, 1936) The trial finished and the guilty verdict received, the prisoner, Walter Miller, was taken by the National Guardsmen, out of the courtroom. With bayonets and machine guns ready, the hustled miller into an Army ambulance and accompanied him to Kilby Prison at Montgomery. He arrived at the prison early the next morning and placed on Death Row, to await his execution. He was executed on June 19, 1936, less that ninety days after he killed Vivian Woodward. (The *Huntsville Times* March 1936)

[654] See footnote references 652 and 653.
[655] *The Weekly Mercury* (November 22, 1905).

"*It would be pretty to think so*, but reality was something else."[657]

Postcard Collection of Fred Simpson

Alabama State Capitol

---

[657] Phrase associated with the book, *The Sun Also Rises,* Ernest Hemingway.

Confidential.

Huntsville, Ala., Sept. 20th, 1904.

Hon. R. M. Cunningham, Governor,

Montgomery, Ala.

My Dear Sir:-

I have been intending to write you for several days, but it has been impossible to write you before, as fully as I desired. You asked me over the 'phone to write you with reference to the conduct of Sheriff Rodgers. My former letter stated the facts as I understood them, viz: that he was asked to clear the streets during the day and evening, and did not do so; that he failed to summon a posse to assist him; that he went to the jail with the militia and was their superior officer and failed to give the order to fire, notwithstanding they were prepared with arms and ammunition to repel the mob and notwithstanding an open and violent attack was being made upon the jail in his presence for several hours. Upon these facts it is impossible to escape the conclusion that he neglected to perform his duty.

His conduct, too, since the return of the indictments has not been satisfactory. It seems to me he could have made more arrests than have been made, had he and his deputies been at all diligent. He has one deputy, Mr. Thos. W. Ward, who is brave, conscientious and fearless in the discharge of his duty; but his other deputies are political trimmers, and, in my opinion, heartily in sympathy with the mob and the mob element. Although I do not know it certainly, yet it seems evident to me that someone, whose duty it is to keep such things secret, has divulged the names of some of those against whom indictments have been returned, and probably given them warning to get away,- else I do not see how so many of

Letter from Judge Paul Speake to Governor Cunningham

them could have escaped arrest. Twenty-six indictments in all have been returned (7 last night, however,) and have heard of only four arrests. Two of these were made by Deputy Ward with the aid of Capt. Brown, one by Ward individually, and the fourth (I believe) by the sheriff himself with Capt. Brown. These men were all in the vicinity of Huntsville, either in town or in the suburbs, and three out of the four had ample opportunity to get away, had they desired to do so, before they were arrested, although I impressed upon the sheriff the duty of making prompt arrests *in order that I might give* them speedy trials. He stated that his deputies were busy summoning special *and witnesses for the grand jury,* jurors, etc., but I told him (as is the law) that he had the right to summon special deputies if necessary

Last night the grand jury returned its final report, having found twenty-six indictments in all. I have ordered that a certified copy of the report be sent by the clerk to the attorney general in accordance with section 4686 of the Code. The grand jury recommended the impeachment of Sheriff Rodgers, Mayor Smith and Chief of Police Overton. Sentiment of the best people is general that these officers did not do their duty; but at the same time there are many who have ranked as "good citizens" who are really in sympathy with the mob and with the officers who have been derelict in duty. Most of the indictments are for capital offenses, and not more than three or four of them can be tried at the present term (even if they are arrested). I shall of course endeavor to try as many as possible. I fear it will be very difficult, if not impossible, to secure convictions; but at the same time believe, notwithstanding the heavy expense to the state and county, the proceedings will have a good effect in deterring mobs in future and in making officers do their duty.

3.

The members of the grand jury are deserving of especial praise and honor, as their position ~~xxxxxxxxxxxx~~ is more trying and their responsibilities more onerous than those of any of the rest of us. They are being greatly criticized by the aforesaid so-called "good citizens".

As to keeping the militia here, I am somewhat in doubt as to exactly how long they should stay, but am inclined to think they should stay until we are through trying the cases the last of next week. Certain citizens, who really are either in sympathy with the lawless element or are trying to arouse public sentiment in order to secure acquittals, are using, for all they can, the fact that the militia are here and the circumstance especially, that they came into the court-room the other day. I have modified the strictness of the military surveillance somewhat, so as not to incense civilians any more than is necessary, and so as not to give these mob-sympathizers any more room than is necessary to play upon the public passions and prejudices, and have ordered the removal of the pickets on the streets in the day-time. The military protection and surveillance remains the same at night as heretofore, and really I apprehend no effort at a rescue as long as the troops are in town and ready for service on call. If any of the prisoners should be left in jail when the term ends next week, it would probably be well for you (if you can do so) to have them removed to some other county. It seems the statute does not give me authority to order their removal, except upon application by the sheriff, and then only to nearest sufficient jail, which I suppose is at Decatur. Whether the sheriff will ask for their removal I do not know, but I think it

4.

~~extremikely~~ probable that he will not. I will endeavor to get him to do so, however, if any charged with capital offenses are in jail when court adjourns.

I did not want the relief company sent here the other day because of the persistent rumors that a negro regiment was coming here by order of the U. S. Government, and I feared that the actual movement of _any_ troops in this direction just at that time would be adding fuel to the flame and would be misconstrued and magnified so as to cause more trouble. I see no reason now why the troops should not be relieved if they so desire.

I think it altogether likely that the United States Court will take up this mob's proceedings, if there is any law authorizing them to do so, and trust they will do so. It will meet here early in October, and I hardly think it necessary to offer any rewards for those who have escaped until that grand jury acts. If they return indictments, the U. S. Marshal and his deputies may be enabled to make the arrests and thus the payment of rewards saved to the State.

It is rumored that one of the main participants in the mob is across the state line in Tennessee, and that two others have fled to Texas. A great many of the factory hands have scattered to the "four winds."

The first trial will begin to-morrow. I fear that owing to this man's popularity, as well as because current rumor says that he was not one of the most guilty, he will be certainly acquitted, and would have preferred to try the other man Ben Hill first, but in view of his attorney's statements with reference to getting his evidence, etc., I could not, acting impartially, set his case for an earlier date than next Monday. Very respectfully yours, Paul Sh—

HUNTSVILLE, ALA. Sept. 15, 1904.

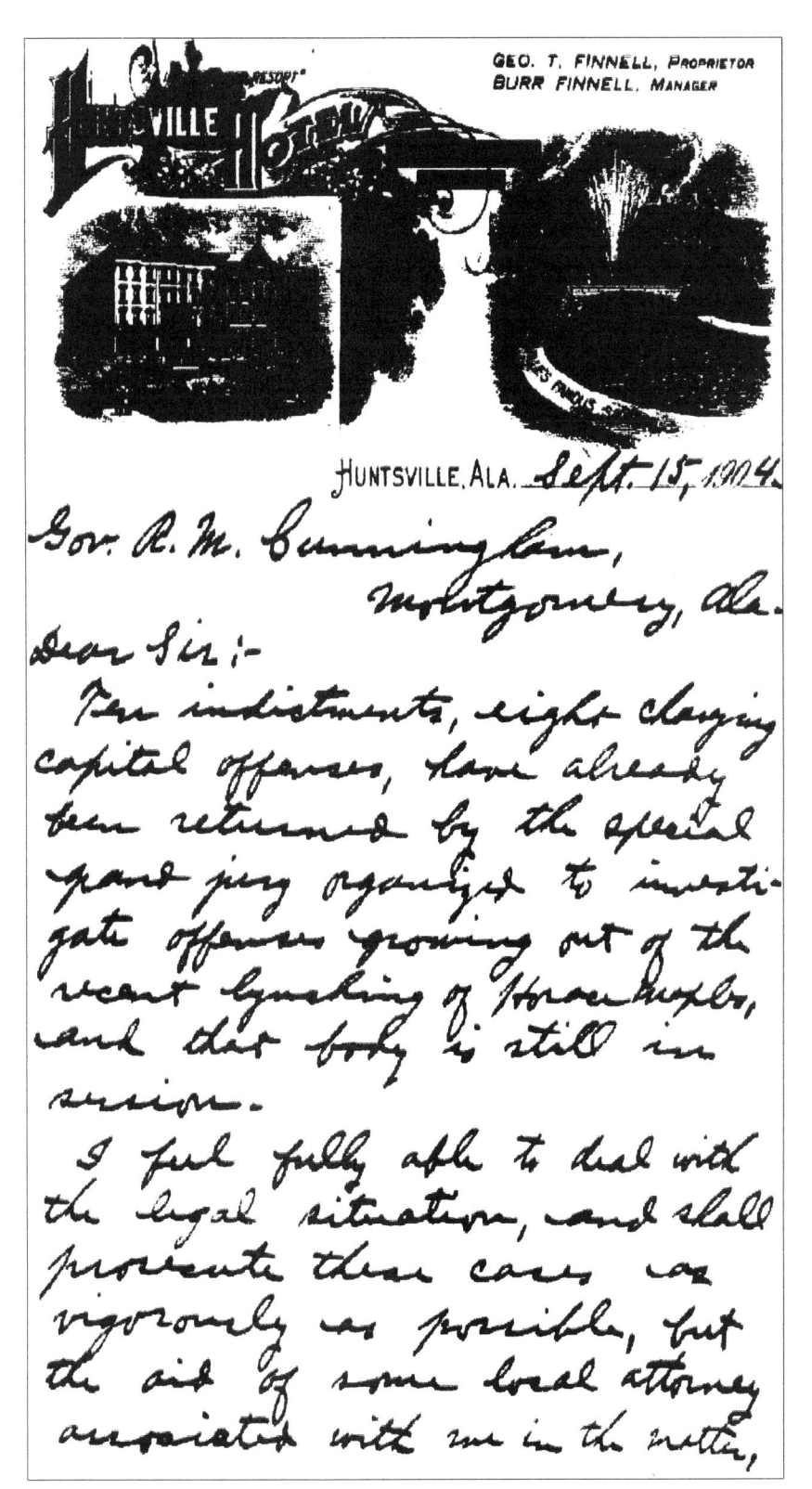

Gov. R. M. Cunningham,
    Montgomery, Ala.

Dear Sir:-

Ten indictments, eight charging capital offenses, have already been returned by the special grand jury organized to investigate offenses growing out of the recent lynching of Horace Maples, and that body is still in session.

I feel fully able to deal with the legal situation, and shall prosecute these cases as vigorously as possible, but the aid of some local attorney associated with me in the matter,

Letter from Solicitor Erle Pettus to Governor Cunningham

HUNTSVILLE, ALA. _____ 190_

who is familiar with the ramifications and connections of the various parties, would no doubt greatly increase the probability of convictions.

Realizing the importance — to the county and the State — of bringing the guilty parties to justice and securing convictions for their offenses, I suggest that, if you deem it advisable, you communicate with D. A. Grayson, Esq., a prominent and influential member of the local bar, who would be competent and fearless in the capacity suggested, and see if he is not willing to serve his people and his State in this emergency —

Very respectfully,
E. W. Pettus,
Solicitor.

Biographies—Chapter Six

The following short biographies are of the people involved in the preceding story. Every effort was made to find information on individuals no matter how small or large a part they played in the story. [657]

Armstrong, James; Alleged Lyncher.
Armstrong was charged with murder and jailed on September 26, 1904, he was held in jail until his court date of September 30, 1904. Judge S. M. Stuart discharged the defendant on a *Writ of Habeas Corpus*,[658] on October 3, 1904. "Jay" was a weaver at the Merrimack Mills. His home was at 239 Rison Avenue. On the same street were other Armstrong's who worked at the mills.[659] [660]

Bailey, Edward A.; Jury—Hill Trial.
Edward A. Bailey, a farmer, was born in October 1850 in Alabama. His wife, Martha Jane, was born in Alabama, in November 1852. Their nine children were: Lisa, born June 1873, in Alabama; Carrie B., born June 1876; Dudley, born December 1879; A. L., a daughter, born September 1881; Sara M., born December 1883; Cornelia born August 1886; Cassie Lee, born November 1891; Robert, born April 1893; and Crutcher, born October 1896. A farm hand, Luke Mitchell [white], born May 1877, lived with the family.

Baldridge, Felix E., Doctor.
A complete biograhpy may be found in Chapter Two.

---

[657] A search was conducted using the Huntsville City Directories; 1900-1910 United States Federal Census; *Madison County Cemeteries*, Vol. 1 & 2; *Maple Hill Cemetery, Phase One;* and private manuscripts regarding the cemetery; Dorothy Scott Johnson; *Merrimack Cemetery*, Ann Maulsby; Confederate *Veterans Census*, Dorothy Scott Johnson; various military records; Madison County Probate and Civil Court Records.

[658] *Black's Law Dictionary*; Fourth Edition, Page 837. The name given to a variety of writs, (of which these were the emphatic works) having for their object to bring a party before a court or judge. The sole function of this writ is to release from unlawful imprisonment.

[659] 1911-The Huntsville City Directory, page 104.

[660] Madison County Sheriffs Bonds, Huntsville-Madison County Public Library. Archives.

Bankhead, William Brockman; Attorney.
William Bankhead was born in April of 1874. He was an attorney in 1904. His practice was located on Bank Row. He lived in a hotel on Franklin Street with his wife, Adelaide Eugene, who was born in July 1880, in Tennessee. They were the parents of the famous movie actress, Tallulah Bankhead. William Bankhead was a member of the United States House of Representatives from 1916 and Speaker from 1936 until his death in 1940. In a television documentary[661] about the life of Franklin Delano Roosevelt, it shows that Roosevelt came to Alabama to attend William Bankhead's funeral. A ramp had to be built so that the presidential car could pull up to the door, behind the funeral procession, to allow the president to enter and exit the church. William Bankhead's wife, Ada, died February 4, 1902, shortly after the birth of her famous daughter. She was buried in Maple Hill Cemetery. Her tombstone reads *"In Tender Memory of Adalaide Eugene, Beloved Wife of Wm. B. Bankhead. Born July 14, 1880 Died February 23, 1902."*[662] William Bankhead died in 1940, and is buried in South Alabama.

Bates, Lonnie (Alonzo) P.; Chief Deputy Sheriff.
By 1911, Bates was married to Dennie, and employed as manager of the Alabama Coal and Oil Company. They lived at 406 Walker Street.[663]

Battle, Jacob William; Special Grand Jury.
Jacob William Battle was born May 2, 1844. In 1900, he was fifty-six years old, and lived near Huntsville and married to Kate. She had been born in Alabama, in December 1845. They were the parents of seven children: B. A. Battle, a son born September 1871; James R., a son born May 1872 (working as a delivery clerk for the Post Office); Katherine, born July 1880; Chester, born October 1883; and Joanna, born April 1885.[664] The 1907 Confederate Census of Alabama shows that Jacob William Battle entered service January 2, 1862, at LaGrange Alabama into Company H of the Thirty-Fifth Alabama Infantry. He served until October 8, 1862 when he was promoted to

---

[661] Aired on the History Channel.
[662] *Maple Hill Cemetery*, page 121, Phase I; Robey, Johnson, Jones, Roberts, Huntsville-Madison County Historical Society, 1995.
[663] 1911 Huntsville City Directory.
[664] 1900 United States Federal Census, Madison County, Alabama, Vol. 38 Enumeration District 100, Sheet 9 line 93.

Second Lieutenant and transferred to Company C of the Fiftieth Alabama. On July 5, 1863, Jacob was promoted to First Lieutenant. He was transferred to the Cavalry on September 4, 1864 where he commanded a scout troop under General Nathan Bedford Forrest, until the surrender of the Confederacy. He was paroled at Pond Springs, near Courtland, Alabama, on May 16, 1865.[665] He is buried in Maple Hill Cemetery with a C.S.A. marker on his grave.[666]

Beadly, William R.; Jury—Frame Trial.
William R. Beadley was born February 18, 1860, in Alabama. He was a farmer. In 1900, people in the home were: Ollie Powell, an eighteen year old niece, and several boarders who were black; Kit Bradley, thirty-years old; and Isaac Ellerson and his family, who are listed as farm laborers.[667] William died January 14, 1926 and was buried in Maple Hill Cemetery, Section 16 Row 4. His tombstone reads, *"Having finished life's duty, He now sweetly rests."*[668]

Berryhill, Count; Witness—Worley Trial.
A diligent search of all resources was performed without results. Many Berryhills worked at the Merrimack Mill and lived in the village. However, a search of those families did not turn up anyone named "Count." Probably this was a nickname.

Blair, Louis C.; Jury—Worley Trial.
Louis C. Blair worked at a hotel. He was single and lived at 121 Gallatin Street.[669] Louis is buried in Mt. Zion Church Cemetery in Madison County. His tombstone gives his birth as May 14, 1870, and his death as May 29, 1947. Also buried there is Epsien A. Blair born June 23, 1880 died August 11, 1963.[670]

Bragg, George T.; Jury—Hill Trial.
George T. Bragg worked at the Ninth Avenue Grocery, located at the corner of Ninth Avenue and Sixteenth Street. His wife Nancy also

---

[665] *1907 Confederate Census of Limestone, Morgan and Madison Counties*, page 1, Johnson Historical Publications, 1981, Dorothy Scott Johnson.
[666] *The Valiant Survivors: the United Confederate Veterans of Madison County—A Record of Their Services 1861—1865*; 2nd Edition, page 31, Charles Wells.
[667] 1900 United States Federal Census, Madison County, Alabama; Vol.38, Enumeration District 99, Sheet 35, line 24.
[668] Manuscripts of Maple Hill Cemetery Records, by Dorothy Scott Johnson.
[669] 1911 Huntsville City Directory.
[670] *Madison County Cemetery Book*, Vol. #1, Page 219, Dorothy Scott Johnson, Johnson Historical Publications.

worked in the grocery store.[671] They were buried in Maple Hill Cemetery in the family plot. George's tombstone reads 1860-1935 and is located in Section 23 Row 22; Nancy J.'s tombstone reads 1873-1936.[672]

Brickell, Robert C., Committee.
A complete biography may be found in Chapter Two.

Bridges, Joe; Jury—Frame Trial.
Joseph Bridges was born August 1842 and lived at Cluttsville, Alabama, on a farm. He was married to Martha A. who was born in Georgia, October 1843. Children were: Charles L. born September 1880; John H. born June 1882; Altho S. born December 1844; Allie born January 1887; Nana Born 1889; The birthday of the oldest son, James, is unknown.

Brigham, Walter L.; Witness—Frame Trial.
Walter L. Brigman worked for the Dallas Manufacturing Company and was married to Mary. They lived on McCullough Avenue.[673] After his death his widow, Mary, continued to work at the Lowe Mills until 1916. In 1920, she lived at a boarding house on Ninth Avenue, but no employment was listed.[674] No death or burial information could be found.

Buckner, William D.; Jury—Hill Trial.
A diligent search was made for William D. Buckner without results. Material was found on William J. Buckner, who was employed at Dallas Mills in 1896, and lived on Stevens Ave. In 1911, he was employed at Abington Mills, and lived on Humes Avenue in East Huntsville. His wife's name was Jessie. In 1916, he was employed at Dallas Mills.[675]

Buford, Robert Stanfield; Jury—Hill Trial.
In 1850, Robert S. Buford lived with his father, Duncastle and his wife Susan (Roach).[676] This was a third marriage for Duncastle.[677]

---

[671] 1916-17 Huntsville City Directory, page 114.
[672] Manuscript records of Maple Hill Cemetery Records, by Dorothy Scott Johnson.
[673] 1896 Huntsville City Directory, page 23.
[674] 1911-1916-1917, Huntsville City Directory.
[675] 1911-1916-1917, Huntsville City Directory, page 120.
[676] 1850 United States Federal Census, Madison County, Alabama, page 119.
[677] Madison County, Alabama Marriage Records.

Buford was born January 15, 1847. His wife, Mary C. was born January 17, 1846. He died April 30, 1932, and she died February 26, 1899.[678]

Burke, John; Made Speech.
John Burke was born June 23, 1875 and died July 9, 1905. He was buried in section 9 of Maple Hill Cemetery, next to his wife Alice Burke.[679]

Cantrell, Malcolm M.; Special Grand Jury.
Malcolm M. Cantrell was born in Tennessee January 1857. His wife, Margaret Ellen, was born in July of 1858 in Alabama. Malcolm and Ellen were married in 1882. Their children were: Lizzie, born November 1884; James R. born December 1886; Addie L. born August 1887; Estelle born November 1892; and Malcolm Jr. born January 1896.[680] Malcolm and Ellen lived at 306 Walker Street. Malcolm worked at Cantrell & Allen. By 1916, Malcolm worked at Cantrell and Stoltzenberg and was President and Manager of the Huntsville Ice and Coal Company and Vice-President of Huntsville Grocery Company.[681] By 1920, he was manager of Cantrell Drug Company and still lived on Walker Street.[682]

Carrager, Albert John; Jury—Frame Trial.
John Albert Carringer was buried in Maple Hill Cemetery, Section 23 Row 11. The tombstone reads "1874-1952."[683]

Christian, Cleveland B.; Jury—Hill Trial.
Cleveland B. Christian worked at Lowe Mills. He lived with his wife Jennie on Douglas Hill.[684]

---

[678] *Cemeteries of Madison County, Vol. #3,* page 54, Neal Chapel Cemetery, Dorothy Scott Johnson, Johnson Historical Publications.
[679] Maple Hill Cemetery Phase One, page 65, Robey, Johnson, Jones, Roberts; Huntsville-Madison County Historical Society.
[680] 1900 United States Federal Census, Madison County, Alabama, Vol. 38, Enumeration District 99, Sheet 21 Line 53.
[681] 1911, Huntsville City Directory, Page 123; 1916 Huntsville City Directory page 121.
[682] 1920, Huntsville City Directory, Page 136.
[683] Manuscript's of Maple Hill Cemetery Records, by Dorothy Scott Johnson.
[684] 1911-12, Huntsville City Directory, page 127.

Cleveland, Archie; Witness—Worley Trial.
In 1900, young Archie Cleveland lived at home with his mother Mindy Echols and her husband Harvey Echols. His mother, Mindy, was forty-one years old at the time. Archie's siblings were: George, born December 1877 [worked at a cotton mill]; Lee, born February 1880 [worked as farm labor]; Robert, born September 1881 [worked as farm labor]; Archie, born October 1883 [worked as farm labor]; Lula, born December 1885, [worked on the farm]; Beaula, born July 1887; Willie, [male] born September 1891; Step-brother Gene Echols, born March 1897.[685] Several of the Cleveland Family was buried in Merrimack Cemetery, just off Triana Blvd. in Southwest Huntsville.[686]

Cobb, Samuel L.; Jury—Hill Trial.
Samuel L. Cobb Sr. lived on Oak Avenue with his wife, Annie, in the home of Lucy Hutchens. Samuel worked as a salesman. He was born December 1869. Samuel and Annie had a child, Samuel Jr., born April 1899.[687] In 1896, the couple lived at 401 Madison Street.[688] In 1920 they lived at 327 Randolph Avenue.[689]

Cooper, Lawrence; Attorney.
Lawrence Cooper was born in January of 1852, in Alabama. He was a lawyer with the law firm of Cooper & Cooper, located in the Struve Building.[690] He and his wife Eliza, [born May 1855], lived on West Holmes Street. They married in 1880, and had two children: George P., born March 1879; and Elizabeth, born July 1891.[691] Lawrence was also the Vice President of the Southern Building and Loan Association.[692] He was buried in Maple Hill Cemetery, Section 20 Row 1. The tombstone reads "1850-1931."[693]

Crowson, John J.; Jury—Hill Trial.
John J. Crowson was born August 1859, in Alabama. He was a farmer. His wife Eliza was born in Alabama, in 1864. In 1900 they

---

[685] 1900 United States Federal Census, Madison County, Alabama.
[686] *Merrimack* Cemetery, Page 28, Ann Maulsby.
[687] 1900 United States Federal Census, Madison County, Alabama.
[688] 1896 Huntsville City Directory, page 27.
[689] 1920 Huntsville City Directory, page 144.
[690] 1911 Huntsville City Directory, page 132—1920, page 147.
[691] 1900 United States Federal Census, Madison County, Alabama, Vol. 38, Enumeration District 100, Page 77, Line 59.
[692] 1920 Huntsville City Directory.
[693] Manuscript of Maple Hill Cemetery Records, by Dorothy Scott Johnson.

had been married seventeen years. The children were: William, born in March 1884; Benjamin, born February 1891; Allie, born February 1898.[694] John and Eliza were buried at Ragsdale [Pultite] Cemetery, on Tipton Road, near Maysville. John J. died in 1929 and Eliza in 1940. Their tombstones do not give specific dates.[695]

Culver, Frank Pugh; Minister.
Frank Culver was born July 31, 1863, at Lawrenceville, Alabama. He was the son of Major Isaac Franklin and Nancy (McSwean) Culver. Rev. Dr. Culver received the degree of M. A. from Southern University in 1888, and an honorary degree of Doctor of Divinity from Southwestern University, Texas, in 1912. In 1888, he was an ordained minister of the Methodist Episcopal Church of the South. He served at Oxford 1888-91; Anniston, 1892-96; Tuscaloosa, 1897-1902; Huntsville, 1903-05; Eleventh Avenue Church in Birmingham, 1906-08, presiding elder, Birmingham district 1909-11; president Polytechnic college, Ft. Worth, Texas, 1911-15; pastor, Waco, Texas, 1915-18; First Church, Ft. Worth, Texas,1918. He was a Democrat, a Mason, and a member of the Kappa Alpha college fraternity. He was married to Ella Taylor of Greensboro, Alabama; then to Mary Lee White, of Meridian, Mississippi. They lived at Ft. Worth, Texas.

Cunningham, Russell McWhortor; Governor [acting].
Dr. Russell McWhortor Cunningham, a physician, as well as a statesman, was born August 25, 1855, at Mt. Hope in Lawrence County. He began teaching school when he was seventeen. He used the income from his teaching and also from farming to pay for his medical education. He attended the Medical College in Louisville, Kentucky and Bellevue Medical College in New York City. He received his degree from Bellevue. He later established a large private practice in Birmingham. In 1880-81 he represented Lawrence County in the legislature. From 1896-1900, he was their representative in the State Senate, and was chosen President of the Senate in 1898. He was a delegate to the Alabama Constitutional Convention of 1901. He was elected to the office of Lieutenant Governor, and became acting governor during the illness of Governor Jelks. At the end of this term as Lieutenant Governor, he retired from office and returned to his medical practice near Birmingham. He later

---

[694] 1900 United States Federal Census, Madison County, Alabama, Vol. 38 Enumeration District 98, page 14, line #4
[695] *Cemeteries of Madison County, Volume II*, 1978, page 301, Dorothy Scott Johnson, Johnson Historical Publications.

authored several articles that were published in medical journals, one of the more notable articles was entitled "*Morbidity and Mortality of Negro Convicts.*" Dr. Cunningham was married August 13, 1876 to Sue L. Moore, daughter of Judge J. E. Moore of Franklin County. He later wed Annice Taylor of Birmingham. He was a Baptist. Russell Cunningham died in Birmingham, June 6, 1921.[696]

Dennis, James D.; Special Grand Jury.
James D. Dennis was born in August of 1848, in Alabama. In 1900, he lived on East Clinton Street with his wife Mary E., who had been born May 1848, in Alabama. James was working as a fish dealer. The children were: Ethel, born March 1876 (worked as a telephone operator); Denie, born September 1880 (worked as a saleslady at a dry goods store); Ola O., born April 1888 (attending school); Anna, born August 1878, and her husband, Rue Hawk, born September, 1875, and Anna's daughter. Rue Hawk worked as a brakeman for the railroad. By 1910, the family lived on Holmes Avenue. James and Mary were then 64 years old; they had been married 44 years. He worked as a grocery salesman.[697] By 1916, James had died and Mary lived at 107 Calhoun Avenue. A son, Jessie T., was buried in Madison Cross Roads Cemetery.[698]

Drake, Zack; Attorney.
Zack Drake was born about 1878. He was an attorney, who passed the Bar on December 23, 1903. He worked in the Milligan Building. His wife's name was Ruth and their home was called "*Heartsease.*"[699] Zack was an assistant solicitor from 1911-1916. His home was on East Clinton Avenue. He was disbarred in May of 1927. The charge was of procuring and attempting to introduce false testimony in a divorce case.

Esslinger, William W.; Special Grand Jury.
William W. Esslinger was born August of 1857, in Alabama. His wife's name was Annie. She had been born in Georgia in 1863. They had been married four years but the two did not have any children together. However, children of William's previous marriage were in

---

[696] *The Governors of Alabama*, Page 154-155, John Craig Stewart, Pelican Publishing Co. Inc.
[697] 1910 United States Federal Census, Madison County, Alabama.
[698] *Madison County Cemetery Book #1*, page 19, Dorothy Scott Johnson, Johnson Historical Publications.
[699] 1911 Huntsville City Directory, page 142.

the home in 1900: Edgar, born January 1881 (worked as farm labor); Jason D., born July 1882 (worked as farm labor); Thomas, born January 1886 (worked as farm labor); Willie (male), born July 1887; Marlon, born July 1889; Irene, born February 1891; and Donnie, born September 1892.[700] The couple on Randolph Avenue.[701]

Farley, Pryor; Jury—Frame Trial.
The 1850 United States Federal Census listed William P. Farley, 24, working as a farmer. He lived with his mother, Sarah, and a brother, James W., twenty years old.

Fletcher, Shelby S.; Special Grand Jury.
Shelby S. Fletcher lived with his parents at their home on Randolph Avenue during 1900. His father, A. S. Fletcher, was born April 1833, in Virginia He was a lawyer. Shelby's mother died and his father remarried in 1896. In 1900, his stepmother was forty-six years old. Her son from a previous marriage lived in the home. His name was R. H. Lowe, and he was forty years old. Children that lived in the home were: W. H. Fletcher, (a banker) born in March 1868; Charles, (a bookkeeper) born in December 1870; Shelby S. (a lawyer) born in March 1873; and Martha L., born April 1879.[702] By 1911, Shelby S. was a cotton buyer working for Harris Cortner & Company. He lived at 121 Williams. The business was located at 11 1/2 Bank Row.[703] In the 1920's Shelby Fletcher became President of the Margaret (Cotton) Mill, but was also an agent of Harris Cortner & Company.[704]

Ford, Lee D.; Special Grand Jury.
Lee D. Ford was born in Alabama in January 1876. He lived with his grandmother, Mrs. Lucy J. Ford in 1900, and was a foreman on her farm. They had five black laborers working for them.[705] By 1911,[706] Lee lived at the "*Ford Place*." However, by 1916[707] he and his wife, Ellen, lived at 428 Eustis.

---

[700] 1900 United States Federal Census, Madison County, Alabama, Vol. 39 Enumeration District 105, Sheet 12 Line 69
[701] 1911 Huntsville City Directory.
[702] 1900 United States Federal Census, Madison County, Alabama Vol. 38 Enumeration District 100, Sheet 8, line 57.
[703] 1911 Huntsville City Directory, page 149.
[704] 1920 Huntsville City Directory, page 172.
[705] 1900 United States Federal Census, Volume 39 Enumeration District 112, Sheet 9, line 84.
[706] 1911 Huntsville City Directory, page 150.
[707] 1916 Huntsville City Directory, page 145.

Foster, Ephraim H.; Attorney.
Ephraim practiced law with the firm of Grayson & Foster, at 303 Franklin Street. He resided at the McGee's Hotel.[708] He died December 2, 1926, and was buried in Maple Hill Cemetery, in Section 16 Row 8.[709]

Frame, George W.; Alleged Lyncher.
In 1896, George W. Frame lived in the home of John Frame, at 423 Rison Avenue, who is presumed to be George's father. They both worked at the Dallas Manufacturing Company.[710] George married Rebecca and had a grocery store by 1900, located on Fifth Avenue. He also worked at the Dallas Mills.[711]

Frazier, T. S.; President of the Military Court of Inquiry.
Sydney Thomas Frazier was born in Union Springs, Alabama, March 17, 1872, the son of Sydney T. and Cornelia Frazier. T. S. Frazier graduated from the University of Alabama, in 1894, and law school in 1896. He practiced law in Union Springs after receiving his law degree. He was elected to the State Senate in 1903, 1911, and 1935. He was a member of the Alabama House of Representatives in 1931. In 1904, he was appointed Colonel on the staff of Governor Jelks. He served on the State Democratic Executive Committee and on two occasions served as delegate to the National Democratic Convention. During the first World War he served in the department of Provost Marshall. He was a Methodist, and had served as president of the Alumni Association of the University of Alabama. He was a member of the Bullock County Bar Association. It was remembered in his obituary that he was immaculate in dress, correct and respectful in demeanor, chaste in speech, and had an inbred, natural elegance and refinement that made him at ease in any company. He was always willing to assist any worthy young person struggling to succeed and to aid those to whom he might render some service. T. S. Frazier died in a Montgomery hospital on July 2, 1941.[712]

---

[708] 1911 Huntsville City Directory, page 150; 1916 page 145.
[709] Manuscript's of Maple Hill Cemetery Records, by Dorothy Scott Johnson.
[710] 1896 Huntsville City Directory, page 35.
[711] 1916 Huntsville City Directory, page 146.
[712] *Biography of Notable Men of Alabama.*

Gardiner, J. Ed.; Special Grand Jury.
John E. Gardiner was born in 1842 in Alabama. His parents were David and Sarah Gardnier. David Gardiner was born at sea while his parents, James and Elizabeth (Wylie), were emmigrating from Ireland. His brothers were: Davies, C. B., William F., Elisha J., and Matthew. His sisters were: Cyntha Ann, Elizabeth J., Mary E., Charity E., and Sarah E.[713]

Giles, Grant H.; Jailer.
Grant Giles lived at #11 Wells Avenue, with his wife Julia.[714] In 1916, he was married to Bertha, and they lived at 213 Steele Street; He was a driver for the Huntsville Manufactoring Company.[715]

Giles, William; Sergeant, National Guard.
In 1900, William was twenty-eight years old. He lived in West Huntsville.[716] William was buried in Maple Hill Cemetery, Section 16 Row 7. Tombstone information: *"William A. Giles, August 8, 1871- January 16, 1952- Susan B. Giles [no dates]"* Above the names is the family name *"Giles."*[717]

Givens, Robert A.; Special Grand Jury.
Robert A. Givens was born in Alabama, August 27, 1867. He worked as a salesman in the dry goods business. He married Nannie F. around 1890. Nannie was born September 17, 1873. She was the mother of two children: Henry G. born September 1891, and Marvalene born March 1897. A sister-in-law, Emma Beane, nineteen years old and single, lived with them during 1900, as well as a brother-in-law Shirley Beane, seventeen years old and single.[718] Robert died January 16, 1907, and was buried in the Gurley Cemetery. Nannie next married a man named, Joplin, but is buried next to Robert. She died April 25, 1948. Also buried with them are the children, Marvalene Given, who died September 16, 1904, and Henry G. Givens, who died July 19, 1933. Henry's wife, Gladys, is

---

[713] 1850 United States Federal Census, Madison County, Alabama, Page 343.
[714] 1911 Huntsville City Directory, page 153.
[715] 1916 Huntsville City Directory, page 148.
[716] 1900 Poll Tax list.
[717] Manuscript's of Maple Hill Cemetery Records, by Dorothy Scott Johnson.
[718] 1900 United States Federal Census, Madison County, Alabama, Vol. 39 Enumeration District 117, Sheet 6, line 20.

also buried there. Her birth date is January 25, 1900, and her death date is September 14, 1974.[719]

Glassford, Edward; Witness—Worley Trial.
Glassford, Kate (daughter of Edward); Witness—Worley Trial.
Edward was born in Canada or England [both are listed in the place of birth]. His father was born in England and his mother in Canada or England. Edward was born in March 1838. He married Nancy E., who was born in August of 1837, in New York.[720] A search for their graves was condutcted without results. There was no further information about Kate Glassford.

Goldsmith, Oscar; Special Grand Jury.
Oscar Goldsmith was born in October of 1849 in New York to German-born parents. In 1896, he was the manager of M. M. Newman, a dry goods store, married to Bettie, and lived at 112 Gates Avenue. Their children were Therissa, a daughter, born June, 1880; and Lawrence born in April, 1883. Also in the home was his brother, Henry, born in February, 1840, and a sister-in-law, Sophia Bernstein born in September, 1859. Oscar remained owner/manager of the Goldsmith Grocery Company and lived on Gates Avenue for the rest of his life.[721] Oscar was buried in Maple Hill Cemetery. His tombstone information reads, "1849-1937." Bettie's tombstone reads "1859-1928," Annie S. Goldsmith's reads "1886-1959;" and Lawrence B.'s reads "1883-1972." Another daughter, Irma Shiffman's stone reads "1889-1956." These graves are in the old Hebrew Section of the Cemetery.[722]

Grayson, David A.; Attorney.
David Grayson was an attorney with the firm of Grayson & Foster, and lived at the McGee Hotel.[723] He was born August, 1871. The 1900 Census shows him as a single lawyer. By 1920, David had married Juliet W. and lived at 219 Madison Street. He worked at 5 1/2 Bank Row on the West Side Square. Mrs. David A. Grayson was

---

[719] *Madison County Cemeteries, Vol. 3* page 9, Dorothy Scott Johnson, Johnson Historical Publications.
[720] 1900 United States Federal Census, Madison County, Alabama.
[721] 1896-1911-1916 Huntsville City Directories (1896-page 37) (1911-page 240) (1916-page 226).
[722] Maple Hill Cemetery, Phase One, page 69, Robey, Johnson, Jones, Roberts; Huntsville-Madison County Historical Society.
[723] 1896 Huntsville City Directory, page 37.

listed as the secretary of The Women's Club.[724] David is buried in Maple Hill Cemetery, Section 20 Row 4. His tombstone information reads "1871-1947," Also, there is a tombstone which reads, *"Nannette Dubose Grayson, Beloved Wife of David A. Grayson October 6, 1877-April 24, 1903."* An infant son is also buried there with a reference that he was the *"Infant Son of David A. and Nannette D. Grayson."*[725]

Grayson, James G.; Special Grand Jury.
James was born in January 1866, in Alabama. He was married about 1895 to Nannie E. and worked in the dry goods business. Nannie had been born in Virginia in October of 1874. The couple's children were: Ethel, born in November 1897, and William G., born in July 1899.[726]

Hall, Walter Fulgham Sr.; Jury—Frame Trial.
Walter F. Hall was a bartender. He operated his business in the Struve Building. His residence was 360 Walker Street. About 1886, Walter married Alice D. who was born in February, 1868. They had three children: Fulghram W., born August, 1891; Richard L., born August 1894; and William S., born June 1899. In 1900, his grandmother, Margarette Stol, seventy-nine years old, lived with them, as did his mother, Mollie E. Hall, fifty-four years old.[727] In 1920, Walter was a clerk for Coca-Cola Bottling Works.[728] Walter was buried in Maple Hill Cemetery in Section 21 Row 12. Tombstone information reads, "1860-1942" for Walter, Alice D. "1868-1951," Richard L. "1894-1914," and William Fulgham Jr. "1891-1944. His mother's tombstone reads, "Sophronia E. Hall 1818-1902".[729]

Halsey, William L.; Special Grand Jury.
In 1896, William Halsey was in the grocery and provisions business selling liquors and foodstuff, "Wholesale and Retail." His business was located at 223 Jefferson. His wife was Laura, and their home was located on the corner of Eustis and Lincoln Streets. The business is

---

[724] 1920 Huntsville City Directory, page 183.
[725] Manuscript's of Maple Hill Cemetery Records, by Dorothy Scott Johnson.
[726] 1900 United States Federal Census, Madison County, Alabama.
[727] 1900 United States Federal Census, Madison County, Alabama Vol. 38 Enumeration District 101 Sheet 7 Line 71.
[728] 1920 Huntsville City Directory, page 189.
[729] Manuscript's of Maple Hill Cemetery Records, by Dorothy Scott Johnson.

still viable and prosperous today. It has passed from one generation to the next. William was buried in Maple Hill Cemetery. Tombstone information: "1854-1938," for William, "*Laura Lanier, wife of W. L. Halsey 1855-1927*;" "*Katherine Halsey 1881-1974*." Section 9 Row 10.[730]

Hatcher, Archer Wood; Doctor—Jury—Hill Trial.
Archer Hatcher was born in Tennessee, August 1852. His second wife Maggie (Margaret[731]) was born July 1876, in Tennessee. They were married in 1895. They had two children: Mary, born September 1896, and Floyd, born in May of 1900. Children by his first wife were: Dillard, born March 1884, and Lizzie, born January 1890.[732]

Hawkins, Archie; Witness—Worley Trial.
Archie R. Hawkins and wife, Elizabeth, lived at 64 First Street. He was a foreman at Lowe Mill Manufacturing Company.[733]

Hawkins, John W.B.; Character Witness—Worley Trial.
In 1911, John W. B. Hawkins was married to Virginia, and they lived at 710 Pratt Avenue. He was an attorney with his office located at 119 1/2 East Side Square.[734] He was the Judge of the Inferior Court for Madison County.[735] John Hawkins and his wife are buried in Maple Hill Cemtery, Section 18 Row 12. Tombstone information only gives John's information as "1851-1924."[736]

Hay, Robert L.; Captain, National Guard.
Robert was born in June 1867, in Alabama. His father was born in England and his mother in Alabama. Robert was a co-owner of T. P. Hay & Brothers. His home was at 214 Walker Street in 1896.[737] In 1900, he was working as a printer, and lived on Greene Street. His sisters, Annie and Kate, lived with him, and all were single. Next door to him was, John L. Hay, probably a brother, who was thirty-

---

[730] *Maple Hill Cemetery Phase One*, page 66, Robey, Johnson, Jones, Roberts; Huntsville-Madison County Historical Society.
[731] 1916-17 Huntsville City Directory, page 157.
[732] 1900 United States Federal Census, Madison County, Alabama, Vol. 38, Enumeration District 99, Page 9, line 82.
[733] 1920 Huntsville City Directory page 194.
[734] 1911 Huntsville City Directory, page 163.
[735] 1916 Huntsville City Directory page 157; 1920 page 194.
[736] Manuscript's of Maple Hill Cemetery Records, by Dorothy Scott Johnson.
[737] 1896 Huntsville City Directory, page 40.

five years old.[738] In 1911, Robert was working for the *Huntsville Daily Times*, and lived at 208 Meridian Street.[739] In 1916, he worked as a printer for M. R. Murray, but still lived on Meridian Street.[740] He died in 1948,[741] and is buried in Maple Hill Cemetery. Tombstone inscriptions reveal that he was a *"Captain in the Alabama Infantry during the Spanish American War."*

Hay, Thomas P.; Lieutenant, National Guard.
Thomas P. Hay was the brother of Robert Hay. In 1896, he was the co-owner of the family business called T. P. Hay & Brothers, listed as a news agent. He lived at 214 Walker Street, and the business appears to be located in the Huntsville Hotel.[742] In 1911, he was married to Inez and was in the cigar and newspaper business. They lived at 203 Randolph Avenue.[743] In 1916, he was the co-owner of Anderson's Drug Store.[744] The only changes during the next few years are that the family moved to 109 Lincoln Street by 1920.[745] Thomas P. Hay is buried in Maple Hill Cemetery, Section 17 Row 13. He died in 1947.[746]

Hill, Ben; Alledged Lyncher.
A diligent search was made through the Hill's in Madison County without results.

Holder, Charles; Found the Victim
Charles W. Holder was a photographer for S. W. Judd Photography Studio. Holder is buried in the Cameron Methodist Church Cemetery but no tombstone date appears there. It is not certain that this is the Charles Holder in the story, but no one else by this name has been found.

---

[738] 1900 United States Federal Census, Madison County, Alabama, Vol. 38, Enumeration District 101, Sheet 1, line 95.
[739] 1911 Huntsville City Directory, page 163.
[740] 1916-17 Huntsville City Directory, page 158.
[741] Maple Hill Cemetery Phase One, page 59, Robey, Johnson, Jones, Roberts; Huntsville-Madison County Historical Society.
[742] 1896 Huntsville City Directory, page 40.
[743] 1911 Huntsville City Directory, page 163.
[744] 1916 Huntsville City Directory, page 158.
[745] 1920 Huntsville City Directory, page 194.
[746] Manuscript's of Maple Hill Cemetery Records, by Dorothy Scott Johnson.

Hooper, William P. Dr.; Jury—Hill Trial.
William P. Hooper was born March 16, 1841 in Caswell County, North Carolina. He entered Confederate service as a private on February 7, 1862, at Yanceyville, North Carolina. He served in Company C of the Third North Carolina Cavalry, until his discharge on disability.[747] In 1896, Dr. W. P. Hooper listed his occupation as a dentist, with his home located at 101 Williams Street.[748] In 1900, he was married to Martha . They lived at 302 Oak Avenue.[749] A Confederate Iron Cross #231 marks his grave in Maple Hill Cemetery. The tombstone information states that Dr. W. P. Hooper died in 1920. His wife, Martha Ann McCalley,[750] was born 1841, and died 1915, and is buried beside her husband. Also buried there is May Hooper, whose tombstone information gives no dates but has the inscription *"Death Lies heavily upon her; like the cruel frost upon a beautiful flower."* William's son, Thomas McCalley Hooper, is buried in the family plot as is Thomas's wife Mollie Catherine Hooper. A daughter, Mary Kate Dunivant (sic), wife of Hillis A. Dunivant, is also buried there, in Section 12 Row 3.[751]

Howard, Cleve; Witness—Hill Trial.
A Clinton C. Howard was found. He was married to Belle B., and was a dentist whose office was located in the Hundley Building. Their home was on Meridianville Pike at *"Abington Place."* It was not determined if Clinton C. and "Cleve" Howard were the same person.[752]

Hughes, Robert Lee; Special Grand Jury.
Robert Lee Hughes was born November 29, 1865. He married Nannie Vaughn who was born April 13, 1867. He died April 8, 1932, and she died August 8, 1958. They are buried in Folkes Cemetery, located at Vaughn Corners, near Capshaw Road.[753]

---

[747] *1907 Confederate Census of Limestone, Morgan and Madison Counties*, page 12, Johnson Historical Publications, 1981, Dorothy Scott Johnson.
[748] 1896 Huntsville City Directory, page 42.
[749] 1911 City Directory, page 167.
[750] See the McCalley's in Chapter one.
[751] *Maple Hill Cemetery Phase One*, page 59, Robey, Johnson, Jones, Roberts; Huntsville-Madison County Historical Society.
[752] 1911 Huntsville City Directory.
[753] *Cemeteries of Madison County, Vol. I* page 206, Dorothy Scott Johnson.

Humes, Milton; Captain.
A complete biography for Milton Humes may be found in Chapter One.

Hundley, Oscar R.; Committee.
Oscar R. Hundley was born in December of 1830, in Alabama. In 1896, he was an attorney practicing law at 6 Bank Street. His home was at 113 Jefferson Street.[754] He His wife, Mary, was born in December of 1836. The couple had one child, but the name was not readable in the census.[755] Oscar's father, Dr. John H. Hundley, was born in Halifax Co., Virginia, on March 5, 1796, and he died at his residence in Limestone County, January 3, 1881. His wife, Melinda R., was born in Greenville Co., Virginia April 3, 1804, and died January 23, 1852. She was the only daughter of Daniel Robinson, a merchant and planter in Limestone County, Alabama. They married in Greenville Co., Virginia in September 1824. Oscar's brother, Daniel R., [A Confederate Soldier] was the author of *"Social Relations in our Southern States"* (1860). No graves for Oscar R. Hundley and wife Mary, have been found. It is believed they were buried in Maple Hill, near his parents.

Hutchens, R. T.; Committee.
A search for R. T. Hutchens was made, however nothing was found. After much consideration and investigation, it is believed that this is W. T. (William Thomas) Hutchens. His complete biography may be found in Chapter Two.

Jelks, William D., Governor of Alabama
William D. Jelks was born in Macon County, Alabama, but grew up in Union Springs in Bullock County, Alabama. He graduated from Mercer University in Georgia, then returned to his hometown to work at the *Union Springs Herald*. He married Alice Shorter and later worked for the *Eufala Times,* where he gained a reputation as a talented journalistic writer. Jelks was elected to the State Senate from Barbour County. He was elected to the position of president of the senate, and became next in line for governor. Governor Samford died in 1901, and Jelks finished Samford's term. In 1902, he ran for the Governor's office and was elected. Due to an illness he was

---

[754] 1896 Huntsville City Directory, page 43.
[755] 1900 United States Federal Census, Madison County, Alabama, Vol. 39 Enumeration District 100, Sheet 19 line 22.

temporarily replaced by Dr. R. M. Cunningham who acted as Governor during 1904-1905. Jelks served five years and eight months as Governor. Jelks died December 14, 1931.[756]

Johnson, Thomas; Prisoner.
Thomas Johnson and his wife, Ella, were employees of the Dallas Manufactoring Company. Their home was located on Beirne Avenue.[757]

Jones, J. Rowe; Special Grand Jury.
J. Rowe Jones worked for Nolen & Jones Co., an agricultural implement business, which was located in the same block as the Huntsville Hotel. His residence was 415 West Clinton Street.[758] In 1911, he was working at the Huntsville Foundry and Machine Works. His home address had changed to 316 East Clinton Avenue.[759]

Jones, John J.; Witness—Worley Trial.
John J. Jones worked at a lab. His home was listed as 506 Stevens Avenue. While there are several people by the names of John Jones, this is the only one found with the same middle initial.[760]

Kirk, Tom; Witness—Frame Trial.
W. T. Kirk, born about 1851, lived in West Huntsville. No further information could be found regarding Thomas Kirk.[761]

Lewis, Samuel Ragland; Grand Jury.
Samuel Ragland Lewis was born November 20, 1842 at Triana, Madison County, Alabama. He entered Confederate service, as a private on January 3, 1862 at Mooresville in Limestone County, Alabama. He was in Company D of the Thirty-Fifth Alabama Infantry and continued until the surrender June 10, 1865. While in the army he served on the staff of John C. Breckinridge, as an express messenger, from January until October when he was transferred from

---

[756] *The Governors of Alabama*, page 149-150, John Craig Stewart, Pelican Publishing Co., Gretna, 1975.
[757] 1916 Huntsville City Directory, page 169.
[758] 1896 Huntsville City Directory, page 47.
[759] 1911 Huntsville City Directory, page 178.
[760] 1896 Huntsville City Directory, page 46.
[761] 1900 Poll Tax list for Madison County, Alabama, page 459.

the Mississippi Department to the Tennessee Department.[762] In 1896, Samuel worked for A. Metzger & Company, located at 123 West Side Square. His home was on Greene Street and his wife's name was Musa, [Alice D].[763] They are buried in Maple Hill Cemetery, Section 6 Row 1. Tombstone information states, "Alice D. Lewis 1845-1926," "Samuel R. Lewis 1845-1914;" and "Merrie D. Lewis January 16, 1870-November 30, 1888."[764]

Lowe, Robert H.; Witness—Frame Trial.
Robert H. Lowe was born July of 1859.[765] He was an attorney; with his law office located at 111 Eustis Avenue. His home was at 120 Williams Street.[766] He was the step-son of A. S. Fletcher, and lived with him during 1900.

Lowenthal, Henry J.; Special Grand Jury.
Henry J. Lowenthal was born in December 1856, to German-born parents. In 1896, he worked at Herstein & Lowenthal as a dry goods merchant, and his home was located at 449 Franklin Street.[767] Lowenthal married Lina about 1882. Their two children were: Etha, born June of 1880; and Robert H., born January of 1885. Henry lived with his mother-in-law, Rosa Herestein, who was born in 1839, in Maryland, to German-born parents.[768] In 1900, he and Lina lived at 309 South Franklin Street. He was owner of H. J. Lowenthal & Son. Henry J. Lowenthal died in 1921, and Lina died in 1930. They are buried in Maple Hill Cemetery, Section 10, in the old Hebrew section of the cemetery.[769]

Lowry, Samuel Hickman; Doctor.
A complete biography may be found in Chapter One

---

[762] *1907 Confederate Census of Limestone, Morgan and Madison Counties*, page 15, Johnson Historical Publications, 1981, Dorothy Scott Johnson.
[763] 1896 Huntsville City Directory, page 50, 1911 page 189, 1920.
[764] *Maple Hill Cemetery Phase One*, page 37, Robey, Johnson, Jones, Roberts; Huntsville-Madison County Historical Society.
[765] 1900 United States Federal Census, Madison County, Alabama, Vol. 38, Enumeration District 100, Sheet 8 line 57.
[766] 1896 Huntsville City Directory, page 51.
[767] 1896 Huntsville City Directory, page 51.
[768] 1900 United States Federal Census, Madison County, Alabama, Vol. 38, Enumeration District 100, Sheet 13, Line 28.
[769] *Maple Hill Cemetery Phase One*, page 76, Robey, Johnson, Jones, Roberts; Huntsville-Madison County Historical Society.

Lyne, R. L.; Jury—Worley Trial.
The only information that could be found is of Robert D. Lyne who is buried in Maple Hill Cemetery, Section 18 Row 6. Tombstone information: "1852-1932."

Manning, Richard A.; Jury—Worley Trial.
Richard A. Manning lived at 112 Washington Street (a hotel).[770] Richard and his wife, Mary Sue, are buried in the middle section of Taylor Cemetery. This cemetery is located in Section 13 Range 1, Township One East, off Butler Road. The tombstone information reads: "Richard A. 1869-1942;" and "Mary Sue 1874-1958."[771]

Maples, Horace; Lynched.
Horace Maples was known to have had a bad reputation. He worked at the Owl resturant and once operated a café on Jefferson Street. No other information was found.

Mason, Tom Jr.; Witness at the lynching.
Thomas Mason Jr. lived at 444 Gallatin Street, and worked at the feed stables on East Clinton Street.[772] He was married to Louise and lived at 41 Oak Avenue, in 1911.[773] He later went to work at the Indian Refinery Oil Company and lived at South Race Street, west of Cross Street.[774] He is buried in Maple Hill Cemetery in Section 21 Row 14. The tombstone inscription reads, *"June 12, 1918—Sgt. Co. D., 167 Infantry Rainbow Division, died with honor in his service to his country, June 12, 1918"* [on ribbon: Dum Tacet Clamat].[775]

Matthews, Albert E.; Special Grand Jury.
Albert E. Matthews is buried in Maple Hill Cemetery. Tombstone reads "1865-1907." It is located in Section 21 Row 19.[776]

Matthews, Elliott R.; Foreman Special Grand Jury.
Elliott R. Matthews was born in Alabama, September 4, 1845. His wife, Fannie, was born November 16, 1848. They were married about

---

[770] 1896 Huntsville City Directory.
[771] *Cemeteries of Madison County, Alabama*, Vol. II, page 84, Dorothy Scott Johnson.
[772] 1896 Huntsville City Directory, page 54.
[773] 1911 Huntsville City Directory.
[774] 1916 Huntsville City Directory.
[775] Manuscript's of Maple Hill Cemetery Records, by Dorothy Scott Johnson.
[776] Manuscript's of Maple Hill Cemetery Records, by Dorothy Scott Johnson.

1869. Their children were: Ellie R., born December 1876; Frank, born October 1878; and Erskine M., born May 1881. Mary Scruggs lived with them, as well as a cousin, Jessie May Harris. The Matthews lived on Lincoln Street.[777] Elliott Matthews was also a member of the Grand Jury in the 1900 Clark case. Elliott R. Matthews is buried in Maple Hill Cemetery, Section 11 Row 3, with his wife Fannie W. Scruggs. He died July 26, 1907. She died May 26, 1920. Also buried in the same plot are Elliott Robertson Matthews II, Margaret Burns Matthews, and Adelaide B. Matthews.[778]

Mayhew, Sidney J.; Made Speech—Committee.
Sindey J. Mayhew was born in May of 1829, in Williamsburg Massachusetts. He was married to Fanny E. about 1849. Sidney worked as a banker at the Huntsville Bank. Fanny had been born March of 1829 in Ohio. In 1900, a nephew, Sidney J. Mayhew, lived with them and attended school. He was 13 years old, born, August of 1886.[779] Sidney was the brother to Carolyn Mayhew Speake, wife of Judge Henry Clay Speake. Mayhew entered service with the Confederate Army as a topographical engineer on November 1862, in Richmond Virginia. He was with the Topographical Bureau, under Captain Albert Campbell, until the close of the war. Meyhew also published a map of Madison County in 1881. Mayhew was buried in Maple Hill Cemetery in Section 11, Row 16. The tombstone simply reads "1829-1912." His wife, Fanny E.'s tombstone reads, "1828-1916."[780]

McCalley, Charles Sanford.;Special Grand Jury.
Charles S. McCalley was born April 6, 1844, in Huntsville, Alabama. He was the son of Thomas Sanford McCalley and Caroline Matilda. Lanford. Caroline Matilda was the daughter of Robert & Ann Lanford, one of Madison County's first settlers. Charles McCalley entered service for the Confederacy, as a private, in March of 1862, in Company Q, of the Fourth Alabama Infantry. He served until the surrender and was paroled at the Appomattox Courthouse on April 9,

---

[777] 1900 United States Federal Census, Madison County, Alabama, Vol. 38 Enumeration District 100, Sheet 9, Line 2.
[778] *Maple Hill Cemetery Phase One*, page 83, Robey, Johnson, Jones, Roberts; Huntsville-Madison County Historical Society.
[779] 1900 United States Federal Census, Madison County, Alabama, Vol. 38 Enumeration District 100, Sheet 10, line 47.
[780] *Maple Hill Cemetery Phase One*, page 93, Robey, Johnson, Jones, Roberts; Huntsville-Madison County Historical Society.

1865.[781] In 1896, Charles was a cashier at A. R. Campbell & Company. His residence was at 101 Williams Avenue.[782] Charles later became a cotton buyer. In 1900, Charles was a farmer.[783] Charles Sanford McCalley died in 1925, but the tombstone does not give an exact date.[784]

McClain, T. E.; Private in the National Guard.
Thomas Elwood McLean was born December 14, 1878 and died December 19, 1910. He is buried in Maple Hill Cemetery, Section 17, Row 12.[785]

Mitchell, James L.; Alleged Lyncher.
James L. Mitchell was born October 10, 1833 in Van Buren County, Tennessee. He entered Confederate service as a Private on May 15, 1861 with Company Q of the 16th Tennessee. He continued until taken prisoner at Missionary Ridge, Tennessee in September of 1863. He remained in prison until the close of the war. At the time of the 1907 Confederate Census,[786] he gave his mailing address as Taft, Tennessee, but he actually lived in Madison County. He is buried in Mt. Sharon Cemetery, located in Section 21 of Township 1S Range 2W, on Charity Lane, in the church yard of the New Sharon Church of God. "*Lickskillet*" was the early name of this pioneer settlement. Also buried there is his infant son. His wife, Mary E., was born March 17, 1844, and died May 16, 1911. Several members of the Mitchell family are buried there.

Mitchell, John; Jury—Hill Trial.
There is a John Mitchell buried in the same cemetery, (Mt. Sharon) as well as James Mitchell. However, without evidence to substantiate the relationship, there is no proof that this is the same John Mitchell who appears in the story. There is no tombstone information.

---

[781] *1907 Confederate Census of Limestone, Morgan, and Madison Counties Alabama*, page 18, Dorothy Scott Johnson.
[782] 1896 Huntsville City Directory
[783] 1900 United States Federal Census, Madison County, Alabama, Vol. 38 Enumeration District 100, Sheet 6, Line 4.
[784] *Maple Hill Cemetery Phase One*, page 58, Robey, Johnson, Jones, Roberts; Huntsville-Madison County Historical Society.
[785] Manuscripts of Maple Hill Cemetery Records, by Dorothy Scott Johnson.
[786] *1907 Confederate Census of Limestone, Morgan, and Madison Counties Alabama*, page 17, Dorothy Scott Johnson.

Mitchell, Will; Son of James.
Five "Wills" or William Mitchells, are listed in the 1911 Huntsville City Directory. There is no information to indicate which one is the person in the story.[787]

Mitchell, William L., Night Chief of Police
There is a William Mitchell buried in Maple Hill Cemetery, in Section 22 Row 6. Tombstone information has a birthdate of July 17, 1860 and death date of March 29, 1926. Also buried there is, Mary E., born July 2, 1860 and died February 22, 1941. John Edgar Mitchell Sr. [believed to be a son] born September 19, 1888 and died November 20, 1965, is located in the next row. No other Mitchells are in the Section.[788]

Murdock, Andrew J.; Special Grand Jury.
Andrew J. Murdock was born in Kentucky, in April of 1861. His mother was born in Connecticut, and his father in Ireland. He worked as a plumber. He married Myra about 1887. Myra was born in Alabama, in July 1866.[789] In 1916, Andrew and Myra lived at 317 West Clinton Avenue. He had his own business, Enterpise Real Estate Company, located at 112 Jefferson Street.[790] In 1920, the business was called Murdock and Weakly, located in the Hutchens Building. The Murdocks then lived at 201 Oak Avenue.[791] No burial information could be found.

Newby, Thomas; Worley—Trial.
Thomas Newby was born in Alabama, in March of 1878. He was married to Nannie. They had three children: James P., born in June 1887; Thomas, born in November 1888; Zennie (daughter), born in September 1891.[792]

Nunnally, Wesley; Prisoner.
Wesley Nunnally was born in December of 1874. He married Anna B., around 1891. Anna was born in Tennessee in April of 1873. They

---

[787] 1911 Huntsville City Directory.
[788] Manuscripts of Maple Hill Cemetery Records, by Dorothy Scott Johnson.
[789] 1900 United States Federal Census, Madison County, Alabama Vol. 38 Enumeration District 100, Sheet 27, Line 100.
[790] 1916 Huntsville City Directory, page 199
[791] 1920 Huntsville City Directory.
[792] 1900 United States Federal Census, Madison County, Alabama; Vol. 39, Enumeration District 114, Sheet 6, line 9.

had five children: John, born in November 1891; Monroe; born in April 1893; Bettie, born in November 1894; Thomas, born in February 1897; and Eva, born in June of 1899.[794] No death information could be found.

O'Neal, Robert L.; Special Grand Jury.
Robert O'Neal was listed as the Huntsville Postmaster in 1916. His wife, Kate C., was the President of the *Mercury Publishing Company*, and Editor of the *Mercury-Banner*. Their home was at 313 South Franklin Street. They later moved to 203 N. Green Street.[795] Robert and Kate are buried in Maple Hill Cemetery, Section 22 Row 14. Tombstone information for Robert reads "1854-1931," and for Kate "1857-1941". Several people with the last name of O'Neal are buried in the family plot.[796]

Overton, Ambrose E.; Coroners Jury.
Ambrose worked as a watchman and lived at 329 Walker Street.[797] He and wife, Lucy, later moved to 809 Randolph Avenue. He was the tax assessor for Madison County 1909-1917.[798] During 1916, he owned the Overton-Green Printing Company but still worked as the county tax assessor.[799] In 1920, he was connected with the Overton Land Company and lived at 618 E. Holmes Avenue; their phone number was 325-W.[800] No death information could be found.

Overton, David D.; Chief of Police.
A complete biography may be found in Chapter Five.

Overton, James; Policeman.
James Overton was a city policeman and lived with his brothers, Ambrose and David Overton, at 329 Walker Street, in 1896.[801] In 1911, he was married to Nannie E., but still lived on Walker Street.[802] Nannie died in 1912. James then married, Mattie L., and by 1916, was the the proprietor of Overton Transfer Company. His home was

---

[794] 1900 United States Federal Census, Madison County, Alabama Vol. 39 Enumeration District 114 Sheet 6 line 9.
[795] Huntsville City Directory, 1916-page 202; 1920-page 266.
[796] Manuscripts of Maple Hill Cemetery Records, by Dorothy Scott Johnson.
[797] 1896 Huntsville City Directory.
[798] 1911 Huntsville City Directory.
[799] 1916 Huntsville City Directory.
[800] 1920 Huntsville City Directory.
[801] 1896 Huntsville City Directory.
[802] 1911 Huntsville City Directory, page 215.

307 North Greene Street.[802] [803] James is buried in Maple Hill Cemetery, Section 23, Row 15. He died in 1929. Several Overtons are buried in this section.[804]

Parm, Richard H.; Jury—Hill Trial.
Richard Parm was born October 30, 1861, in South Carolina. In 1891, he married Tommie A., who was born in August 1871, in Tennessee. They had one child, Joe Will Parm. They lived in the Hazel Green area.[805] Richard died May 15, 1916. His wife, Tommie A, who died December 1, 1917, was buried beside him. They are buried in the "State Line Cemetery" located on the Tennessee state line. Also, buried with the Parms are two infant sons and an infant daughter [with no dates]. Their son, Joe Will, who was born January 10, 1890, and died February 13, 1967, is buried there along with his wife, Zemma S., born June 18, 1900, and died April 27, 1965. The brother of Richard, Joe Parm, born December 11, 1853, and died December 26, 1935, is buried there also.[806]

Pettus, Richard Erle; Solicitor.
Erle Pettus was born February 4, 1877, in Elkmont, Limestone County, Alabama. He was the son of Dr. Joseph Albert and Musie (Cartwright) Pettus and the grandson of Thomas Coleman and Mary (Fowlkes) Pettus. He was educated at the University of Alabama, in Tuscaloosa. He was the editor-in-chief of the *"Crimson-White"*, the class representative in the law department, and University representative in intercollegiate debate in Talladega, in 1897. He attended law scool at Cumberland University, Lebanon, Tennessee. He entered the practice of law in Athens. Richard Pettus was a former member of the Alabama Legislature; a member of the Constututional Convention of Alabama in 1901; and was appointed to be the United States Attorney for the Sixteenth Judicial Circuit in 1903, by Governor Jelks. He was a member of the Alabama State Bar Association. He continued to practice law in Athens until 1906, when he moved his practice to Birmingham. The First National Bank

---

[802] 1916 Huntsville City Directory.
[803] 1920 Huntsville City Directory.
[804] Manuscripts of Maple Hill Cemetery Records, by Dorothy Scott Johnson.
[805] 1900 United States Federal Census, Madison County, Alabama Vol. 39 Enumeration District 114, Sheet 15, line 69.
[806] *Madison County Cemeteries, Volume II*, page 10, Dorothy Scott Johnson, Johnson Historical Publications.

Building on Sixteenth Avenue was the location of his practice with his partner, Judge Zell Gaston. He was the author of an anti-trust law (1900-01), and the author of the first primary election law ever placed on the Alabama statute books, (1900-01). Pettus was a Methodist, a 32nd Degree Mason; a Shriner (Zamora Temple); and a member of Sigma Alpha Epsilon (college fraternity). He married Ellelee Chapman on November 27, 1907. She was the daughter of Reuben and Rosalie[807] (Sheffey) Chapman; and the granddaughter of Reuben and Felicia (Pickett) Chapman, Ex-Governor of Alabama. Richard and Ellelee had two children: Erle Pettus Jr., and Rosalie Pettus.

The Birmingham Bar Association submitted a very fitting memorial address to the *Birmingham Messenger* regarding Pettus' death, July 5, 1960, which read: *"Words are inadequate to express the great loss in the passing of Erle Pettus, Sr. He was indeed a partiarch of the Birmingham Bar, having lived a full 83 years. Active to the very last, Mr. Pettus was engaged in the law practice for more than 62 years. To the writer, Mr Pettus will be remembered for other reasons. As a speaker and an advocate to the courts, he had few equals. His closing arguments to the jury in the many cases he tried were masterpieces. His words were eloquent and his logic, unsurpassed. He had the knack of 'getting to the point' and his knowledge of the law and his respectfulness won him the respect and admiration of his fellow lawyers, his clients and the judges. Although a devoted practitioner at the bar, Mr Pettus loved the land and spent many happy days on his farm near Selma, his eyes would sparkle when he talked of his farm. Mr. Pettus found the secret of a long and wonderful life, and that secret was in staying active, of finding new interest, and of working, of never quitting and in this he left a rich heritage to all members of the Bench and Bar. We lost a great lawyer and wonderful friend."* (The Memorial Committee)1960.[808][809][810][811]

---

[807] Rosalie became one of Alabama's finest artists.
[808] *History of Alabama and Dictionary of Alabama Biography*, Thomas McAdory Owen, page 1352, The Reprint Company, Spartanburg, SC, 1978.
[809] *History of Birmingham and Its Environs*, Vol. II, 1920, page 20, George M. Cruikshank, The Lewis Publishing Co.
[810] *Alabama Blue Book and Social Register*, page 163, Blue Book Publishing Co., Inc. Edited by Nelson P. Hoff, Birmingham, Alabama, 1929
[811] The Birmingham Bar Association.

Petty, Turner; Attorney.
Turner F. Petty was married to Margaret E. and they lived at 709 Randolph Avenue.[812] He worked at 4-6 Struve Building. His office phone number was 298-2. No death information could be found.

Phillips, William L.; Constable.
William L. Phillips was born in October 1859, in Tennessee. William married Louanna about 1895. In 1900, they were the parents of two children. There were two other older children in the home from William's first marriage, Pat W., a son, born in February 1886; and Telin I., a daughter, born in February 1884. Also in the home was a nephew, John Phillips, who was born in 1879, and worked as a farm laborer.[813] William became a policeman and lived on Meridian Street.[814]

Pleasants, Shelby, Attorney
Shelby Pleasants was born in May of 1878. He was a United States Assistant District Attorney in the early 1900's. In 1904, he was thirty-one years old, single in the home with his mother, Mary S. Pleasants. Mary was a widow. They lived at a hotel on Jefferson Street.[815] By 1911, Shelby's law practice was at 103 1/2 bank row, and he lived at 241 Walker Street.[816] His wife, Marie, died in 1940, and was buried in Maple Hill Cemetery, Section 13 Row 22. Shelby committed suicide in 1916, during the investigation of the killing of Judge Lawler. Samuel Pleasants who died in 1873, is buried near-by, who is probably the father of Shelby.[817]

Pollard, James B.; Witness at the lynching.
James B. Pollard became a bartender at the J. R Stegall Hotel about 1896. His home was at 528 Madison St.[818] He was later employed at a restaurant on 115 Washington Street and his home was at 317 W. Clinton Street.[819] He and his wife, Hattie, born in Tennessee, had

---

[812] 1911 Huntsville City Directory, page 219.
[813] 1900 United States Federal Census, Madison County, Alabama Vol. 39 Enumeration District 114, Sheet 3 line 72.
[814] 1911 Huntsville City Directory, page 219.
[815] 1900 United States Federal Census, Madison County, Alabama Vol. 38 Enumeration District 100, Sheet 18, line 42.
[816] 1911 Huntsville City Directory, page 221, and 1916, page 208.
[817] *Maple Hill Cemetery Phase One*, page 123, Robey, Johnson, Jones, Roberts; Huntsville-Madison County Historical Society.
[818] 1896 Huntsville City Directory.
[819] 1911 Huntsville City Directory.

three children: Vermer, born in 1898; Nell, born in 1900; and Edith born in 1905.[821] Pollard was buried in Maple Hill Cemetery. Tombstone information reads, J. B. born 1864 and died 1934. Hattie O., was born in 1867 and died in 1938. Irma [a daughter] was born September 30, 1887 and died November 18, 1887. They are buried in Section 21 Row 9.[822]

Popejoy, James E.; Jury—Worley Trial.
James E. Popejoy married Laura Yarbrough, November 11, 1869.[823] James was the tax assessor from 1892-1896. He lived at New Market in 1896.[824] James was born 1842, and died September 25, 1917. James and Laura are buried in Rice Cemetery, Madison County Alabama.[825]

Powell, John P., Ex-Sheriff
John Peyton Powell was born in Alabama, July 1857. He was married to Conlie [Cornelia], who was born in August 1850. They had several children: Fenos D. [daughter] born in November 1877; Hattie born in March 1878 [shown as the mother of two children, Broney Bonds, born in May 1897, and Powell Bonds born in July 1898, both are granddaughters, born in Tennessee.] John P. Jr., born in March 1879; Robert W., born in September 1881; Cornelia S., born in October 1889; James S, born in March 1886; and Bell D., born in November 1890.[826] John later became a cotton buyer for F.C.O. & F. Company. Powell served as sheriff from 1892-1896. Their home was at 400 W. Clinton Avenue.[827] Powell is buried in Maple Hill Cemetery, Section 21 Row 18. Tombstone information reads "1851-1915."[828]

Pulley, Ed. L.; Witness.
Edward Pulley was a senator, lawyer, and President of the Madison Loan and Trust. His business was located at #1 and #2 Provost Building and he lived at 148 Calhoun Street.[829] He was born May 21,

---

[821] 1910 United States Federal Census, Madison County, Alabama.
[822] Manuscripts of Maple Hill Cemetery Records, by Dorothy Scott Johnson.
[823] Madison County, Alabama Marriage Records.
[824] 1896 Huntsville City Directory.
[825] *Madison County Cemeteries Vol. II,* page 148, Dorothy Scott Johnson, Johnson Historical Publications.
[826] 1900 United States Federal Census, Madison County, Alabama Vol. 39 Enumeration District 113, Sheet 2.
[827] 1911 Huntsville City Directory.
[828] Manuscripts of Maple Hill Cemetery Records, by Dorothy Scott Johnson.
[829] 1896 Huntsville City Directory.

1870, September 7, 1910. He was buried September 9, 1910, in Maple Hill Cemetery. Edward was buried next to his father and mother, Robert L. and Georgia S. Pulley.[830]

Rafford, T. N.; Private National Guard.
T. N. Rafford paid his poll tax in 1900, listing himself as twenty-one years of age.[831] No further information was found.

Richardson, William; Judge.
A complete biography regarding Judge William Richardson may be found in Chapter One.

Riggins, Thomas W.; Alleged Lyncher.
Thomas Riggins was born February 1857. In 1900, he was a restaurant keeper, and rented a home on Greene Street. Thomas was married to Idella, who had been born in November of 1865. In 1900, they had one child still at home, Edgar, was born in June 1879. Edgar worked in the restaurant business with his father. Thomas and Idella had been married twenty-four years.[832] In 1911, Thomas was the owner of the 'new' Stegall Hotel and lived at the hotel.[833] In 1916, he was the manager of the Alabama Tire Repair Company.[834] In 1920, he was still in the tire repair business and lived at 609 Ward Avenue.[835]

Rodgers, Augustus D.; Sheriff
Augustus D. Rodgers was born in 1846, in Alabama. He married Zoro V. and lived at 504 West Clinton Avenue. Augustus ran a livery stable at 110 West Clinton Avenue. He was elected Sheriff from 1900-1907,[836] but lost the election then to William Mitchell.[837] In 1910, he was sixty years of age and had been married thirty-five years. He listed his occupation as horse trader. A son, Kilner, who was a store owner, and his wife, Minnie, who was thirty-two years

---

[830] *Maple Hill Cemetery Phase One*, page 119, Robey, Johnson, Jones, Roberts; Huntsville-Madison County Historical Society.
[831] Madison County Poll Tax list.
[832] 1900 United States Federal Census, Madison County, Alabama Vol. 38 Enumeration District 101, Sheet 6, line 25.
[833] 1911 Huntsville City Directory, page 228.
[834] 1916 Huntsville City Directory, page 216.
[835] 1920 Huntsville City Directory, page 288.
[836] 1896 Huntsville City Directory.
[837] *A Dream Come True*, Vol. II, James Record, 1978, John Hicklin Printing Co., Huntsville, Alabama; Library of Congress Card Number: 76-11880.

old and lived with Rodgers.[837] The Rodgers family is buried in Maple Hill Cemetery, Section 11, Row 1.

Sharpe, Albert D.; Jury—Worley Trial.
Albert D. Sharp was born in Alabama, in April of 1860. He married Annie around 1881. Annie was born in Alabama, in September of 1864. They were the parents of five children: Joe W., born in January 1882; Eddie L., born in July 1883; Mary O., born in April 1889; Arthur L., born in September 1893; and Albert E., born in February 1897. They were farmers.[838]

Shelby, Anthony Bouldin; Doctor.
Dr. Anthony Bouldin Shelby was born in Huntsville, December 10, 1845. He was the son of Dr. David and Mary [Bouldin] Shelby. His education was interrupted by the War Between the States, when at sixteen years of age, he joined Company I, Fourth Alabama Infantry, commanded by Captain Egbert J. Jones. Shelby participated in the battles of Manassas, Seven Pines, and the Seven Days Battle before Richmond. He later joined Captain Frank Gurley's company of the Fourth Alabama Cavalry. He participated in the battle of Chickamauga, the campaign of Atlanta, and General Hood's Tennessee campaign. He next served under General Nathan Bedford Forrest, and was wounded at Benton, Tennessee. Returning home following the surrender, Anthony began the study of medicine in 1866, with his father. After a course of lectures at Jefferson Medical College in Pennsylvania, he received his Doctor of Medicine Degree on May 4, 1872. After his father's retirement, he succeeded him in his practice. Dr. Shelby was the jail physician for Madison County from 1882-1883. Dr. Shelby remained a bachelor and lived with his two sisters Mariam and Yancy at 508 Madison Street. His 1900 Poll Tax listed him as fifty-six years of age. He retired in 1912 due to his health. Dr. Shelby died August 2, 1923, and is buried with his family in Maple Hill Cemetery.[839]

Sibley, William J.; Jury—Worley Trial.
William J. Sibley was born, April 1878. He married Mimia, about 1898. She was born January, 1870.[840]

---

[837] 1910 United States Federal Census, Madison County, Alabama.
[838] 1900 United States Federal Census, Madison County, Alabama.
[839] *Medicine Bags and Bumpy Roads*, page 157, Goldsmith & Fulton, Valley Publishing Co., 1985.
[840] 1900 United States Federal Census, Madison County, Alabama.

Simmons, Saxe, Witness—Worley Trial.
Saxe Simmons was a traveling salesman. In 1900, his home was at 407 W. Holmes Avenue. By1916, he boarded at the McGee Hotel.[841]

Slaton, John; Jury—Frame Trial.
John Slaton was born July 31, 1849, in Alabama. He was married to Jane S. about 1880. They were the parents of nine children, but only six were known: Johnnie, born in November 1885; Sarah, born in 1887; Slaughter, born in May 1890; Mattie, born in October 1892; and Lanford, born in July 1894.[842] Slaton died May 5, 1922 and was buried in Maple Hill Cemetery, Section 9 Row 1. Also buried there was his son, J. Slaughter Slayton, who died in July 1919; and two babies. Mrs. Jane Slaughter Slaton is buried in the next row of the cemetery, along with three daughters: Mary, who died in August 1887; Lottie who died in 1897; and Martha who died in January 1919.[843]

Smith, Edward D.; Military Commander from Birmingham.
Edward D. Smith was the city attorney for Birmingham, Alabama. He was born in Livingston, Sumter County, Alabama, September 5, 1876. He was the son of Addison G. and Florence D. (Hopkins) Smith. Edward's father was also a Birmingham attorney. Edward was solicitor for the Sixth Judicial Circuit, for about twelve years. He was chosen chairman of the Democratic State Executive Committee during the Jones-Kolb campaign. Edward was educated in the Livingston private schools, then at the University High School at Tuscaloosa. He graduated with a medal for mathmatics, in the spring of 1893. That fall he entered the sophomore class of the University of Alabama, and graduated in 1896. He was the president of his class in his junior year. He entered Georgetown Law School, Washington, D.C., graduating as president of his senior class in 1898. He worked a short while for the Southern Railway law agency in Birmingham. On January 1, 1902, he was elected city attorney for Birmingham, and was re-elected in 1903 and 1904. He was the Captain of Battery D,

---

[841] 1911-1916 Huntsville City Directory, page 237.
[842] 1900 United States Federal Census, Madison County, Alabama.
[843] *Maple Hill Cemetery Phase One*, page 61, Robey, Johnson, Jones, Roberts; Huntsville-Madison County Historical Society.

First Alabama Artillery, National Guard, at its beginning, in Birmingham, September 23, 1902.[845]

Smith, Thomas W.; Mayor.
Thomas W. Smith was a carriage maker, operating on Jefferson Street, between Union Street and Halsey Street. He was born in 1850. Around 1875, he married Callie L., who was born in 1855. Callie was a dressmaker, and they lived at 302 West Clinton Avenue.[846] [847] Thomas died in 1928, and Callie died in 1933. Both are buried in Maple Hill Cemetery.

Speake, Daniel Webster; Judge.
Daniel Webster Speake was a lawyer and farmer. He was born July 8, 1856, at Oakville, Lawrence County, Alabama. He was the son of James B. and Sarah Brooks (Lindsey) Speake. Daniel received his early education in the schools of Lawrence County and the University of Alabama. He received his LL. B. in July, 1879. He began his law practice at Moulton, in September 1879. Speake was Solicitor for Jackson County from 1885-89, and appointed Judge of the Eighth Judicial Circuit, July 23, 1904, and re-elected in November. He was a Democrat and served as deacon of the Presbyterian Church. He married Caro (sic.) McCalla (sic.) on December 14, 1881, in Tuscaloosa. She was the daughter of Major R. C. and Margaret E. (Lewis) McCalla. Their children were Richard, Elizabeth, Charles Lewis, Daniel W. Jr., Carolee, Neal, and Margaret Lindsey. The family resided in Decatur where he maintianed his law practice. Daniel Speake died January 3, 1915, in Decatur.[848]

Speake, Paul; Judge.
Paul Speake was born in Morgan County, Alabama June 17, 1871. His parents were Judge Henry Clay and Carrie Olivia (Mayhew) Speake. His early education was received in Huntsville, and he later attended the University of Alabama, but was unable to finish because of failing health. While working as a stenographer in the law office of Humes, Walker & Sheffey, he studied law, and in 1890, was admitted

---

[845] Notable Men of Alabama, page 68, Vol. II, Hon, Joel C. DuBose, The Reprint Company, Spartanburg, South Carolina, 1976.
[846] 1911 Huntsville City Directory.
[847] 1900 United States Federal Census, Madison County, Alabama Vol. 38 Enumeration District 100, Sheet 25, line 86.
[848] *History of Alabama and Dictionary of Alabama Biography*, Thomas McAdory Owen, page 1604-1605, The Reprint Company, Spartanburg, SC, 1978.

to the bar. He became a member of the law firm of Humes, Sheffey & Speake, which subsequently became Spragins and Speake. In November of 1903, he was appointed judge of the Sixteenth Judicial District, and was nominated for re-election in the 1904 Democratic primary. The act creating the judgeship was declared unconstututional and the office was abolished. He was a Democrat, a Presbyterian, serving as an Elder, a Mason, and a Woodsman of the World. He married Florence Inez Hoy, daughter of Clarence E., and Clara Hoy, on January 17, 1895. Paul and Florence's children were; Dorothy Clare, born in 1901 (married Joe Helm. She died 1980), Margery Mayhew, born in 1906 (she died February 24, 1941); and son Paul Meredith, born in 1909 (married Anne Hawkins Armstrong, his second marriage was to Anne Canterberry.)[848] Judge Speake was again appointed as Judge of the Twenty-third Judicial Circuit Court in 1937, and served until his death. The family was buried in Maple Hill Cemetery, Section 11, and Row 17. Florence Hoy Speake, "August 31, 1874- January 17, 1960." Paul Speake, "June 17, 1871-December 6, 1937."[849]

Spraggins, Robert S.; Attorney.
Robert Spraggins was the law partner of Paul Speake for many years. Robert was born in October of 1861. He was married to Susie E. Echols, (Susie was the daughter of William H. Echols, president of the First National Bank). Susie was born in February, 1864, in Georgia. They married around 1886. The couple had four children: William E., born in March 1887; Marion, born in October 1892; Robert L., born in March 1890; and Susie E., born in October 1899. The family home was atop Echols Hill, and is still there today. Robert and Susie resided in this home.[850] Robert was president of the Farmer's Cotton Oil & Fertilizer Company and vice-president of the Huntsville Ice & Coal Company. In 1916, he was the president of the First National Bank, and was associated with the YMCA (Young Men's Christian Association).[851] Robert and Susie are buried in Maple Hill Cemetery, in Section 13, Row 16. Robert's tombstone reads, *"Robert Elias Spraggins October 14, 1861-October 17, 1935."*

---

[848] *History of Alabama and Dictionary of Alabama Biography*, Thomas McAdory Owen, page 1605, The Reprint Company, Spartanburg, SC, 1978.
[849] *Maple Hill Cemetery Phase One*, page 93, Robey, Johnson, Jones, Roberts; Huntsville-Madison County Historical Society.
[850] 1900 United States Federal Census, Madison County, Alabama Vol. 38 Enumeration District 100, Sheet 11, line 10.
[851] Huntsville City Directory, 1911-page 141, 1916-page 227, 1920-page 309.

Susie's reads, "*Susie Patton Echols Spraggins, wife of Robert Elias Spraggins, February 17, 1864- March 25, 1918.*" They are buried near her father and mother.[852]

Steger, Joseph M.; Jury—Hill Trial.
Joseph M. Steger was born in May of 1851, in Alabama. He married Calley D. in 1871. She was born in October of 1852. In 1900, five of their children were at home with them: Walter J., born in March 1874 (worked as a carpenter); Lina, born in December 1878; Willie H., born in April 1880 (worked as farm labor); Ollie, born in May 1884 (worked as farm labor); and Thomas B., born in May of 1887, (was in school).[853]

Stephens, Robert L.; Witness—Frame Trial.
There is no information regarding this person.

Stewart, E. B.; Coroner.
E. B. Stewart was born in December of 1871, in Alabama. Stewart was the Deputy Circuit Clerk in 1896, and lived in a room at the County Courthouse.[854] He was the Coroner from 1900-1908, and he lived alone on Bank Row. He was a lawyer, and lived next door to three other lawyers, Charles J. Stone, John Burke, and Robert E. Smith.[855]

Stewart, Samuel Morgan, Sr.; Lieutenant National Guard.
Samuel Morgan Stewart, Sr. was born in Alabama, October 17, 1849. He was the Probate Judge of Madison County from 1896-1904. He and Zoe married about 1896, and in 1900, they had one child, Margaret, born in July of 1897. Samuel had children at home from his first marriage to Catherine A., who had died, January 5, 1892. Children by his first marriage were: Samuel M., born in June 1876; Thomas T., born in March 1878; Francis G.[son], born in April 1881; Douglas, born in April 1884; Laura G., born in March 1886; John B., born in July 1887; Mildred, born in December 1891.[856] Children that

---

[852] *Maple Hill Cemetery Phase One*, page 117, Robey, Johnson, Jones, Roberts; Huntsville-Madison County Historical Society.
[853] 1900 United States Federal Census, Madison County, Alabama Vol. 39 Enumeration District 100, Sheet 12, line 44.
[854] 1896 Huntsville City Directory, page 72.
[855] 1900 United States Federal Census, Madison County, Alabama Vol. 39 Enumeration District 100, Sheet 4, line 20.
[856] 1900 United States Federal Census, Madison County, Alabama.

died young were, Catherine A., (born in November 20, 1882, died August 1, 1884), Lawrence B., (born March 1, 1890-March 1,1890) and Percy Hendree, (born November 13, 1888 and died August 1889).[858] Also in the home was Zoe's child from a previous marriage, Zannie Hale, born March 1888. Stewart resigned his position as Probate Judge in 1904. He took a job as Clerk of the Superior Court in 1920. The Stewart home was at 309 Franklin Street. The home was called 'San Aqua Wells.'[859] Samuel died June 18, 1924. Zoe S. died March 28, 1962, at 94 years of age. Buried next to Samuel is his first wife Catherine A., born October 23, 1851, then Zoe is next to Catherine. They are all buried in Maple Hill Cemetery, Section 13 Row 20.[860]

Talley, Tom; Jury—Hill Trial.
Thomas Talley was born in March of 1853, in Tennessee. He was a farmer. He married Ellen between 1873-74, who had been born in November of 1859. They were the parents of ten children: Elijah, born 1875; John, born September 1878; Bygie (sic.), born in May 1882; Sallie, born in August 1885; Sofa (sic.), born in December 1888; Nellie J. born in October 1891; and Annie, born in December 1897.[861] The Talleys are buried in Plainview Cemetery, three miles northwest of Meridianville. Tombstone information shows that Thomas died January 16, 1905, at fifty-one years of age. Ellen died June 13, 1917, at sixty-three years of age. Thirty-five Talleys are buried in this cemetery.[862]

Terry, Jefferson H.; Jury—Mitchell Trial.
Jefferson H. Terry was born in December 1879. In 1900, he lived at home with his father, G. L. Terry, and worked in the family dry-goods business. His brother was Edwin T., born in November 1871.[863] Jefferson H. Terry married Alma. Later he worked for the Ezell Brothers—Terry Co. and General Merchandise, located at 235 Jefferson Street. He and Alma's home was at 403 East Holmes.[864]

---

[858] *Maple Hill Cemetery Phase One*, page 122-123, Robey, Johnson, Jones, Roberts; Huntsville-Madison County Historical Society.
[859] Huntsville City Directory, 1896-page 72, 1911-page 144, 1916-page 229, 1920-page 312.
[860] *Maple Hill Cemetery Phase One*, page 122-123, Robey, Johnson, Jones, Roberts; Huntsville-Madison County Historical Society.
[861] 1900 United States Federal Census, Madison County, Alabama.
[862] Madison County Cemeteries, Vol. I, page 54.
[863] 1900 United States Federal Census, Madison County, Alabama.
[864] Huntsville City Directory, 1911-page 248, 1916- page 233.

Thompson, Joseph Robert; Grand Jury.
Joseph Robert Thompson and his wife, Mary, lived at 410 East Holmes Avenue. He worked at W. I. & J. R Thompson Company.[864] In 1916, Mary was a widow who lived at 305 Randolph Avenue.[865]

Thrift, J. R; Jury-Worley Trial.
John. R. Thrift was a carpenter. He and his wife Laura lived at 803 Wells Avenue.[866]

Waldrop, Elias D.; The Victim
Waldrop, Jack; Son of E. D. Waldrop
Elias D. Waldrop was born June of 1833, in Alabama. He was seventy years old when he was murdered, September 6, 1904. Elias worked as a farmer. His father had been born in North Carolina, and his mother was born in Alabama. His wife, Nancy C., was born in Tennessee. The Waldrops had been married twenty-four years when he was murdered. They had three children: Andrew Jackson, born March in 1880, Charley, born in April 1888; and Cara, born in August 1890. Jackson [known as Jack] was helping his father farm.[867] Elias D. Waldrop is buried in Locust Grove Baptist Cemetery, located in what is now called Sharpe's Cove Community. It used to be called the Moulder Community, and is located off of Winchester Road and County Lake Road.[868]

Walker, Richard W.; Attorney.
In 1911, Richard W. Walker was a lawyer. His office was at # 7 ½ Bank Row. His wife's name was Shelby W., and they lived at 421 McClung Avenue. His law firm was Walker & Spraggins.[869] In 1920, Richard was the United States Circuit Court Judge for the Fifth District.[870] The Walkers are buried in Maple Hill Cemetery. Tombstone information reveals that Richard was born March 11, 1857, and died April 10, 1936.[871]

---

[864] 1911 Huntsville City Directory, page 248.
[865] 1916 Huntsville City Directory.
[866] 1920 Huntsville City Directory, page 321.
[867] 1900 United Stated Federal Census, Madison County, Alabama.
[868] *Madison County Cemeteries, Vol. II*, page 224, Dorothy Scott Johnson, Johnson Historical Publications.
[869] Huntsville City Directory, 1911-page 254 checked 1916, same information as in 1911.
[870] 1920 Huntsville City Directory.
[871] Manuscripts of Maple Hill Cemetery Records, by Dorothy Scott Johnson.

Wallace, John H; Attorney.
John H. Wallace was born June of 1835, in Alabama. He married Mary C., around 1871. John was an attorney. They lived on Adams Street. Mary was born February 1849, in Alabama. John and Mary had four children: John H., Jr., born December 1872 (also a lawyer); W. J., born October 1874 (was married to Nellie Ryan. He worked as a life and fire insurance agent); Mamie Sue, born September 1878; and Logan S., born September 1878.[872] In 1911, John Jr. worked for the State of Alabama Game Commission. In 1916, the family home was at 512 Adams Street.[873]

Ward, Thomas W.; Deputy Sheriff.
Thomas W. Ward was born in 1851, in North Carolina. In 1896, he was a policeman with the Huntsville Police Department. He had married Virginia in about 1872, and they lived at 211 Jefferson Street. In 1900, the children at home were: Janella, was born in April 1879, in Tennessee; and Herman, was born in November 1891, in Alabama.[874] In 1904, Thomas was a Deputy Sheriff. Ward died in 1906, and was buried in Maple Hill Cemetery next to his wife, Virginia F. Ward, who was born April 1854, and died 1942.[875]

Watts, John Parks, Doctor; Special Grand Jury.
Dr. John Park Watts was born in Green County, Georgia, March 28, 1854. He was the son of William Thomas and Mary Margaret (Williams) Watts. In 1860, William sold his landholdings in Georgia and moved to the Hillsboro-Courtland area of Lawrence County Alabama. With the War Between the States imminent, the family moved to Brazos River, Texas. Beginning in 1873, John Parks began attending the University of Louisville School of Medicine and received his Doctor of Medicine degree in 1876. Dr. Watts began his practice in Lawrence County before moving into Madison County. In 1893, he interrupted his practice to accept a position as Staff Physician of the Haguey Institute in Savannah, Georgia. His letterhead, printed at this institute, stated that he treated his patients for *"liquor, opium, morphine, tobacco and cocaine diseases."* On

---

[872] 1900 United States Federal Census, Madison County, Alabama Vol. 38 Enumeration District 100, Sheet 15, line55.
[873] Huntsville City Directory, 1911-page 255; 1916-page 240.
[874] 1900 United States Federal Census, Madison County, Alabama.
[875] *Maple Hill Cemetery Phase One*, page 135, Robey, Johnson, Jones, Roberts; Huntsville-Madison County Historical Society.

March 3, 1884, he married William (Willie, as she was called) Ette McCrary at the "*Old McCrary Place*." This house was built about 1814. Willie died four days before her thirty-sixth birthday, leaving John Park with four young children to rear alone. In 1899 John Park retired entirely from medical practice to have time for his family responsibilities. When he retired from farming and the children were grown, he moved into Huntsville Twickenham District, 427 Locust Avenue. He served the county as tax adjuster during 1927-28. A devout, dedicated and active Christian throughout his entire life, he attended the Church of Christ on Randolph Avenue where he served as an Elder. John Park Watts died on December 22, 1933, at the age of seventy-nine. He and Willie are buried in Maple Hill Cemetery. His saddlebags, instruments in the case, and medicine bottles are on loan to the Burritt Museum.[877]

Williams, James N.; Special Grand Jury.
James N. Williams worked for the Williams Brothers Hardware. He and wife Minnie lived at 1006 Pratt Avenue, in East Huntsville. His business address was 404 Church Street.[878]

Wilson, H. P.; Policeman.
The 1900 Poll Tax list for Madison County listed H. P. Wilson, twenty-one years of age, in Huntsville. No other information was found.

Winkle, Tom; Alledged Lyncher.
A complete search was conducted for information without results.

Worley, Jim (James); Brother of Silas Worley.
James G. Worley lived next door to his brother, Silas Worley Jr., his father, Silas, Sr. and his mother, Eliza Jane. James's daughter, Henretta, born in May of 1896; Aunt Marion LeRow, born in 1828; as well as her daughter Mary, born in 1868; and Marion LeRow's grandson named Leo, born in 1886, all lived in the home.[879] In 1911, James lived with his wife, Jimmie, at 310 O'Shaughnessy Street. James worked at Dallas Mills.[880] Later James was a laborer, and their

---

[877] *Medicine Bags and Bumpy Roads*, page 171-172, Goldsmith & Fulton, Valley Publishing Co., 1985.
[878] 1911 Huntsville City Directory, page 262.
[879] 1900 United States Federal Census, Madison County, Vol. 38, Enumeration District, 98, Sheet #3, line 52.
[880] 1911 Huntsville City Directory, page 266.

home was on Beirne Avenue, near the corner of Fourth Avenue.[880] James was buried in Maple Hill Cemetery, Section 24 Row 11. Tombstone information reveals that James was born June 1, 1875, and died January 18, 1957.[881]

Worley, Silas H. Jr.; Alleged Lyncher.
Silas H. Worley was born in January of 1839. In 1900, he had been married to Eliza Jane for thirty years. They had sixteen children, of whom ten survived. Silas was born in Alabama; his father was born in North Carolina, and his mother in South Carolina. Silas was a farmer. Silas died June 26, 1914. He was buried in Maple Hill Cemetery. Tombstone information reveals that Silas was born January 6, 1839. The inscription reads, *"A loving husband and father."* Eliza J. was buried next to him. She was born August 15, 1850, and died April 3, 1927. The inscription reads, *"She was the sunshine of our home."* Their graves are located in Section 26 Row 12.[882]

Young, John; Attorney.
John Bassett Young was born in 1860. He was an attorney. His practice was located at 107 Franklin Street. He resided at the same address.[883] In 1920, he was married to Elizabeth, and lived at 317 Eustis Street.[884] He is buried in Maple Hill Cemetery, Section 22 Row 17. Tombstone information reveals that he was born in 1860, and died in 1936.[885]

---

[880] 1916 Huntsville City Directory, page 249.
[881] Manuscripts of Maple Hill Cemetery Records, by Dorothy Scott Johnson.
[882] Manuscripts of Maple Hill Cemetery Records, by Dorothy Scott Johnson.
[883] 1900 United States Federal Census, Madison County, Alabama.
[884] 1920 Huntsville City Directory.
[885] Manuscripts of Maple Hill Cemetery Records, by Dorothy Scott Johnson.

Bibliography

Books

Ames. Jessie Daniel. (1942) *The Changing Character of Lynching.* Atlanta, Georgia: Commission on Interracial Cooperation, Inc.

Ayers, Edward L., (1992) *The Promise of the New South: Life After Reconstruction.* New York: Oxford University Press.

Ayers, Edward L., (1984) *Vengeance and Justice: Crime and Punishment in the Nineteenth-Century American South.* New York: Oxford University Press.

Beck, E. M., (1994) *Violence Toward African-Americans in the Era of the White Lynch Mob.* Albany: State University of New York Press.

Betts, Edward Chambers (1909) *Early History of Huntsville, Alabama.* Montgomery, Alabama: The Brown Printing Company.

Brewer, W., (1872) *Alabama: Her History and Public Men.* Tuscaloosa, Alabama. Republished by Photo Lithography, Willo Publishing Company. (1964).

Brownstone, David and Franck, Irene, (1990) *Dictionary of 20th Century History*; New York: Prentice Hall.

Brundage, W. Fitzhugh (1993) *Lynching in the New South.* Urbana and Chicago: University of Illinois Press.

Chamberlain, David. 1997. *Storied Ground: Facts and Fictions About Huntsville's Maple Hill Cemetery.* .Huntsville, Alabama: Fell house Publishing.

Chapman, Elizabeth Humes (1989) *Changing Huntsville, 1890–1899.* Huntsville, Alabama: Historic Huntsville Foundation Inc.

Cash. W. J., (1969) *The Mind of the South.* New York: Random House.

Cowart, Margaret Matthews, *Old Land Records of Madison County,* (1988).

Cutler, James E. (1905) *Lynch-Law: An Investigation Into the History of Lynching in the United States*. New York: Longmans, Green, and Co.

Downey, Dennis B., (1991) *No Crooked Death, Coatesville, Pennsylvania, and the Lynching of Zachariah Walker*. Urbana and Chicago, University of Illinois Press.

DuBose, Joel C., (1908) *Alabama History*. Atlanta: B. F. Johnson Publishing Company.

Flynt, Wayne, (1987), *Mine, Mill and Microchip*; Windsor Publication, Inc., Northridge, California.

Fisk, Sarah Huff, (1997) *Civilization Comes to the Big Spring: Huntsville, Alabama 1823*. Huntsville, Alabama: Pinhook Publishing Company.

Fisk, Sarah Huff, (1997) *Found Among the Fragments*. Huntsville, Alabama: Pinhook Publishing Company

Gaither, Gerald H., (1977) *Blacks and the Populist Revolt: Ballots and Bigotry in the "New South."* University: University of Alabama Press.

Garrett, *Biography of Notable Men of Alabama*

Ginzburg, Ralph, (1962) *100 Years of Lynchings*. Baltimore, Md. Black Classic Press.

Goldsmith & Fulton, (1985), *Medicine Bags and Bumpy Roads*, Valley Publications, Huntsville, Alabama.

Griffith, Lucille, (1968) *Alabama, A Documentary History to 1900*. University, Alabama. The University of Alabama Press.

Griffith, Lucille (1962) *History of Alabama*. 1540-1900. Northport, Alabama: Colonial Press.

Johnson, Dorothy Scott, (1981) *1907 Confederate Census—Limestone, Morgan, & Madison Counties Alabama*; Johnson Historical Publications, Huntsville, Alabama.

Johnson, Dorothy Scott, (1971) *Cemeteries of Madison County, Alabama, Vol. I*. Huntsville, Alabama. Johnson Historical Publications.

Johnson, Dorothy Scott, (1978) *Cemeteries of Madison County, Alabama Vol. II, Huntsville, Alabama*; Johnson Historical Publications.

Johnson, Dorothy Scott, *Cemeteries of Madison County, Alabama Vol. III*, Huntsville, Alabama; Johnson Historical Press.

Jones, Virgil Carriagton, (1992) *True Tales of Old Madison County*. Dorothy Scott Johnson, Editor, Huntsville, Alabama, Johnson Historical Publications.

Linton, Calvin D., Ph.D., (1985) *American Headlines, Year by Year*; Nashville, Thomas Nelson, Inc.

McAdory, Owen Thomas, (1978) *History of Alabama and Dictionary of Alabama Biography*; The Reprint Company, Spartanburg, S.C.

Maulsby, Ann, (1999) *Merrimack Cemetery*.
Stewart, John Craig, (1975) *The Governors of Alabama*; Pelican Publishing Co. Inc., Gretna.

Moore, Albert Burton, (1934) *History of Alabama*; University of Alabama; University Supply Store.

Murphey, Dwight D., (1995) *Lynching—History and Analysis*; Washington D.C.: Journal of Social, Political and Economic Studies. Monograph Number 24.

McGovern, James R., (1982) *Anatomy of a Lynching: The Killing of Claude Neal*; Baton Rouge, Louisiana State University Press.

National Association for the Advancement of Colored People (1919—1969), *Thirty Years of Lynching in the United States, 1889-1918*; New York: Arno Press.

Raper, Arthur (1933) *The Tragedy of Lynching*; Chapel Hill: University of North Carolina Press.

Record, James (1970) *A Dream Come True. The Story of Madison County and Incidentally of Alabama and the United States*; Vol. 1; Huntsville, Alabama: John Hicklin Printing Company.

Record, James (1970*) A Dream Come True. The Story of Madison County and Incidentally of Alabama and the United States*; Vol. II; Huntsville, Alabama: John Hicklin Printing Company.

Roberts, Barbara Baker. *Early History of Calera, Alabama*; Montevallo, Alabama, Times Printing Co. (No copyright date.)

Robey, Diane, Johnson, Dorothy S., Jones, John Rison, Jr. Roberts, Frances C., *Maple Hill Cemetery Phase One, Huntsville, Alabama*; The Huntsville-Madison County Historical Society. (1995).

Schlesinger, Arthur M., Jr., (1983) *The Almanac of American History*; New York, Bramhall House.

Smead, Howard (1986) *Blood Justice: The Lynching of Mack Charles Parker*; Oxford: Oxford University Press.

Stewart, John Craig, (1975) *The Governors of Alabama*; Gretna, Louisiana. Pelican Publishing Co.

Tolnay, Stewart E., (1992) *A Festival of Violence. An Analysis of Southern Lynchings*, 1882- 1930; Urbana and Chicago. University of Illinois Press.

Urdang, Laurence, (1983) *The Timetables of American History*; New York. Touchstone.

Walker, Samuel, (1980) *Popular Justice: A History of American Criminal Justice*; New York: Oxford University Press.

Wells, Charles Reed, Sr., *The Valiant Survivors: the United Confederate Veterans of Madison County—A Record of Their Services 1861—1865*; 2nd Edition.

Wells-Barnett, Ida B., (1991) *On Lynchings*; Salem, New Hampshire: Ayer Company, Publishers, Inc.

White, Walter (1969) *Rope and Faggot. A Biography of Judge Lynch*; Salem, New Hampshire: Ayer Company Publishers, Inc.

Whitfield, Stephen J., (1988) *A Death in the Delta: the Story of Emmett Till*; New York: Free Press.

Woodward, C. Vann, (1966) *The Strange Career of Jim Crow*; New York: Oxford University Press.

Manuscripts

Manuscript History of the Lanier Family, told by Felix Robertson Lanier, and written by John Fulton Lanier.

Alabama Governor's Papers, Governor Jelks Correspondence, 1905; The State of Alabama Department of Archives and History; Montgomery, Alabama.

The Birmingham Bar Association Records.

Microfilm Records

1850—1860—1870—1880—1900—1910—1920 United States Federal Census, Madison County, Alabama.

1850 United States Federal Census, Russell County, Virginia, 54th District.

Newspapers

The Huntsville Times
USA Today
The Independent
The Huntsville Gazette
The (Huntsville) Weekly Democrat
The (Huntsville) Daily Mercury
The (Huntsville) Weekly Mercury
The Daily Age (Birmingham, Alabama)
The Daily Age-Herald News (Birmingham, Alabama)
The Republican

Birmingham News
The Weekly Tribune
The Journal

Pamphlets

Ryan, Patricia H., *Northern Dollars for Huntsville Spindles*; Huntsville Planning Department, Special Report No. 4, 1983.

Periodicals

The Huntsville Historical Review, (1994-1999) The Huntsville-Madison County Historical Society.

The Historic Huntsville Quarterly, (1974-1999) Historic Huntsville Foundation.

Valley Leaves, (1964-1999) The Tennessee Valley Genealogical Society.

Index

A

Adams, Charlie, 4, 53, 58, 59, 66, 81, 89, 90, 92, 94, 98, 99, 100, 101, 102, 103, 104, 105, 107, 109, 131
Adams, Daniel A., 261
Adams, Private, 226
Almon, David, 285, 286
Anderson, Alice, 51
Anderson, Amanda, 51
Anderson, Charles, 51
Anderson, Charles C., 195
Anderson, Charlie, 102
Anderson, Harvey, 51
Anderson, James, 51
Anderson, Jenny C, 51
Anderson, John B., 5, 51, 195
Anderson, Lila (Lelia), 195
Anderson, Lucille C., 195
Anderson, William, 51
Ansley, 100
Armstrong, 281
Armstrong, James, 265, 268, 280, 281, 297
Arnold, J. H., 204
Austin, Birdie, 119
Austin, Eliza Virginia, 119
Austin, Ellie, 119, 120, 121, 123, 124, 126, 127, 128, 129, 130
Austin, Ellie Sando, 119, 132
Austin, James, 129
Austin, James A., 131
Austin, James Alexander, 119
Austin, Johnson, 119
Austin, Mary Elizabeth, 119
Austin, Mary Elizabeth (Skeen), 119
Austin, Mildred, 131
Austin, Mildred J. (Duryee), 119
Austin, Thomas, 119

B

Bailes, E. T., 245
Bailey, A. L., 297
Bailey, Carrie B., 297
Bailey, Cassie Lee, 297
Bailey, Crutcher, 297
Bailey, Dudley, 297
Bailey, Edward A., 297
Bailey, Lisa, 297
Bailey, Martha Jane, 297
Bailey, Mattie, 109
Bailey, Sara M., 297
Baldridge, Alice (Boarman), 109
Baldridge, F. E., 247
Baldridge, Felix, 109, 113, 146, 155, 297, 341
Baldridge, Felix Edward, 109
Baldridge, Milton C., 109
Baldridge, N. C., 109
Baldridge, Vira B. (Mrs. Davis), 109
Bankhead, Adalaide Eugene, 298
Bankhead, Attorney, 253
Bankhead, Tullala, 214
Bankhead, Tullula, 298
Bankhead, W. B., 235
Bankhead, William, 272, 274, 281
Bankhead, William B, 219
Bankhead, William B., 253, 269, 279, 285
Bankhead, William Brockman, 298
Barclay, 48
Bates, Dennie, 298
Bates, Lonnie (Alonzo) P., 298
Battle, B. A., 298
Battle, Chester, 298
Battle, J. W., 245
Battle, Jacob, 52
Battle, Jacob W., 5, 51
Battle, Jacob William, 51, 298
Battle, James R., 298
Battle, Joanna, 298
Battle, Kate, 298
Battle, Kate E., 51
Battle, Katherine, 298
Battle, Mary, 51
Baubaugh, George, 15
Baubaugh, Sara, 15
Bauhough, George, 66
Bauhough, Sarah, 66
Bayless, John, 262
Beadly, William R., 299
Beane, Emma, 307
Beane, Shirley, 307
Beiderman, Adale, 54
Beiderman, Eliza, 54
Beiderman, Jennie, 55
Beiderman, Leo, 54
Beidermann, Rudolf, 23
Beiren, Nona Plunkett, 52
Beirne, Eliza Carter Gray, 52
Beirne, Eliza Gray, 53
Beirne, Elizabeth Gray, 52
Beirne, Ellen, 52
Beirne, George P., 39, 52

Beirne, George Plunket, 53
Beirne, George Plunkett, 52
Beirne, Jane Patton, 52
Beirne, Lucey, 52
Beirne, Mary, 52
Beirne, Nona, 52
Beirne, Nona Plunkett, 53
Bernstein, Sophia, 308
Berryhill, Count, 269, 299
Betts, Charles Edward, 53
Betts, Augusta, 54
Betts, Augusta Ada, 54
Betts, Edward C., 5, 39, 54, 88
Betts, Edward Chambers, 53
Betts, Elisha, 53
Betts, Martha Cousins [Chambers], 53
Betts, Mary [Parrot], 53
Betts, Maud M. (Brown), 54
Betts, Tancred, 54
Betts, Victor, 54
Betts, Virginia, 54
Betts, Virginia Augusta, 53
Biederman, Rudolf (Henry), 54
Bierne, George, 39
Bierne, George P., 5
Billingsley, John, 236, 273
Billingsly, John, 274
Binford, Cornelia Clopton, 61
Binford, Henry, 61
Blair, Epsien A., 299
Blair, Louis C., 299
Blair, Nancy, 299
Blair, S. M., 279
Blake, H. C., 118
Blocker, Angie, VII
Blunt, A. L., 120, 122, 129
Blunt, Algernon L., 119, 132
Blunt, Birdie, 119, 129
Blunt, Byrdie, 132
Blunt, Eliza Virginia, 132
Blunt, Elizabeth (Austin), 129
Blunt, James, 119
Blunt, James A., 129
Blunt, James A., Jr., 132
Blunt, Maysie, 119, 129, 132
Blunt, Mazie, 132, 133
Blunt, Melvina, 123, 129
Blunt, Odell, 129
Blunt, Odelle, 119, 132
Blunt, Susie, 119, 129, 132
Blunt, William, 119, 129, 132
Bonds, Broney, 324
Bonds, Powell, 324
Bone, Annie L., 55
Bone, C. P., 55
Bone, G. P., 40

Bone, Houston, 55
Bone, Hugh Phillips, 55
Bone, James, 55
Bone, Lane, 55
Bone, Laura G., 55
Bone, Lillian, 55
Bone, Lily, 55
Bone, Louisa, 55
Bone, M. H., 55, 70
Bone, Martha, 55
Bone, Mary, 55
Bone, Matthew H., 55
Boykin, Manly, 81
Bradley, J. C., 103
Bradley, Kit, 299
Bragg, G. T., 274
Bragg, George T., 299
Brandon, Robert, 88
Brandon, William W., 277
Brasher, Sonya, VIII
Breckinridge, John C., 314
Brickell, Benjamin Fitzpatrick, 110
Brickell, Eliza M., 109
Brickell, Mary J., 109
Brickell, Robert, 243
Brickell, Robert C., 235, 247, 261, 300
Brickell, Robert C., Jr., 109
Brickell, William, 73
Bridges, Allie, 300
Bridges, Altho S., 300
Bridges, Charles L., 300
Bridges, James, 300
Bridges, Joe, 300
Bridges, John H., 300
Bridges, Martha A., 300
Bridges, Nana, 300
Brigham, Mary, 300
Brigham, W. L., 234
Brigham, Walter L., 300
Brigham, Will, 273
Brigman, W. L., 275
Brigman, Will, 277
Brock, George P., 223, 259, 261
Brown, Captain, 237, 251, 255, 257, 272
Brown, Lucien E., 250
Brown, R. K., 203
Brown, Wesley, 72, 89, 90, 94, 96
Bryson, John H., 92, 110
Buckner, Jessie, 300
Buckner, William D., 300
Buckner, William J., 300
Buford, Duncastle, 300
Buford, Mary C., 301
Buford, Robert Stanfield, 300
Buford, Susan (Roach), 300
Burgess, Sam, 103

Burke, Alice, 301
Burke, Carolyn, 56
Burke, Dr. James P., 56
Burke, Ella K., 56
Burke, Henrietta E. (Strong), 56
Burke, James P., 19, 56
Burke, John, 56, 247, 301, 330
Burke, Mat O., 56
Burke, Thomas G., 56
Burnett, Clark, 74
Burnett, John L., 76
Burnett, Mary, 74
Burns, Tom, 127
Burwell, Ann (Walker), 195
Burwell, Carrie (Davis), 195
Burwell, David, 155
Burwell, E. D., 169
Burwell, Edwin Dudley, 195
Burwell, Edwin Dudley, Jr., 195
Burwell, Howard Beirne, 195
Burwell, James R., 156
Burwell, James William, 195
Burwell, Jennie, 143, 150, 154, 155
Burwell, Sue (Kelly), 156

C

Cabaniss, (Septimus) Douglas, 57
Cabaniss, Charles, 56
Cabaniss, Charles E., 56
Cabaniss, Ellen D., 56
Cabaniss, Fanny, 56
Cabaniss, Frances (Fannie), 57
Cabaniss, Lucy, 56
Cabaniss, Mariah, 18
Cabaniss, Septimus, 44, 56
Cabaniss, Septimus D., 49, 56
Cabaniss, Virginia (Shepherd), 56
Cabaniss, Virginia C., 56
Cabaniss, William, 56
Cabannis, Bud, 57
Cabannis, Mariah, 31
Cage, Abraham, 51
Campbell, Albert, 317
Campbell, E., 88
Campbell, Gay, II, IX, XIV, 287
Campbell, Gay Cushing, IV
Campbell, Kathie, IV
Cantrell, Addie L., 301
Cantrell, Estelle, 301
Cantrell, James R., 301
Cantrell, Lizzie, 301
Cantrell, Malcolm Jr., 301
Cantrell, Malcolm M., 301
Cantrell, Margaret Ellen, 301

Carney, Tom, VIII
Carrager, Albert John, 301
Carter, J. S., 226, 262
Carter, James Lee, 276
Chambers, Henry C., 53
Chapman, Felicia (Pickett), 322
Chapman, Reuben, 287, 322
Chapman, Reubin, 67
Chapman, Rosalie (Sheffey), 322
Charlie, 13, 37
Chase, Charles, 118
Chase, Henry, 118
Chase, Herbert, 118
Chase, Robert, 118
Childs, Jane H., 75
Christian, Cleveland B., 301
Christian, Jennie, 301
Clark, Elijah, 163, 168, 169, 170, 171, 180, 183, 185, 186, 190, 196, 225, 246
Clark, Peter, 168, 170, 196
Clay, Clement C., 57
Clay, J. Withers, 21, 33, 39, 57, 58
Clay, Jennie, 58
Clay, John Withers, 49, 57, 58
Clay, Mary Louisa, 57
Clay, Susanna W., 57
Clay, W. L., 39
Clay, William L., 57
Cleveland, Archie, 269, 302
Cleveland, Beaula, 302
Cleveland, George, 302
Cleveland, Lee, 302
Cleveland, Lula, 302
Cleveland, Robert, 302
Cleveland, Willie, 302
Cloyd, Henry, 127, 132
Cloyd, Julia, 132
Cloyd, Lula May, 132
Cloyd, Nannie L., 132
Clutts, Reuben, 236, 274
Cobb, Annie, 302
Cobb, Rufus W., 113
Cobb, Samuel Jr., 302
Cobb, Samuel L., 302
Cole, William, 66
Coleman, Daniel, 39, 58, 59, 145, 180, 196
Coleman, LeVert, 58
Coleman, Vera, 58
Connally, 178
Connally, John W., 196
Connally, Mary T. (Wright), 196
Connelly, Jailor, 185
Connutt, James M., 196
Cooper, Attorney, 251, 256

Cooper, Carol, 111
Cooper, Eliza, 302
Cooper, Eliza H. (Thomas), 111
Cooper, Elizabeth, 302
Cooper, George P., 302
Cooper, J. T., 242
Cooper, John W., 90, 92, 98, 99, 110, 111
Cooper, Joseph E., 111
Cooper, Lawrence, 111, 253, 254, 267, 302
Cooper, Lou T., 111
Cooper, William, 111
Cornatt, James, 175, 178, 180
Costantino, Jeanette, VII
Couch, Jim, 236, 274
Coulson, Alexis, IV
Coulson, Kenysha, IV
Coulson, Kristina, IV
Coulson, Tony, IV
Cox, William, 44
Craft, Arthur, XXIV, 288
Craft, Frank, 126, 132
Craft, M. J., 132
Craft, W. N., 126
Cramer, Carl Ernest, 55
Cramer, Jennie Beiderman, 55
Crawford, Austin, 59
Crawford, Emma, 59
Crawford, Fletcher, 59
Crawford, Frank, 59
Crawford, Sarah, 59
Crawford, Thomas B., 5, 59
Crowson, Allie, 303
Crowson, Benjamin, 303
Crowson, Eliza, 302
Crowson, John J., 302
Crowson, William, 303
Culver, Ella Taylor, 303
Culver, F. P., 245
Culver, Frank P., 221
Culver, Frank P. Reverend, 236
Culver, Frank Pugh, 303
Culver, Isaac Franklin, 303
Culver, Mary Lee (White), 303
Culver, Nancy (McSwean), 303
Culver, Reverend, 221, 222, 232, 245, 247, 277, 278, 283
Cunningham, Annice (Taylor), 304
Cunningham, Governor, 100, 214, 218, 223, 225, 231, 233, 243, 246, 248, 249, 250, 256, 257, 262, 263, 265, 272, 277, 282, 291, 303
Cunningham, R. M., 314
Cunningham, Russell McWhorter, 243
Cunningham, Russell McWhortor, 303

Cunningham, Sue L. (Moore), 304

D

Dallas, Trev B., 165
Daniel, Frank (Kenny), IV
Daniel, Kendra, IV
Daniel, Mary, IX, XIII, 287
Daniel, Mary Neyman, IV
Daniel, Trent, IV
Darwin, Doctor, 184
Darwin, James, 197
Darwin, James L., 197
Darwin, Mary (Lanier), 197
Darwin, Sidney Sledge, 197
Davis, Zebulon Pike, 49
Davis, Anna E., 59
Davis, Effie, 59, 60
Davis, George Lane, 59
Davis, Henrietta, 60
Davis, Jefferson, 141
Davis, Martha H., 59
Davis, Nancy, 79
Davis, Nicholas, 60, 75
Davis, Nicholas Jr., 88
Davis, Nora, 60
Davis, Norah, 289
Davis, Willimetta Davis Eason, 59
Davis, Zabulon, 44, 60
Davis, Zabulon Jr., 60
Davis, Zabulon P., 59
Dement, Henry, 61
Dement, John J., 19, 70
Dement, John Jefferson, 60
Dement, Robert S., 61
Dement, Sarah, 61
Dennis, Anna, 304
Dennis, Denie, 304
Dennis, Ethel, 304
Dennis, James D., 304
Dennis, Jessie T., 304
Dennis, Mary E., 304
Dennis, Ola O., 304
Devore, Bessie (Snead), 131
Devore, John, 131
Doak, Hugh, 287
Douglas, Annie R. (Pettus), 158
Dox, Eliza E., 62
Dox, I. M., 58
Dox, Matilda M., 61
Dox, Peter M., 5
Dox, Peter Myndert, 61
Drake, Lizzie, 158
Drake, Ruth, 304
Drake, Zack, 277, 279, 281, 304

Dryer, James Edmund, 155
Dryer, Mabelle Rose (White), 155
Dryer, Sara Caroline, 155
Dryer, Thomas, 143
Dryer, Thomas E., 154
Dryer, Thomas Edmund, 155
Duaney, 100
Dunivant, Hillis A., 312
Dunivant, Mary Kate (Hooper), 312

E

Early, Jeremiah, 53
Early, John, 53
Early, Jubal A., 53
Early, Peter, 53
Easley, Hugh, 53
Echols, Gene, 302
Echols, Harvey, 302
Echols, Mindy, 302
Echols, William H., 329
Eliza, 79
Ellerson, Isaac, 299
Elliott, James C., 80
Elliott, Major, 237
Elliott. John, 225
Ellis, C. K., 5
Ellis, Clara L., 62
Ellis, Clarence B., 62
Ellis, Clarence K., 62
Ellis, Kellogg, 62
Ellis, Lavisa, 62
Ellis, Nelson, 62
Elllis, Nettie, 62
Elway, John, XXVI
Esslinger, Annie, 304
Esslinger, Donnie, 305
Esslinger, Edgar, 305
Esslinger, Irene, 305
Esslinger, Jason D., 305
Esslinger, Marlon, 305
Esslinger, Thomas, 305
Esslinger, W. W., 245
Esslinger, William W., 304
Esslinger, Willie, 305
Euneline, 89, 90, 97, 111
Evans, Ben, 7, 8, 13, 17, 18, 22, 23, 24, 25, 26, 27, 28, 29, 30, 31, 32, 33, 34, 35, 36, 37, 41, 45, 47, 48, 62, 69, 297
Evans, Josie, 7, 8, 17, 18, 19, 23, 24, 26, 27, 28, 29, 31, 32, 33, 34, 35, 37, 62
Evans, Lizzie, 95

F

Falls, Gregory, 289
Farley, James W., 305
Farley, Pryor, 305
Farley, Sarah, 305
Fearn, Thomas, 52
Finney, D. C., 277
Fisk, J. B., 214
Fleming, Kate, 68
Fletcher, A. S., 315
Fletcher, Charles. 305
Fletcher, Martha L., 305
Fletcher, S. S., 245
Fletcher, Shelby S., 305
Ford, Ellen, 305
Ford, John, 4
Ford, Lee D., 305
Ford, Lucy J., 305
Forrest, Nathan B., 75
Forrest, Nathan Bedford (General), 51, 72, 299
Foster, Attorney, 251, 256
Foster, E. H., 268, 270, 274
Foster, Ephraim, 253
Foster, Ephraim H., 306
Frame, 275, 276
Frame, George, 265, 274
Frame, George W., 306
Frame, John, 306
Frame, Rebecca, 306
Franklin, Martha, 131
Franks, Alameda E., 63
Franks, Amanda, 149
Franks, Amanda (Mandy), 143
Franks, Brittain, 16, 41, 63
Franks, Brittian, 17, 18, 19, 21, 22, 23, 24, 26, 27, 28, 29, 30, 31, 33, 34, 35, 38, 49, 62, 63
Franks, Eleanor P., 63
Franks, James, 63
Franks, Mandy, 147, 148, 149
Franks, Rufus B., 63
Franks, William, 63
Franks, William W., 63
Frazer, Thomas Sydney, 257
Frazier, Cornelia, 306
Frazier, Sydney Thomas, 306
Freeman, C. W., 280
Fulgham, Oscar, 106, 117, 147, 154, 170, 173, 182, 183, 184, 187, 188, 191, 198, 221, 244
Fullington, John, 280
Fuston, H. F., 48

G

Gardiner, C. B., 307
Gardiner, Charity E., 307
Gardiner, Cyntha Ann, 307
Gardiner, David, 307
Gardiner, Davies, 307
Gardiner, Elisha J., 307
Gardiner, Elizabeth (Wylie), 307
Gardiner, Elizabeth J., 307
Gardiner, J. E., 270
Gardiner, J. Ed, 307
Gardiner, James, 307
Gardiner, Mary E., 307
Gardiner, Sarah, 307
Gardiner, Sarah E., 307
Gardiner, William F., 307
Gaston, Ada, 30, 89, 90, 107, 111
Gaston, Addie, 111
Gaston, Zell, 287, 322
Gifford, Frank, 100
Giles, Grant H., 307
Giles, Jailer, 232, 261, 267, 275
Giles, Julia, 307
Giles, Sergeant, 233, 268
Giles, Susan B., 307
Giles, W. T., 227, 261
Giles, William, 268, 270, 307
Giles, William A., 224
Gill, George B., 15, 63, 90
Gill, Mariah, 64
Gill, Octie, 64
Gill, Thomas, 64
Given, Henry G., 307
Given, Marvalene, 307
Givens, Henry G., 307
Givens, Marvalene, 307
Givens, Nannie F., 307
Givens, Robert A., 307
Glassford, Edward, 270, 308
Glassford, Kate, 269, 308
Glassford, Nancy E., 308
Goldsmith, Bettie, 308
Goldsmith, Henry, 308
Goldsmith, Lawrence, 308
Goldsmith, Oscar, 308
Goldsmith, Therissa, 308
Gooch, Sergeant, 227
Gooch, Sgt., 261, 262
Gooch, Victor, 263
Gordon, E. C., 47, 64
Gordon, E. C. A., 74
Graves, Bibb, 286, 288
Graves, Tom, 139
Grayson, Claude A., 249
Grayson, D. A., 249
Grayson, David A., 274, 277, 278, 308
Grayson, Ethel, 309
Grayson, J. G., 245
Grayson, James G., 309
Grayson, Juliet W., 308
Grayson, Nannette Dubose, 309
Grayson, Nannie E., 309
Grayson, William G., 309
Greene, Maxwell, 57
Griffin, M. U., 287
Guinn, Birdie, 132
Guinn, Birdie (Blunt), 132
Guinn, Birdie Blunt, 129
Guinn, Lawrence, 129, 132
Gulley, Reuben A., 230, 269
Gully, Preacher, 275

H

Hale, Zannie, 331
Hall, Alice D., 309
Hall, Benton, 178, 188
Hall, Benton McMillian, 198
Hall, Cicero, 198
Hall, Ephraim, 7, 18, 19, 29, 30, 31, 32, 33, 34, 35, 36, 37, 38, 41, 45, 46, 47, 48, 64
Hall, Fulghram W., 309
Hall, Mary Susan (Wallace), 198
Hall, Mollie E., 309
Hall, Richard L., 309
Hall, Sophronia E., 309
Hall, Walter Fulgham, Sr., 309
Hall, William S., 309
Halsey, Katherine, 310
Halsey, Laura, 309
Halsey, Laura Lanier, 310
Halsey, W. L., 214
Halsey, William L., 309
Hamlett, Frank, 124
Hammond, Etta, 64
Hammond, Hubert, 64
Hammond, J. J., 5, 40, 64
Hammond, John J., 64
Hammond, Nancy (McCrary), 64
Hammond, Otho Conrad, 64
Hammonds, Lee P., 73
Hampton, J. P., 40
Hampton, John P., 65
Hampton, Mary T. (Battle), 65
Hampton, Placebo, 65
Hampton, William B., 65
Hardie, John Byron, 65
Hardin, B. H., 5

Hardy, 33, 38, 42
Hardy, Harriet M. (Saxon), 65
Hardy, John Byron, 65
Harris, Arthur L., 66
Harris, Epps, 65
Harris, George, 112
Harris, George M., 5
Harris, George Milton, 65
Harris, Jessie May, 317
Harris, Lula Allen (Weaver), 66
Harris, Mahala, 65
Harris, Mary A. E. (Ford), 65
Harrison, Carrie, 66
Harrison, Elizabeth, 14, 15
Harrison, Elizabeth L. (Daniel), 66
Harrison, Florence (Cochran), 66
Harrison, Harriet, 66
Harrison, Hattie, 17
Harrison, Kibble J, 66
Harrison, Lizzie (Elizabeth), 15
Harrison, Perry, 11, 13, 14, 15, 22, 66
Harrison, Perry I., 41
Harrison, Perry Jr., 66
Harrison, Perry L., 14, 19
Harrison, Sue, 14, 17
Harrison, Susan, 66
Harrison, Todd, 14, 15, 66
Hatcher, Archer Wood, 310
Hatcher, Dr., 274
Hatcher, O. R., 40
Haw, J. P., 5
Hawk, Rue, 304
Hawking, Archie, 236
Hawkins, Archie, 310
Hawkins, Elizabeth, 63, 310
Hawkins, J. W. B., 270
Hawkins, John W.B., 310
Hawkins, Nancy, 63
Hawkins, Virginia, 310
Hay, Annie, 310
Hay, Captain, 243, 246, 258, 262
Hay, Inez, 311
Hay, John L., 310
Hay, Kate, 310
Hay, Leonard, 262
Hay, Robert, 61, 71, 75, 82, 84, 87, 88, 109, 117, 162, 189, 198, 213, 223, 224, 226, 259, 260, 261, 262, 297, 311, 332
Hay, Robert L., 310
Hay, T. P., 310
Hay, Thomas, 88, 162, 175, 189, 198, 223, 224, 225, 228, 246, 258, 262
Hay, Thomas P., 258, 259, 311
Hayes, Rutherford B., XXII
Hearn, Rev., 48

Helm, Joe, 329
Henry, Patsey, 28
Herestein, Rosa, 315
Heron, Melissa, VIII
Hickman, Samuel Hickman, 70
Hill, Archie, 273
Hill, Ben, 249, 253, 254, 255, 272, 285
Hill, Tom, 273
Holder, Charles, 215
Holder, Charles W., 311
Holloway, Peggy, IV
Hooper, Martha Ann (McCalley), 312
Hooper, May, 312
Hooper, Mollie Catherine, 312
Hooper, Thomas McCalley, 312
Hooper, W. P., 236, 274
Hooper, William P., 312
Howard, Belle B., 312
Howard, Cindy Simpson, IV
Howard, Cleve, 273, 312
Hoy, Clara, 329
Hoy, Clarence E., 329
Huddleston, Amelia, 11, 67
Huddleston, Bovell, 67
Huddleston, Edgar, 67
Huddleston, Henry, 11, 13, 16, 22, 37, 67
Huddleston, James, 67
Huddleston, Mildred, 67
Huddleston, Ora, 67
Huddleston, Oscar, 67
Huddleston, Walter D., 67
Huddleston, Willie, 67
Huffman, Annie, 83
Huffman, Emma, 83
Hughes, Henry M., 287
Hughes, Nannie (Vaughn), 312
Hughes, Robert Lee, 312
Humes, Ellelee (Chapman), 67
Humes, Milton, 15, 19, 41, 67, 68, 75, 180, 198, 223, 313
Humphrey, Bessie, 68
Humphrey, Harmon, 80
Humphrey, Herman, 15, 68
Humphrey, Mary, 68
Humphrey, Matthew, 68
Humphrey, Thomas, 68
Humphrey, Thomas W., 68
Humphrey, Virginia Sneed, 68
Hundley, John H., 313
Hundley, Mary, 313
Hundley, Melinda, 313
Hundley, O. R., 247
Hundley, Oscar R., 247, 313
Hunt, Silas, XXIV, 288
Hunton, Maria, 52
Hutchens, Allen Vick, 111

Hutchens, Lucy, 302
Hutchens, Mary Elizabeth, 111
Hutchens, Maude Elise, 111
Hutchens, Morton McAllister, 111
Hutchens, R. T., 313
Hutchens, Vernon Fisher, 111
Hutchens, W. T., 90, 103, 247, 313
Hutchens, Willard Coxey, 111
Hutchens, William Jefferson, 111
Hutchens, William T., 90
Hutchens, William Thomas, 111
Hutchens, Willie Thomas (Armstrong), 111

I

Irwin, Lurinda, 66

J

Jackson, J. Kirk, 243
Jackson, James H., 50, 79
Jamar, Jack, 170
Jamar, John, 262
Jasper, Will, 170
Jelks, William D., 191, 214, 218, 225, 232, 233, 243, 246, 248, 249, 250, 256, 257, 262, 263, 265, 289, 306, 313, 321, 341
Johnson, Dorothy Scott, VIII
Johnson, Debbie, 153
Johnson, Deborah, VII
Johnson, Ella, 314
Johnson, Thomas, 269, 314
Johnston, Governor, 180
Johnston, Jos., 183, 187, 189
Johnston, Jos. F., 181
Jones, Edwin, 288
Jones, G. W., 118
Jones, J. Rowe, 314
Jones, John, 269
Jones, John J., 314
Jones, Judge, 282
Jones, Mary, 68
Jones, Thomas G., 248
Jones, Thomas W., 287
Judd, S. W., 311
Julia, 56, 144

K

Kage, Abraham, 51
Kage, DeWitt C., 51

Kelly Aaron, 28
Kelly, Aaron, 69
Kelly, Adelene (Rhyne), 157
Kelly, David, 69, 144, 154
Kelly, David E., 139, 146, 156
Kelly, Delia, 69
Kelly, Ellen H.(Pettus), 158
Kelly, Eula (Russell), 157
Kelly, Eva, 144, 146, 147, 154
Kelly, Eva (Thompson), 156
Kelly, Frank, 8, 15, 20, 23, 24, 29, 32, 33, 34, 36, 37, 45, 48, 49, 68
Kelly, G. L., 144, 146
Kelly, George Lawson, 154
Kelly, J. O., 140, 156
Kelly, Joshua, 157
Kelly, Joshua O., 145, 146, 156, 157
Kelly, Joshua O. Jr., 144, 156
Kelly, Joshua O., III, 153
Kelly, Joshua Oscar, 139
Kelly, Lawson, 142, 156, 157
Kelly, Lula, 156, 157
Kelly, Major, 141
Kelly, Nancy, 69
Kelly, Sally, 146
Kelly, Sally (Strong), 139
Kelly, Sally B. (Strong), 156
Kelly, Thompson R.., 157
Kelly, William Solon, 69
Kennard, G. W., 14, 15, 16, 17, 18, 19, 22, 27, 41, 69
Kennard, Maggie F. (Pryor), 69
Kennard, Mattie, 69
Kennard, Thomas, 69
King, Mickey, VII
King, Rodney, XXVII
Kirk, Tom, 234, 236, 275, 314
Kortrecht, Augusta Ada, 54

L

Lackey, Malinda, 158
Lane, Charles P., 251
Lanford, Ann, 71, 317
Lanford, Robert, 71, 317
Lang, C. P., 247
Lanier, Alexander, 3, 94
Lanier, B. C., 113
Lanier, Burwell Clinton, 89, 94, 99, 100, 101, 103, 105, 107, 113, 341
Lanier, Burwell Clinton Jr., 112
Lanier, Burwell Clinton, III, 112
Lanier, Isaac Alexander, 113
Lanier, Joseph B., 113

350

Lanier, Laura Prudence America (Ford), 112
Lanier, Mattie (Ashford), 94
Lanier, Mattie C. (Ashford), 113
Lassiter, Jan, VII
Lawler, Judge, 323
Lawler, W. T., 192, 200
Lawler, William, 201
Leddy, Sallie, 88
Lehman, John H., 262
Lemburg, Henry, 63
LeRow, Marion, 334
LeRow, Mary, 334
LeRoy, Leo, 334
Lewis, Alice D. (Musa), 315
Lewis, Betty Washington, 155
Lewis, John, 57
Lewis, Merrie D., 315
Lewis, Percy, 144, 146
Lewis, Samuel Ragland, 314
Lifcar, Carbri, 53
Lifer, Ann, VII
Lowe, 276
Lowe, Ella, 28
Lowe, R. H., 305
Lowe, Robert H., 236, 315
Lowe, W. H., 305
Lowenthal, Etha, 315
Lowenthal, Henry J., 315
Lowenthal, Lina, 315
Lowenthal, Robert H., 315
Lowry, Doctor, 184
Lowry, Elizabeth, 71
Lowry, Elizabeth (Mrs. William Halsey, Jr.), 70
Lowry, Georgia, (Mrs. Birnie Spraggins), 70
Lowry, J. T., 11, 19, 41
Lowry, John, 72
Lowry, John Tate, 15, 70, 71
Lowry, Lucy James (Pulley), 70
Lowry, S. H., 19, 41
Lowry, Samuel, 15, 71
Lowry, Samuel H., 19, 198
Lowry, Virginia H. (Miller), 70
Lurind, 15
Luten, Mary Lena (Kelly), 157
Lynch, Charles, XVII
Lynch, John, XVII
Lynch, William, XVII
Lyne, R. L., 316
Lyne, Robert D., 316

M

Madden, T. F., 269
Magennis, P. M., 80
Malone, George, 156
Malone, Henry B., 156
Malone, Lena (Kelly), 156
Malone, Minerva, 27
Malone, Nanny (Kelly), 156
Manning, Mary Sue, 316
Manning, Richard A., 316
Maples, Horace, 215, 217, 218, 219, 222, 233, 234, 236, 237, 241, 242, 245, 254, 258, 260, 267, 273, 278, 281, 316
Maples, Peter, 196
Martin, Ausborne, 71
Martin, Ella F., 71
Martin, Emmett W., 71
Martin, John William, 71
Martin, John William Jr., 71
Martin, Malisa E., 71
Martin, Mary L., 71
Martin, Mattie L., 71
Martin, Mollie Mary (Wilmore), 71
Martin, Peny, 71
Martin, Robert Eldridge, 71
Martin, Seny, 71
Mason, Louise, 316
Mason, Tom Jr., 236, 274, 316
Mastin, 102
Mastin, Edmond, 103
Mastin, Edmund, 95, 106
Mastin, Edmund I., 113
Mastin, Frank, 79
Mastin, William, 56, 79
Mastin, William J., 145
Matthews, Adelaide B., 317
Matthews, Albert E., 316
Matthews, E. R., 245
Matthews, Ellie R., 317
Matthews, Elliott R., 198, 316
Matthews, Elliott Robertson II, 317
Matthews, Erskine M., 317
Matthews, Frank, 317
Matthews, Margaret (Burns), 317
Matthews, Fannie W. (Scruggs), 316
May, Frank, 178
May, Frank H., 199
Mayhew, Fanny E., 317
Mayhew, S. J., 247
Mayhew, Sidney, 103, 131, 317
Mayhew, Sidney J., 317
McAllister, Captain, 182

McCalla, Margaret E. (Lewis), 328
McCalla, R. C., 328
McCalley, Ann (Lanford), 71
McCalley, C. S., 245
McCalley, Caroline M. (Lanford), 199
McCalley, Caroline Matilda (Lanford), 71, 317
McCalley, Carrie L., 72
McCalley, Charles, 71, 199
McCalley, Charles S., 71
McCalley, Charles Sanford, 317
McCalley, Connie L., 199
McCalley, J., 4
McCalley, John, 71, 199
McCalley, Kate T., 72, 199
McCalley, Martha Ann, 71
McCalley, Robert, 71
McCalley, Robert L., 71, 104
McCalley, Thomas, 71
McCalley, Thomas S., 5, 72, 199
McCalley, Thomas Sanford, 71, 113, 317
McClain, Private, 261
McClain, T. E., 262
McClain, Thomas, 226
McClellan, W. C., 204
McClung, F. A., 5
McCravey, Elizabeth, 23
McCravey, Leroy, 13, 14, 16, 17, 19, 22, 23, 25, 37, 41, 72
McCravey, Leroy W., 11, 14
McCravey, Rebecca L., 72
McCravey, Sarah, 14, 72
McDavid, Blanche, 73
McDavid, Edmund, 73
McDavid, John J., 39, 73
McDavid, Mary, 73
McDavid, Mary Thompson, 73
McDavid, Mollie, 73
McDavid, Neddie, 73
McDavid, Robert, 73
McDonald, Christopher (Christ), 199
McDonald, Mary L., 199
McEachin, John, 288
McKelby, 169
McKelby, William, 199
McKelvey, William, 199
McLean, Thomas Elwood, 318
McLellan, Thomas C., 191
Metz, Henry, 72
Miller, George T., 180, 199
Miller, John, 70
Miller, Lillie, 199
Miller, Mary, 70
Mitchell, James, 221, 223, 232, 266, 280, 281, 318
Mitchell, James H., 277, 278

Mitchell, James H. (Jim), 265
Mitchell, James L., 318
Mitchell, John, 318
Mitchell, John Edgar Sr., 319
Mitchell, Lilly, 8, 18, 19, 23, 24, 26, 27, 28, 29, 31, 32, 33, 34, 79
Mitchell, Luke, 297
Mitchell, Mary E., 318, 319
Mitchell, Will, 232, 277, 278, 319
Mitchell, William, 270
Mitchell, William L., 319
Mitchells, William, 319
Moore, 177
Moore, Alfred, 187, 188, 192, 200
Moore, Mayor, 181, 182
Moore, R. A., 188
Mormon, John Dement, 61
Mormon, Riley Marion, 61
Mormon, Robert Circy, 61
Mosley, Annie, 127
Mosley, Bradford, 133
Mosley, Columbus, 133
Mosley, Emmy, 127, 133
Mosley, Robert, 104, 109, 110, 120, 121, 122, 123, 124, 126, 127, 133
Mosley, Willie, 127, 133
Moss, James M., 5, 73
Moss, Ella, 74
Moss, Ellen, 74
Moss, Gertrude, 74
Moss, Grant, 74
Moss, Hubert, 74
Moss, Jane T., 74
Moss, Louisa, 74
Moss, Rosalind, 74
Murdock, Andrew J., 319
Murdock, Henry A., 112
Murdock, Myra, 319
Murray, M. R, 311

N

Nance, Jim, 150
Neely, Herman, XXIV, 288
Northington, Captain, 257
Nuckols, Eliza C., 74
Nuckols, Martha Susan (Allen), 74
Nuckols, Samuel O., 74
Nuckols, V. Augustus, 5, 74
Nuckols, Virgil Augustus, 74
Nunnally, 269
Nunnally, Anna B., 319
Nunnally, Bettie, 320
Nunnally, John, 320
Nunnally, Monroe, 320

Nunnally, Wesley, 319

O

O'Halloran, Don, IX
O'Neal, Edward A., 102, 113
O'neal, R. L., 245
O'Neal, Robert L., 320
O'Neal, Wade, 270
O'Shaughnessy, James, 163
Oates, Willliam, 258
O'Neal, Emmet, 77
O'Neal, Kate C., 320
Orgain, J. L., 242
O'Shaughnessy, Michael, 83, 88, 163
Otey, Walter, 170
Overton, A. E., 242
Overton, Ambrose, 200, 320
Overton, Ambrose E., 320
Overton, David, 176, 192, 223, 230, 264, 277, 285, 320
Overton, David D., 184, 200, 320
Overton, David V., 200
Overton, James, 223, 320
Overton, Lucy, 320
Overton, Mattie L., 320
Overton, Nannie E., 320
Overton, Nora, 200
Overton, Sallie H., 200

P

Parm, Joe, 321
Parm, Joe Will, 321
Parm, Richard H., 321
Parm, Tommie A., 321
Parm, Zemma S., 321
Parsons, Elbert, 287
Parton, Joseph, 22, 75
Parton, Joseph J., 64, 74
Parton, Joseph P., 16
Parton, Sarah A. (Scrogins), 74
Parton, William, 74, 75
Patrick, Tina, VIII
Patterson, Ben, 145
Patterson, George C., 200
Patterson, George, Jr., 201
Patterson, Mary, 201
Patterson, Pearle, 200
Patton, 18
Patton, Billie, 157
Patton, Dicey, 75
Patton, I. D., 146
Patton, Irvine D., 144, 157

Patton, James, 75
Patton, John, 15, 75
Patton, Louise, 75
Patton, Marion, 75
Patton, Mary, 75
Patton, Olive B., 157
Patton, Robert, 75
Patton, Robert H., 75
Pegriun, Capt., 187
Penny, (Gus) Augustus, 133
Penny, Gus, 128
Penny, Harriett, 133
Penny, Jesse, 133
Penny, Seelie, 133
Penny, W. E., 50
Pettus, Ann Dew (Brown), 158
Pettus, Eellelle (Chapman), 287
Pettus, Ellelee (Chapman), 322
Pettus, Erle, XV, 123, 143, 154, 157, 158, 211, 219, 220, 223, 231, 235, 241, 245, 246, 247, 248, 249, 250, 251, 253, 254, 267, 268, 271, 274, 277, 278, 284, 286, 287, 288
Pettus, Erle Jr., 322
Pettus, Joseph Albert, 321
Pettus, Mary (Fowlkes), 321
Pettus, Musie (Cartwright), 321
Pettus, Nora E., 158
Pettus, R. E., 245, 247
Pettus, R. R., 123
Pettus, Richard Erle, 321
Pettus, Rosalie, 322
Pettus, Thomas Coleman, 321
Pettus, William, 143
Pettus, William David, 154, 157
Pettus, William H., 158
Pettus, William R., 157
Petty, Attorney, 269
Petty, F. Turner, 268, 270, 274
Petty, Louanna, 323
Petty, Margaret E., 323
Petty, Pat W., 323
Petty, Telin I., 323
Petty, Turner F., 323
Phillips, John, 323
Phillips, Mary B. (Pettus), 158
Phillips, Nancy, 201
Phillips, Robert, 170
Phillips, Robert L., 201
Phillips, W. L., 218
Phillips, William L., 323
Pilgreen, Dorcas, IX
Pleasant, Shelby, 243
Pleasants, Howard, 88
Pleasants, Marie, 323
Pleasants, Mary S., 323

Pleasants, Samuel, 323
Pleasants, Shelby, 285, 323
Pollard, Edith, 324
Pollard, Hattie, 323
Pollard, Hattie O., 324
Pollard, Irma, 324
Pollard, James B., 236, 273, 323, 324
Pollard, Nell, 324
Pollard, Vermer, 324
Pope, Leroy, 197
Popejoy, James E., 324
Popejoy, Laura (Yarbrough), 324
Posey, Adaline, 35
Powell, Bell D., 324
Powell, Conlie (Cornelia), 324
Powell, Cornelia S., 324
Powell, Fenos D., 324
Powell, Hattie, 324
Powell, J. P., 270
Powell, James S., 324
Powell, John P., 324
Powell, John P. Jr., 324
Powell, Lucy T., 82
Powell, Ollie, 299
Powell, Robert W., 324
Power, J. J., 82
Power, Thomas, 67
Pratt, T. W., 118, 138
Pratt, Tracey, 289
Pratt, Tracy W., 165
Price, Nellie (Snead), 131
Price, Walter Harp, 131
Price,Walter, 287
Priest, Daisy, 201
Priest, Greenberry, 168
Priest, Helen, 168, 186
Priest, Marion, 168
Priest, Nellie, 168, 169, 186, 201
Priest, Richard, 168
Priest, Susan, 168, 171, 201
Priest, Susie, 186
Priest, Suzie, 168
Priest, Will, 168, 186, 201
Priest, Woodard, 168
Pruitt, Raneè, VIII
Pryor, Martha, 69
Pulley, Ed L., 237, 274
Pulley, Edward L., 324
Pulley, Georgia S., 325
Pulley, Robert L., 325

R

Radford, Private, 261
Rafford, N. T., 227

Rafford, T. N., 325
Rainey, Ed, 35
Reed, Banister, 67
Reed, Creecy, 68
Rev. Gordon, 64
Reverend Gordon, 64
Richardson, Elizabeth B., 77
Richardson, Patrick W., 240
Richardson, William, XV, 41, 44, 49, 50, 58, 75, 76, 77, 88, 95, 96, 97, 102, 107, 113, 214, 235, 263, 325
Riddick, Frank, 288
Ridge, Elizabeth, 78
Ridge, Jimmy, 23, 25
Riggins, Edgar, 325
Riggins, Idella, 325
Riggins, Thomas, 253, 254, 255, 266, 285
Riggins, Thomas W., 253, 325
Rison, W. R., 180
Roberts, Frances Dr., VIII
Robertson, Vance M., 53
Robinson, Christopher, 78
Robinson, Christopher A., 19
Robinson, Daniel, 313
Robinson, Joanna, 78
Rodgers, A. D., 191, 198, 204, 217, 218, 262, 268
Rodgers, August D., 282
Rodgers, Augustus D., 325
Rodgers, Kilner, 325
Rodgers, Minnie, 325
Rodgers, Sheriff, 191, 198, 204, 218, 223, 224, 226, 228, 230, 244, 246, 257, 259, 260, 262, 264, 273, 275, 285
Rodgers, Zoro V., 325
Rolf, Alecia, 202
Rolf, Charlie, 201
Rolf, Estelle, 201
Rolf, Garth, 201
Rolf, Katie, 202
Rolf, Meghew, 201
Rolf, William, 201
Ross, H. E., 288
Rowe, Aurora (Kelly), 157
Rowe, Homer M., 157
Ruffin, George, 79
Ruffin, Sallie, 79
Russell, Sam, 262

S

Samford, Governor, 313
Samford, J. M., 188

Sanders,, 39
Scales, Joe, 88
Scruggs, Mary, 317
Sharp, Albert D., 326
Sharpe, Albert E., 326
Sharpe, Annie, 326
Sharpe, Arthur L., 326
Sharpe, Eddie L., 326
Sharpe, Joe W., 326
Sharpe, Mary O., 326
Shelby, Anthony Bouldin, 326
Shelby, David, 326
Shelby, Mariam, 326
Shelby, Mary (Bouldin), 326
Shelby, Yancy, 326
Shelly, Judge, 222
Shiffman Irma, 308
Shoenberger, Annie, 8, 9, 27, 79
Shoenberger, Cassander, 50, 78
Shoenberger, Cassender (Lamar), 8
Shoenberger, Fannie, 8, 9, 32, 50, 79
Shoenberger, Fannie Strong (Davis), 8
Shoenberger, George, 7, 8, 9, 11, 12, 13, 14, 15, 16, 19, 20, 22, 23, 24, 25, 29, 30, 31, 32, 35, 36, 37, 38, 39, 41, 43, 44, 45, 46, 48, 50, 56, 67, 68, 72, 75, 78, 114
Shoenberger, Sallie, 8, 9, 50
Sibley, Mimia, 326
Sibley, William J., 326
Simmons, Saxe, 270, 327
Simpson,, IV
Simpson, Bryan, IV
Simpson, Derek, IV, VII
Simpson, Fred, II, IV, X, XVI, 10, 16, 108, 124, 125, 140, 166, 193, 212, 287
Simpson, Fred B., II, X, XVI, 10, 16, 153
Simpson, Fred Bryan, IV
Simpson, Margaret, 62
Simpson, O. J., XXVII
Simpson, Peggy, IX
Simpson, Shannon, IX
Slaton, John, 327
Slaughter, John, 63
Slayton, Jane S., 327
Slayton, Jane Slaughter, 327
Slayton, Johnnie, 327
Slayton, Lanford, 327
Slayton, Lottie, 327
Slayton, Martha, 327
Slayton, Mattie, 327
Slayton, Sarah, 327
Slayton, Slaughter, 327
Sledge, Ada, 30
Smallwood, Richard, IX

Smith, 92
Smith, Addison G., 327
Smith, Ann Adams, 53
Smith, Callie L, 328
Smith, Captain, 237
Smith, Dennis, 212, 220, 222, 243, 251, 256, 281, 286, 287
Smith, Edward D., 257, 327
Smith, Florence D. (Hopkins), 327
Smith, Ida, 158
Smith, Jessie, 158
Smith, Mollie, 143, 145, 147, 148, 149, 158
Smith, Robert E., 330
Smith, Thomas, 287
Smith, Thomas W., 74, 192, 219, 264, 285, 328
Snead, Bessie, 131
Snead, Charlie, 131
Snead, Mary Elizabeth (Austin), 131
Snead, Nellie, 131
Snow, Susanna, 68
Solway, Walter, 249
Speake, James B., 328
Speake, Anne (Canterberry), 329
Speake, Anne Hawkins (Armstrong), 329
Speake, Caro (McCalla), 328
Speake, Carolee, 328
Speake, Carolyn Mayhew, 317
Speake, Carrie, 192
Speake, Carrie O. (Mayhew), 202
Speake, Carrie Olivia (Mayhew), 328
Speake, Charles Lewis, 328
Speake, D. W., 285, 286
Speake, Daniel W. Jr., 328
Speake, Daniel Webster, 328
Speake, Dorothy Clare, 329
Speake, Elizabeth, 328
Speake, Florence H., 287
Speake, Florence Inez (Hoy), 329
Speake, H. C., 175, 180, 181, 183
Speake, Henry C., 192, 211
Speake, Henry C., Jr., 202
Speake, Henry Clay, 202, 317, 328
Speake, James B., 202
Speake, Judge, XV, 68, 175, 180, 183, 192, 202, 211, 220, 221, 222, 223, 224, 233, 241, 245, 248, 250, 251, 253, 255, 256, 262, 264, 265, 266, 267, 269, 271, 272, 276, 278, 280, 283, 285, 288
Speake, Kate M., 202
Speake, Margaret Lindsey, 328
Speake, Margery Mayhew, 329
Speake, Neal, 328

Speake, Paul, XV, 284, 286, 288, 291, 328, 329
Speake, Paul Mayhew, 202, 211, 220
Speake, Paul Meredith, 329
Speake, Richard, 328
Speake, Sarah Brooks (Lindsey), 328
Speake, Susan B. (Lindsey), 202
Spence, Emma, 79
Spence, John, 34, 79
Spence, Laura, 79
Spence, Lillian A., 79
Spence, Sue, 79
Spence, William H., 79
Spraggins, Attorney, 282
Spraggins, Marion, 329
Spraggins, Robert Elias, 329
Spraggins, Robert L., 329
Spraggins, Robert S., 329
Spraggins, Susie E., 329
Spraggins, Susie E. (Echols), 329
Spraggins, Susie Patton Echols, 330
Spraggins, William E., 329
Stainback, Dr., 8
Steele, George, 48
Steele, Matthew, 56
Stegall, J. R., 90, 103, 221, 224, 268, 274
Stegall, J. Rufus, 113
Stegall, Mary E., 113
Steger, Calley D., 330
Steger, Joseph M., 330
Steger, Lina, 330
Steger, Margaret, 203
Steger, Ollie, 330
Steger, Thomas B., 330
Steger, Walter J., 330
Steger, William D., 202
Steger, Willie H., 330
Stephens, R. L., 233, 275
Stephens, Robert L., 330
Steward, Lieutenant, 262
Stewart, Catherine A., 330, 331
Stewart, Charles, 287
Stewart, Coroner, 218
Stewart, Douglas, 260, 330
Stewart, E. B., 215, 216, 242, 273, 330
Stewart, Francis G., 330
Stewart, John B., 330
Stewart, Laura G., 330
Stewart, Lawrence B., 331
Stewart, Lieutenant, 224
Stewart, Margaret, 330
Stewart, Mildred, 330
Stewart, Percy Hendree, 331
Stewart, S. B. Jr., 242
Stewart, S. M., 175, 178, 181, 281
Stewart, S. Morgan, 224

Stewart, Samuel M., 330
Stewart, Samuel Morgan, 191, 203
Stewart, Samuel Morgan Sr., 330
Stewart, Second Lt., 276
Stewart, Thomas T., 330
Stewart, Zoe, 330
Stol, Margarette, 309
Stone, Charles J., 330
Stoner, Amanda, 203
Stoner, John C., 203
Street, Reubin, 56, 114
Street, Rube, 262
Street, W. J., 91
Street, William, 56, 106, 107
Street, William J., 89, 92, 94, 102, 104, 114
Strong, Fanny, 157
Strong, H. N., 249
Stuart, S. M., 297
Sweeney, 18, 22
Sweeney, Alfred, 16, 79
Sweeney, Catherine (Neagle), 80
Sweeney, Mary, 80
Swope, Cyntha [Early], 53
Swope, John M., 53

T

Talley, Annie, 331
Talley, Bygie, 331
Talley, Elijah, 331
Talley, Ellen, 331
Talley, John, 331
Talley, Nellie J., 331
Talley, Sallie, 331
Talley, Sofa, 331
Talley, Thomas, 331
Talley, Tom, 236, 273
Tarks, Mollie, 56
Terry, Alma, 331
Terry, B., 40
Terry, Edwin T., 331
Terry, Eliza, 80
Terry, Elizabeth, 80
Terry, Ellen, 80
Terry, G. L., 331
Terry, George, 80
Terry, Jeff, 278
Terry, Jefferson H., 331
Terry, John, 80
Terry, Susan J. (White), 80
Terry, T. T., 118
Terry, William B., 80
Thomas, John C., 42
Thompson, Albert, 181

Thompson, Mary, 332
Thrift, John R., 332
Thrift, Laura, 332
Tilden, Samuel J., XXII
Tiller, Harriet, 133
Toney, Analon, 81
Toney, Elleck, 82
Toney, Harris, 40, 80, 81
Toney, Hugh L., 40, 82
Toney, J. E, 82
Toney, Mary Bell, 81
Toney, Mary N. (Alexander), 81
Toney, Matthew, 81
Toney, Robert G.,, 82
Toney, Sarah E. (Biggers), 82
Trottman, Willametta, 72
Turner, Ann, 82
Turner, Daniel, 82
Turner, Daniel H., 5
Turner, Fannie L. (Ailed), 203
Turner, H. P., 242
Turner, Henry P., 82, 203
Turner, Jennie H., 82
Turner, John, 82
Turner, John S., 82
Turner, Lucy, 82

V

Vaiden, W. D., 257
Vaughn, James B., 203
Vaughn, James Robert, 203
Vaughn, Mable Evelyn, 203
Vaughn, Martha Louise, 203
Vaughn, Mavalina, 203
Vaughn, William Buford, 203
Vincent, Isaah H., 113
Vining, Lillie, 178
Vining, Will, 188, 204
Vining, William, 178
Vining, William "Ed", 191

W

Wade, Mary P. (Boggs), 204
Wade, Robert B., 204
Waldon, Monica, VII
Waldrop, Andrew Jackson, 332
Waldrop, Cara, 216, 332
Waldrop, Charley, 216, 332
Waldrop, E. D., 241
Waldrop, Elias, 215, 216, 217, 219, 221
Waldrop, Elias D., 215, 332
Waldrop, Jack, 216, 234

Waldrop, Nancy C., 332
Walker, Attorney, 282
Walker, Nellie (Ryan), 333
Walker, Richard W., 332
Walker, Shelby W., 332
Walker, W. J., 333
Wall, John W., 145
Wallace, Capt., 182, 188
Wallace, Captain, 182
Wallace, John H., 180, 333
Wallace, John H. Jr., 333
Wallace, John H., Jr., 204, 235
Wallace, Logan S., 333
Wallace, Mamie Sue, 333
Wallace, Mary C., 204, 333
Ward, Deputy, 233
Ward, Herman, 333
Ward, Janella, 333
Ward, Sheriff, 251
Ward, Thomas W., 232, 265, 333
Ward, Tom, 268, 270, 278
Ward, Virginia F., 333
Ward, willie, 126
Washington, George, 155
Watkins, America, 83
Watkins, Cordelia, 83
Watkins, Isham, 5, 83
Watkins, James, 83
Watkins, Jane Yeatman, 83
Watkins, Mollie, 220, 251
Watkins, Sarah, 83
Watkins, William, 83
Watts, J. P., 245
Watts, John Parks, 333
Watts, Mary Margaret (Williams), 333
Watts, William (Willie) Ette (McCrary), 334
Watts, William Thomas, 333
Weaver, Ann, 114
Weaver, James, 114
Weaver, Mary, 114
Weaver, Matt, 96
Weaver, Nannie, 68
Weaver, S. M., 114
Weaver, Samuel Matt, 114
Webb, Brenda, VII
Webster, J. W., 215
Weeden, Howard, 70
Wesley, Brown, 89, 90, 91, 95, 96, 97, 98, 99, 102, 103
Wheeler, Dr., 267
Wheeler, Joe, 50
Wheeler, Joseph, 162
Wheeler, Joseph (General), 107
White, Anna, 27
White, Elizabeth, 7, 27, 42, 45, 48, 50

White, Elizabeth (Lizzie), 27
White, Elizabeth Huffman, 84
White, Mike, 7, 8, 9, 11, 12, 15, 17, 18, 20, 22, 23, 24, 26, 27, 28, 29, 30, 31, 32, 35, 36, 38, 41, 42, 43, 45, 46, 47, 48, 50, 62, 78, 83
White, Thomas, 49, 60
White, Worley, 43, 50, 83
Whitfield, W. B., 287
Whitman, Albert, 84
Whitman, Alvadora, 84
Whitman, Ann B., 84
Whitman, Dorothy Jones, 84
Whitman, James, 84
Whitman, Mary, 84
Whitman, Pricilla, 84
Whitman, Rebecca, 84
Whitman, Robert, 84
Whitman, Texanna, 84
Whitman, Thomas, 84
Whitman, W. F., 40, 84
Whitman, William Felo, 84
Wilburn, Benjamin O., 139, 140
Wilburn, Mrs., 139
William, 15
Williams, James N., 334
Williams, Minnie, 334
Willisson, Bob, VII
Wilson, H. P., 218, 334
Wilson, Officer, 251
Winkle, Tom, 249, 265, 279
Wise, Abe, 233
Wood, Dillard, 310
Wood, Floyd, 310
Wood, Lizzie, 310
Wood, Maggie (Margaret), 310

Wood, Mary, 310
Woodard, Oakley, 143, 144, 146
Woodard, Oakly, 144
Woods, Thomas, 133
Woodson, Charles, 133
Woodson, Charley, 128, 133
Woodson, Mary J., 133
Woodward, Vivian, 288, 289
Worley, Eliza Jane, 334, 335
Worley, Henretta, 334
Worley, James (Jim), 334
Worley, Jim, 269
Worley, Jimmie, 334
Worley, Silas, 232, 236, 265, 266, 268, 269, 270, 272, 276
Worley, Silas H., 335
Worley, Silas Jr., 334
Worley, Silas Sr., 334
Worley, W. F., 269
Wynn, A. M., 90, 114
Wynn, Alec, 114
Wynn, John, 114
Wynn, Lillie, 114
Wynn, Martha C., 114
Wynn, Mattie, 114
Wynn, Mollie, 114
Wynn, Sallie, 114

Y

Yancey, Douglas, 267
Yeatman, Major, 237
Young, Elizabeth, 335
Young, John, 247
Young, John Bassett, 335

Order Form
Sins of Madison County

Thank you for purchasing and reading Sins of Madison County. We are sure that you will agree this book will make a wonderful gift for anyone on your gift list. Please feel free to make copies of this form, and use it often for all of your ordering needs.

Sins of Madison County
Triangle Publishing Company
105 Northside Square Suite D
Huntsville, Alabama 35801
$28.95 (current 2000 price)
$ 2.32 (Alabama Residents)
$ 4.00 (current S&H)
$35.27 per book ordered

Name _____

Address _____

City _____

State _____ Zip _____

Phone _____

Number Ordered _____ Amt Enclosed _____

Comments about the book _____

Corrections to the book/ and photographs of the people and events are appreciated, but must be accompanied by proof.

Your order is appreciated!

364.134   C1
SIM

   Simpson, Fred B.
   The Sins of Madison
   County
CLY

CLAY CO. LIBRARY
CELINA, TENN.